D1211576

PLEASE ROTATE YOUR BOOK

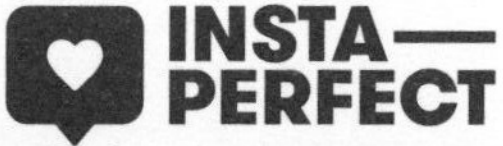

Creative photography for social media today

First published and distributed by
viction:workshop ltd.

viction:ary™

viction:workshop ltd.
Unit C, 7/F, Seabright Plaza, 9-23 Shell Street,
North Point, Hong Kong
Url: www.victionary.com Email: we@victionary.com

@victionworkshop
@victionary_
@victionworkshop

Edited and produced by viction:ary
Concepts & art direction by Victor Cheung
Book design by viction:workshop ltd.
Jacket photography by Eloisa Iturbe, Ice Cream Books/Ben Deezer, Young & Innocent, Daniel Rueda & Anna Devìs, Matter Matters, and Present & Correct.
Icons on Tips & Tricks pages (Rock Music, Mini Heart, Finger Pointing, Drop) by BomSymbols from the Neon Project.

ISBN 978-988-78501-3-7
Printed and bound in China

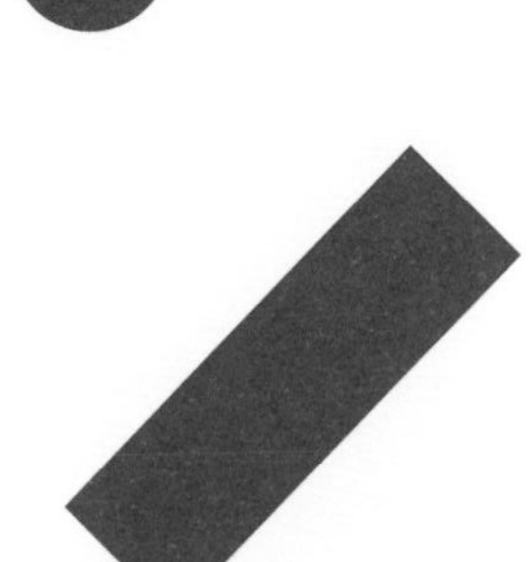

ACKNOWLEDGEMENTS

We would like to thank all the designers and companies who were involved in the production of this book, which would not have been accomplished without their significant contribution to its compilation. We would also like to express our gratitude to all the producers for their invaluable opinions and assistance throughout this entire project. Its successful completion owes a great deal to many professionals in the creative industry who have given us precious insights and comments. And to the many others whose names are not credited but have made specific input in this book, we thank you for your continuous support the whole time.

FUTURE EDITIONS

If you wish to participate in viction:ary's future projects and publications, please send your website address or portfolio to submit@victionary.com

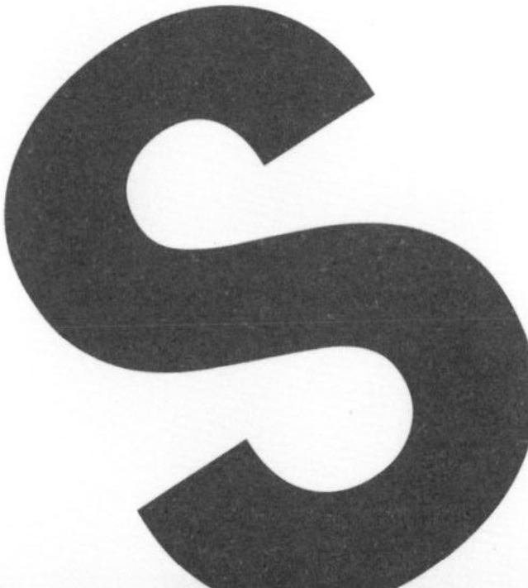

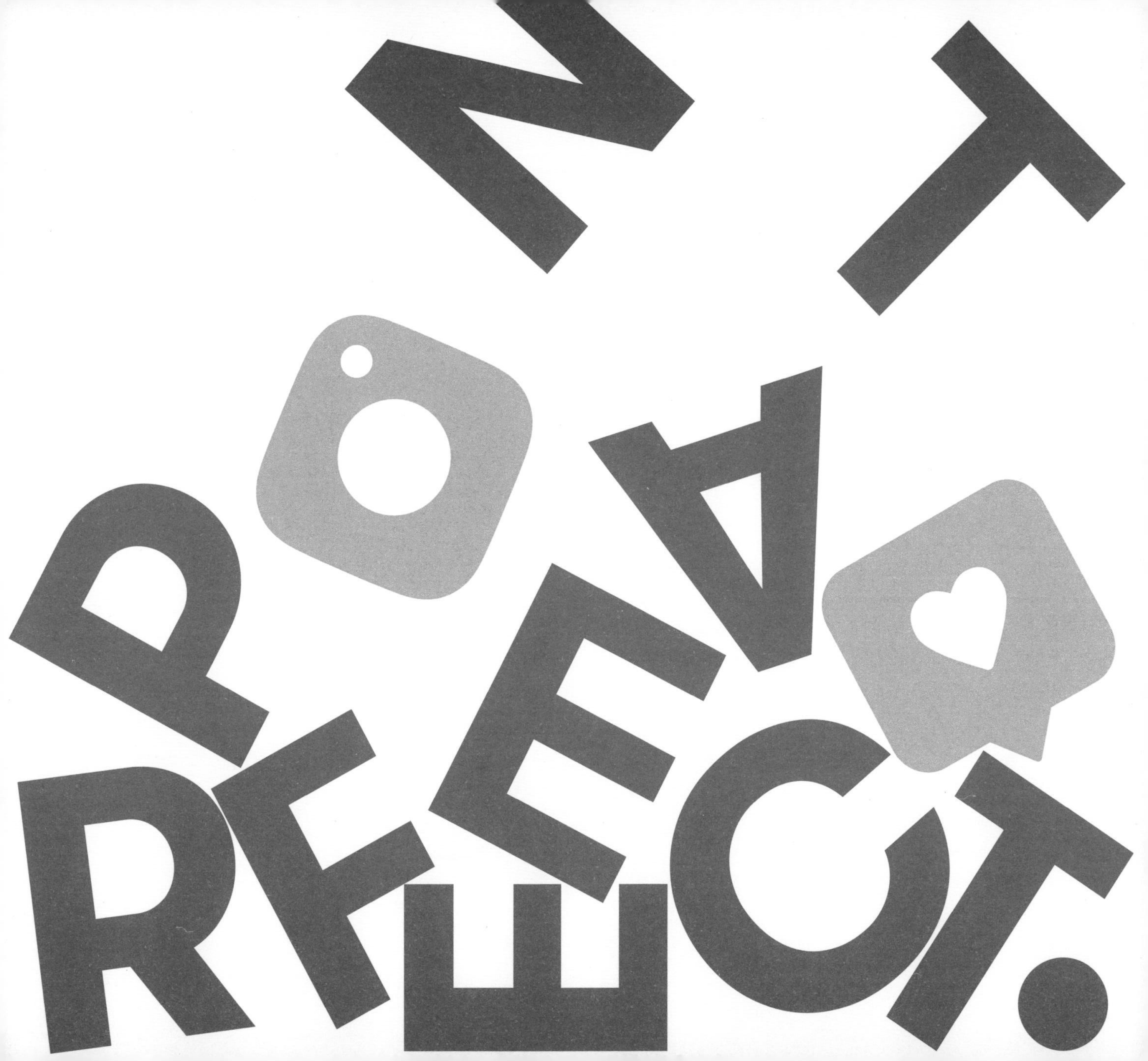

When I first started using Instagram in 2011, I had no real knowledge of social media. I never had Facebook, nor was I ever interested in interacting with anyone through virtual reality. To top it all off, I had no idea what photography was about. While I was no stranger to art as I grew up reading art books and auction catalogues, I was somehow convinced that a photograph was less important than a painting because – to my knowledge at the time – a photograph took only one second to shoot whereas a painting could take hours, sometimes years, to complete.

However, I quickly realised how powerful Instagram could be. By browsing through the popular pages, I came to understand that I was somehow looking at a modern encyclopaedia of photography, as I could discover not only other Instagrammer's creations, but also works by photography masters like Cartier-Bresson, Doisneau, and Brassaï.

The learning process became part of the game, as every Instagrammer's goal was to make a popular page where the challenge lay in creation and originality. I remember how passionate I was and how quickly I achieved that goal to become part of the happy few who shared a 'social passion' for photography.

As passions have their tricky ways of getting to you, I was soon caught up in a daily creative activity that gave energy to my imagination and thirst to my determination. With the overload of information and knowledge I found on Instagram, I probably spent years trying to figure out how to elevate a bad picture into a better one. And even so, I could only have been trying to duplicate other photography masters' creations without learning how the new generation brought a simple picture to picture-perfect status.

Today, when I look back, there is one thing I am certain of. I was far from thinking that my work would end up being exhibited in galleries and art fairs all around the world; and that I would go from being a non-creative (I am a

This is precisely why I never turned my back on Instagram. Other people's works are still a major source of inspiration to me, as you will probably discover through those assembled in this book. INSTA-PERFECT is not only about the Instagrammers who have gone from anonymous to popular, but is also mostly about those who have redefined creativity itself, and by creativity, I mean going beyond the strict comprehension of photography.

The ability to give power to an idea thanks to one's talent and imagination can do wonders these days, and many social influencers exemplify this modern phenomenon. They have the ability to make the most out of the medium through compelling compositions – knowing that the hardest thing is turning simple situations into eye-catching moments through strong aesthetics, personality, and wit.

I often ask myself if there is such a thing as perfection in photography, and if this perfection means holding the truth. My conclusion today would be that there is no such thing as a single truth when it comes to creating, as there are as many truths as one can imagine.

There are also those who excel at breaking the rules by redefining the way we capture the world around us. And, as you will discover in this book, their works form the purest reflection of their unique talents.

FOREWORD BY SERGE NAJJAR @SERJIOS

“THE BEST CAMERA IS THE ONE YOU HAVE WITH YOU.”

— UNKNOWN

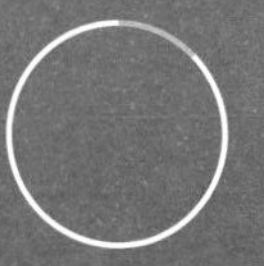

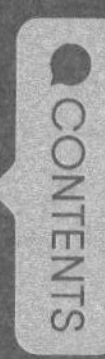
CONTENTS

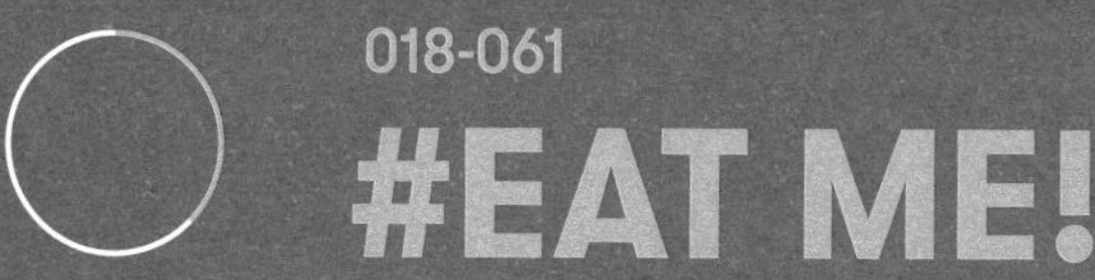

THE ART OF STYLING STATIONERY

Chat with *Neal Whittington* of @presentandcorrect

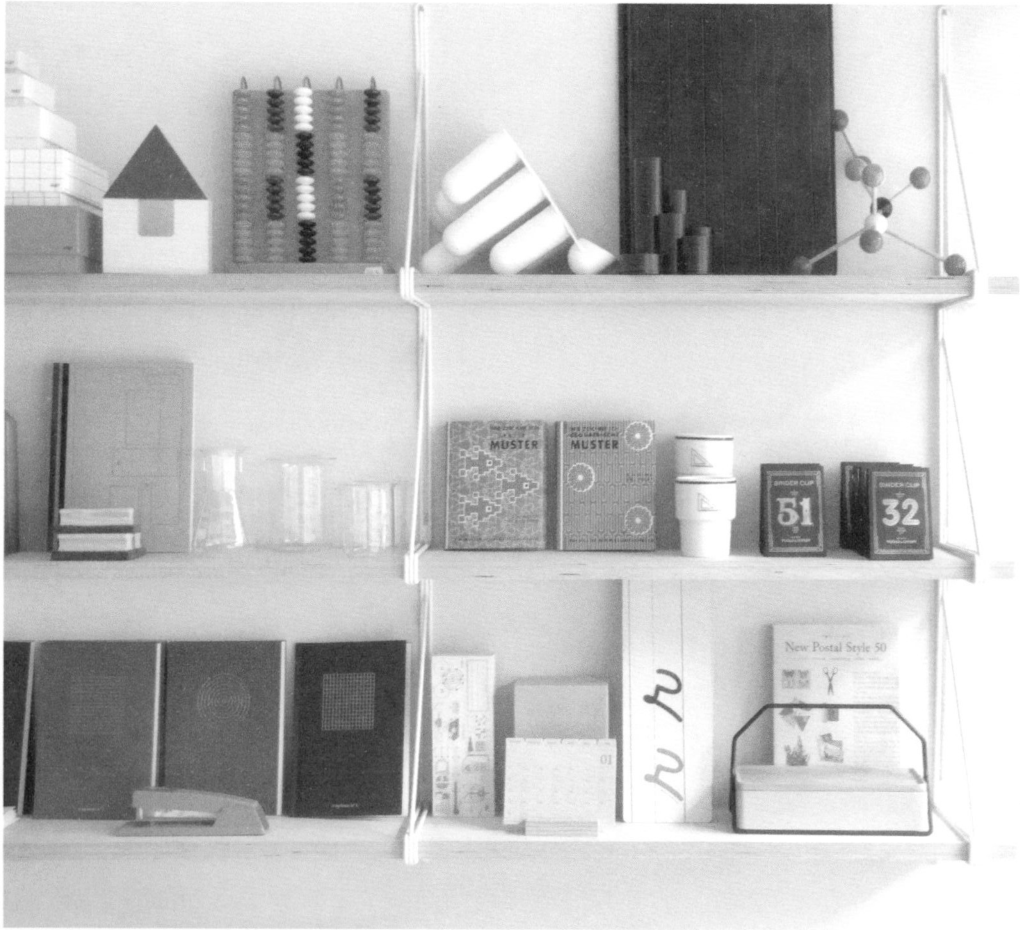

Q: When Present & Correct (P&C) first opened its online doors in 2009, was social media/Instagram the main medium of expression or marketing? If not, when did photography become important for you and how has your style evolved since then? → A: I didn't join Instagram until 2013! Although we had been using Twitter and Facebook for some time, it served us well for marketing and sharing things we liked besides P&C products. Instagram felt like a nice extension of the photography 📸 on our website, where we could create arrangements and have fun with them, in a graphic way. We had always shot our products in a graphic way, but as the website content grew, we slowly made our product shots cleaner and simpler. On Instagram, we get to have fun and 🤹 play around. Our style has evolved naturally because we see how people respond to things, and what people like. I think we have always been playful: it is really important to us that P&C has a sense of fun and humour.

Everybody needs stationery and office supplies at some point, but how much has social media/Instagram influenced your brand and business so far? → For a small business, it is great 🌟. We don't really have a budget for PR, so we have always tried to do our own PR using social media. It helps us spread the word and also emphasise what we are about and what we enjoy. It allows us to show what our world is beyond stationery 📐, in that we enjoy things like buildings, galleries 🏛, nice doors 🚪 – even brilliant signage 🚸.

You showcase stationery and office supplies in a fun light, with thoughtful and stylish art direction/composition. Who comes up with the ideas and concepts behind your photos? How much planning is involved in each shot and what are the challenges you typically face? → We don't plan much, to be honest! If we have an idea 💭, we just do it as soon as possible ⚡. Our popular 'eraser popsicles' post came about because it was really hot 🔥 in London and know how good erasers look stacked up! We restrict ourselves to using things we have in stock. The main challenge is that we don't have a studio! We take photos on the floor. It would be nice to have a permanent photography space set up.

Is having a good eye or instinct important in product photography? What can aspiring photographers do to build that eye or increase their skills? → It's definitely important because your product shots sell your items and also your brand. There are a lot of places that just shoot a product on a white or grey background. While functional and useful, it's nice to have a bit more character I think; to define your business differently from someone else's. That way, you establish a style that people recognise as being yours.

Who is usually in charge of curating your product collections? What drives the theme behind the sourcing process? → I choose everything and the only rule is that I like it. Sometimes, we sell things at no profit just because we love them and want them in the shop. I think that an interesting product mix should be a priority. I love hunting for new and vintage items , and also really try to stock items that a lot of people don't have. That is getting very hard to do. I suppose the only theme is my taste, and that is usually graphic and fairly classic.

Has social media/Instagram been an important tool for you to connect with your customers? How important is building a follower base to you? → It's been really important, and each one brings different interactions. Twitter is great for speedy chats with people, in that they usually use it to ask questions about the shop or certain products. Instagram is brilliant to share places, exhibitions etc. I have always wanted to use social media in a useful way, so we can not only tell people about P&C, but also share tips and ideas.

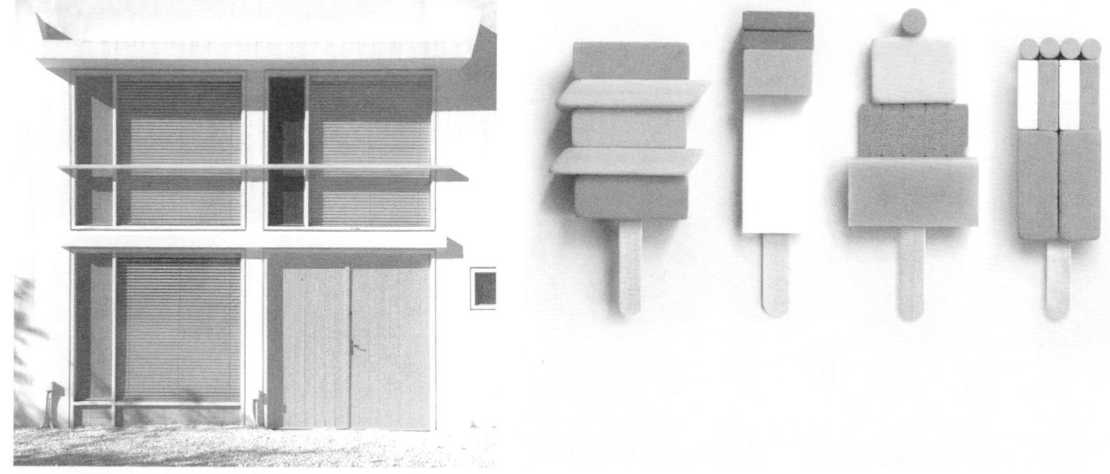

Do you have a dream creative collaboration or project? Who are the digital creatives that inspire you today, and which accounts should we follow for inspiration? → I'd love to team up with a biscuit company and do something stationery-themed. I'd also like to have a gallery space to collaborate with artists and collectors. Accounts that I like include @micahlexier, @virgin_honey, @sovietinnerness, @rrreeepppeeeaaattt, and @erictabuchi.

What would you do if social media/Instagram became irrelevant in the future? Where do you see P&C within the next 10 years? → If social media became irrelevant, we would just have to find new ways to spread the word. Plenty of people survived before it was invented! I love ♥ running P&C, and have a lot of ideas of things I would still like to do. We don't want to be a chain; we want to have one bigger shop and make it as perfect as possible. That's our goal really, and to keep having fun!

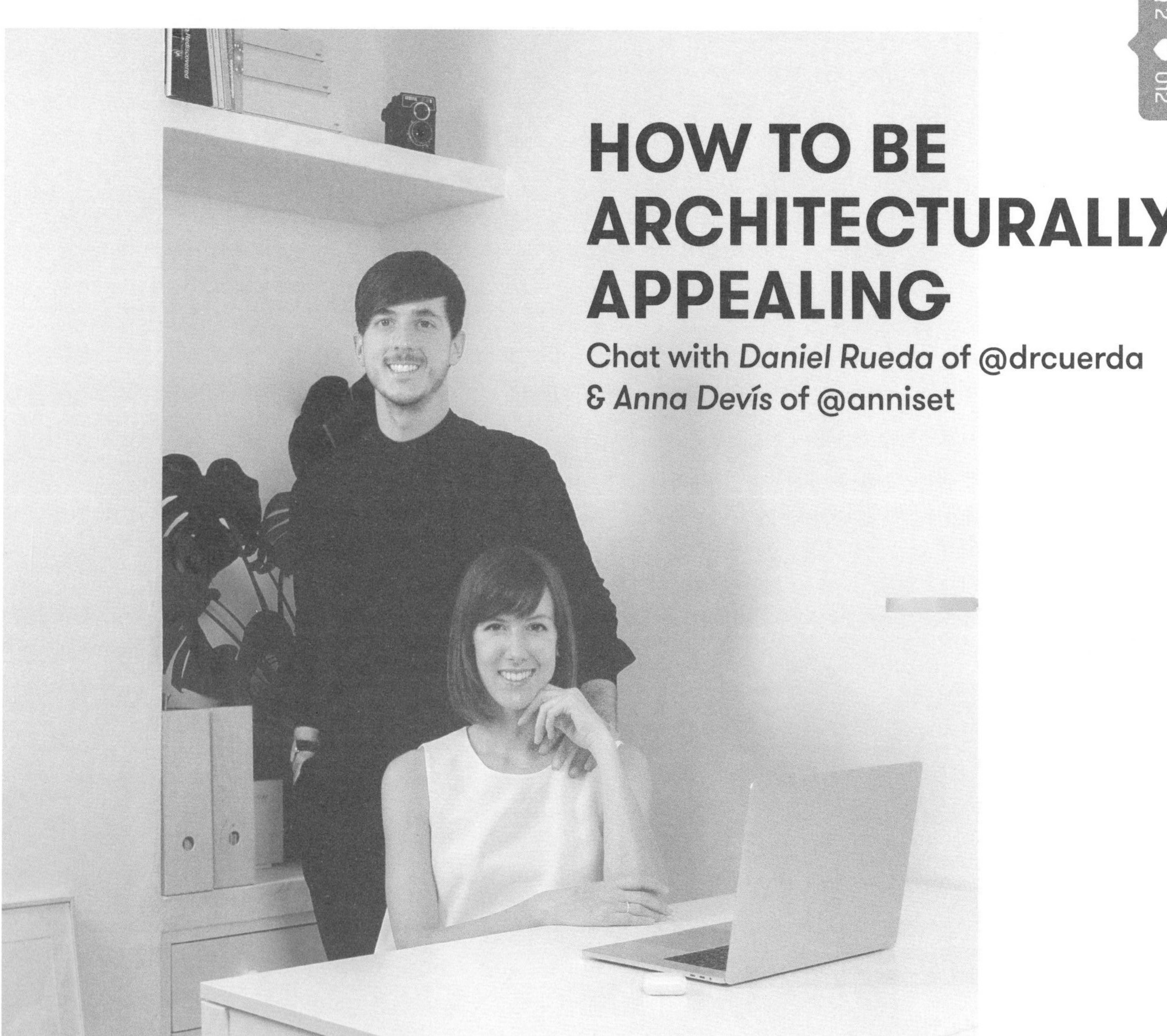

HOW TO BE ARCHITECTURALLY APPEALING

Chat with *Daniel Rueda* of @drcuerda & *Anna Devís* of @anniset

Q: Looking through your work, it becomes apparent that your relationship seems to be a major component of and source of inspiration for your photographs. How and when did you start getting into photography in the first place? D → [Yes, it's] a fact. Whenever we speak about our work, we always try to show what each one of us does separately. [Mine's] architecture-related; very abstract with a lot of geometry, compositions, and literal images, but not very close to the feeling or emotion [whereas] Anna is more creative and freer in that she doesn't pay that much attention to the format. I think we're a mixture of trying to come up with beautiful ideas and creative concepts, but also very passionate about how they look and want to make them very easy to understand. [This is] the result of our two very different approaches to photography combined.

I've always been interested in photography. I was very introverted , so it was something I could enjoy and learn on my own. Also, it's very easy to find a camera lying around [now]. I used to be an architectural photographer's assistant and learned a lot about things like composition, what it means to take pictures of a building, and how you can tell a story → through them, but I was always trying to think outside of the box, and that's how this thing with Anna came about.

It seems like one of the things that drew you to photography is accessibility. Do you think that ties into why social media/Instagram has become one of your chosen mediums for showcasing your work? D → Yes, but I've also been very passionate about technology, social media, and apps, because I was always a little bit of a...geek ? Besides using apps to show my work to friends or teachers, social media also helped me to develop my own style, because when your work is put together, you can see how each picture relates with another to find your own voice. I think it's a very visual way to understand your stuff, what you like to do, and what makes images work best for you. Instagram is also a creative way to improve your work, because you can learn from others.

Do the restrictions on Instagram — for example, size, quality or resolution of the photo —bother you at all? How do you deal with these limitations and still push the boundaries of creative and conceptual photography? A → I think limitations are often a way to improve your work because if you have too much liberty, it's difficult to [crystallise] an idea or a format. In the beginning, the fact that [our photos] had to be [within a] grid ⬛ [on Instagram] because there was no other format, helped us to develop our very specific style. We're [still] fascinated by it, because it shows the amount of things that can be done even with restrictions, and adds a coherent aspect to our work. I think our work needs to be easy to understand, because trying to tell a story with too many elements can affect the impact the viewer will have.

Speaking of viewer impact, your photos always make people smile! How important is building a follower base to you, and what do you hope they take away from your work? D → This is definitely the part that Anna and I love 💓 the most. The first thing that people always comment on – and what we get the most – is, "This picture made my day!" or "This made me smile! 🙂", and I think it's the

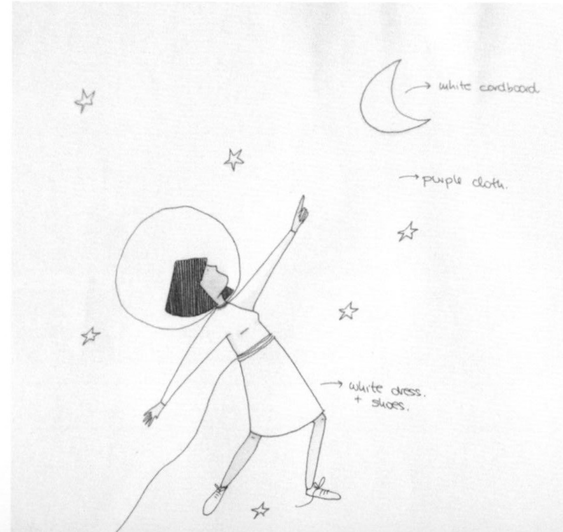

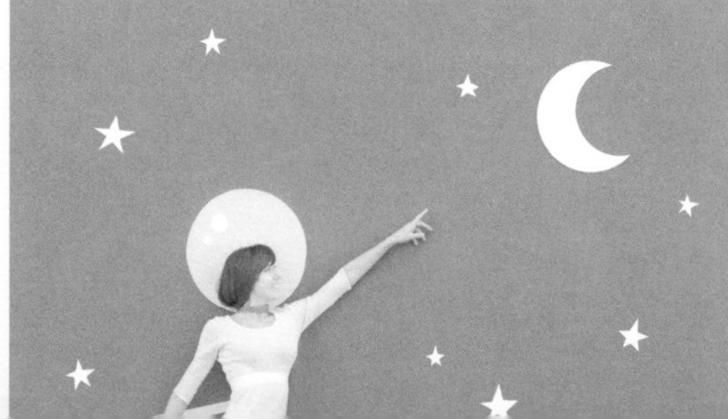

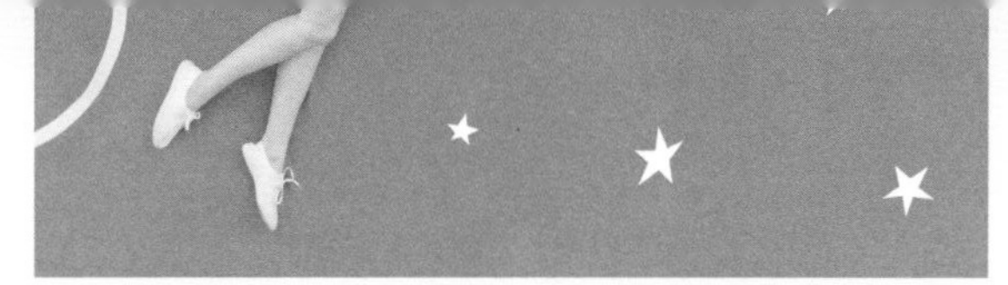

best achievement that we can have. We always try to be neutral and not court controversy to be a safe place for people who enjoy seeing ideas, perspectives, colours, and funny stuff.

In terms of perspectives, why does architecture appeal to you as a concept or a starting point for your photos, as opposed to using products or fashion as the main inspiration? D → The fact that both of us are architects is a very major part of the reason, but I also think that it is because we're truly passionate about it. [Growing up], my family were not as fascinated as I was about what I was studying and it frustrated me, so I've always been trying to show how incredibly interesting a city can be by highlighting the design of some buildings and locations in a way that fascinates people. What we try to do is not for architects or designers. We want it to be for anyone 🌍, really.

How long does it take to come up with an idea and then execute or process and post it? Do you have a complicated equipment set-up? D → We're always walking on two different roads. On one, we're looking for beautiful buildings or locations to highlight an idea or concept that we want translated into photography. On the other, we have the perfect spot – but without a message or story to go with it. These two roads need to align or meet in the middle for us to build an image.
Our ideas are always way too complex to be random, and we always sketch 📝 every idea that we have. For me, this is the most important part of the process and it helps us think of how we can showcase an idea in the most attractive way – right down to the outfit 🧥🌂 to be worn! We don't use our phones to shoot anymore, but in the end, it's not really about the quality of the image itself.

An image is not better or worse because of the camera. It's better or worse because of the amount of ideas and thought that you put into it. Also, many of our images could be easily constructed with Photoshop, but we actually create most of the effects by hand, and if you look closely, everything is a little bit imperfect, like in real life. We only use Photoshop as a polishing tool.

That's very good advice to aspiring photographers! Besides your photos, how do you think your 'punny' captions affect people's reactions? Do you ever have writer's block? A → Coming up with captions and writing those tiny pieces of text actually take up so much more effort than they look like in the end! The fact that our images and the stories we try to tell is so simple, visual, and easy to understand almost makes words redundant. That's why we always like to use puns and jokes 😂 , because we're not going to tell you anything else that's not already in the image. We do everything by ourselves, and rely a lot on ideas and inspiration – which can strike anytime.

In the future, would you be focusing on platforms beyond Instagram, like galleries and museums, or going in an entirely new creative direction? D → It's something that's already happening. There's a gallery in Tel Aviv and Miami where you can buy some limited-edition work of ours, and I think this is really great in that it was something that was unexpected 🐣 — an opportunity that we were not looking out for but has come with a lot of hard work and passion in what we do. [Beyond that,] I really don't want to know. I enjoy the process and the uncertainty of it all. If you had asked me this question two years ago, my answer would have been very different, but I just want to keep doing what I do. I have the crazy luxury of doing what I love with the person I love the most, so I think I'm already in the best position that I could be in. 💘

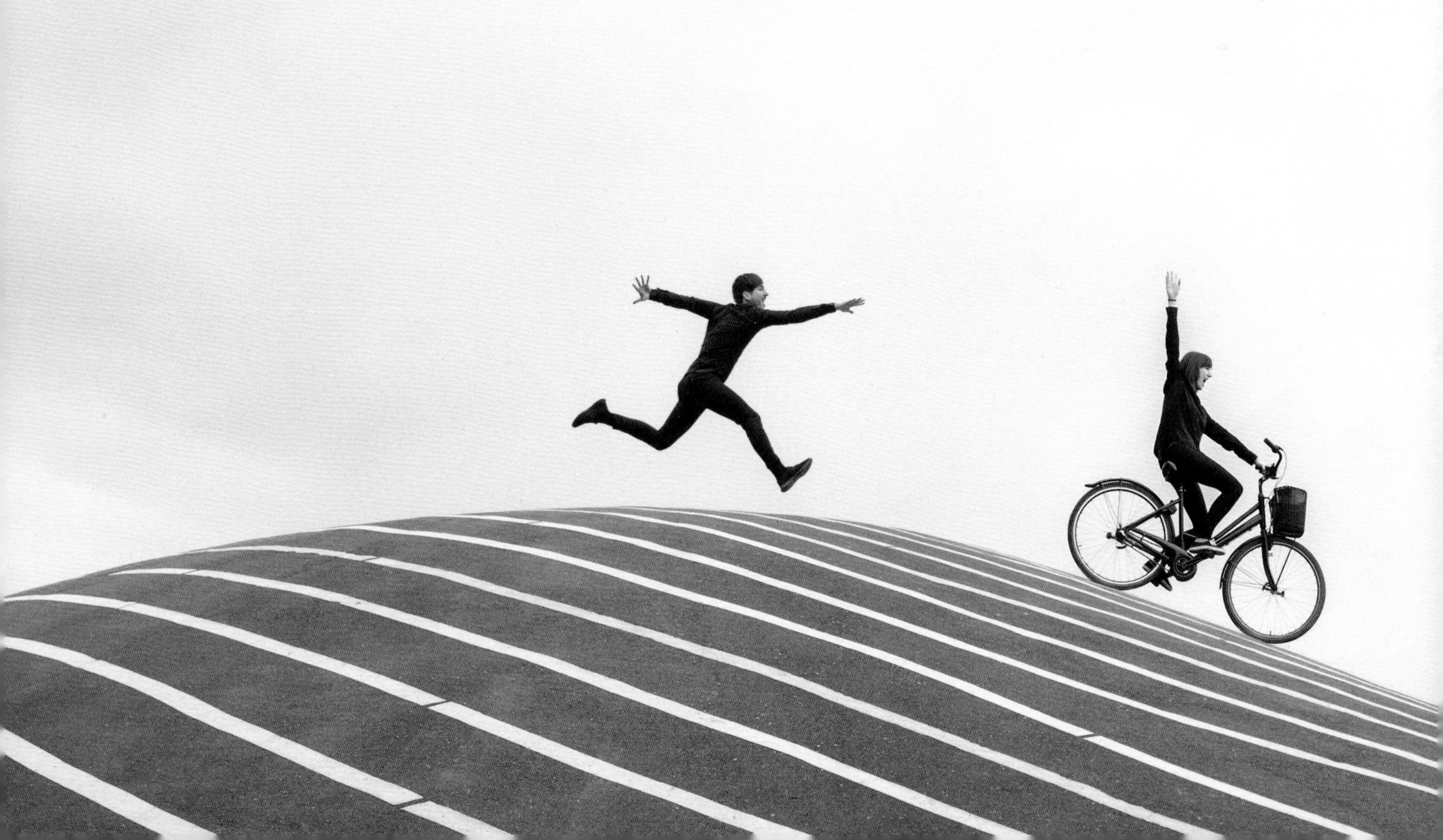

#EAT ME! → Food is always better when shared. From next-level plating and styling to new recipe ideas and ingredients, what better way is there to elevate edibles to art or simply showcase yummy stuff than via an Instagram 'feed'?

Background image by Paloma Rincón

- Eating Patterns / Vega Hernando
- Espacio Crudo
- Russell Smith Photography
- Chung-hui Shen
- Lililoveme & Dmitry Buko
- rvrbr studio
- Paloma Rincón

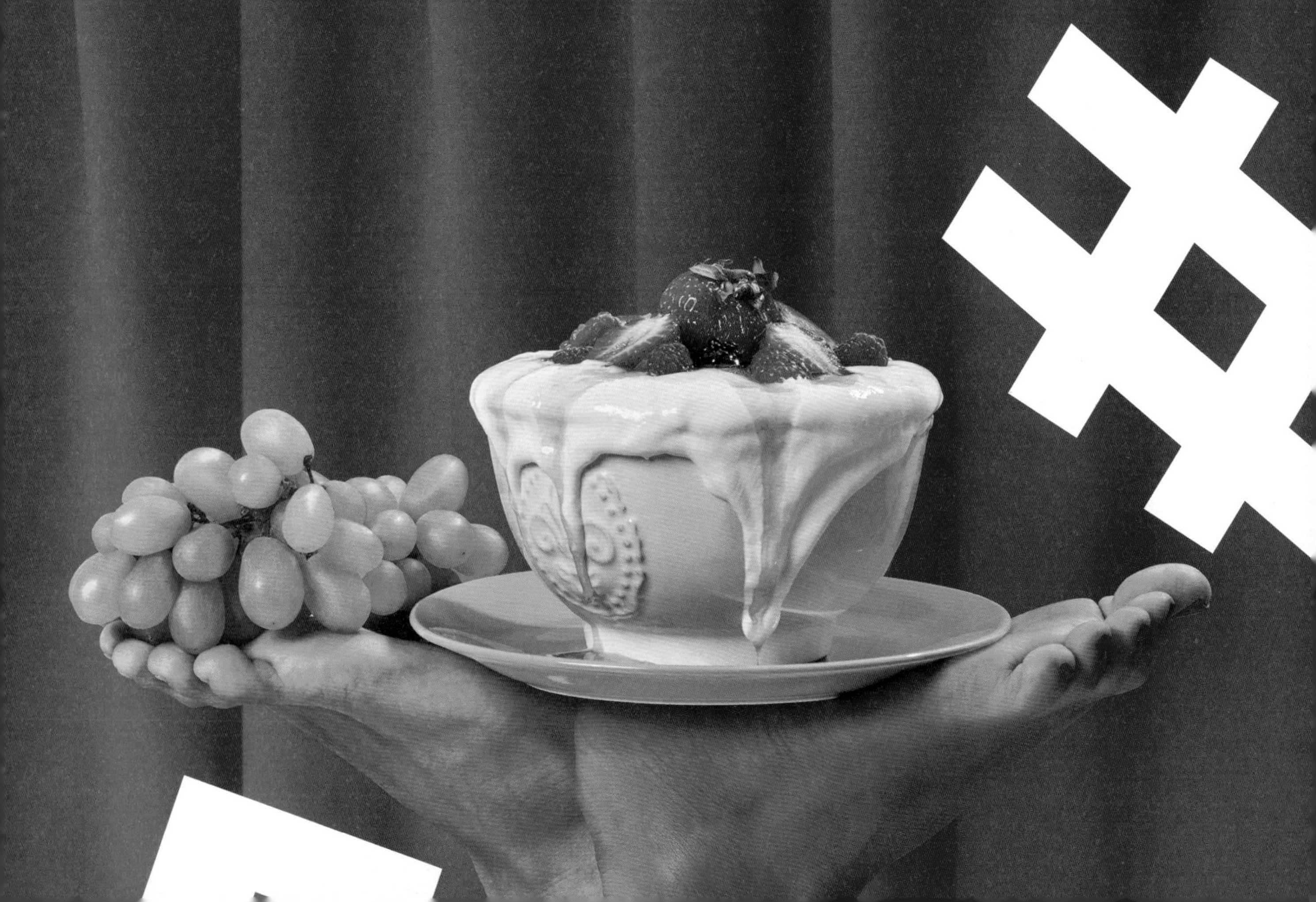

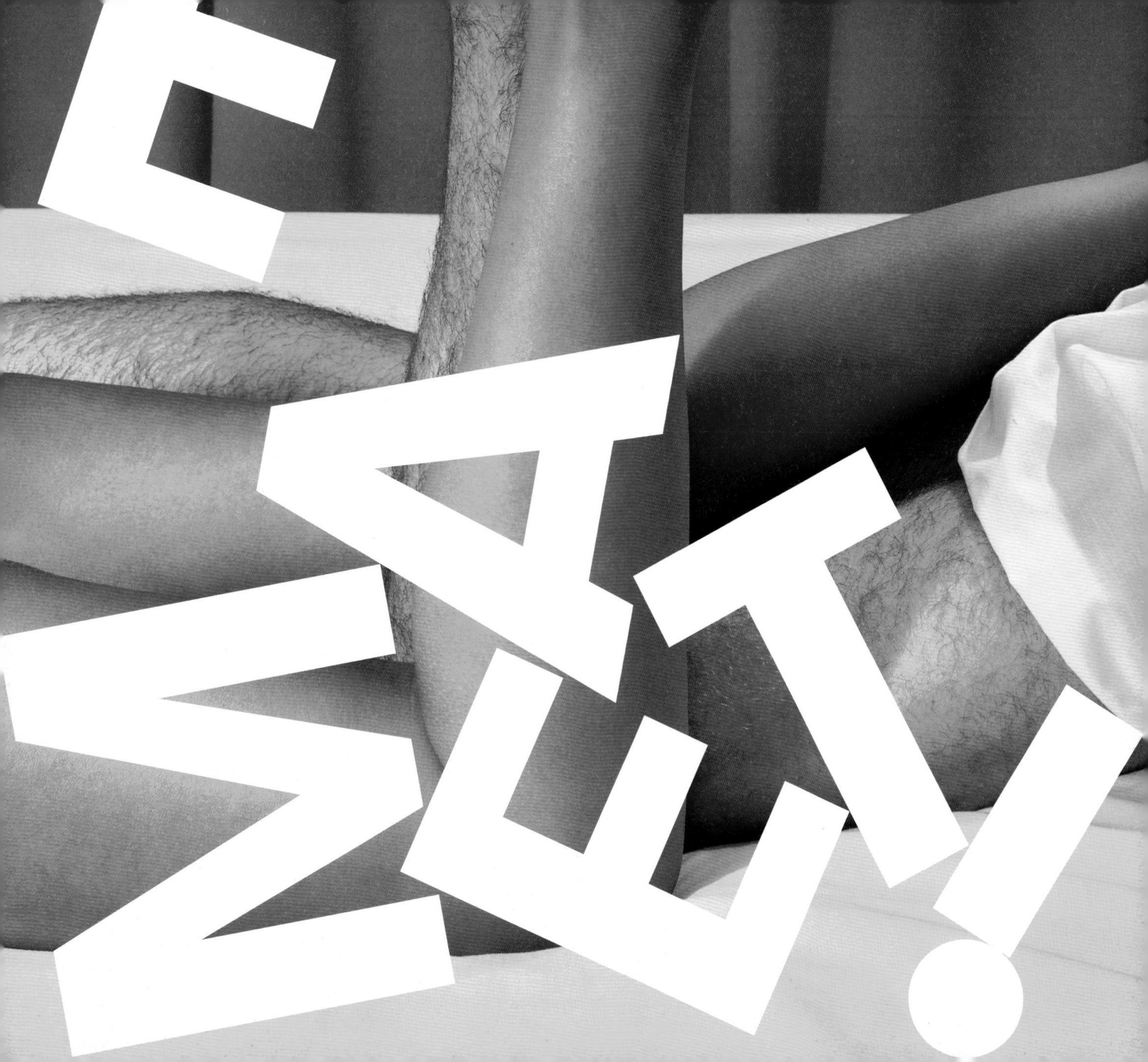
EAT ME!

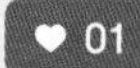

LEARN TO SOLVE PROBLEMS

Technical issues do not stop us. We know pretty much how to solve every issue now, so we just need good ideas.

— Akatre

GO WITH THE FLOW

I rarely use a tripod, as I prefer the freedom of movement to change angles and perspectives by shooting a handheld.

— Eloisa Iturbe

MANAGE YOUR EXPECTATIONS

When your idea seems better on paper than reality, change the lighting or framing from the beginning, so you can still end up with a good image.

— Akatre

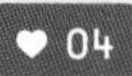

GET IT RIGHT EARLY

We have learnt over a long time that it is way easier to get the shot correct on camera than to fuss about later in Photoshop.

— Compendium Design Store

LOOK AT THE BIG PICTURE

One thing that I especially like, and do not see that often, is the creation of a certain flow in the feed. Sometimes, people have great individual images, but when you look at the whole feed, it is lacking. I like to see some order; some criteria in the way images are presented, and not just a random collection of pictures.

— Eloisa Iturbe

DON'T BE PRECIOUS

The most important design tip I have ever received is: kill your first idea.

— Espacio Crudo

WORK WITH GOOD PEOPLE

It is a full team effort with the buyer, photographer, store staff, and graphic designer to make sure that your feed presents a nice cross-section of products, and that it remains flexible enough to adapt when a new product arrives in-store etc. It is as much planning as it is 'Photoshopping'.

— Compendium Design Store

THINK IN THREE'S

When we make pictures, we do it in multiples of three (3, 6, 9) to have an organised Instagram layout.

— Espacio Crudo

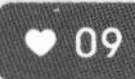

PURPOSE IS IMPORTANT

We develop our images based on a concept. We never take pictures without having a reason why they are made.

— Espacio Crudo

KNOW WHEN TO DITCH THE PLAN

If we are talking about photographs, we do not do any planning. It is 100% improvisation.

— Lililoveme & Dmitry Buko

TIPS & TRICKS FOR PREPARING YOUR SHOOTS

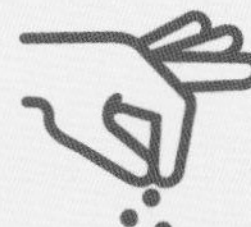

#01-22

BE PATIENT

Shooting products is usually a slow process. Building up the set and trying out lighting take time; and I love that.

— Olivia Jeczmyk

BEGIN WITH A BLANK SLATE

When doing artistic, personal projects, I often do everything from scratch.

— Olivia Jeczmyk

BE FLEXIBLE

I try to have enough space to be able to adapt my image into as many formats as possible.

— Paloma Rincón

GROUP > SINGLE SHOTS

I look at the Instagram grid as a layout, in that I try to keep a balance of tone and types of images so that when you see them as a group, they still look nice. I also try not to crowd the images too much.

— Present & Correct

DRAW, DRAW, DRAW

Everything we shoot always starts with a simple sketch, so we can be sure that the image will have a certain impact.

— Studio Furious

BOUNDARIES BREED CREATIVITY

I think limitations are often a way to improve your work because if you have too much liberty, it is difficult to [crystallise] an idea.

— Daniel Rueda & Anna Devís

LOOK AT EVERY DETAIL

We plan based on themes of colour and tone, regularly making use of negative spaces to create a smooth transition between images and aid highlighting our garments as the main focal point of our feed.

— Olive Clothing

BE FLEXIBLE

When things do not turn out as planned, you just have to be fluid and willing to change.

— Wilson Wong

EQUIPMENT IS NOT EVERYTHING

In my opinion, what still makes the difference today is the ability to rely on sensations, to be able to design the images before they are taken; projecting in the mind a result as precise as possible, and organising the set for this to happen.

— Nicola Galli

SPEND TIME IN THOUGHT

Think about what you are trying to achieve, prepare well before hand, and take your time before a shoot to process it all. Better before than after when it is too late.

— Russell Smith

BE CLEVER WITH TECH

I like to use technology because it shortens the path between what I see in my mind and what the finished work is.

— Nicola Galli

BE SUCCINCT

In social media, especially Instagram, the story is usually told in one image post and it is quite limiting in terms of layouts and different ways to present images.

— Sharon Radisch

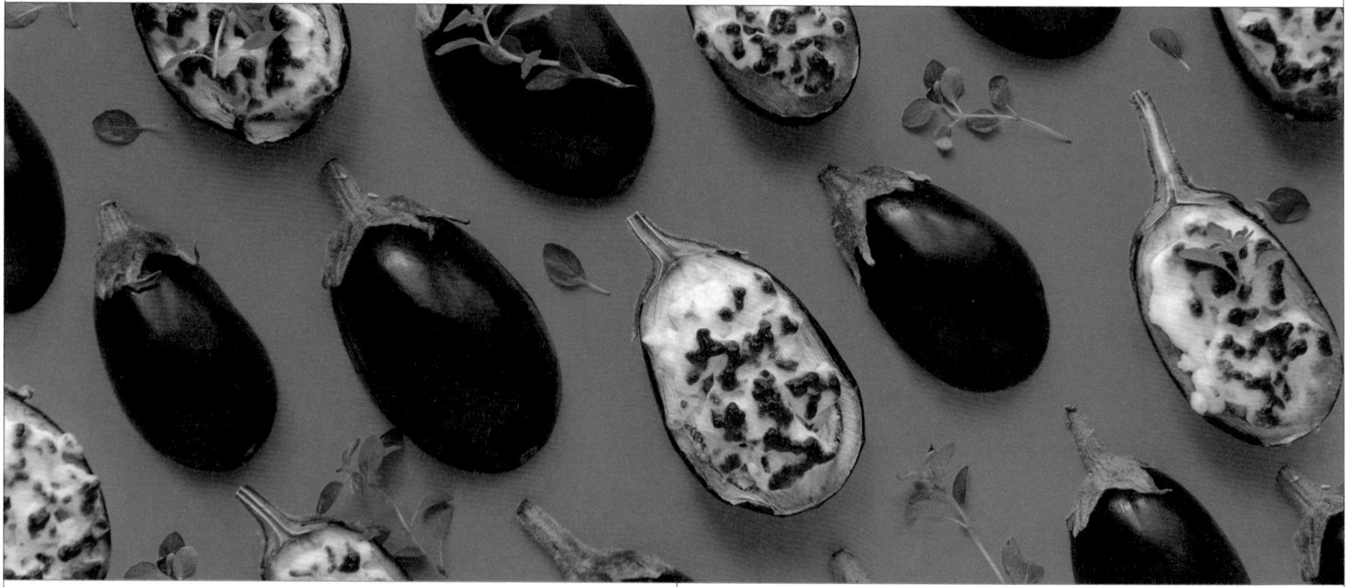

EATING PATTERNS / VEGA HERNANDO

eatingpatterns

Vega Hernando launched Eating Patterns as a means to share her vision for cuisine and the recipes she likes to cook. What started out as a creative exercise has now become her profession, through which she creates content for brands that fuse design and gastronomy.

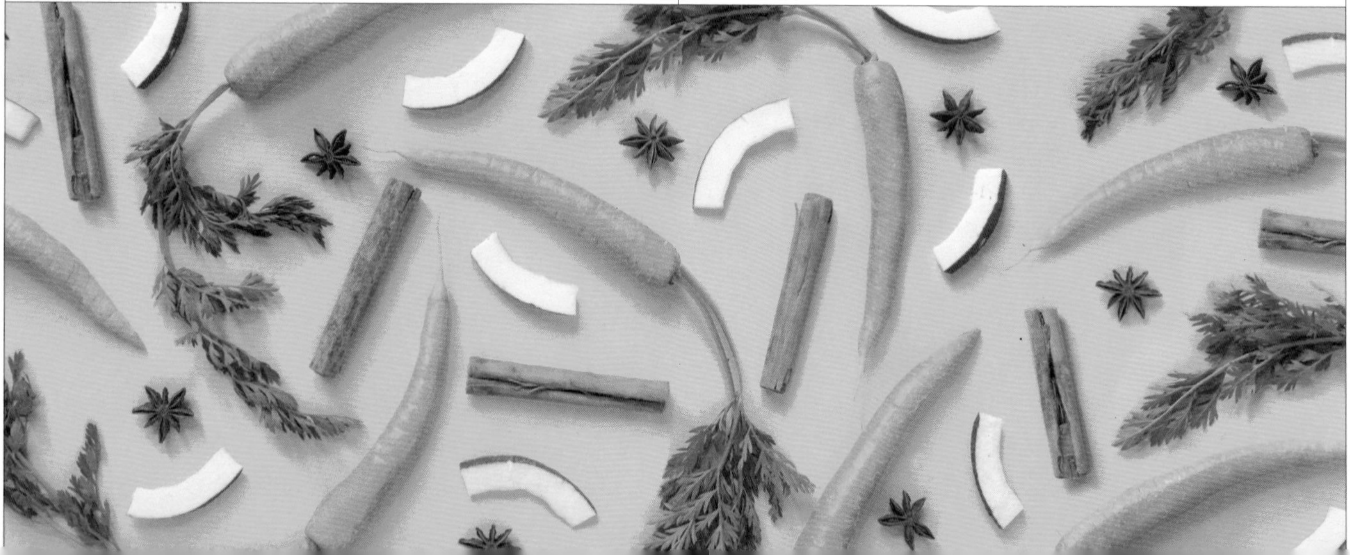

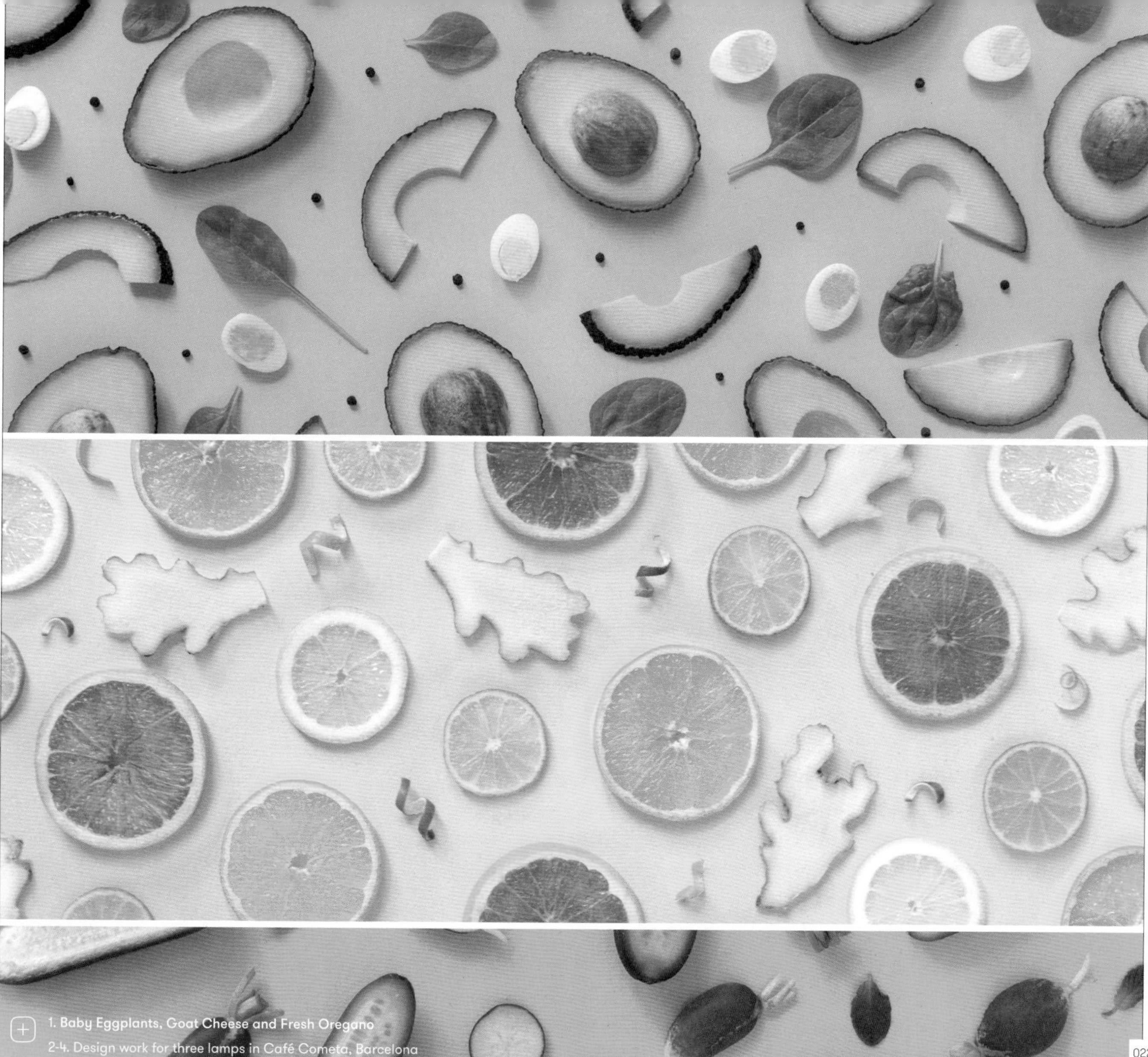

1. **Baby Eggplants, Goat Cheese and Fresh Oregano**

2-4. Design work for three lamps in Café Cometa, Barcelona using ingredients from their top dishes.

Client: Café Cometa

5. **Cucumber, Radish and Mint Salad**

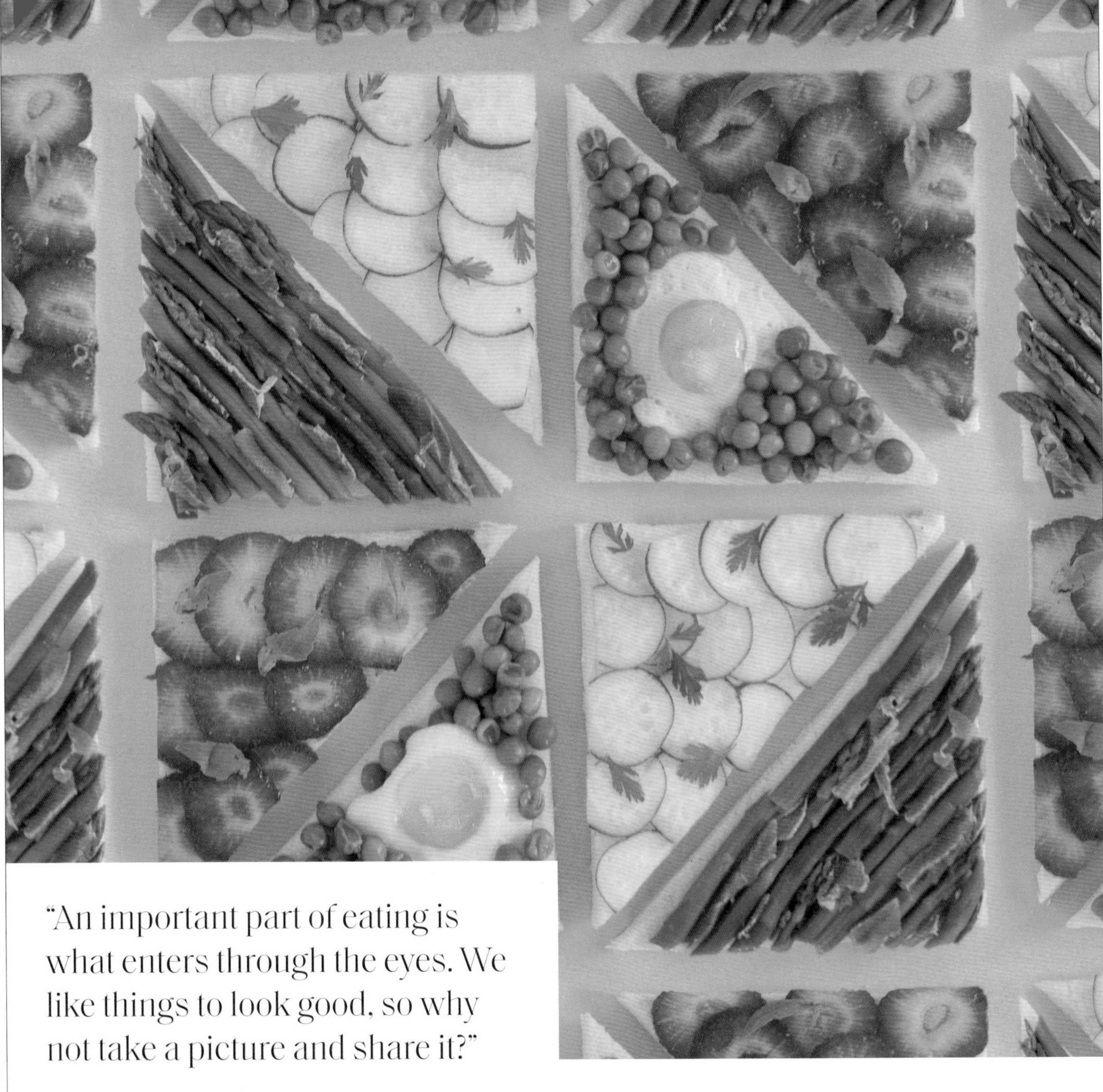

"An important part of eating is what enters through the eyes. We like things to look good, so why not take a picture and share it?"

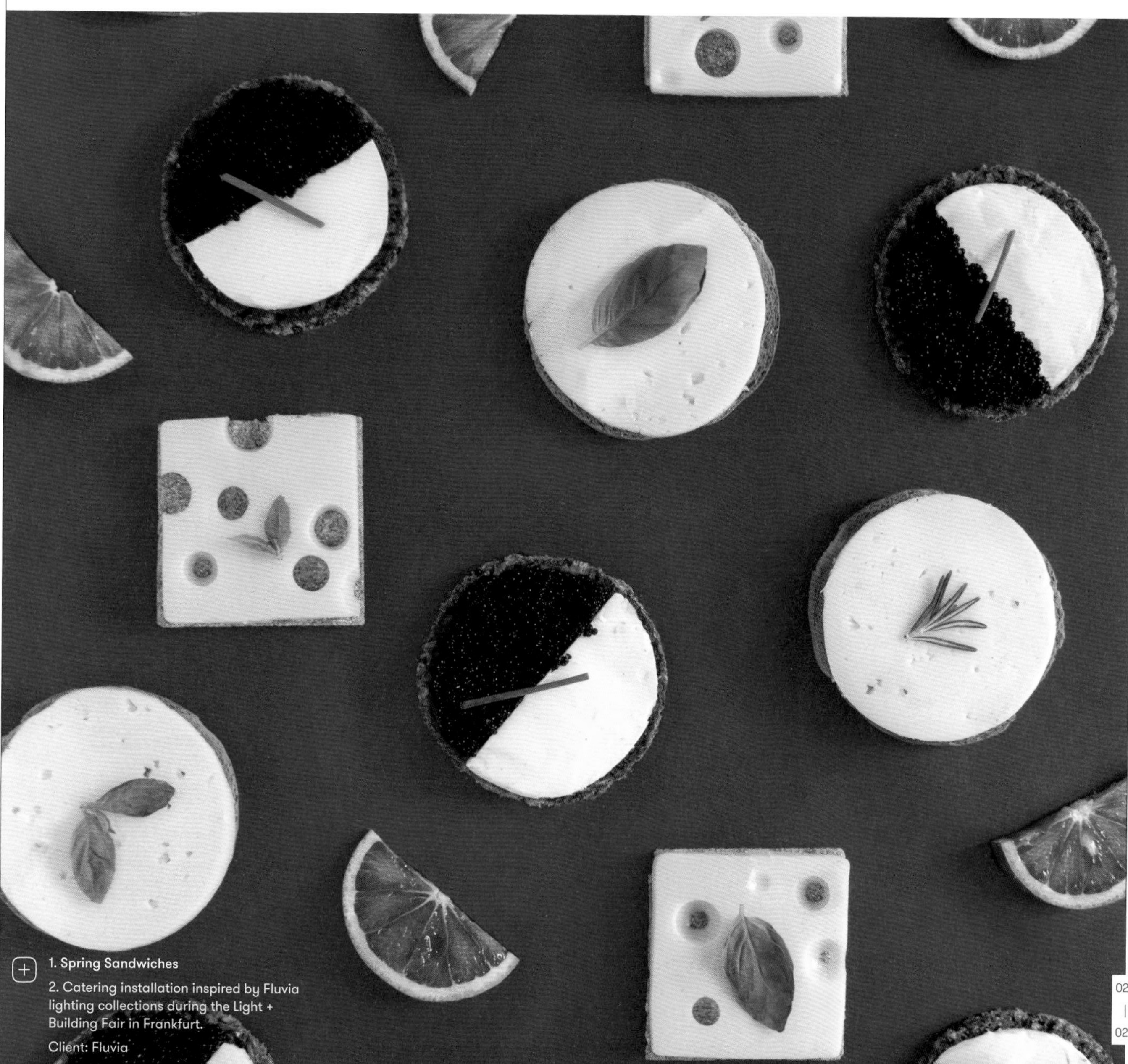

1. **Spring Sandwiches**

2. Catering installation inspired by Fluvia lighting collections during the Light + Building Fair in Frankfurt.

Client: Fluvia

Kumquat Margaritas

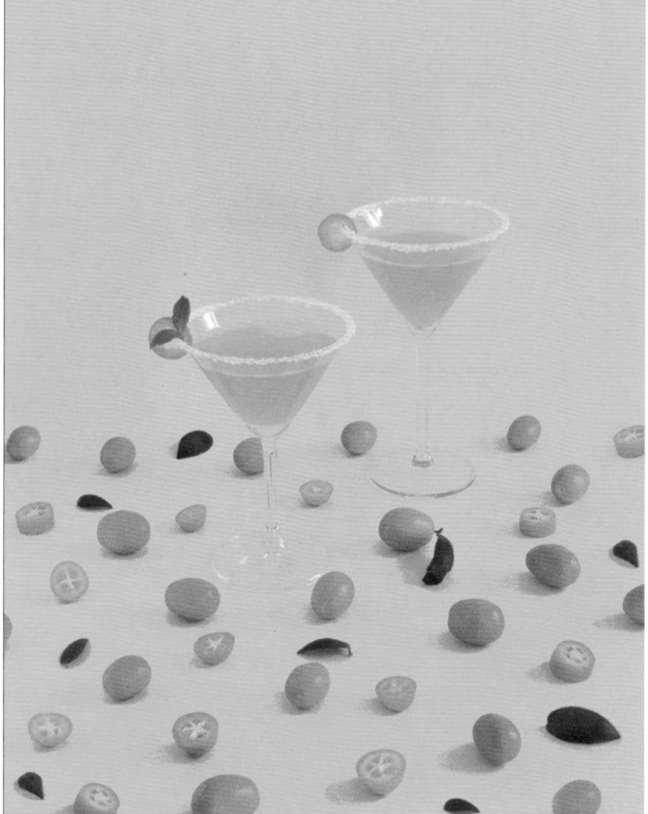

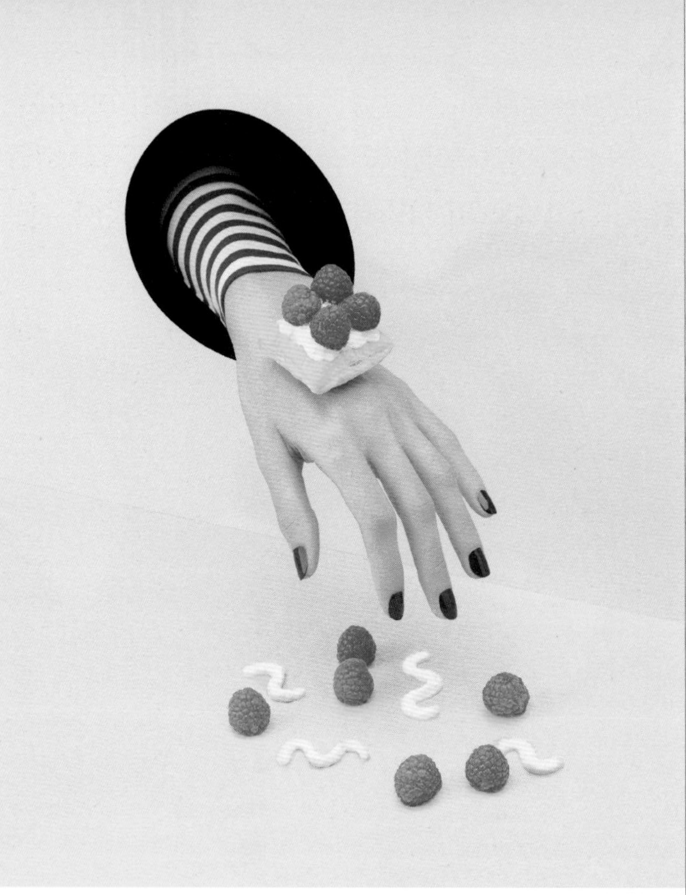

French Desserts
Art direction for the menu of SOMOS night restaurant at Hotel Barceló Torre Madrid.

Client: Barceló / Design: Ele & Uve / Photography: Anne Roig

Family Treasures
Vintage hand-painted plates from Philippines and some fresh herbs from Vega's mother-in-law's garden.

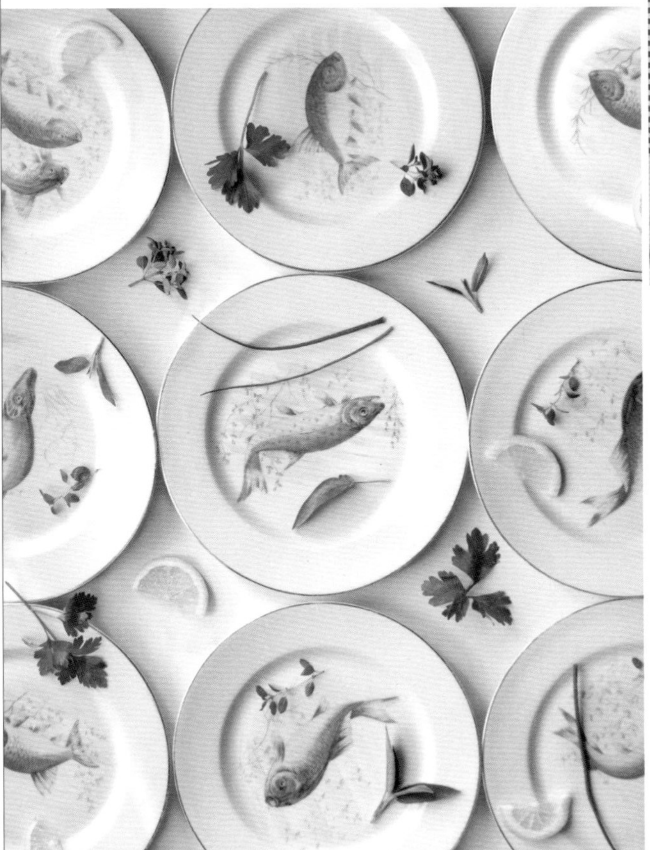

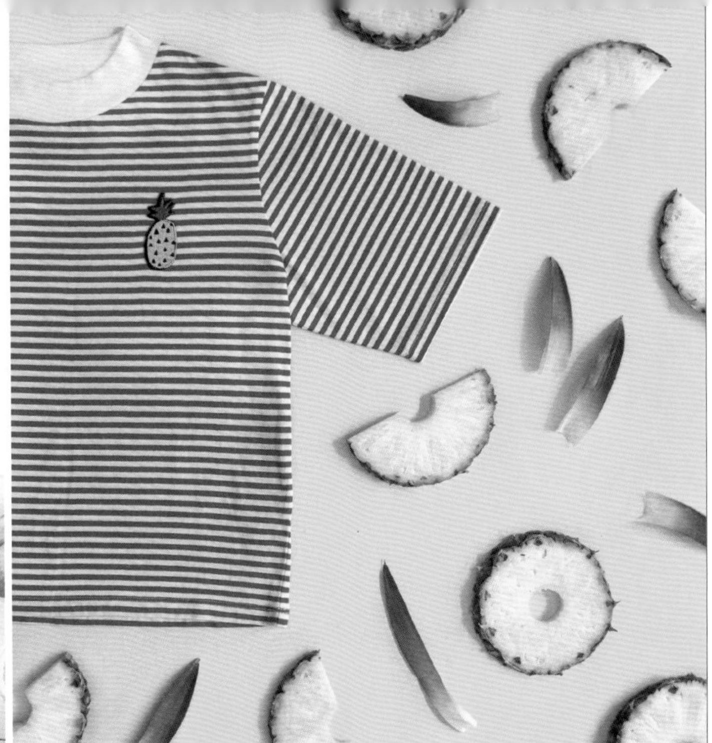

Pineapple Tee
Lazy Oaf's Summer'17 Collection Editorial

Client: Lazy Oaf

"Publishing what we eat allows us to share experiences and knowledge with others."

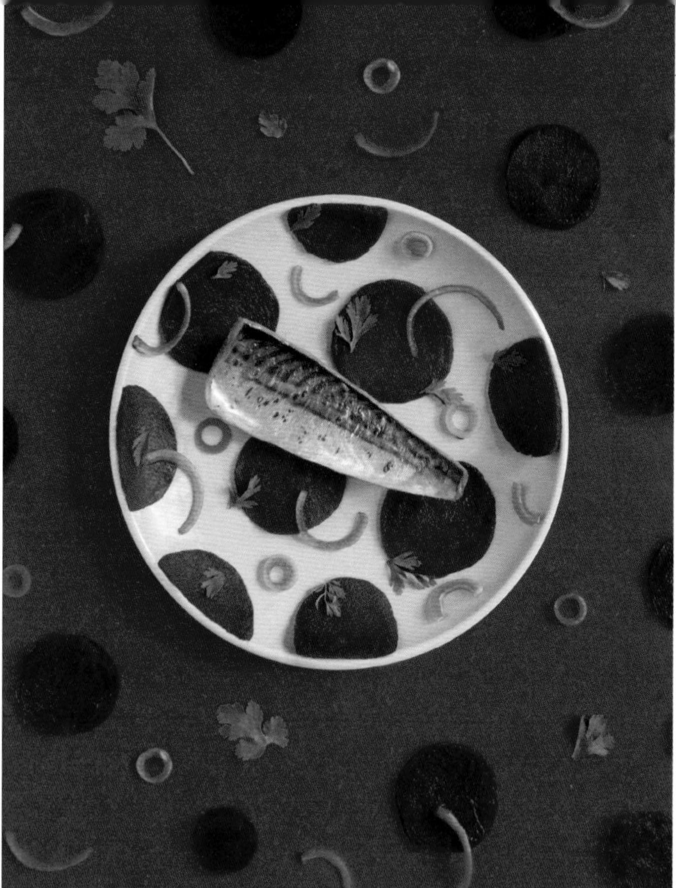

"I think that there is more awareness about what we eat and the relationship between food and health..."

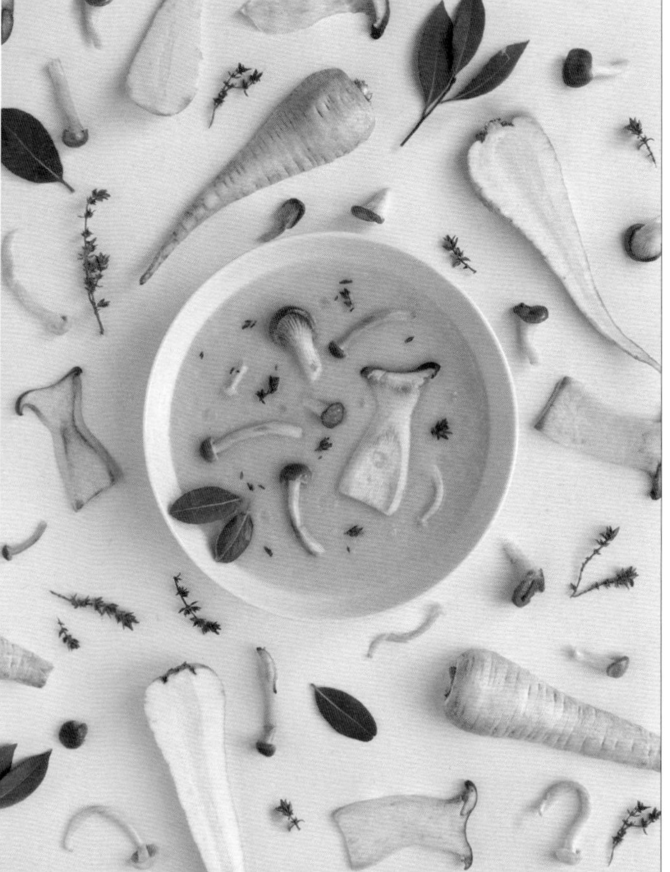

1. Grilled Mackerel with Sweet and Sour Beetroot

2. Parsnip and Mushroom Soup with Thyme and Bay Leaves

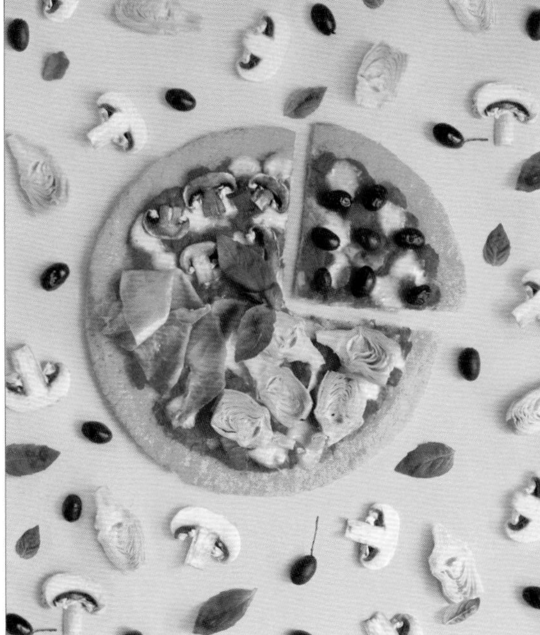

"...that is why we are giving more importance to what we put on our plate than before."

3. Quattro Stagioni Polenta Pizza

4. 'Black is such a happy colour'. Squid Ink Pasta with Cherries, Prawns, and Dill.

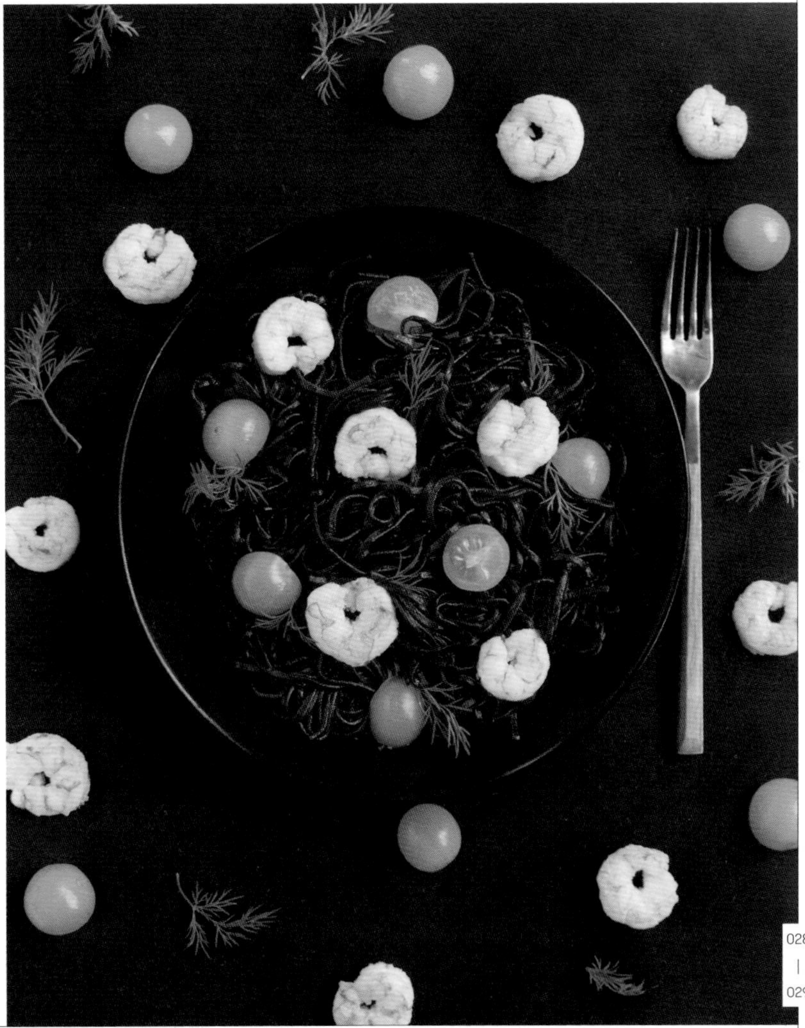

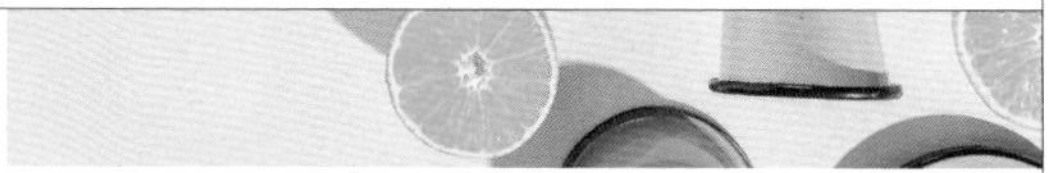

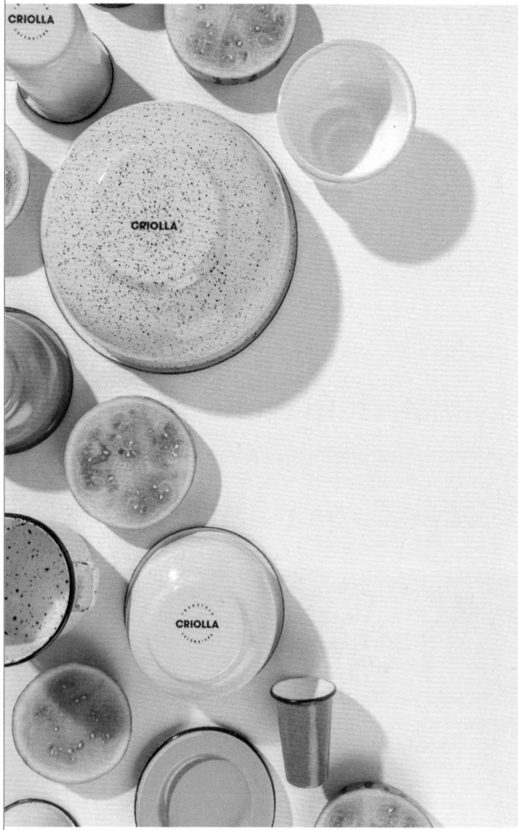

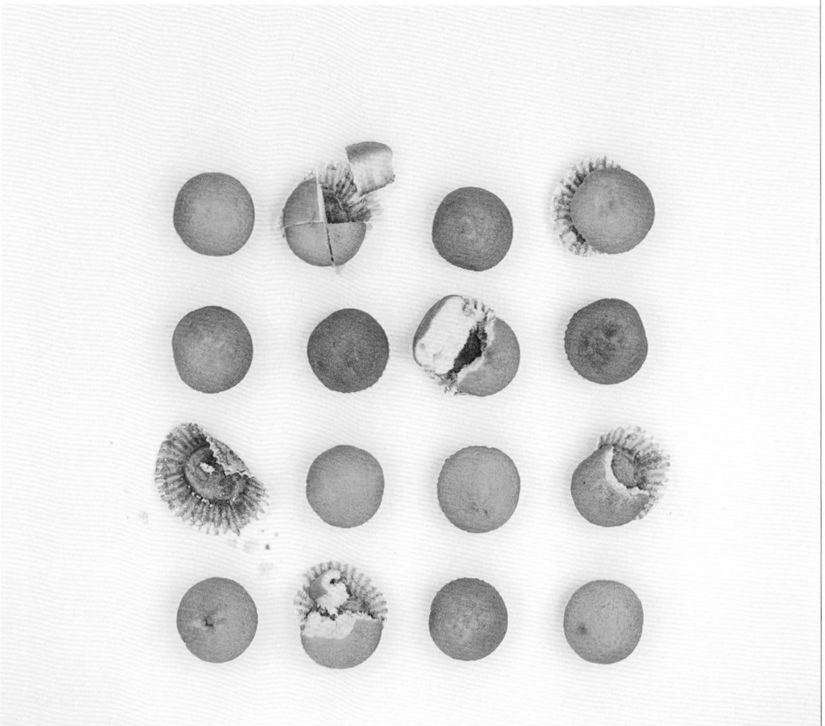

2, 3, 6. **Mecato (Snacks)**
Recreations of 'Proustian memories', where smells or tastes unlock past recollections.

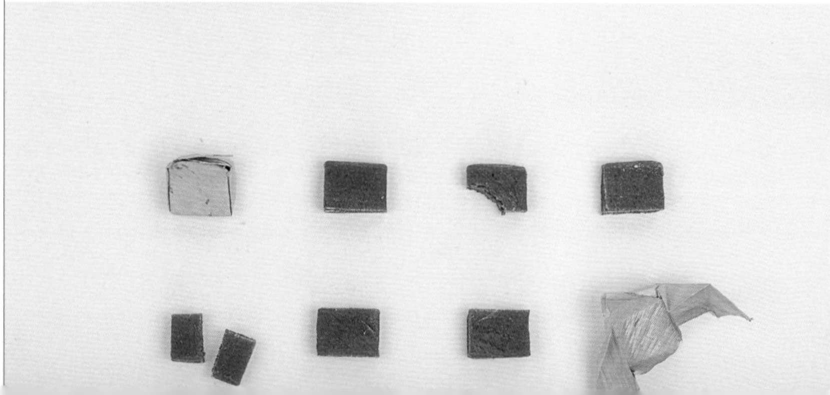

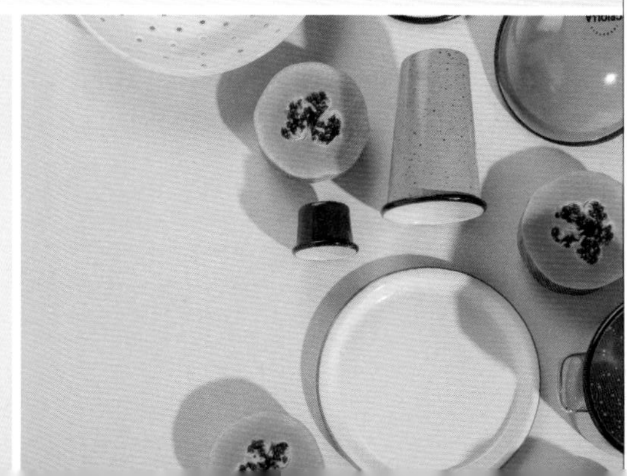

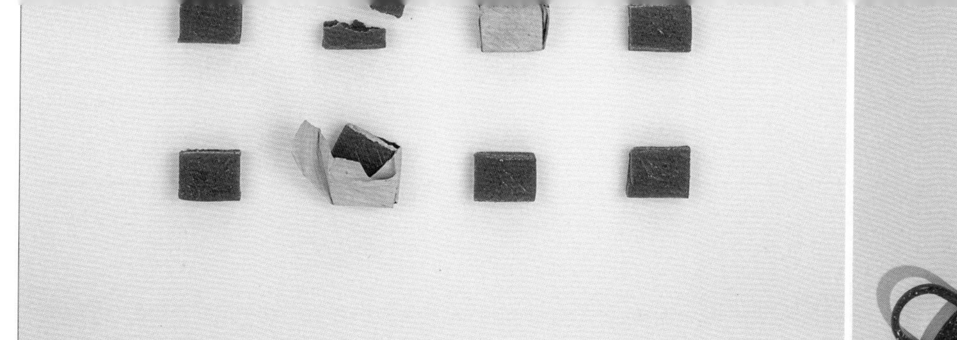

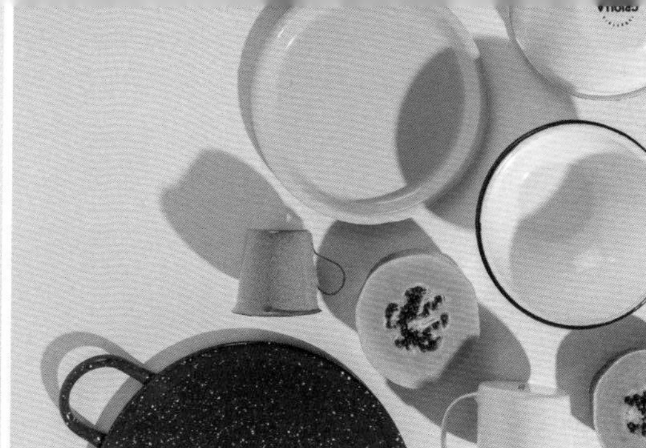

ESPACIO CRUDO

espacio_crudo

Espacio Crudo is a food design and photography studio run by a designer, a photographer, and a food stylist located in Bogota, Colombia. The trio focus on the re-interpretation of aesthetics and concepts around food, where they play with ingredients, recipes, table manners, and traditions.

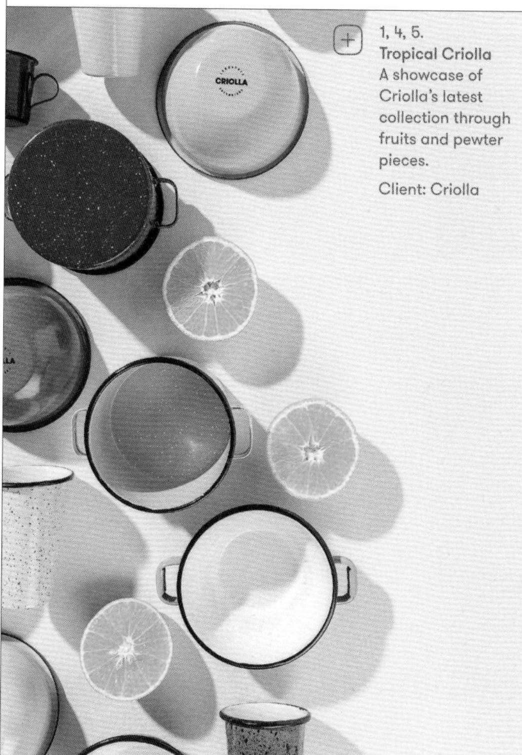

1, 4, 5.
Tropical Criolla
A showcase of Criolla's latest collection through fruits and pewter pieces.

Client: Criolla

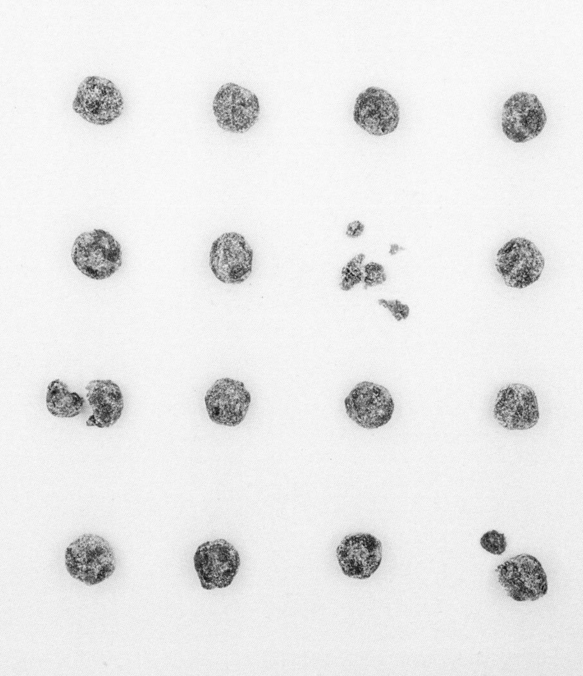

"Social media has helped food photographers show the best dishes and the best plating."

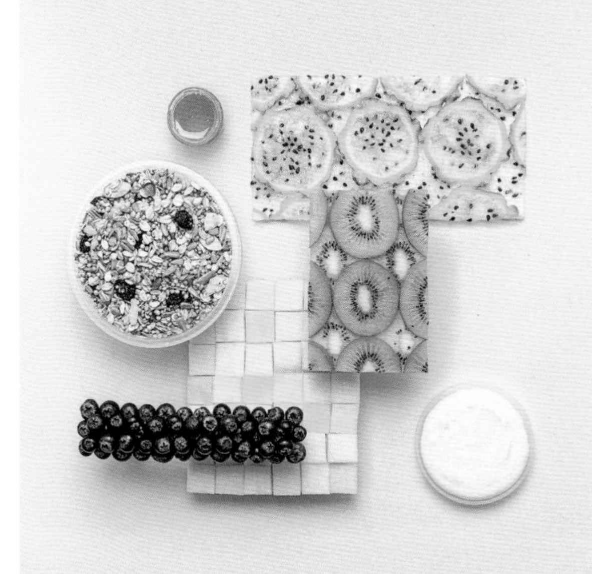

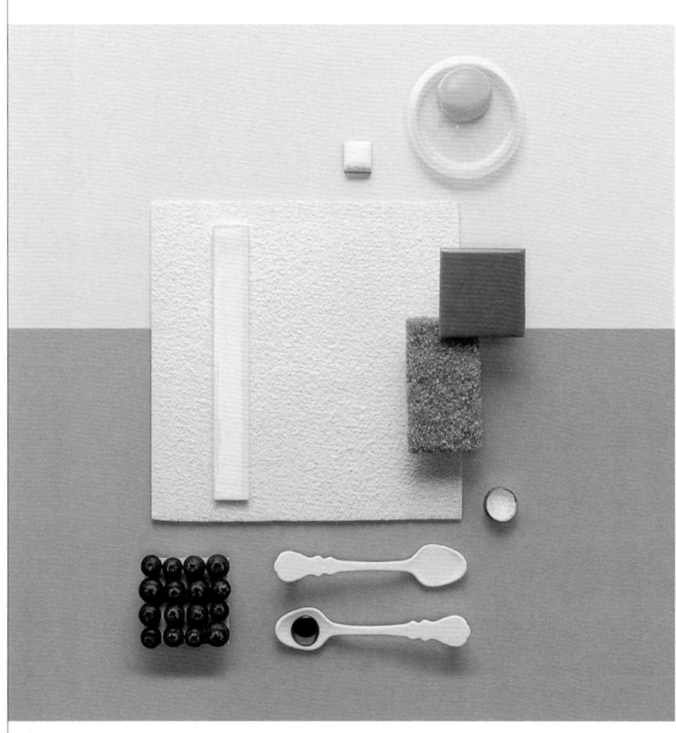

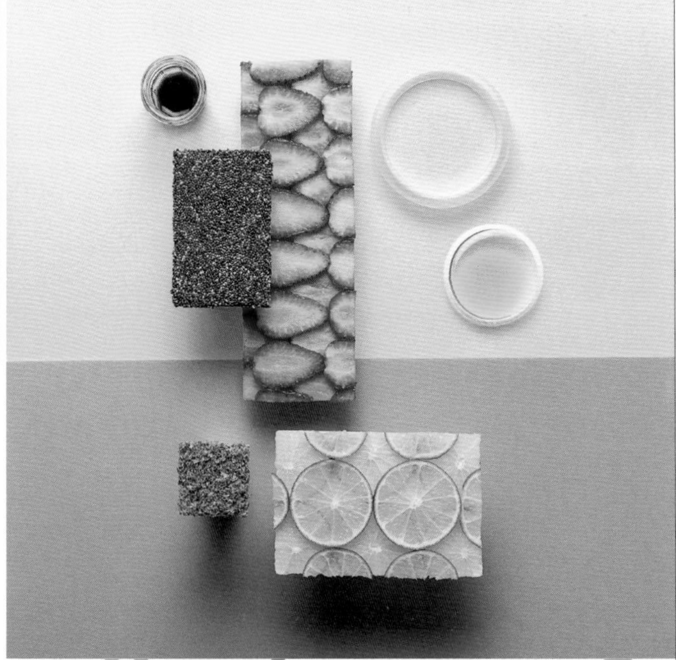

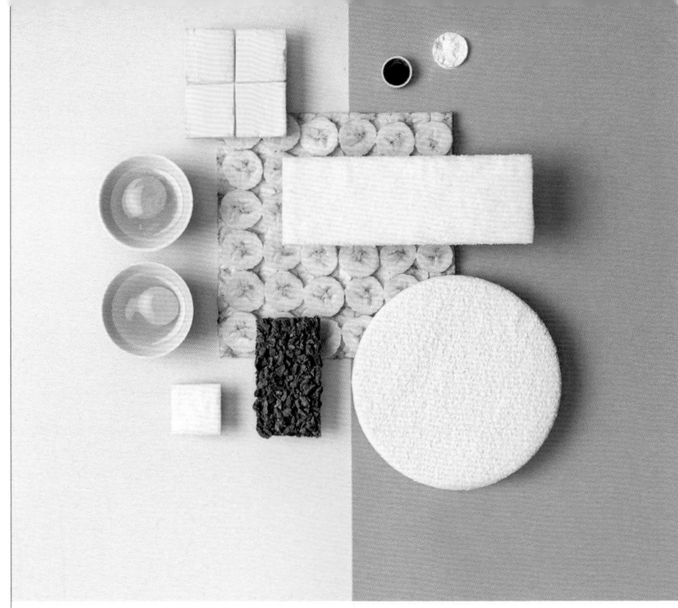

“We help restaurants, chefs, and brands communicate ideas, but with everybody taking pictures all over, people tend to think that our job is easy... :(”

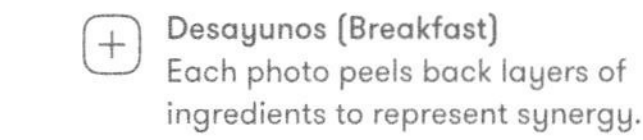

Desayunos (Breakfast)
Each photo peels back layers of ingredients to represent synergy.

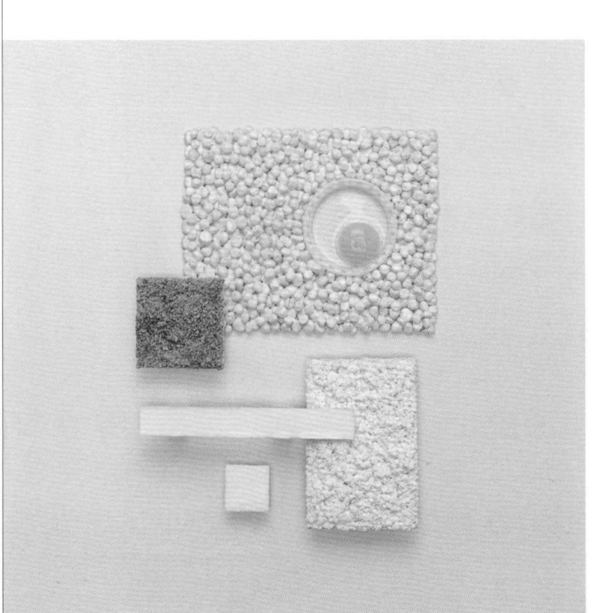

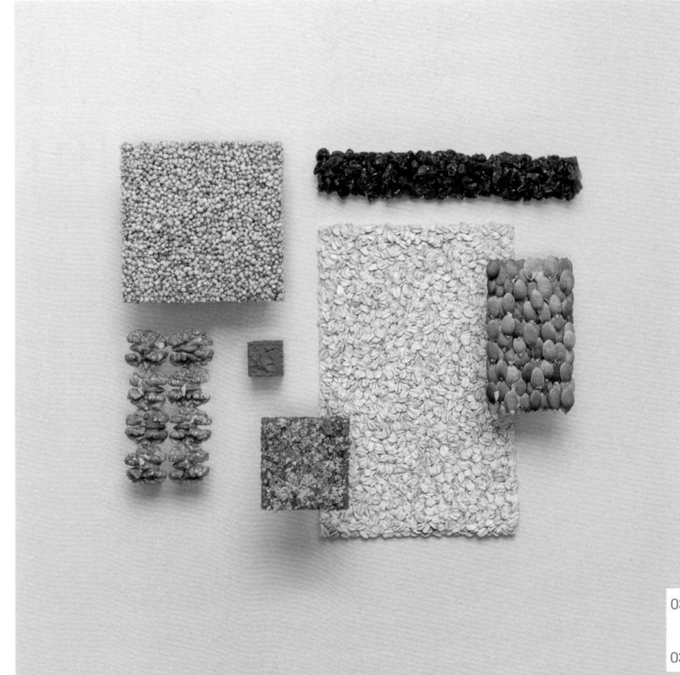

Flapjack, omelette, salad, smoothie, wrap
Client: Numi Health Food Chain

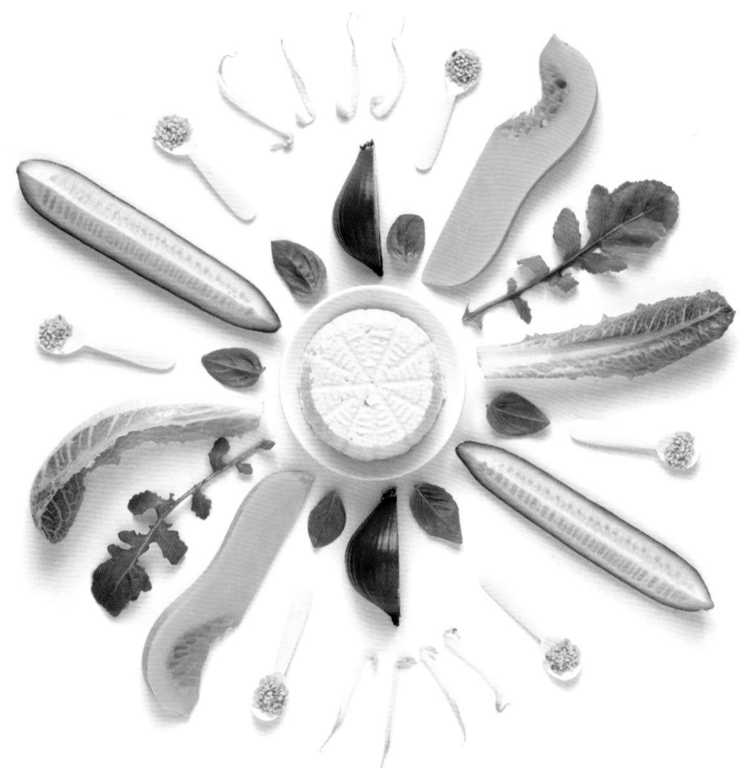

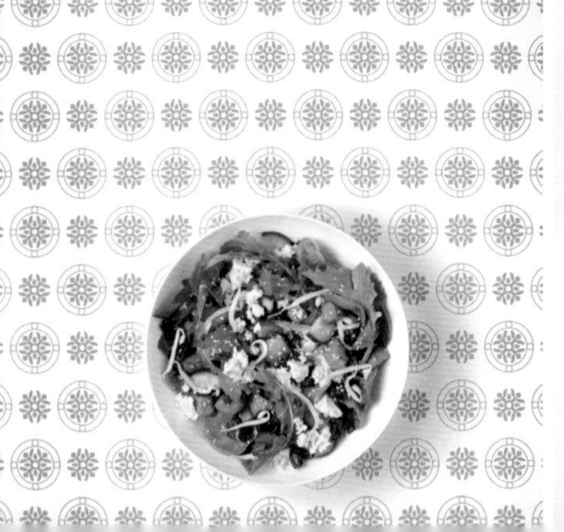

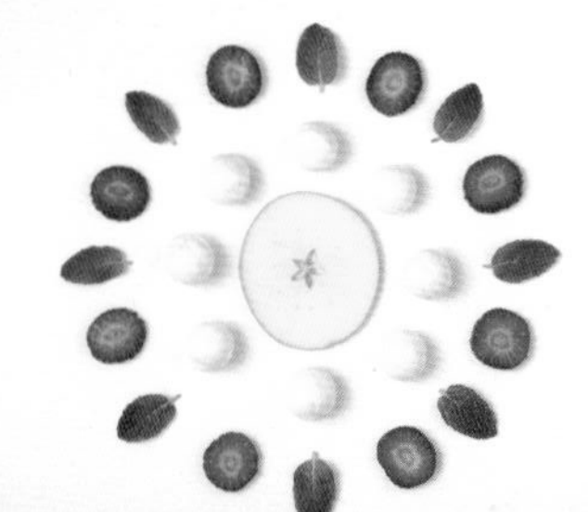

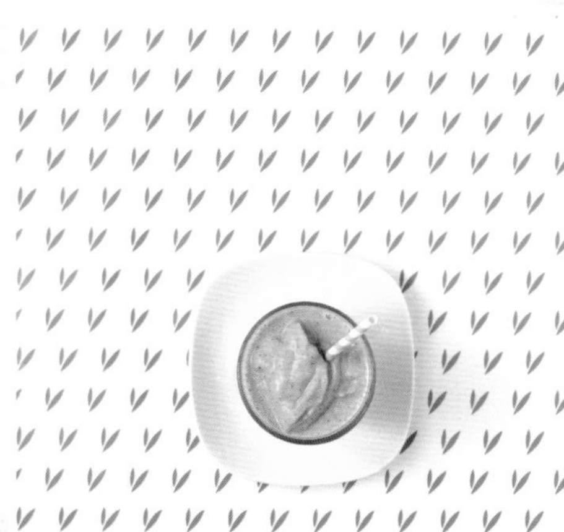

RUSSELL SMITH PHOTOGRAPHY

russmithphotography

Russell Smith has been shooting professionally for 15 years. With a background in art direction, his passion lies in lighting, the little details, and bringing the best concepts to life for his clients.

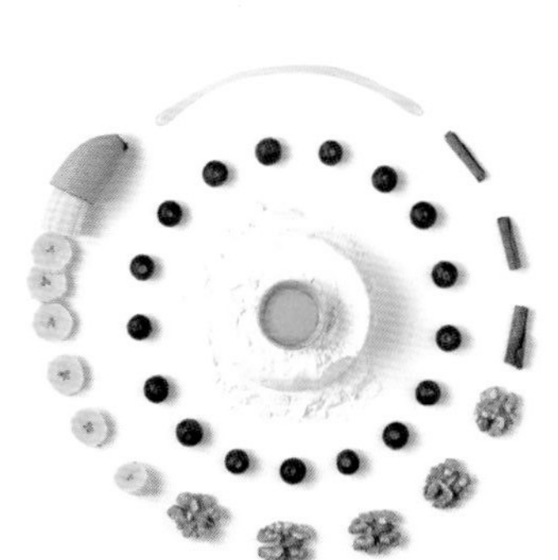

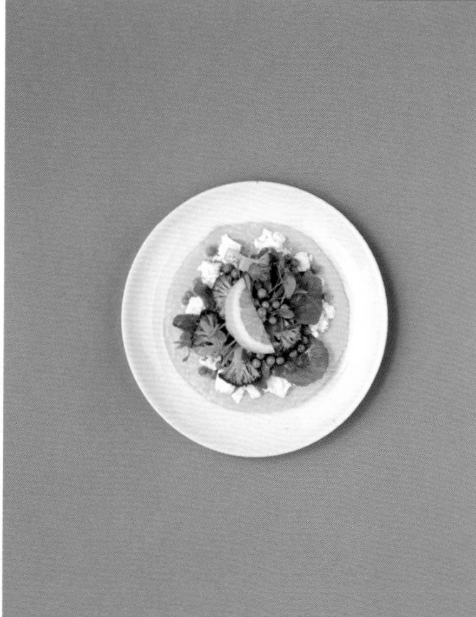

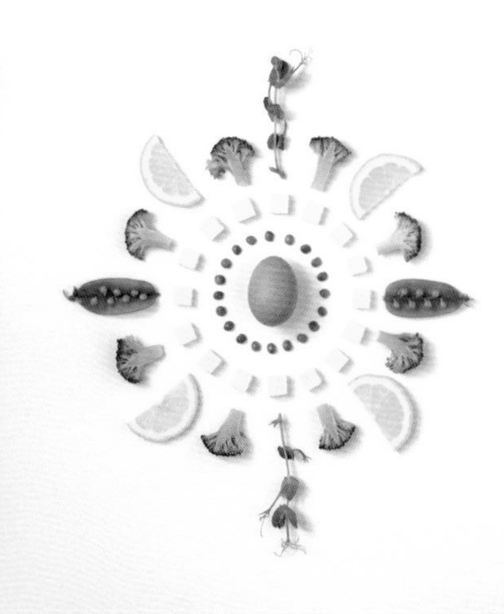

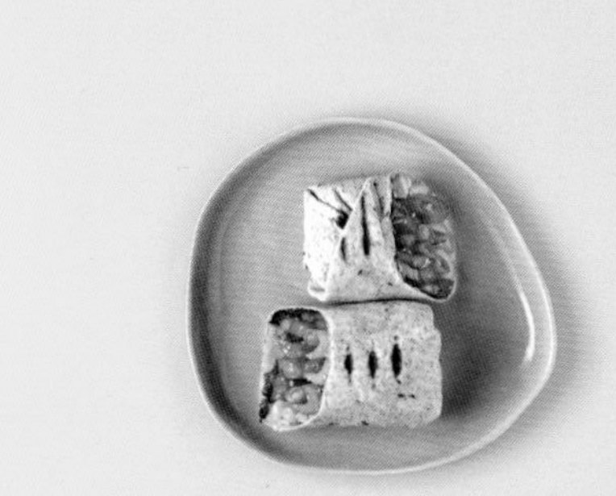

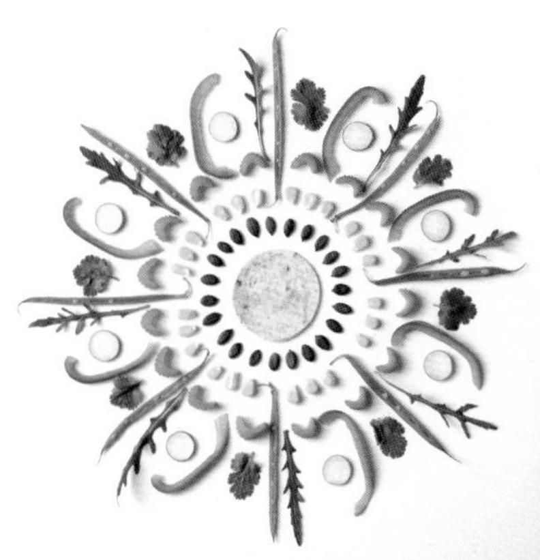

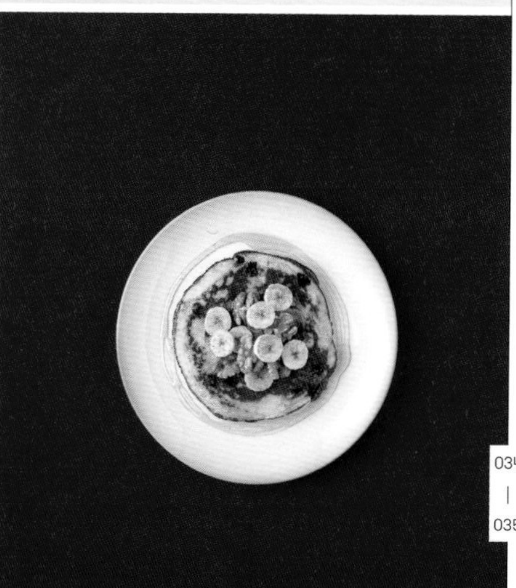

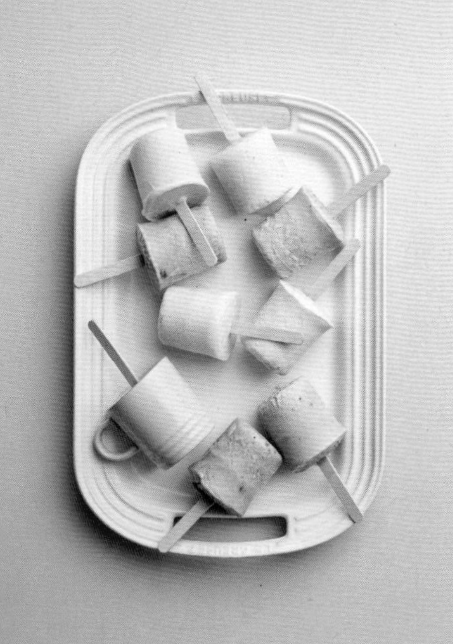

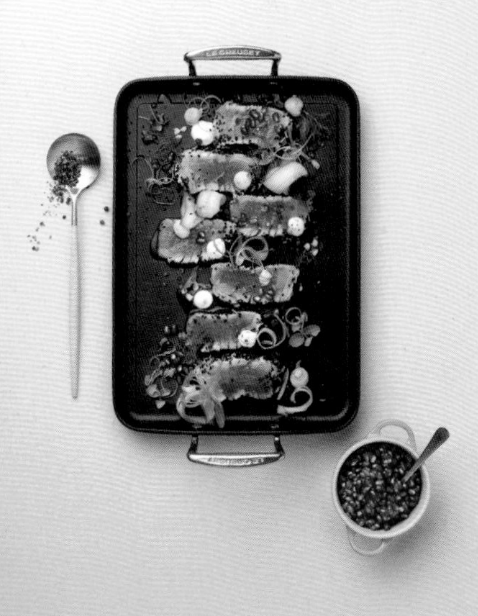

1-2. **Mother's Day Campaign 2018**
Client: Le Creuset

3-4. **Summer Campaign 2017**
Client: Col'cacchio

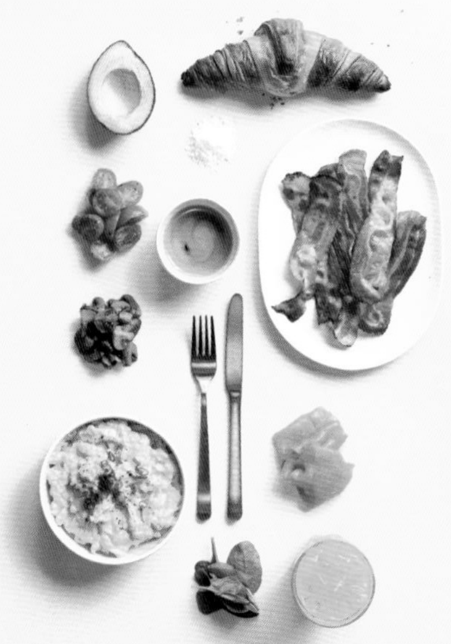

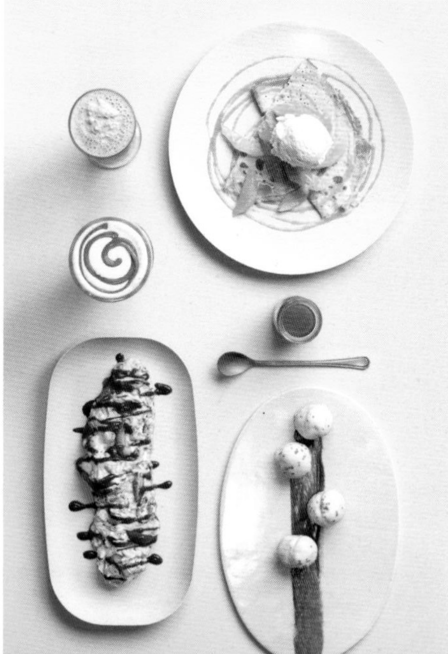

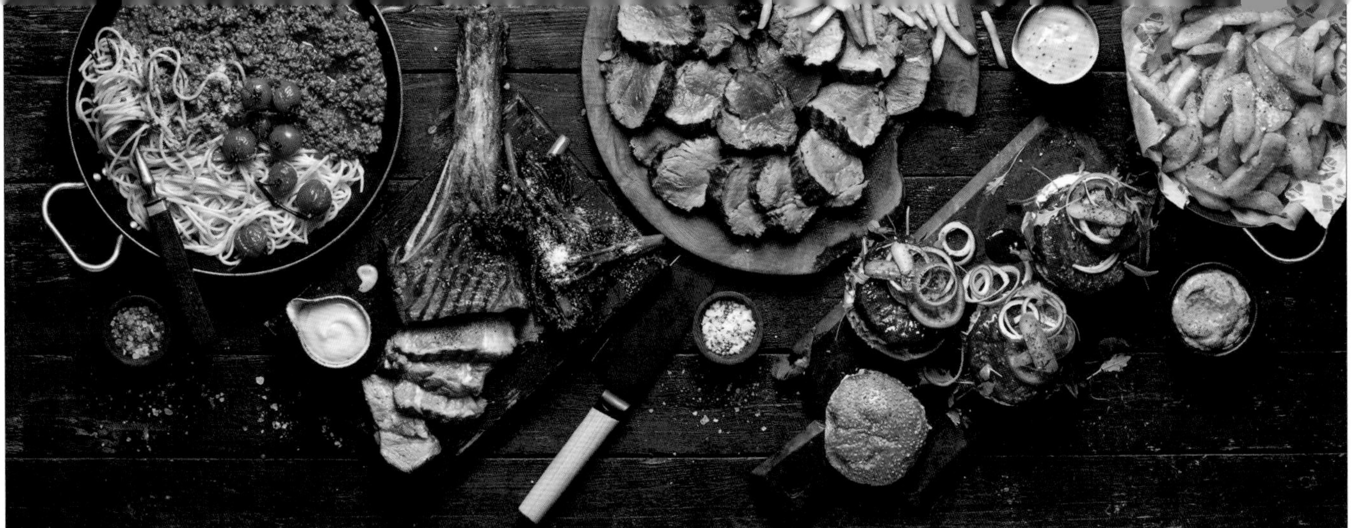

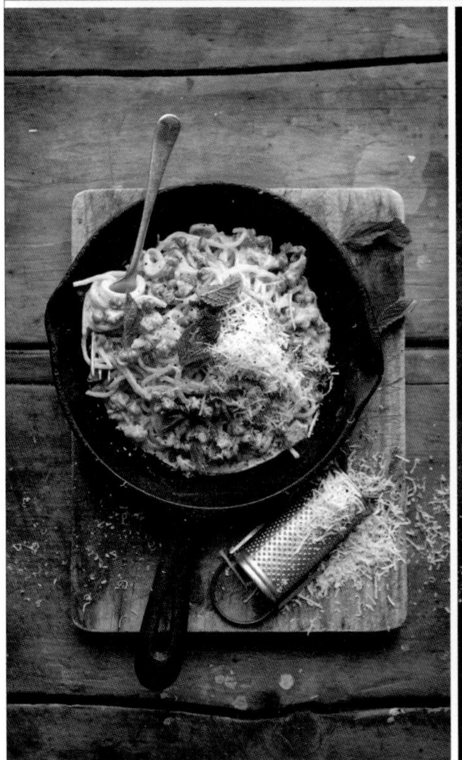

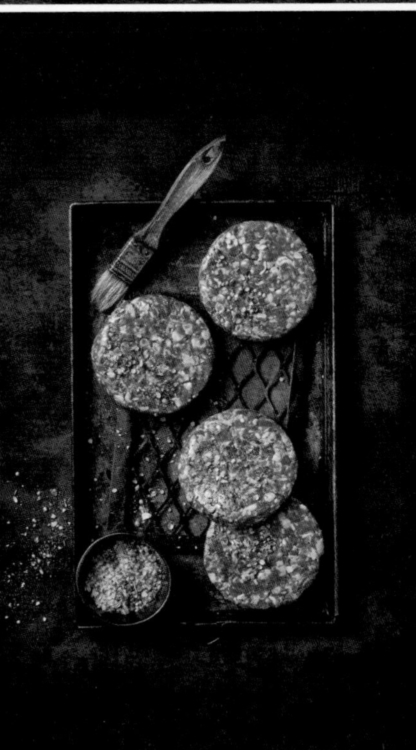

"[Social media] has not only made food photography sexier, but also made people aware that it is not exclusively the domain of the professional."

5. **Online Butchery**
Client: Buyfresh

6. **Italian Restaurant**
Client: Col'cacchio Italian Restaurant

7. **Pie Story**
Client: House & Leisure

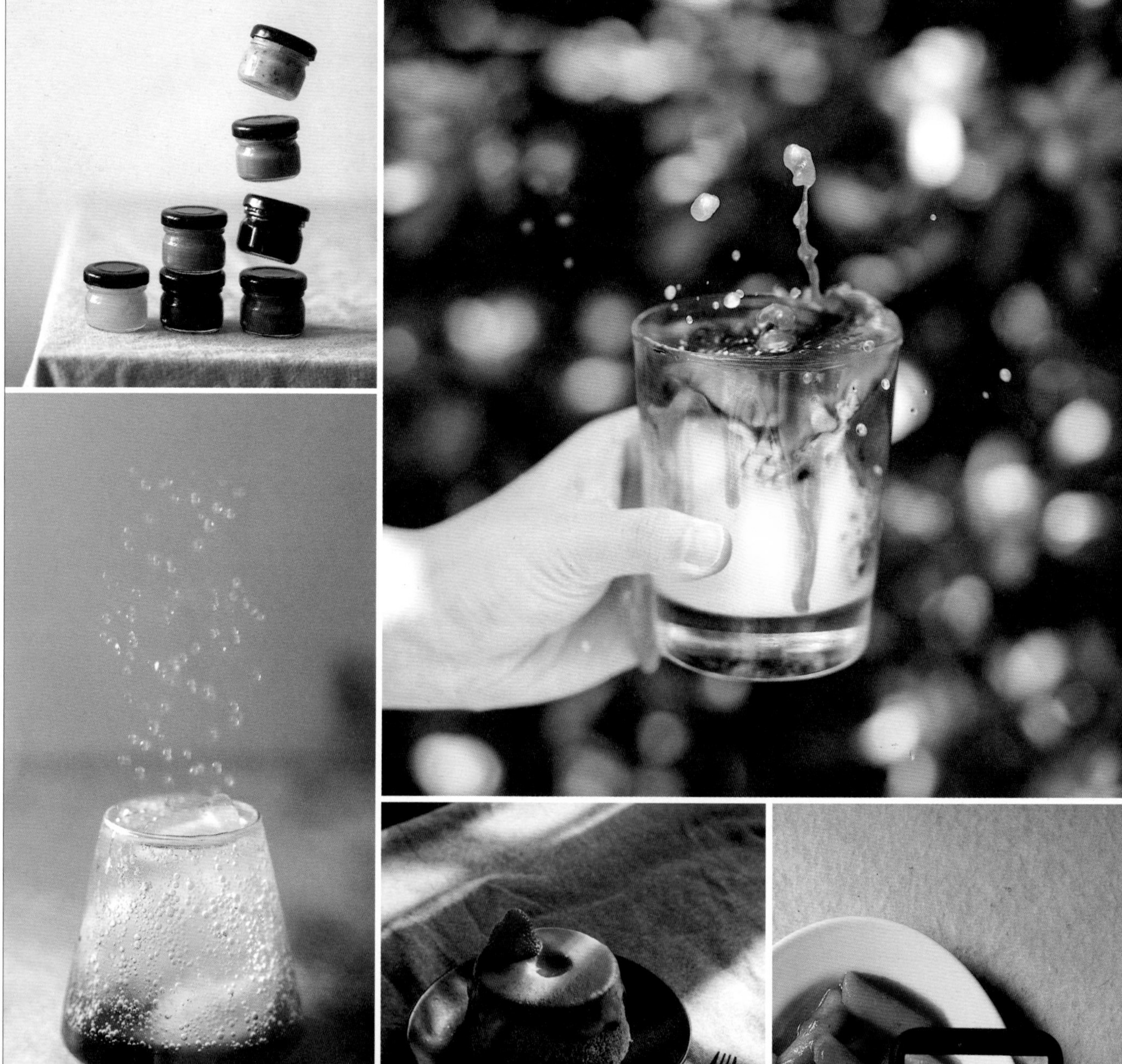

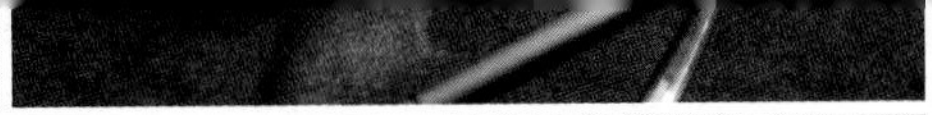

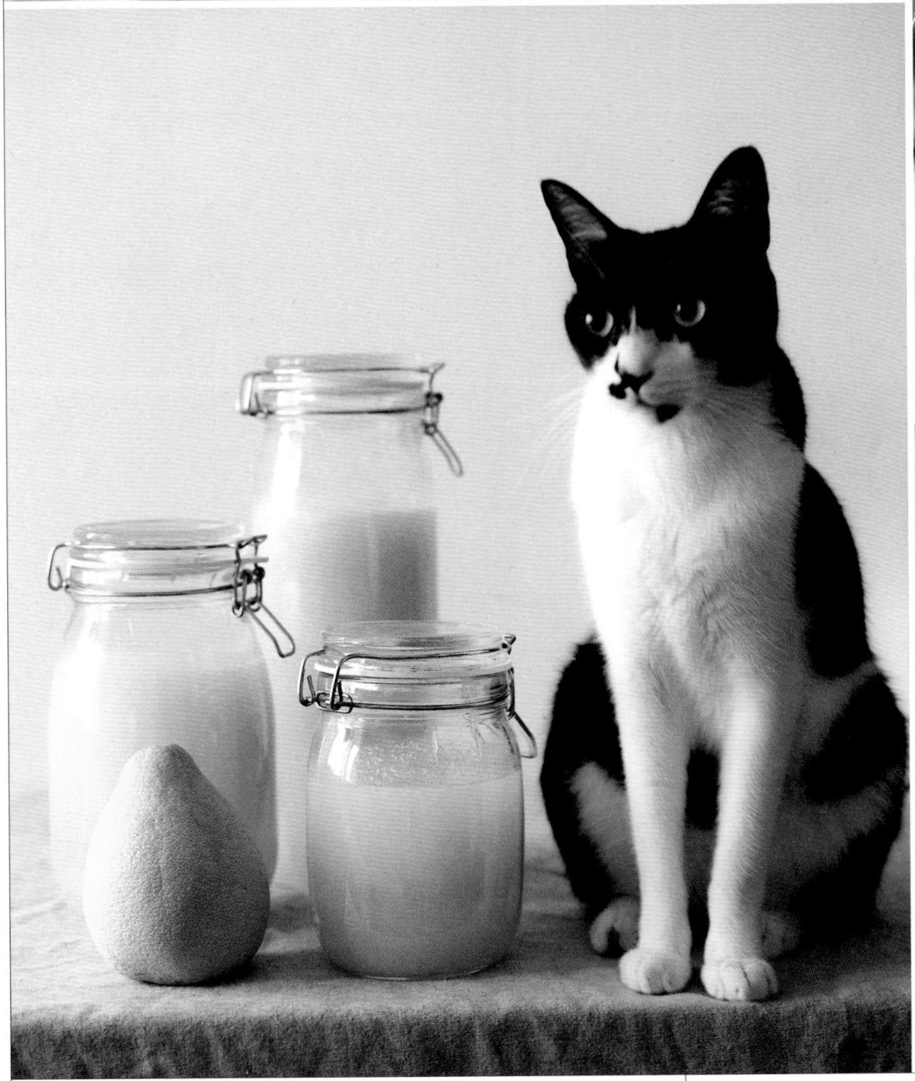

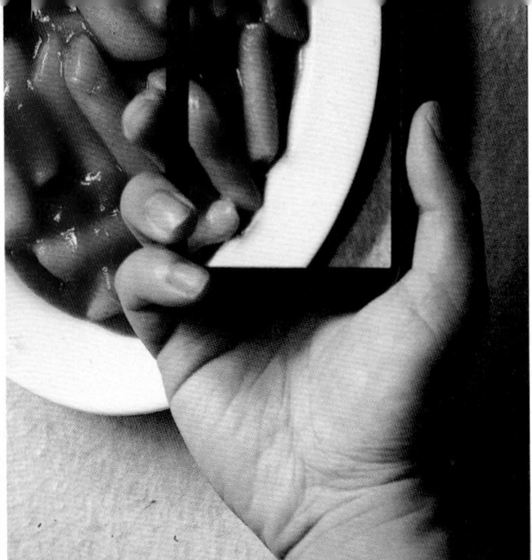

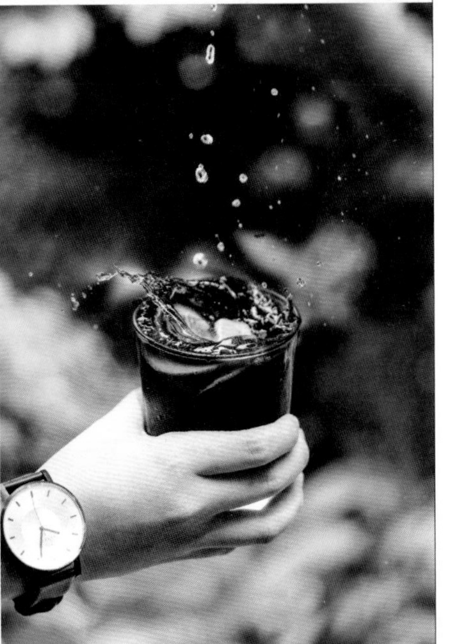

CHUNG-HUI SHEN

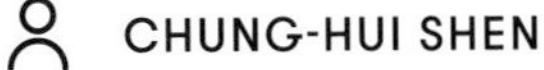

finalefinale

Finalefinale is an Instagram account belonging to Chung-hui Shen. It focuses on food styling and vibrant compositions that look good enough to eat.

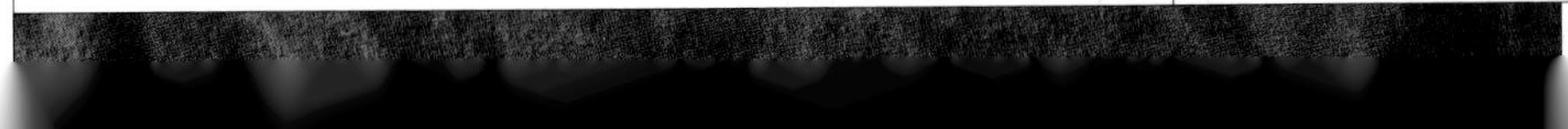

"The starting point for food photography should always be how to present dishes in a way that looks tastier through the lens."

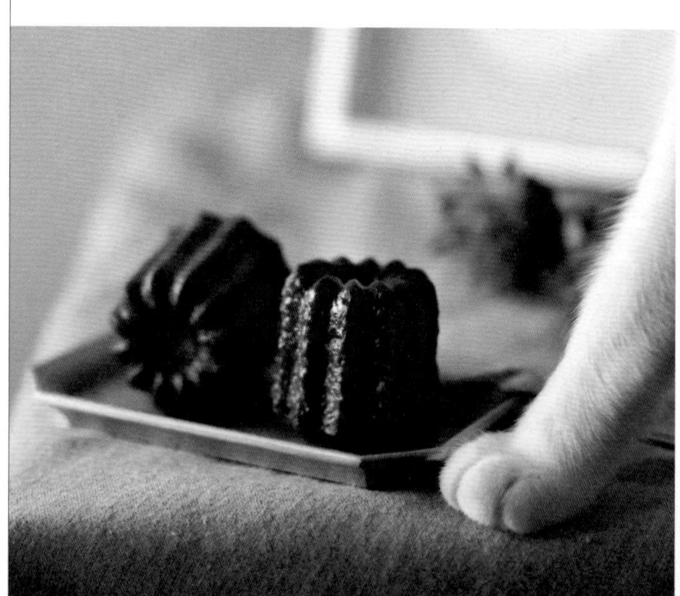

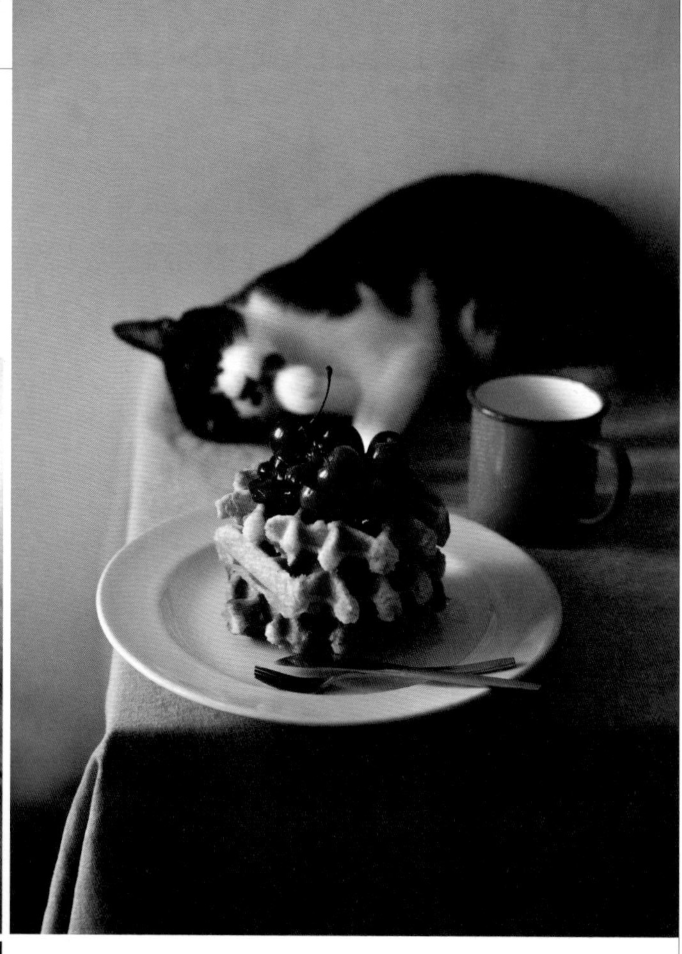

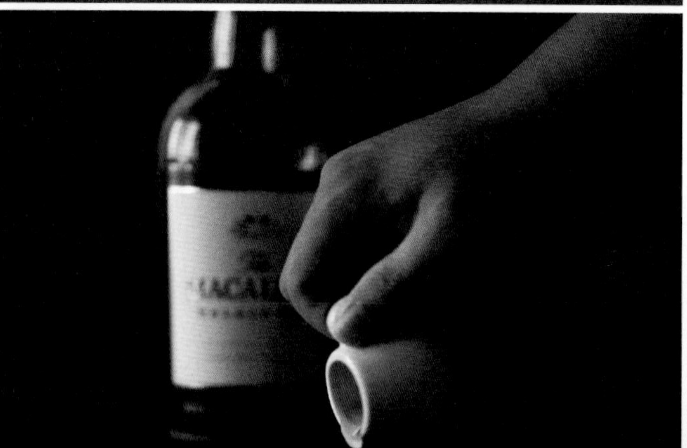

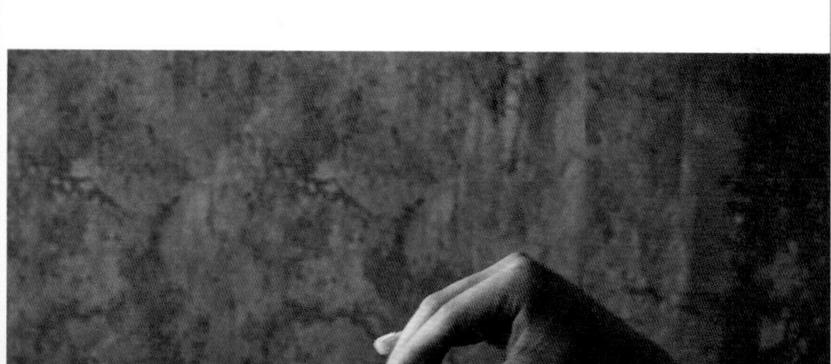

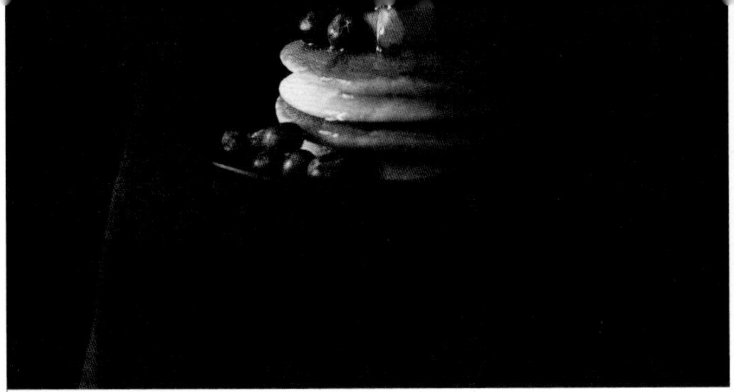

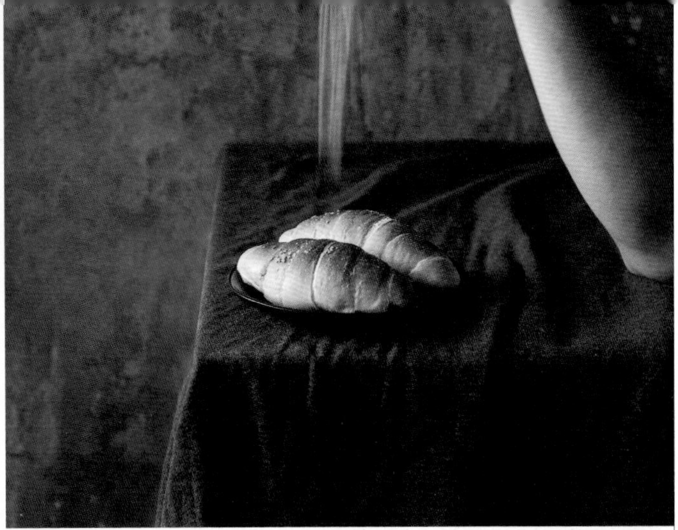

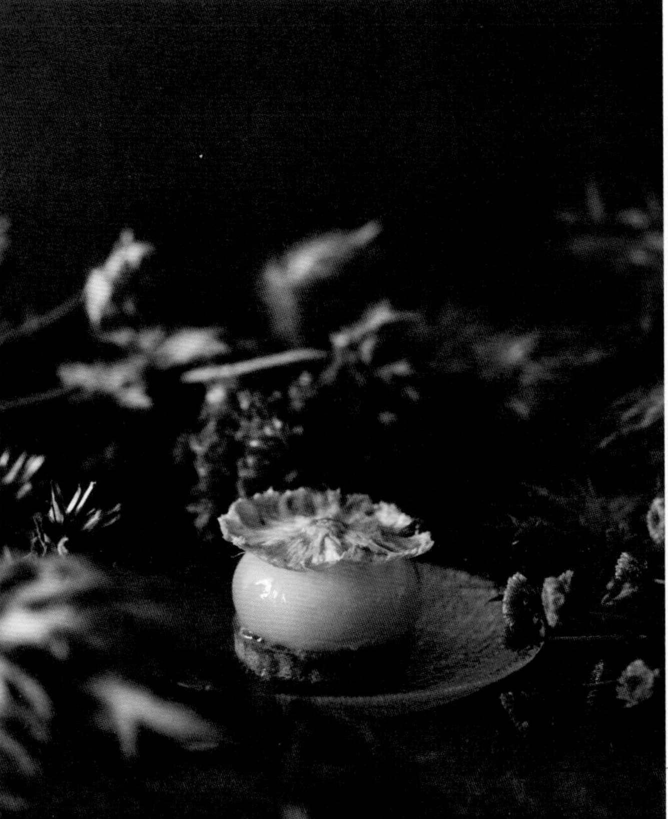

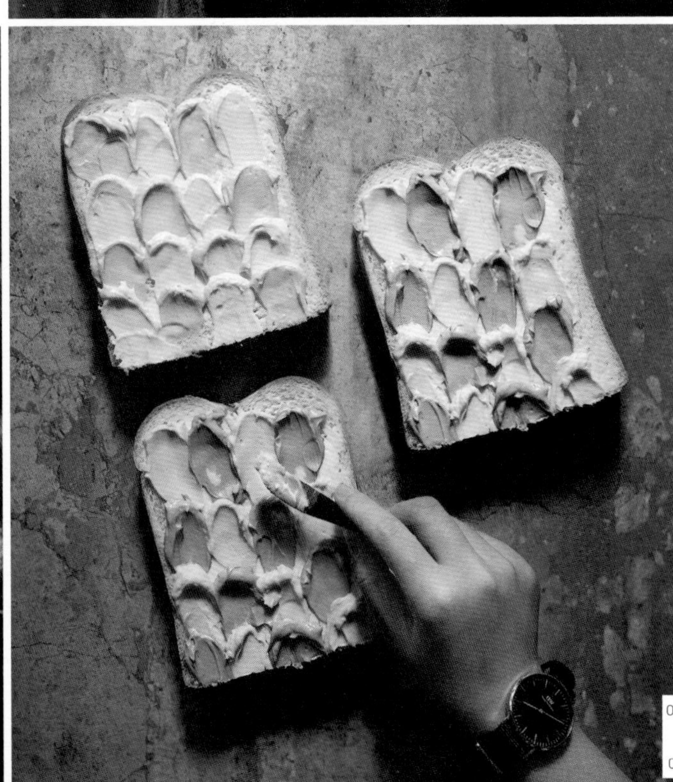

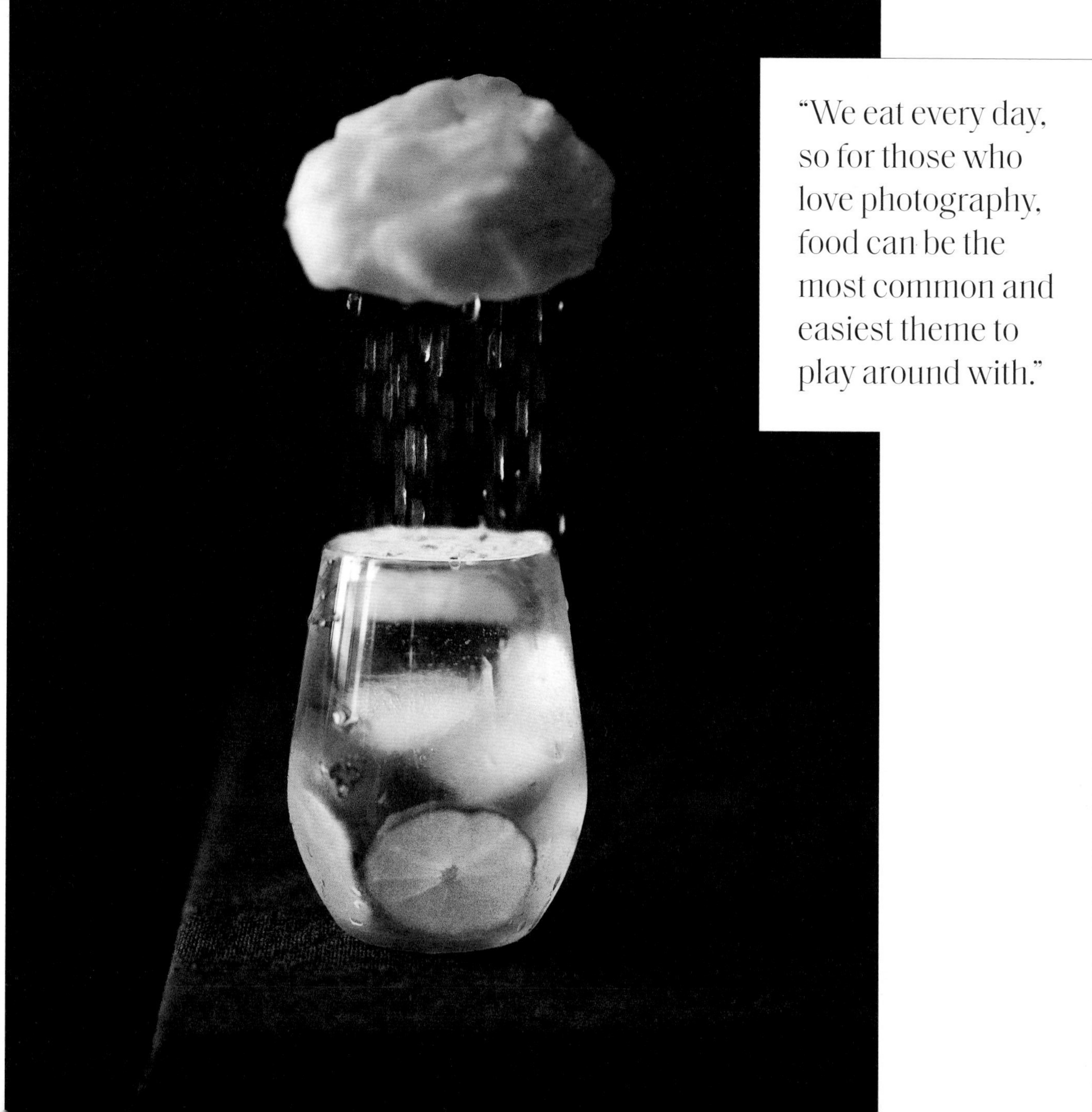

"We eat every day, so for those who love photography, food can be the most common and easiest theme to play around with."

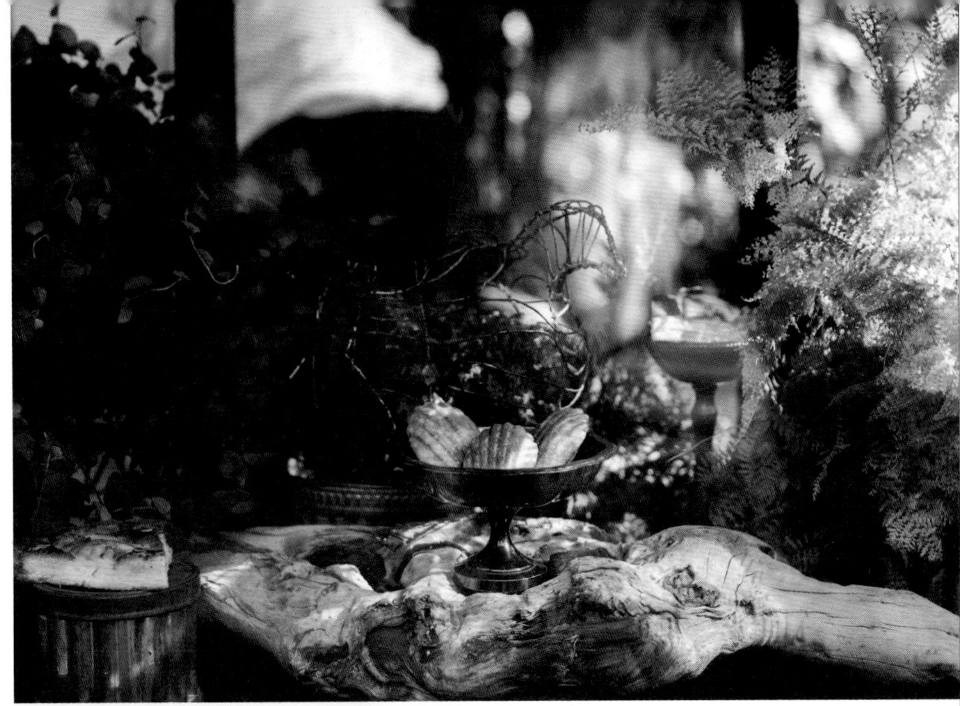

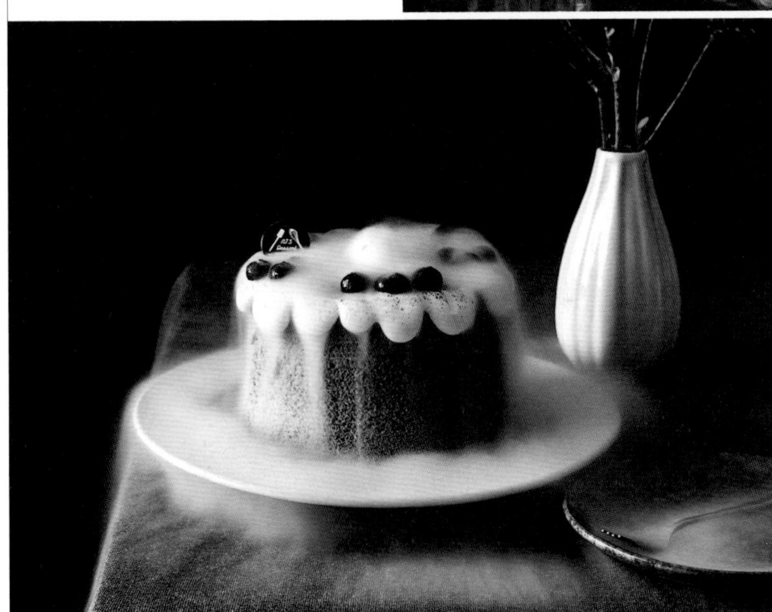

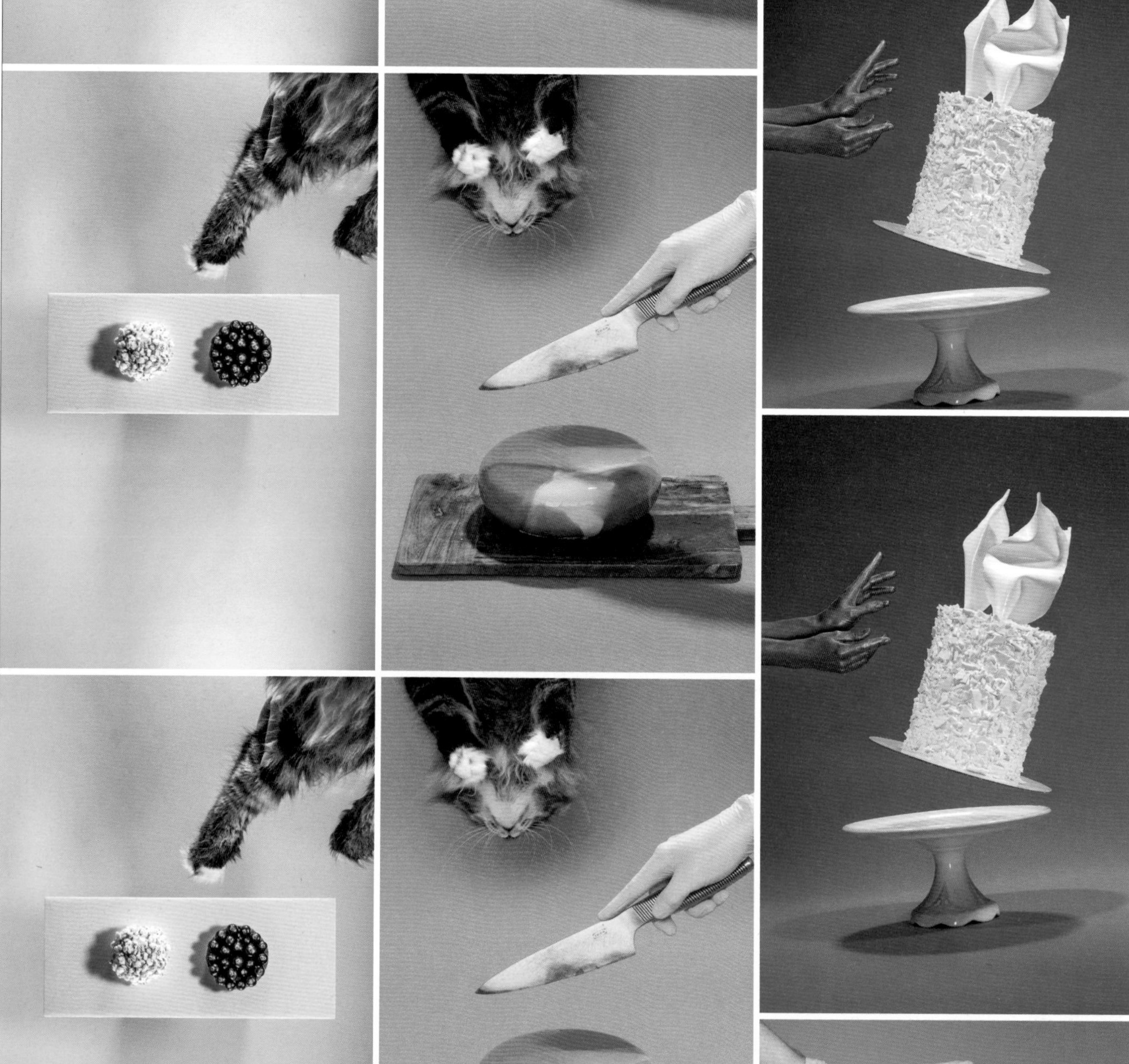

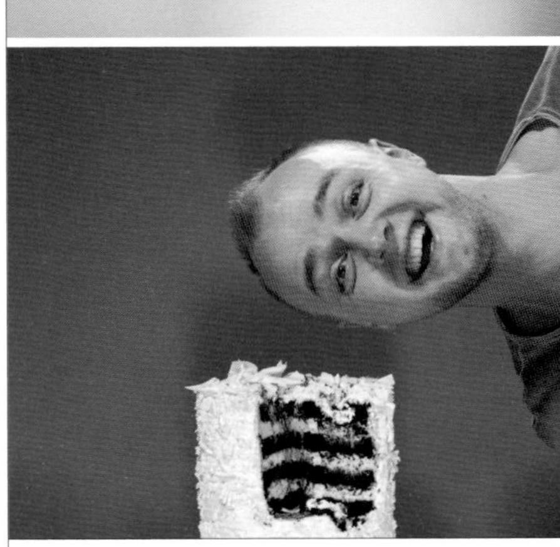
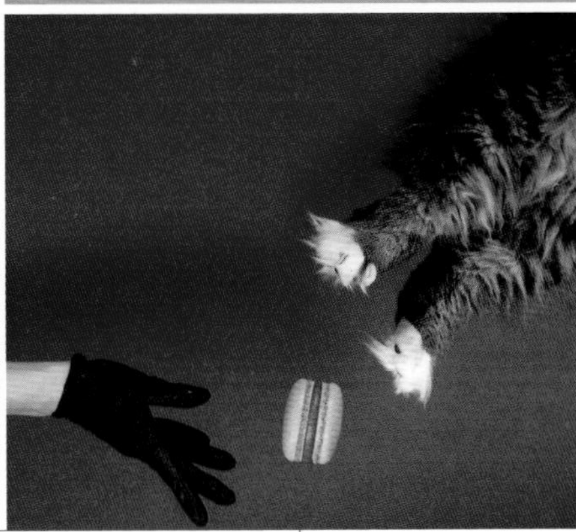
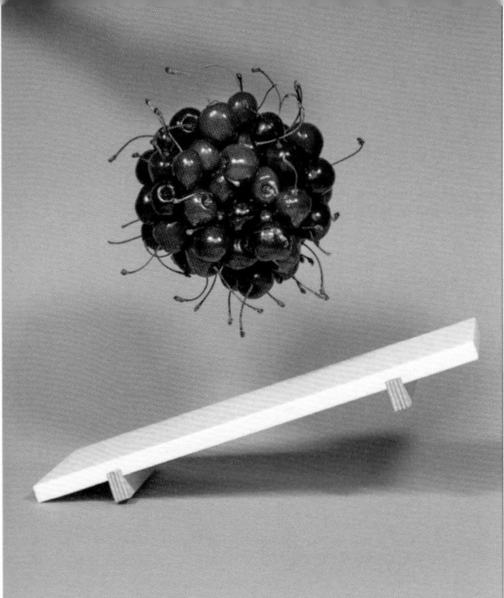

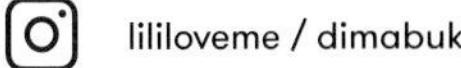

LILILOVEME & DMITRY BUKO

lililoveme / dimabuko

Lililoveme is an online pastry academy where everybody can learn how to create art on a plate at home. Its Instagram account features the beauty of well-executed pastry work through simple and elegant shapes with pops of colour.

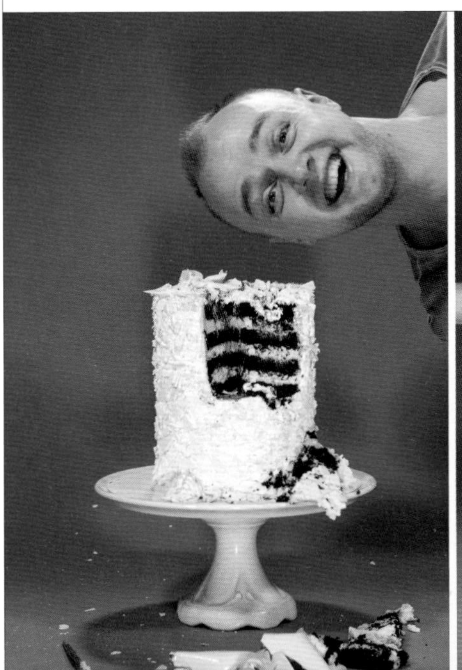
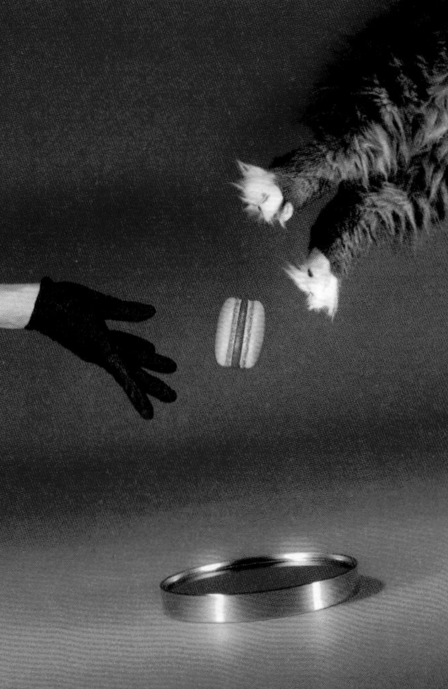
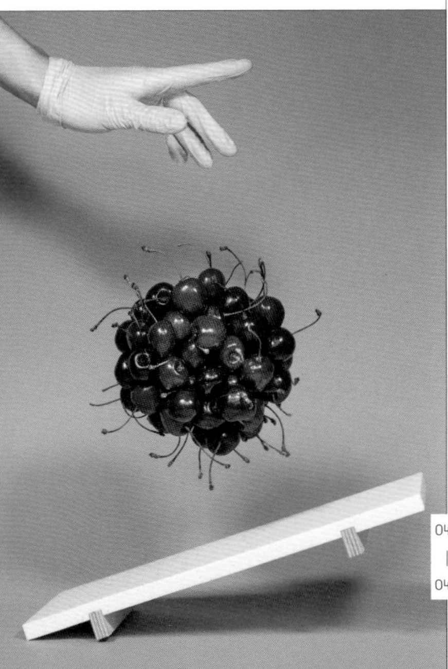

“Now, everyone can explore, see, and learn about this big and incredible world of tastes, ingredients, looks, and philosophies of food.”

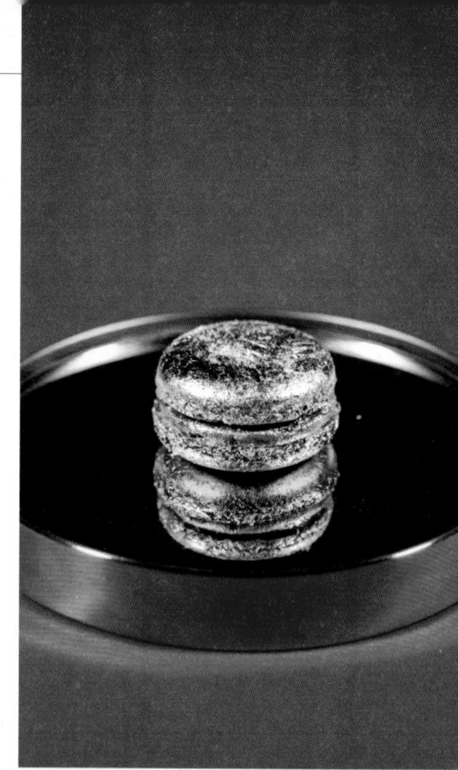

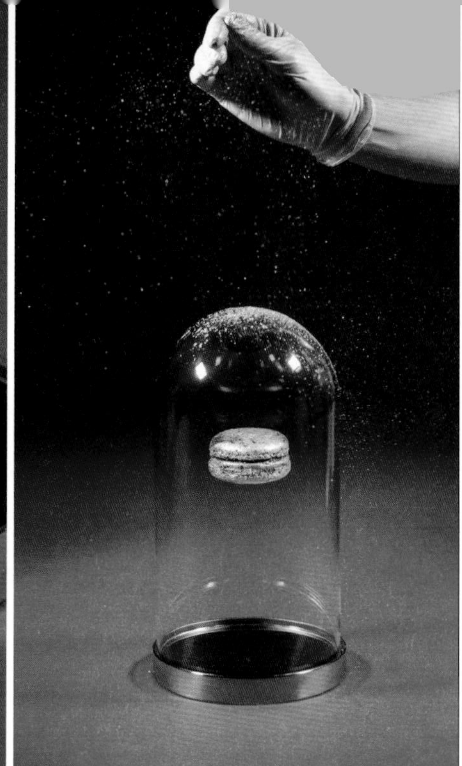

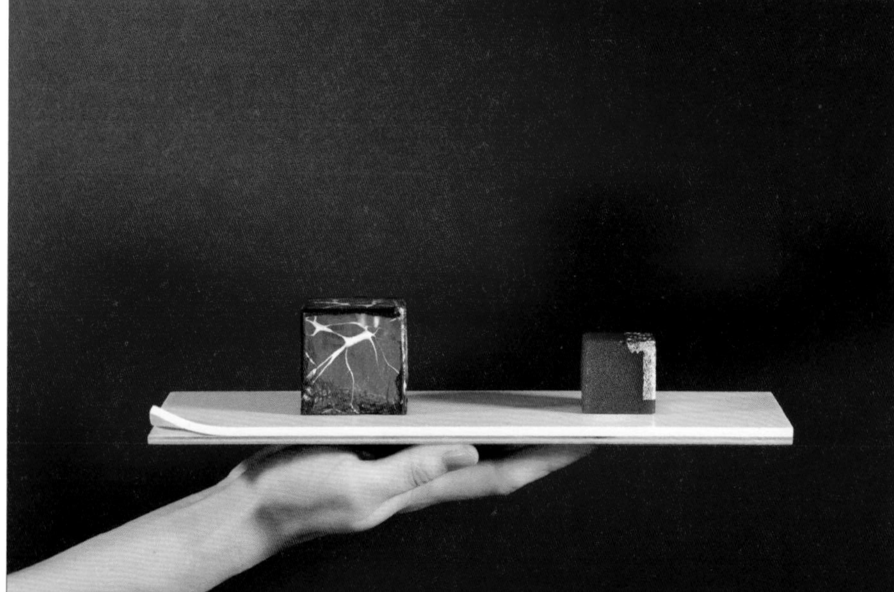

All photos were taken for Pastronomy, an online pastry course in 2017.

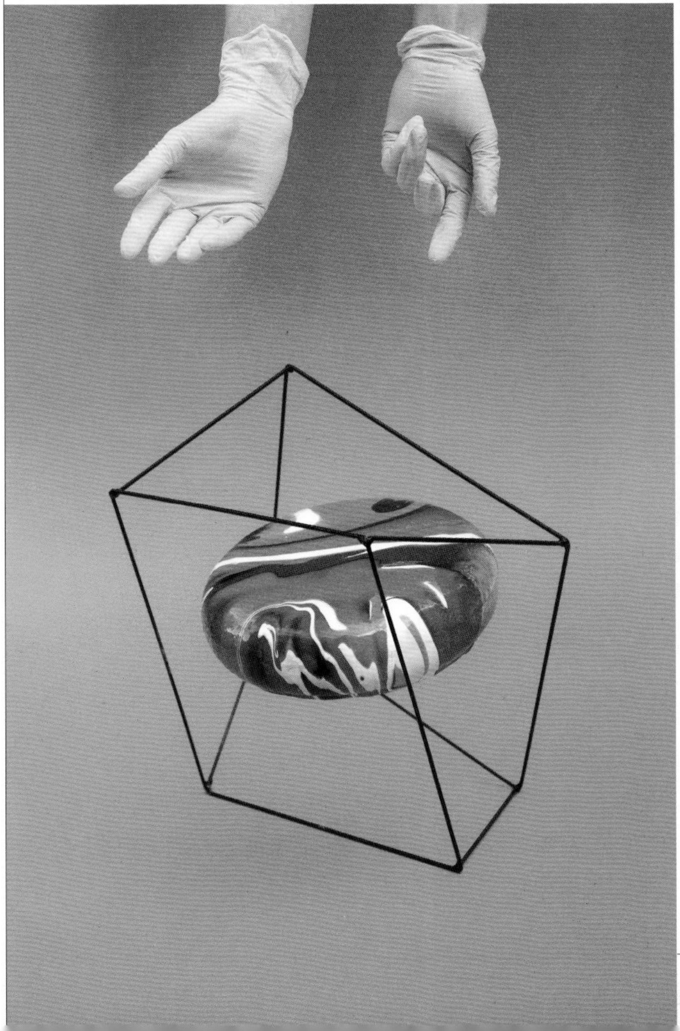

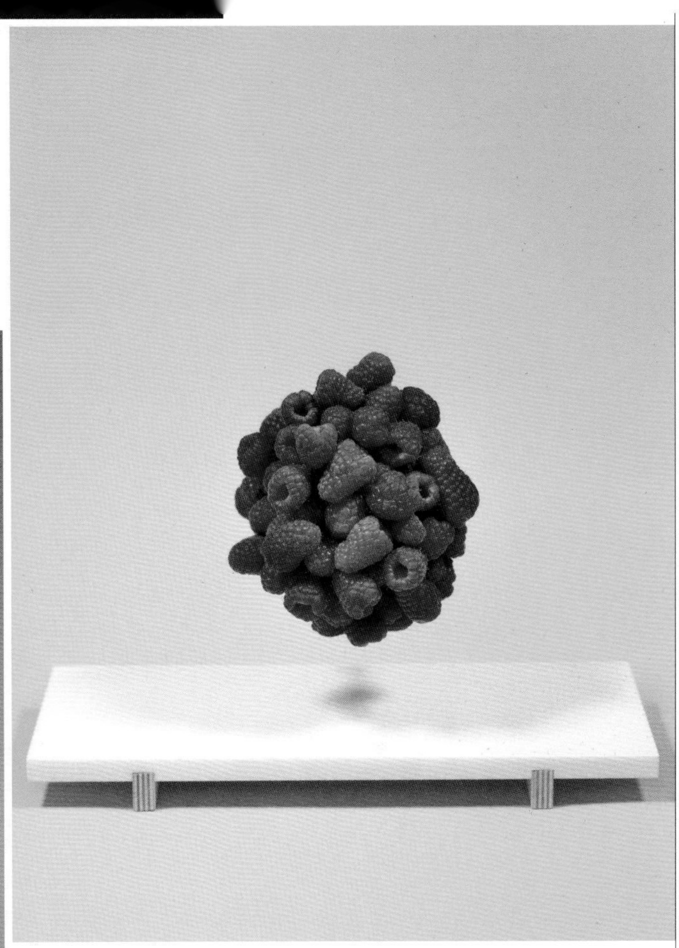

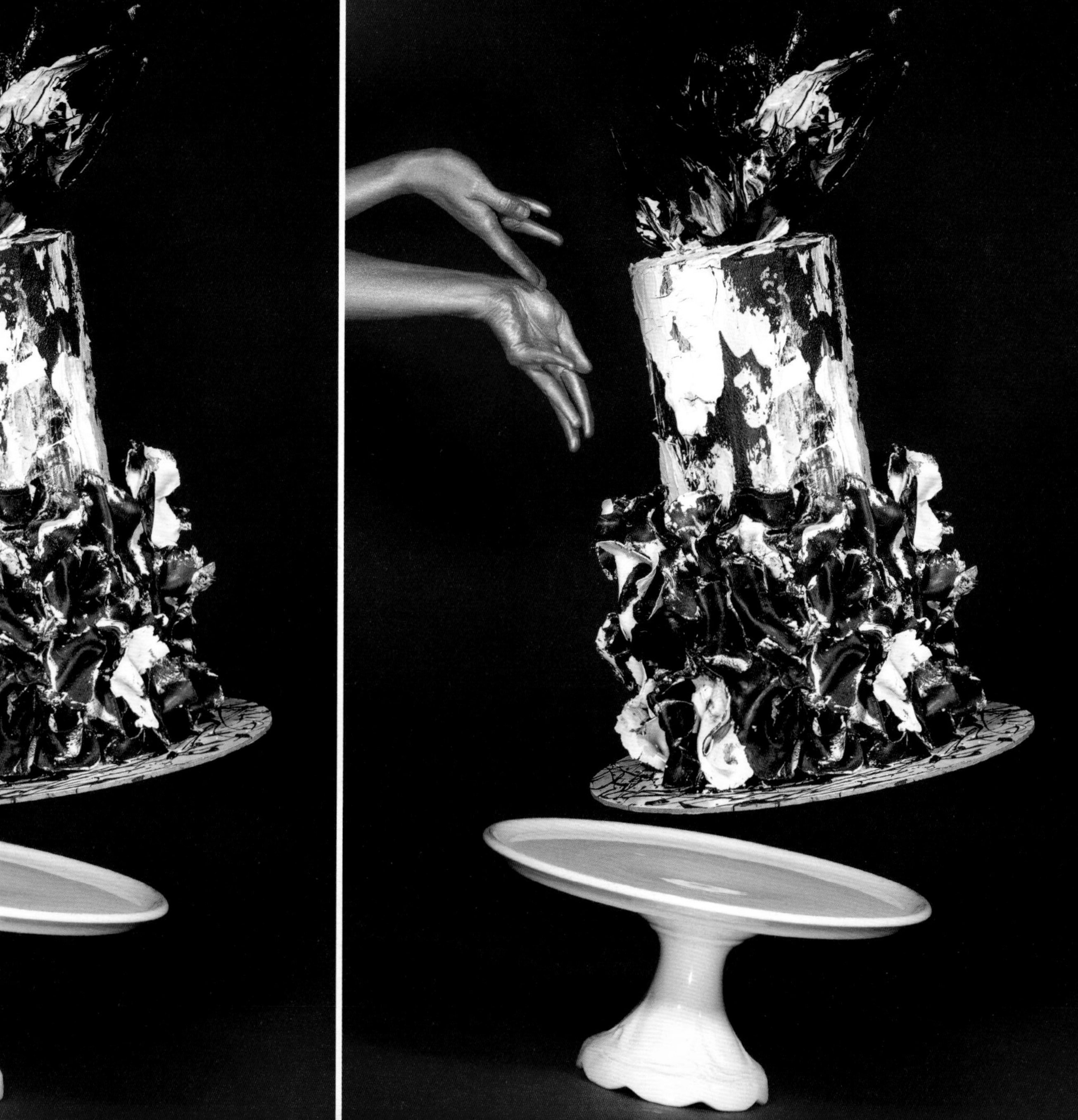

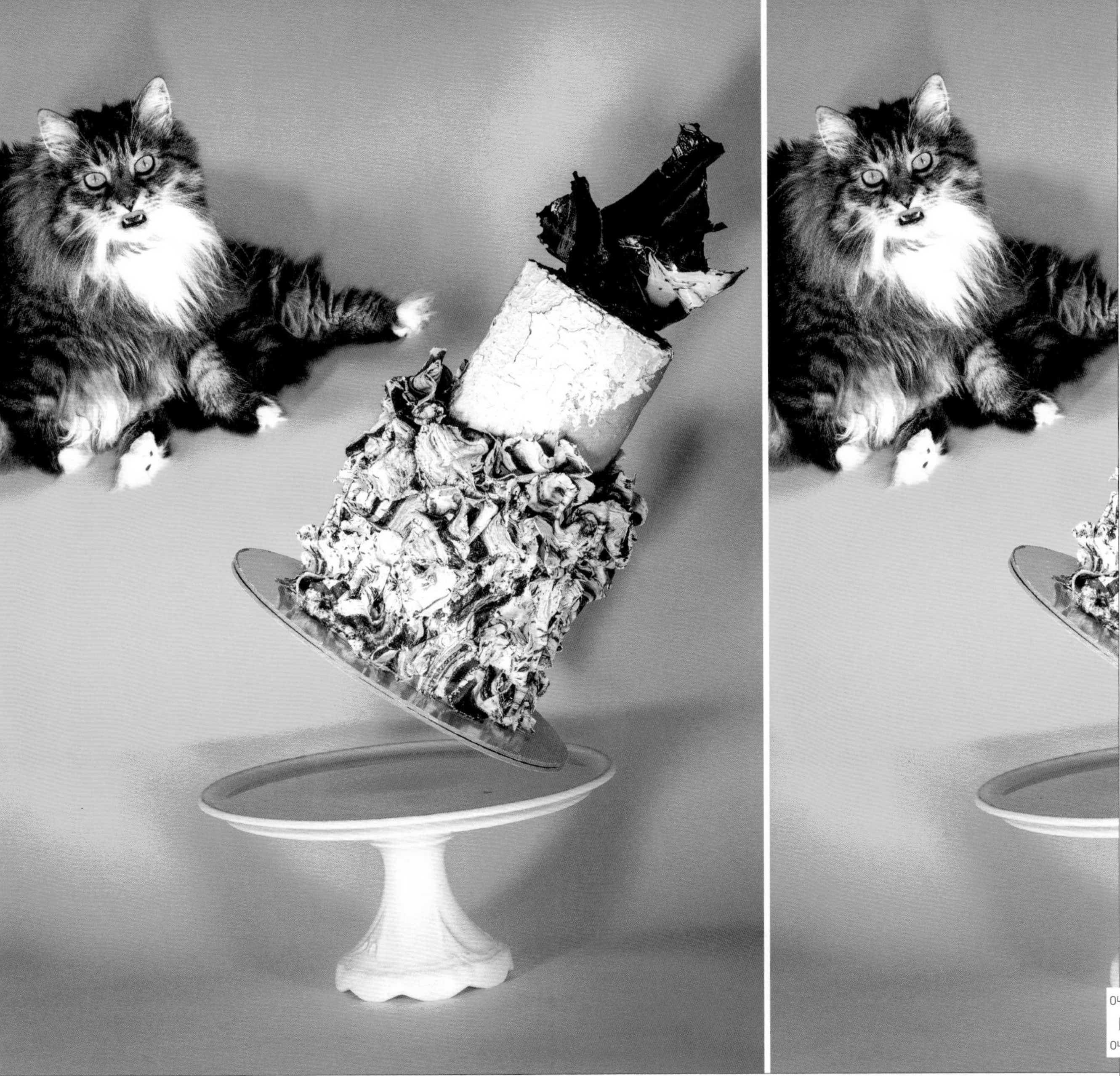

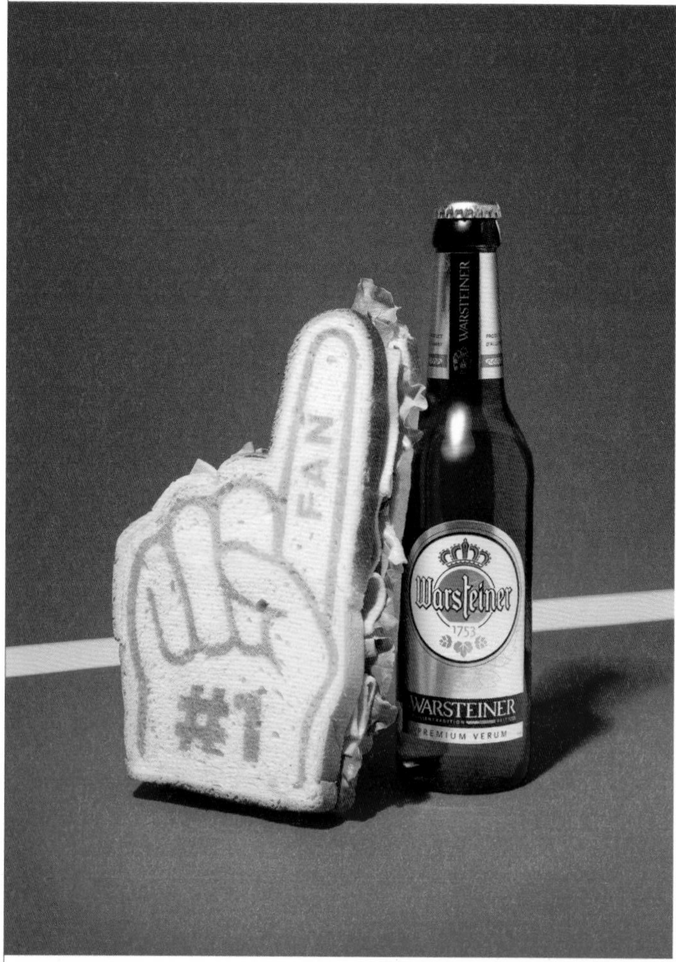

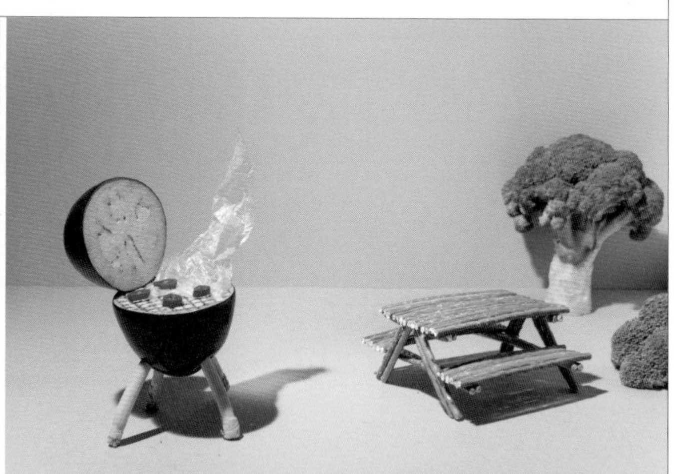

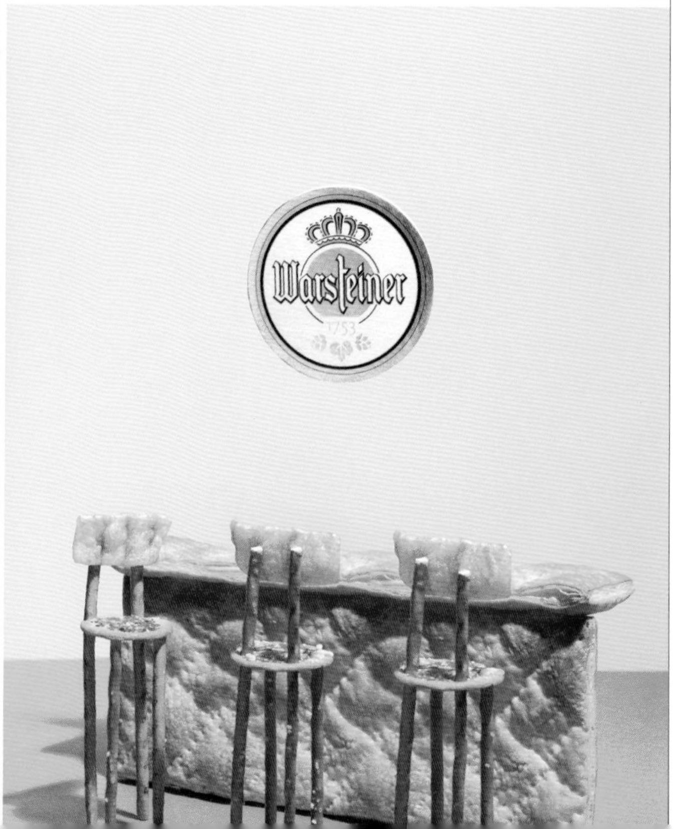

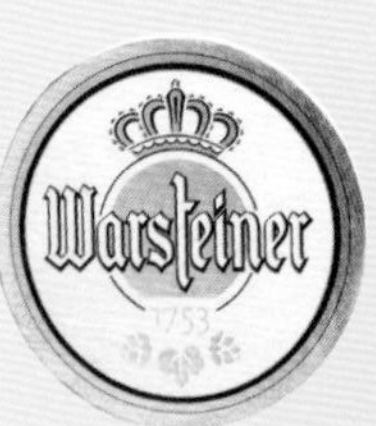
Warsteiner
1753

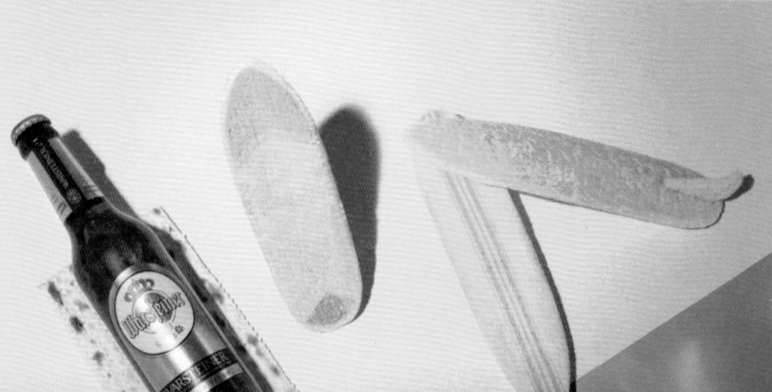

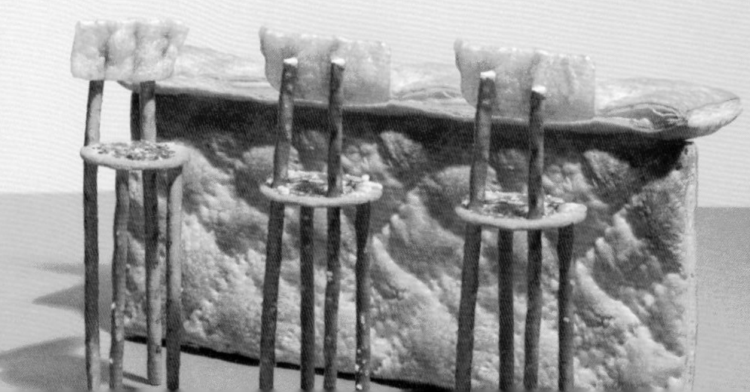

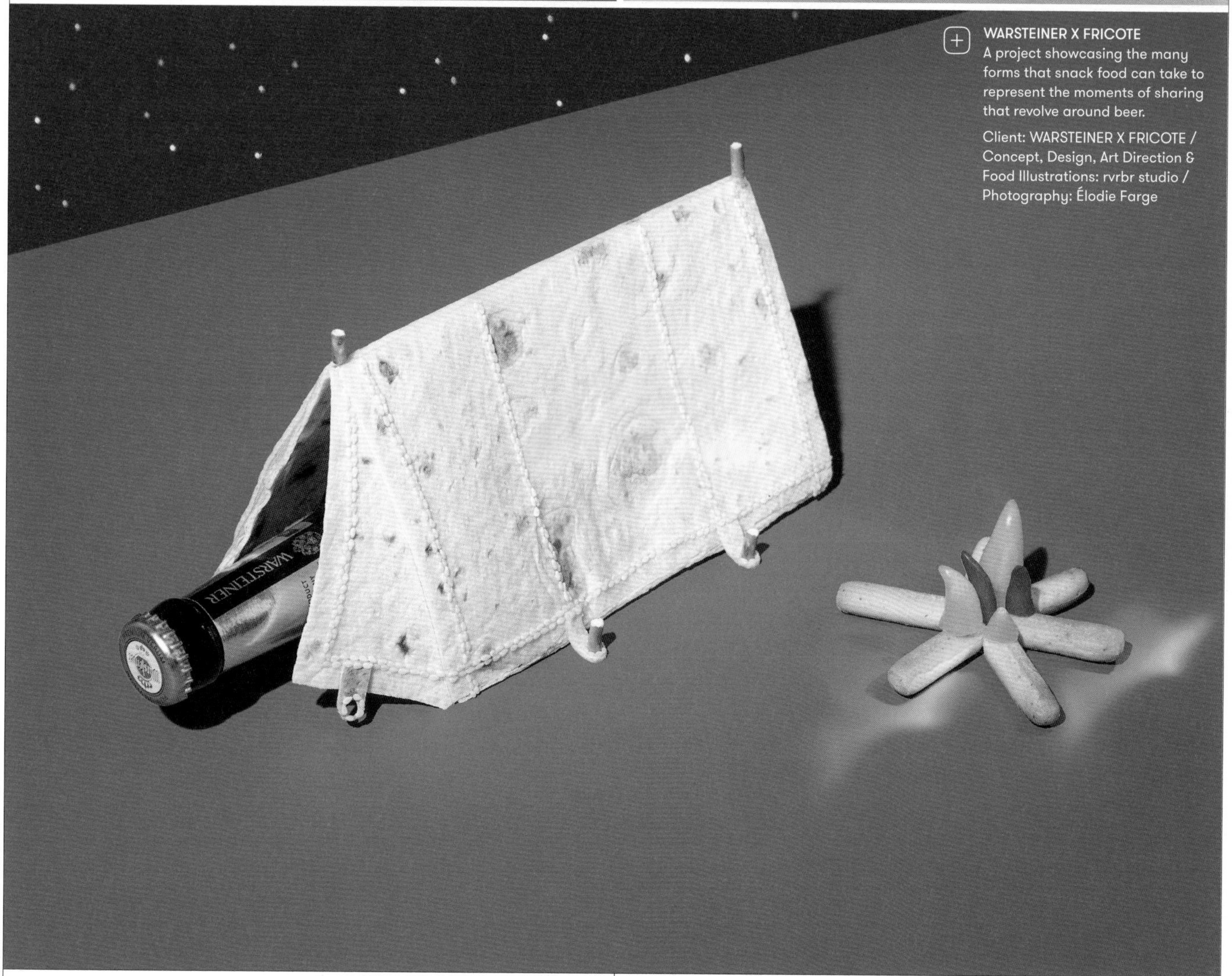

WARSTEINER X FRICOTE
A project showcasing the many forms that snack food can take to represent the moments of sharing that revolve around beer.

Client: WARSTEINER X FRICOTE / Concept, Design, Art Direction & Food Illustrations: rvrbr studio / Photography: Élodie Farge

RVRBR STUDIO

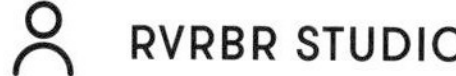

reverberestudio

rvrbr studio is a multifaceted creative outfit based in Paris that creates custom-made solutions for businesses, brands, and creatives. Crafty and curious, the studio is passionate about handmade visuals, experimentation, and visual trickery.

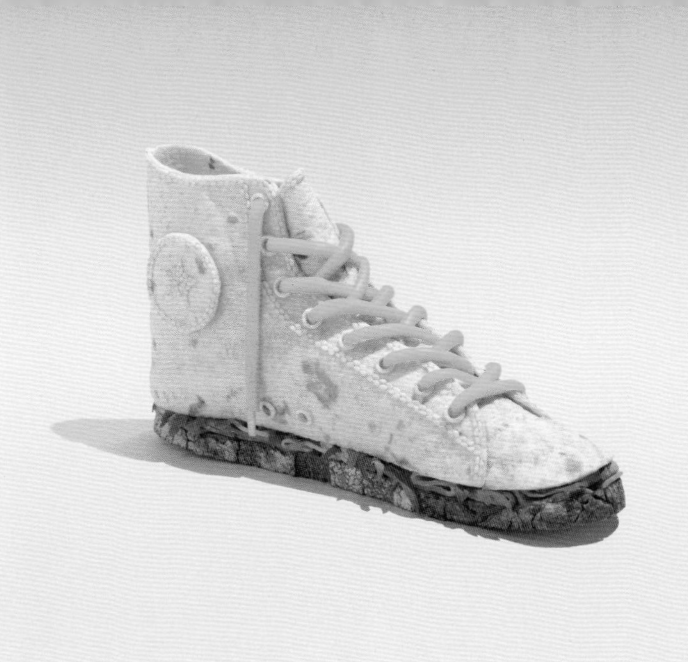

1-3, 5. **Food Works**
A project that sought to turn the old phrase, 'Don't play with your food!' on its head through playful and offbeat imagery.

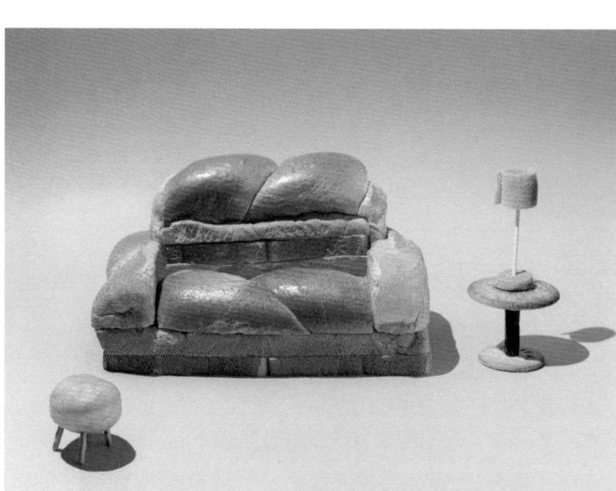

"We try to keep composition simple in order to have powerful images that pop out easily on social media feeds."

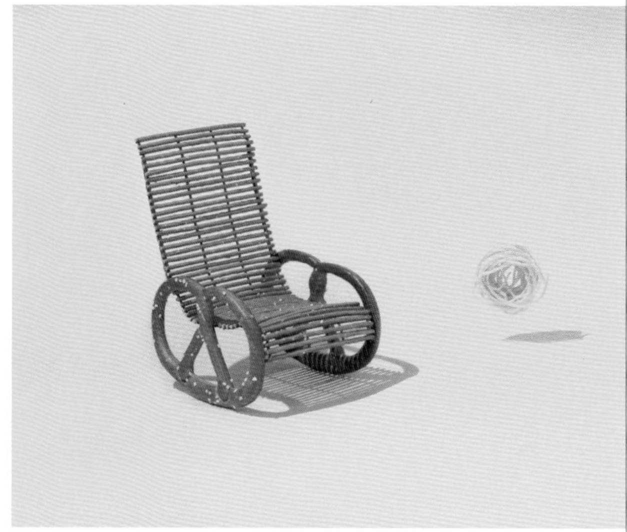

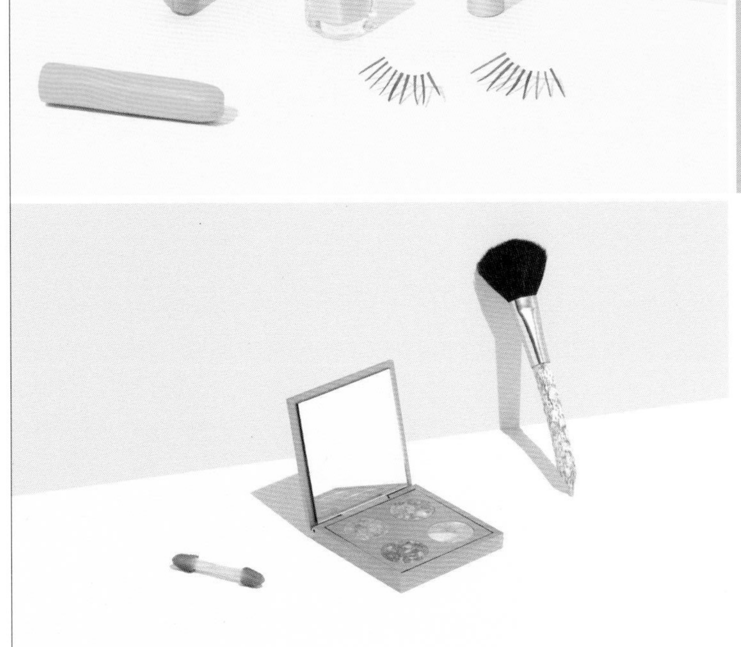

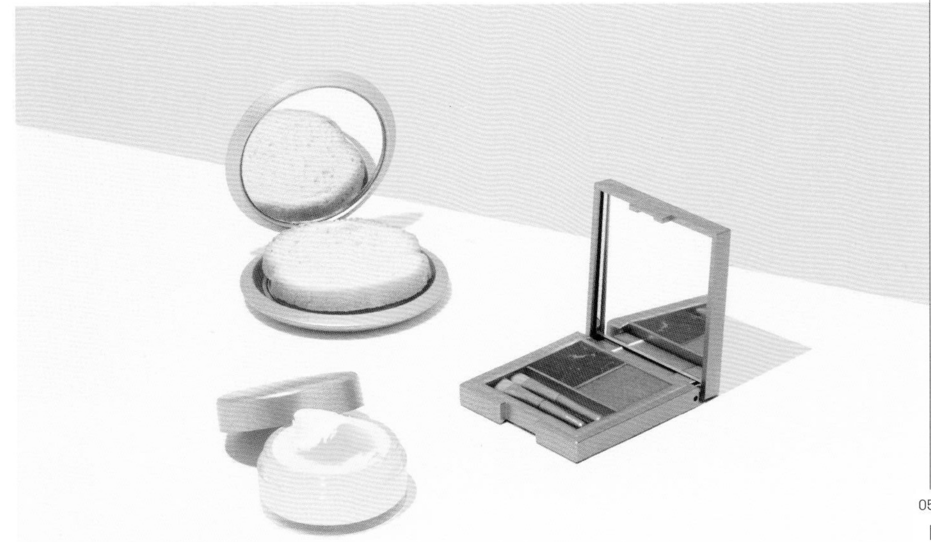

4, 6-7. **Meat You**
A project that represented cosmetics with charcuterie as a nod to contradictory beauty tips.

Concept Design & Design: rvrbr studio / Retouching: Peter Strauli

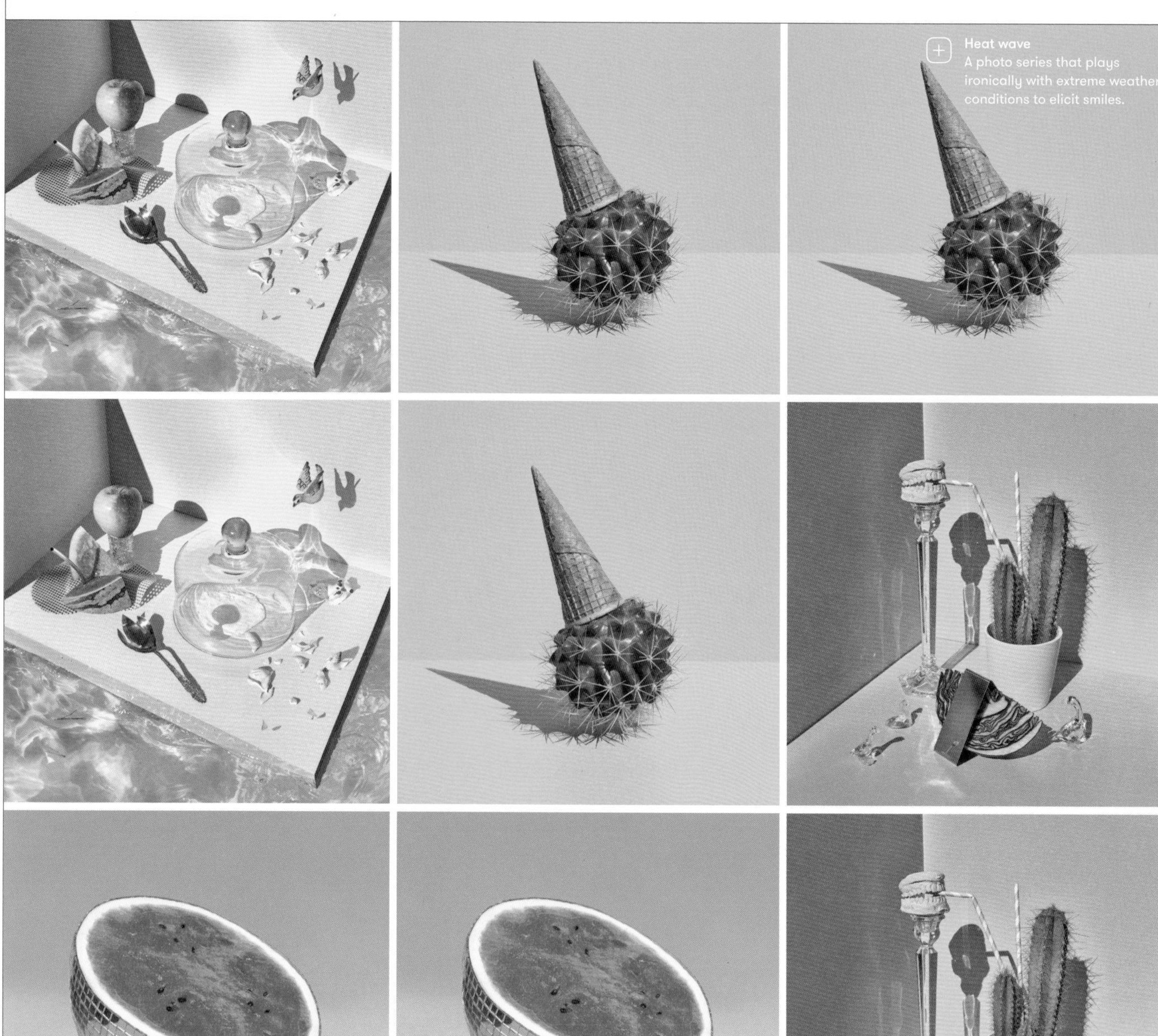

Heat wave
A photo series that plays ironically with extreme weather conditions to elicit smiles.

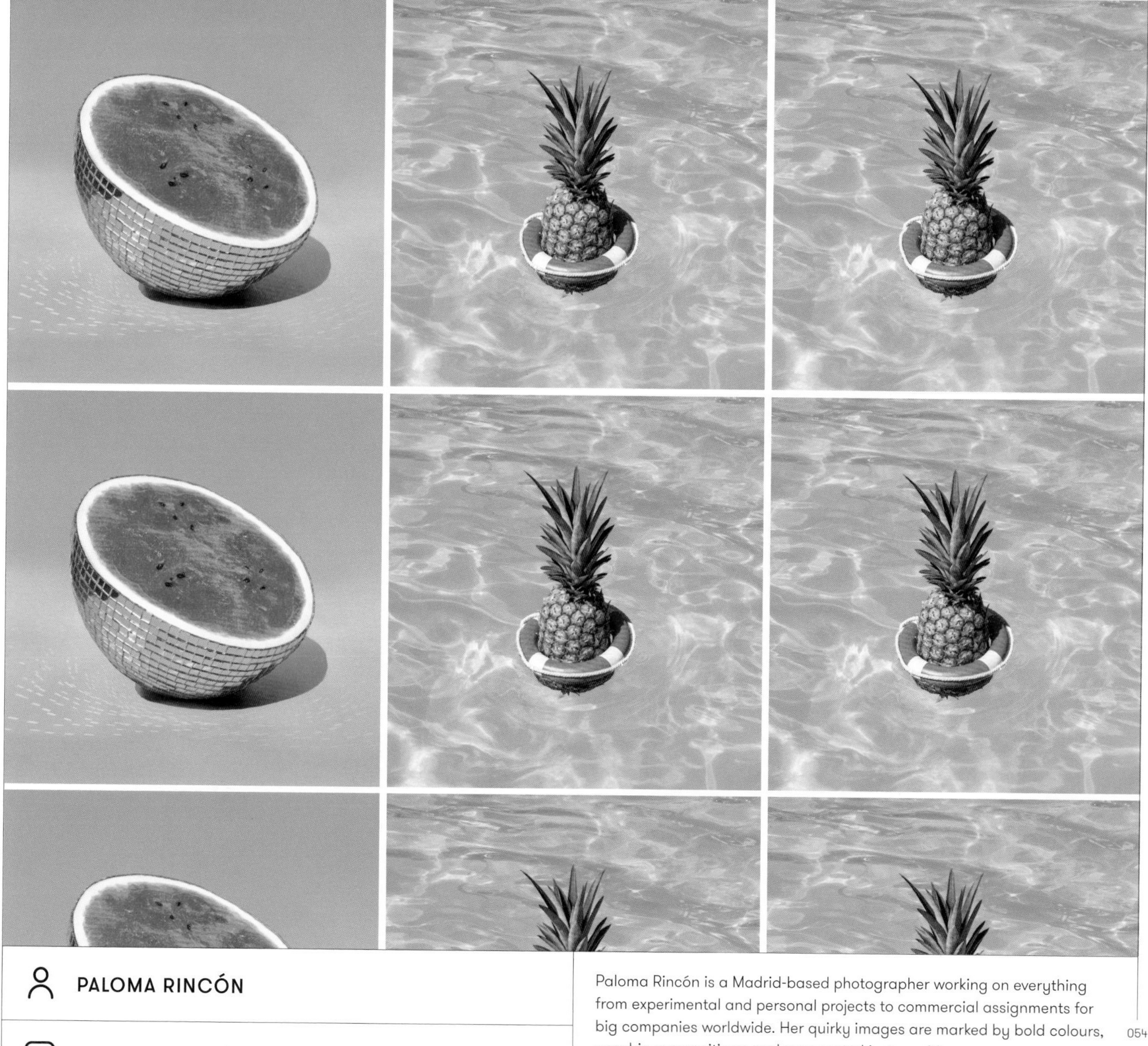

PALOMA RINCÓN

paloma_rincon_

Paloma Rincón is a Madrid-based photographer working on everything from experimental and personal projects to commercial assignments for big companies worldwide. Her quirky images are marked by bold colours, graphic compositions, and unexpected juxtapositions.

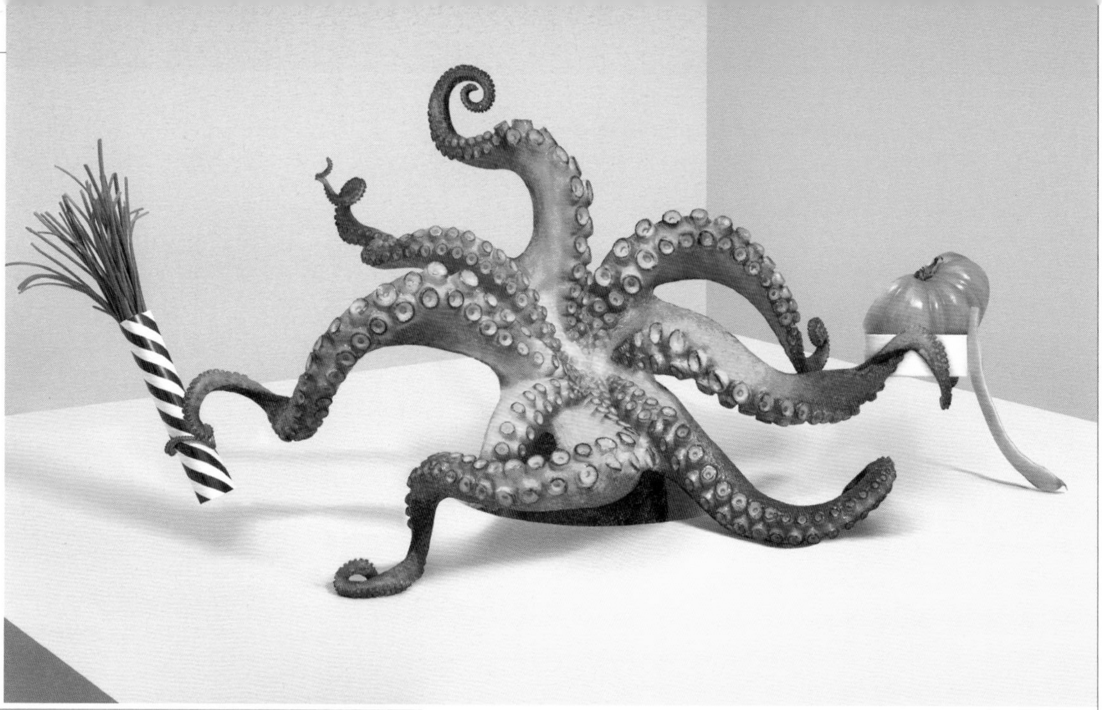

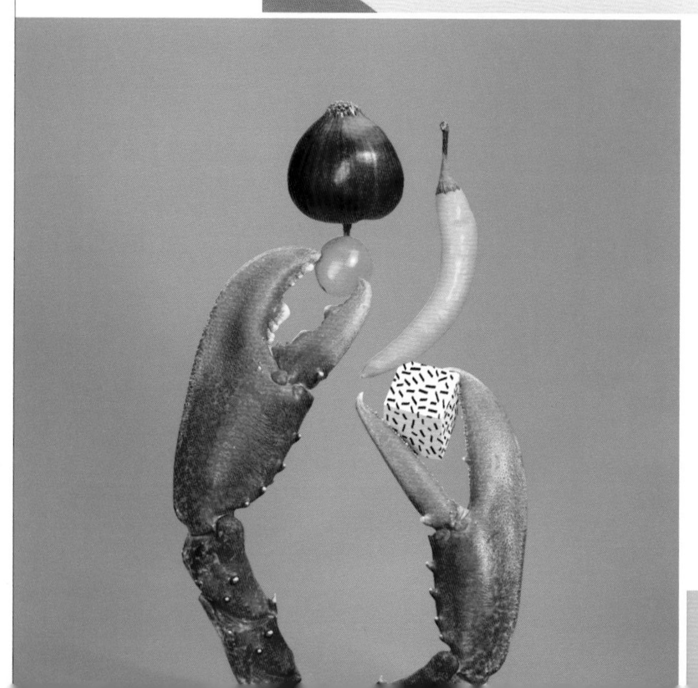

"Food is something that we are all familiar with, and most people like. It's a beautiful and fun subject to play with."

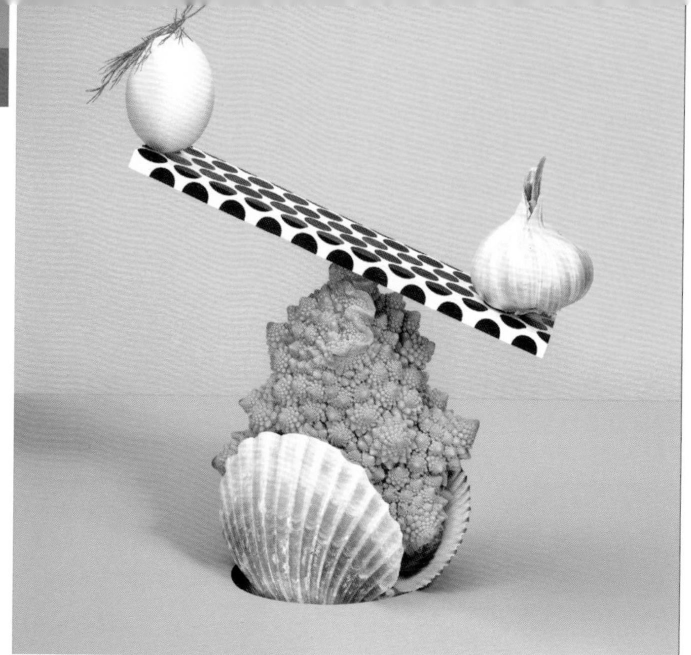

Balanced Diet

A photo series showcasing seafood styled like fancy fashion shoots.

Client: Fricote Magazine / Photography & Set Design: Paloma Rincón / Assisting & Post-production: Nahuel Ojjioni

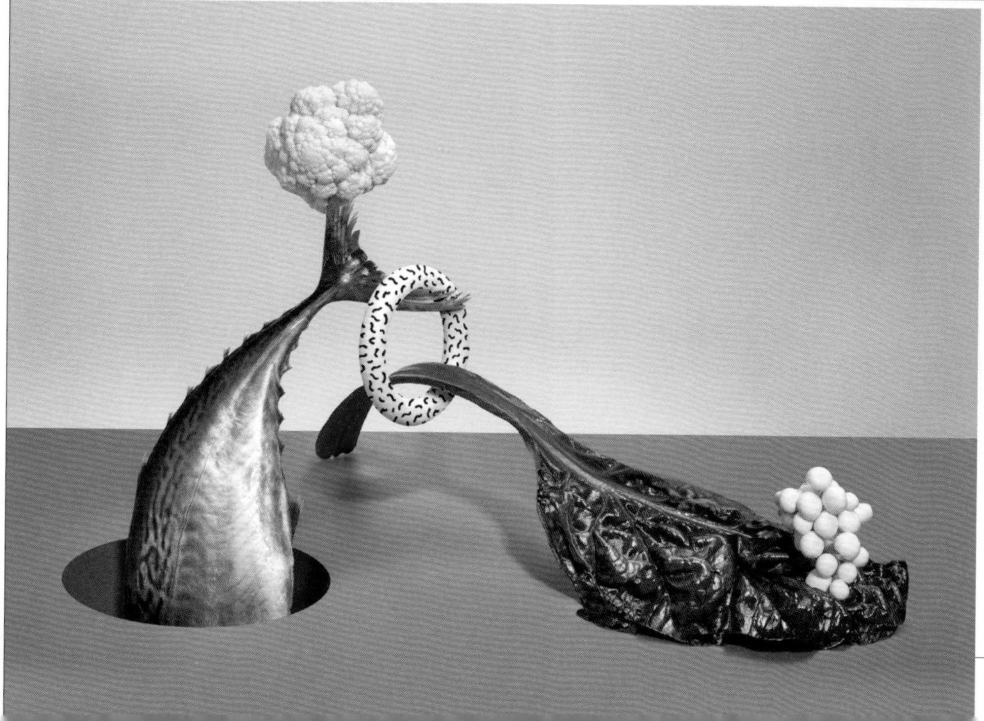

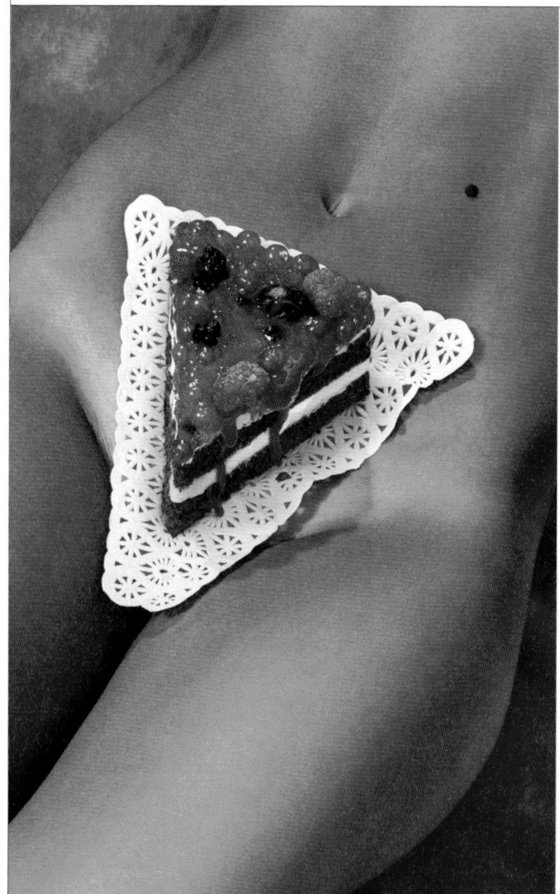

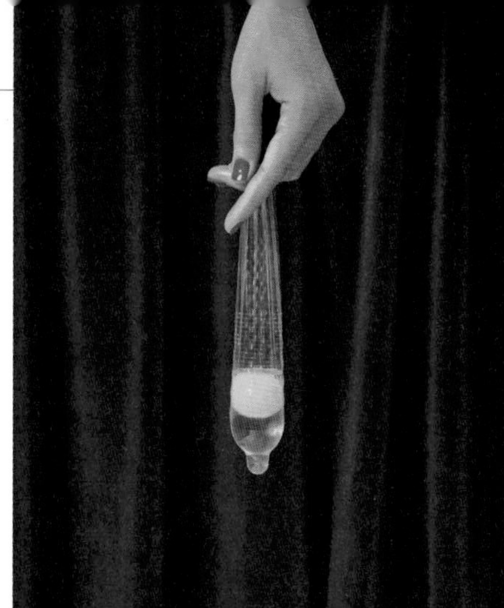

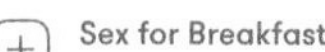

Sex for Breakfast
A playful photo series that explored morning sex, a timeless subject, in a comical yet innocent way.

Creative & Art Direction: Pabli Alfieri, Paloma Rincón / Set Design: Pablo Alfieri / Photography: Paloma Rincón / Production: Antiestatico / Operation: Matias Dumont, Carola Bisci, Vir Herrador / Casting: Nydia Vacas (Va de Casting) / Model: Miriam Larragay

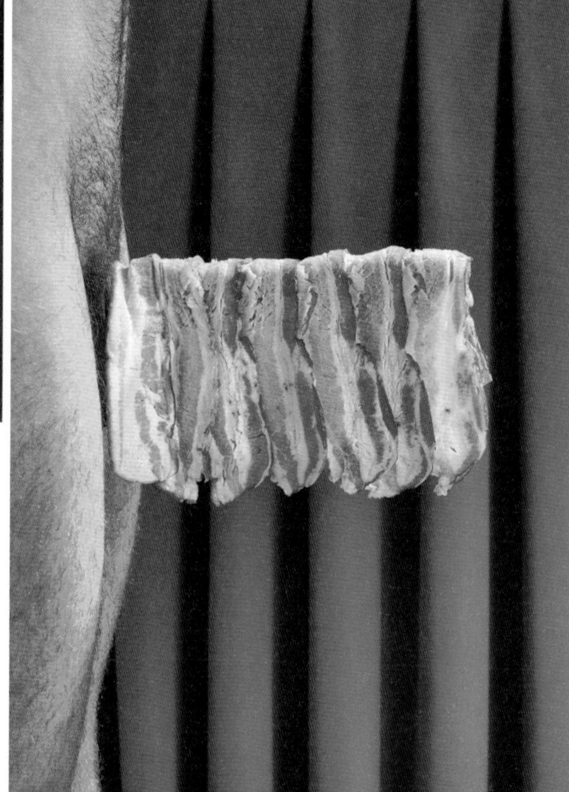

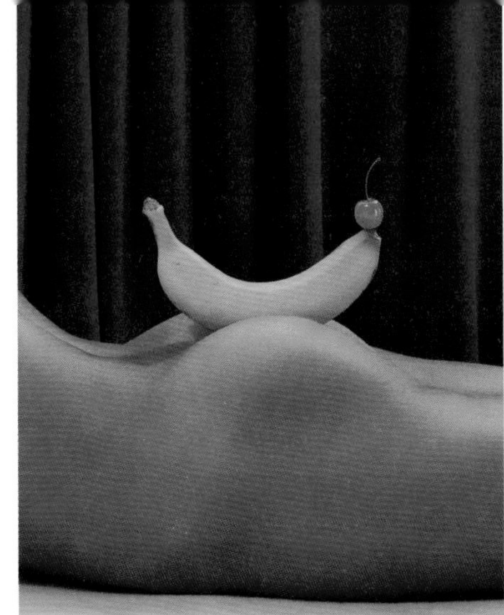
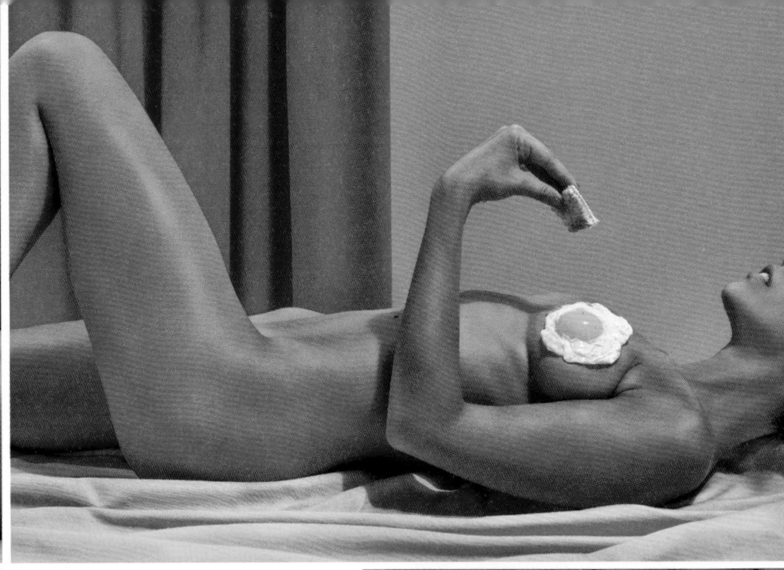
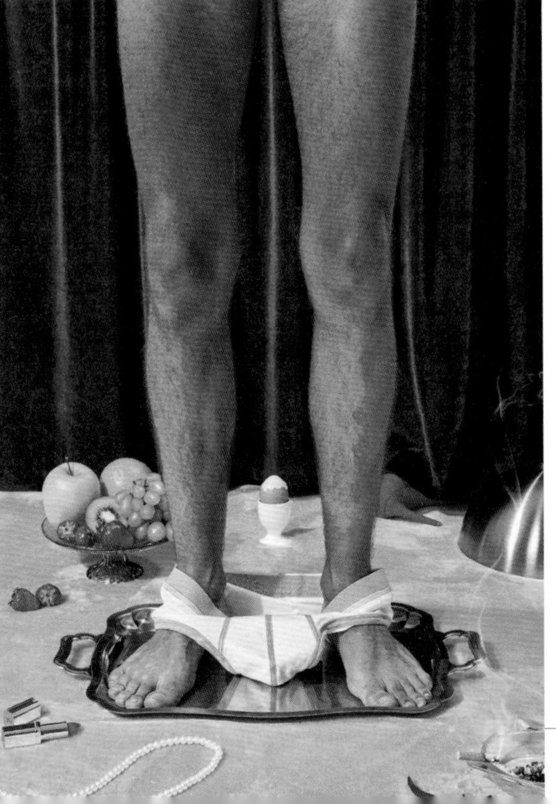
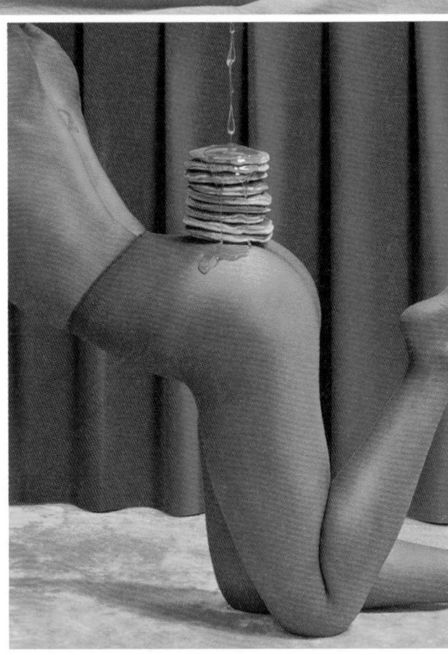

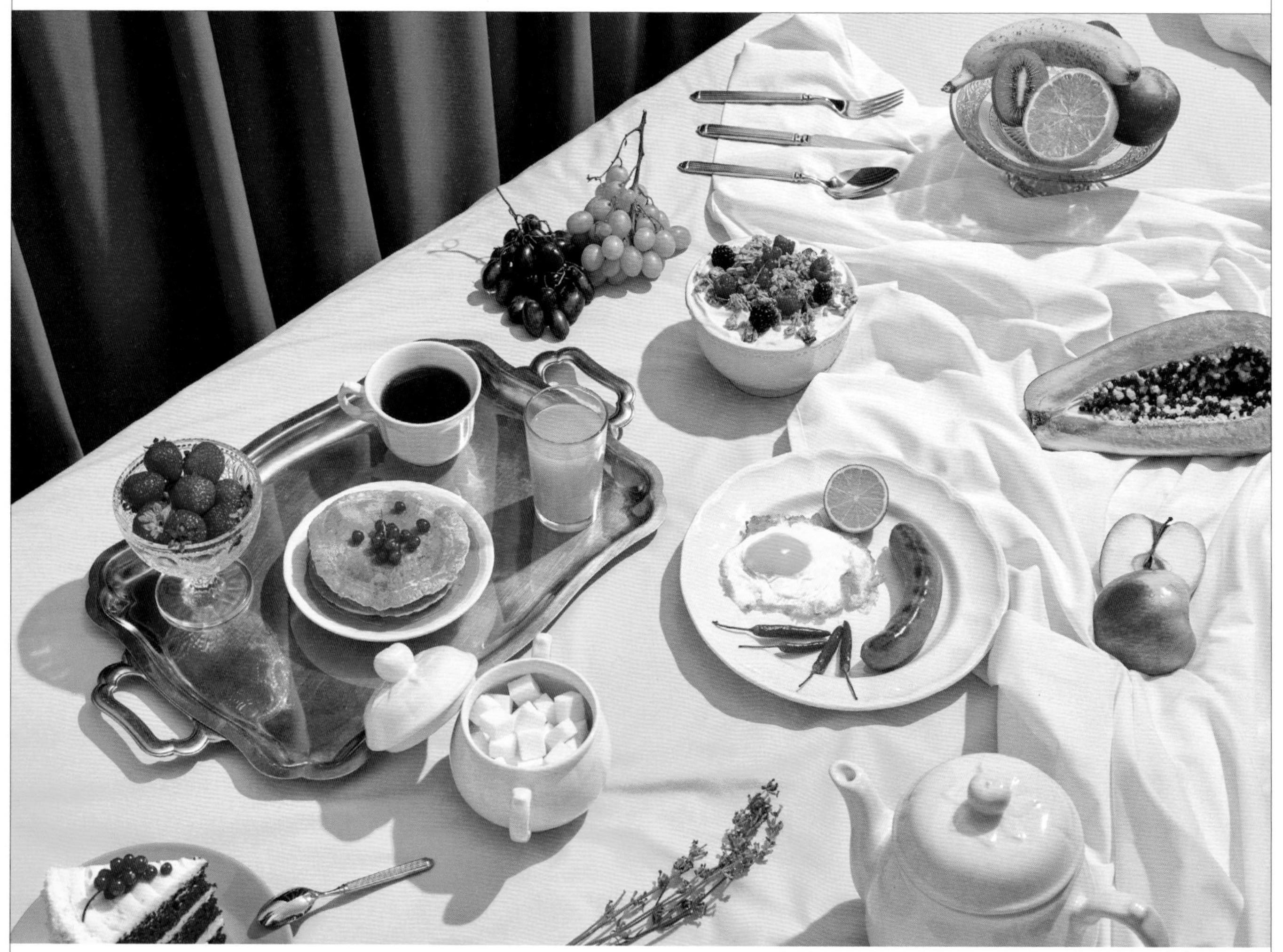

"Since we were children, we were told not to play with our food, and definitely not even talk about sex..."

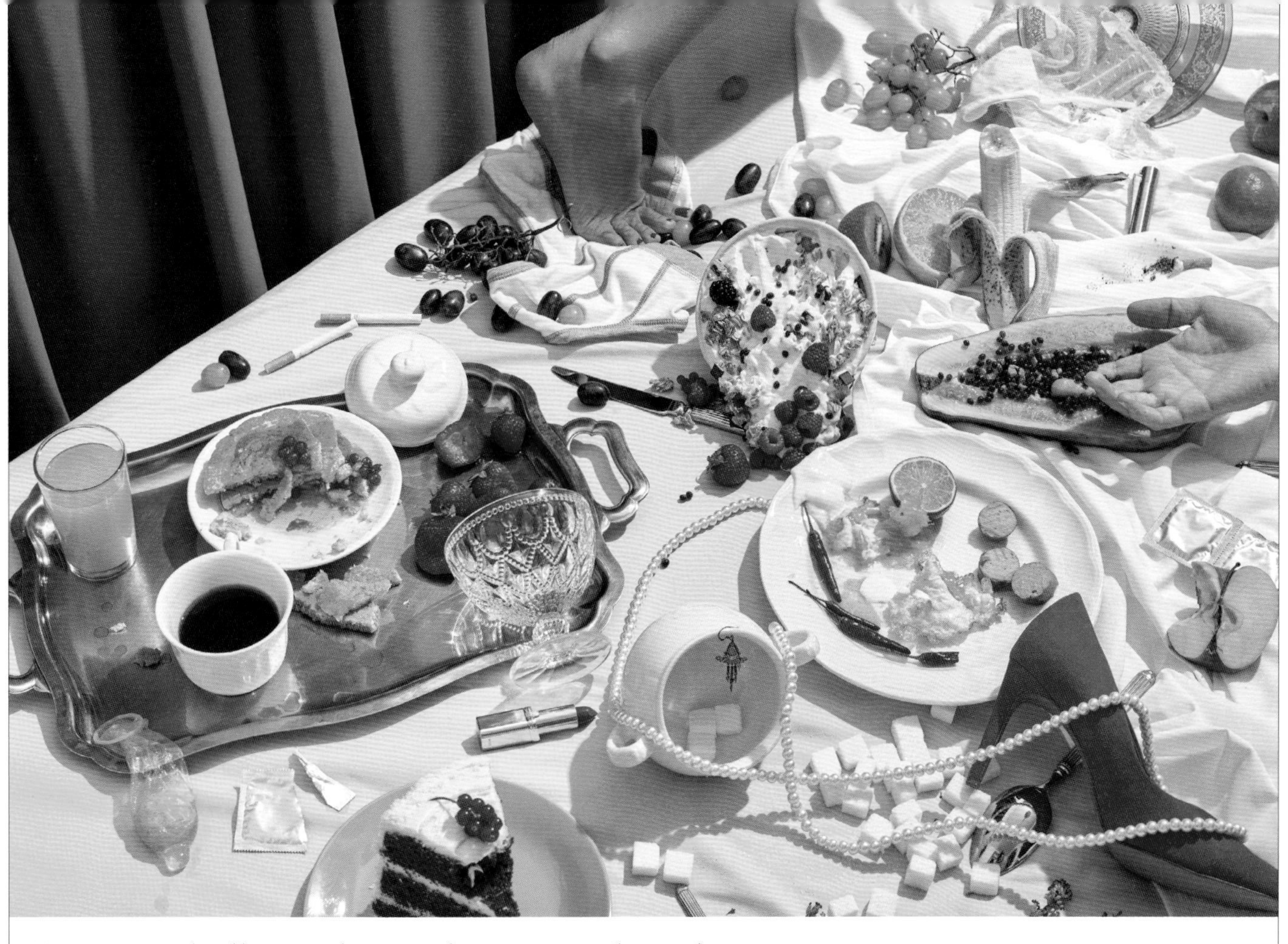

"...so we challenged ourselves to explore these topics in an innocent and direct way – an ode to pleasure, enjoyment, and freedom."

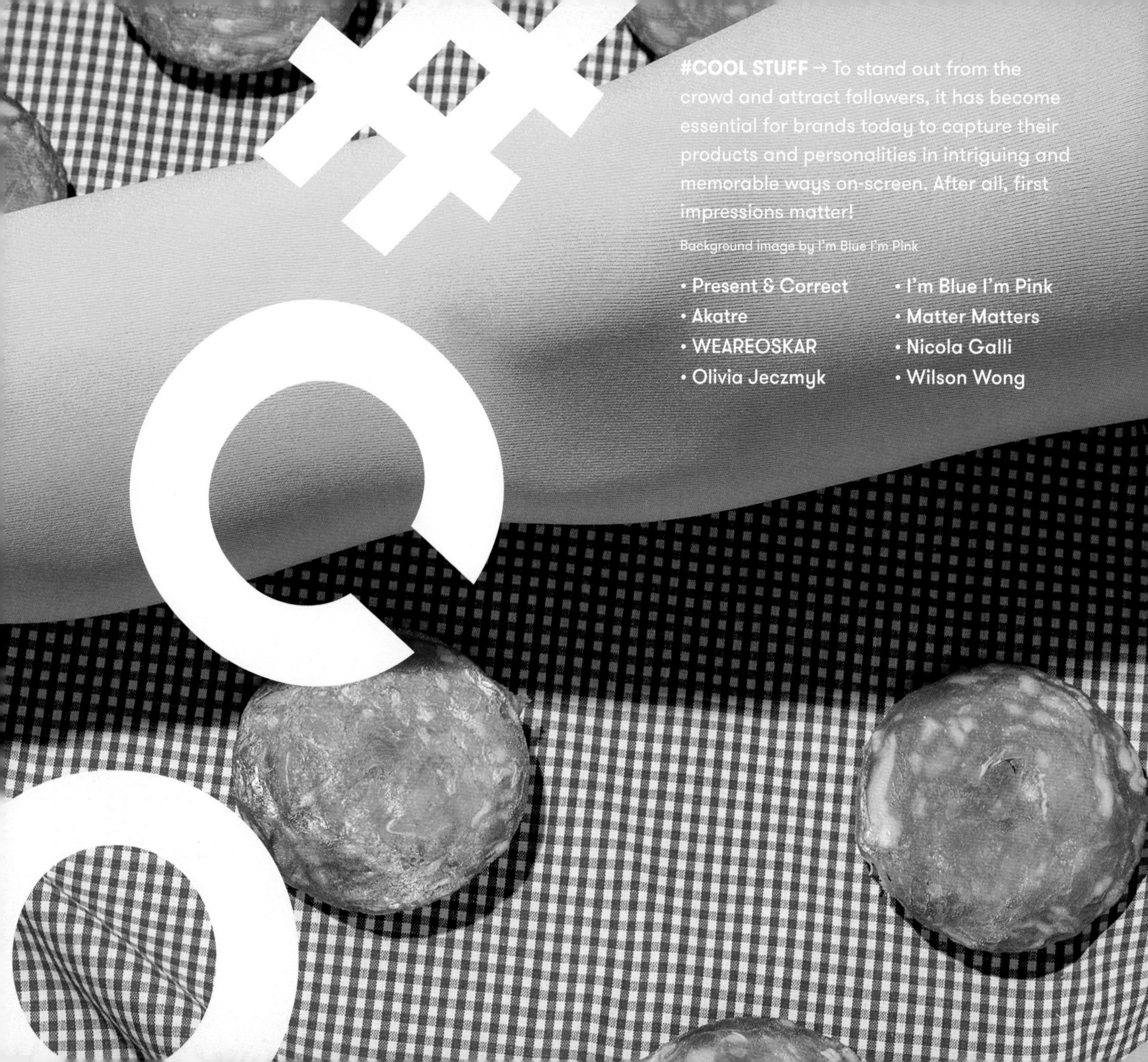

#COOL STUFF → To stand out from the crowd and attract followers, it has become essential for brands today to capture their products and personalities in intriguing and memorable ways on-screen. After all, first impressions matter!

Background image by I'm Blue I'm Pink

- Present & Correct
- Akatre
- WEAREOSKAR
- Olivia Jeczmyk
- I'm Blue I'm Pink
- Matter Matters
- Nicola Galli
- Wilson Wong

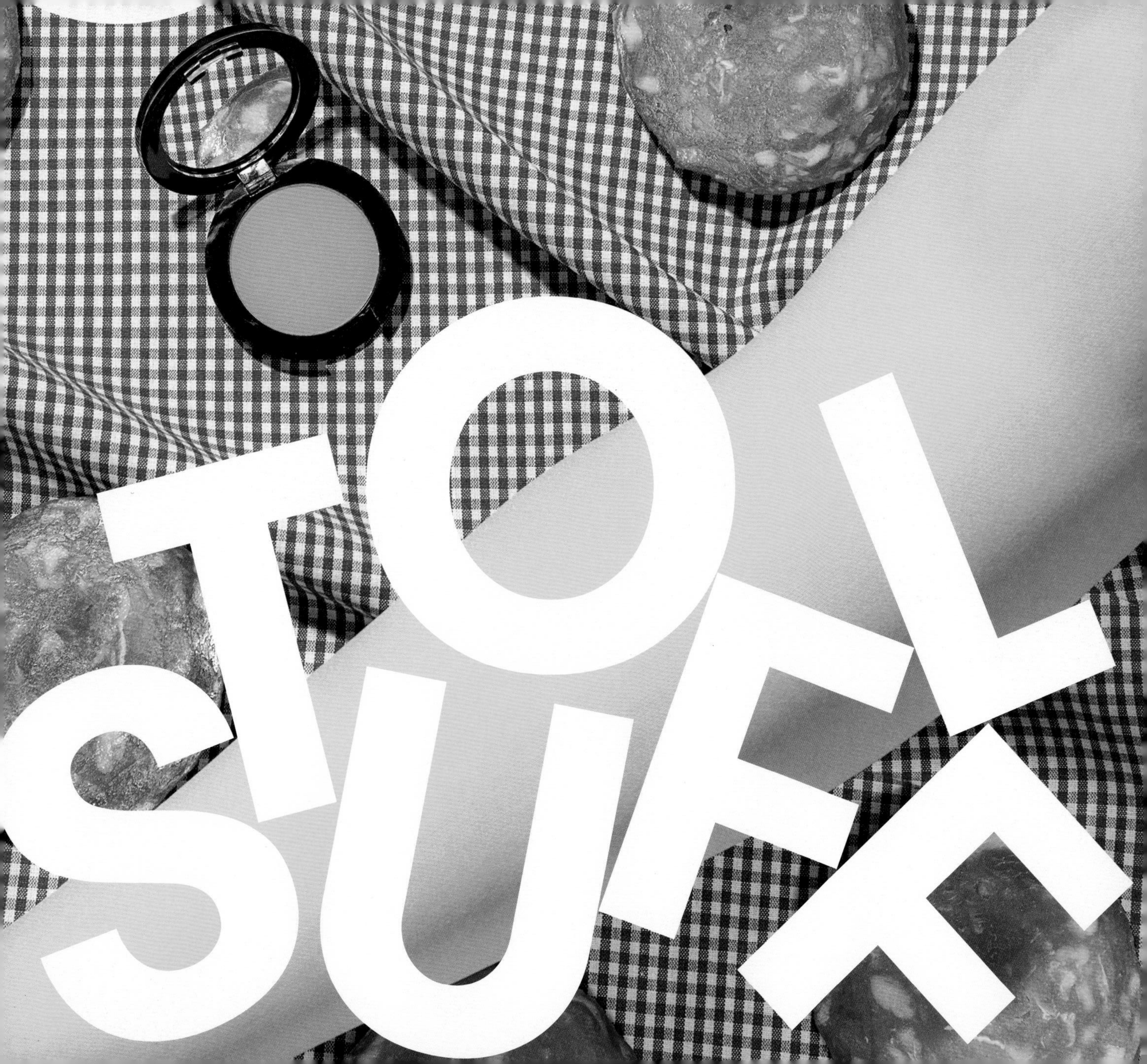

FIRST IMPRESSIONS MATTER

I look for visual impact. I try to publish at least once a week and ensure that the colours on my feed do not repeat themselves.

— Eating Patterns / Vega Hernando

HAVE FUN WITH CAPTIONS

We always like to use puns and jokes, because we are not going to tell you anything else that is not already in the image.

— Daniel Rueda & Anna Devís

MAKE IT POP!

I often work in a playful way, where products become a part of set design. Through lighting and a set created with monochrome colours, materials, or shapes that are in contrast to the products, I try to make the latter stand out.

— Olivia Jeczmyk

LEARN FROM YOUR MISTAKES

Working for almost ten years now has shaped me a lot. I learned the most important lesson through experiences of failure and success – trial and error.

— Olivia Jeczmyk

1 PICTURE = 1,000 WORDS

A good picture is all about storytelling. It should look like a frozen moment amidst on-going action: the viewer has to be able to imagine or know what might happen in the next frame.

— rvrbr studio

BE INSTA-RECOGNISABLE

If someone can look at an image and say it looks like your image, then you are doing something right!

— Olive Clothing

IGNORE THE NEGATIVE VIBES

We pay more attention to good work rather than mistakes.

— rvrbr studio

PERFECTION IS OVERRATED

Sometimes, it is better to keep some imperfections than over-process the image.

— I'm Blue I'm Pink

FOCUS ON THE SUBSTANCE

We are more about the idea, rather than trying to find a specific style.

— Studio Furious

BEING COOL IS NOT ENOUGH

Introduce storytelling, not just a cool set of images empty of meaning.

— I'm Blue I'm Pink

EXPLORE DIFFERENT PLATFORMS

I find it easier (and more fun) to think and design between the physical and the digital.

— Ice Cream Books / Ben Deezer

CELEBRATE YOUR CULTURE

When I photograph, I try to create some art of my own by using my own cultural baggage. My challenge is to show how thin the line is between art and (real life) photography.

— Serge Najjar

MAKE PEOPLE SMILE

It is always rewarding when people like the photos, or they smile or comment in a fun way. When I am happy with the result, that is also nice :-)

— Present & Correct

TIPS & TRICKS FOR ENGAGING YOUR AUDIENCE

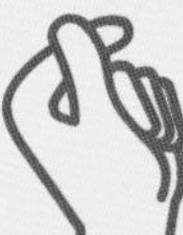

#23-46

NOTHING IS TOO STUPID

What seems to be working best for me is to be disciplined with always trying out things, yet to have a fairly relaxed approach to concepts and ideas. I often try things out and let them grow (or die) in the process. Sometimes, stupid or simple things are what works best.

— Studio Kleiner

PUT YOUR VIEWERS FIRST

Think about what you are trying to achieve, prepare well before hand, and take your time before a shoot to process it all.

— Nicola Galli

GET YOUR PRIORITIES RIGHT

In general, we do not think about photography too much. We are thinking about food – how it tastes and looks.

— Lililoveme & Dmitry Buko

FIND THE BEST TIME

My strategy for social media is weekday-focused. I find that the best time to post on Instagram is between noon and 1pm during the work week, when a large number of users browse through their feeds during their lunch breaks.

— Wilson Wong

SAY NO TO DRAMA

We always try to be neutral and not court controversy to be a safe place for people who enjoy seeing ideas, perspectives, colours, and funny stuff.

— Daniel Rueda & Anna Devís

MINIMISE VISUAL CLUTTER

When you have too many elements, like a very dense story, too many subjects in the image, a very rich background, or a very rich location, you are not going to be able to impact the viewer much.

— Daniel Rueda & Anna Devís

MAKE YOUR ART ACCESSIBLE

What we try to do is not for architects or designers. We want it to be for anyone.

— Daniel Rueda & Anna Devís

KEEP COOL & CALM

I only keep what soothes my eye.

— Serge Najjar

BE PRECISE

For product styling shoots, we build/design all the sets by ourselves to get the exact composition beforehand.

— Young & Innocent

WORK HARD!

It is awesome when people in the know recognise your efforts.

— Compendium Design Store

STAY TRUE TO YOUR ART

The goal is to get an image, not a commercial.

— Akatre

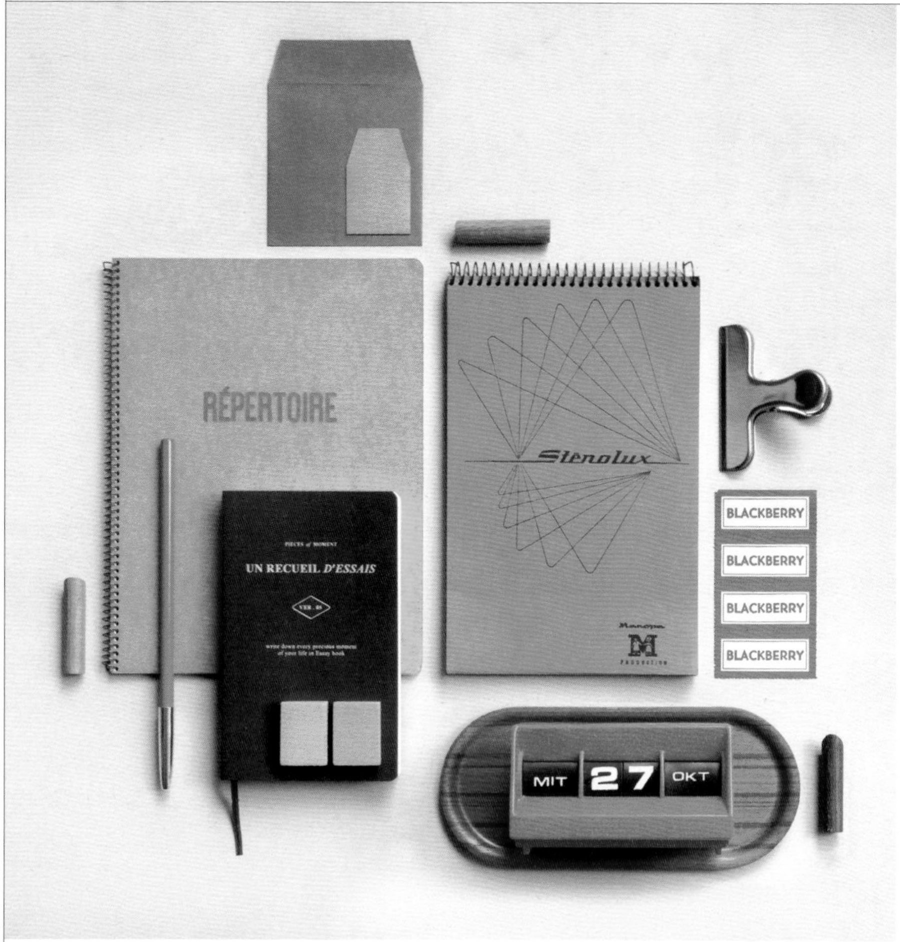

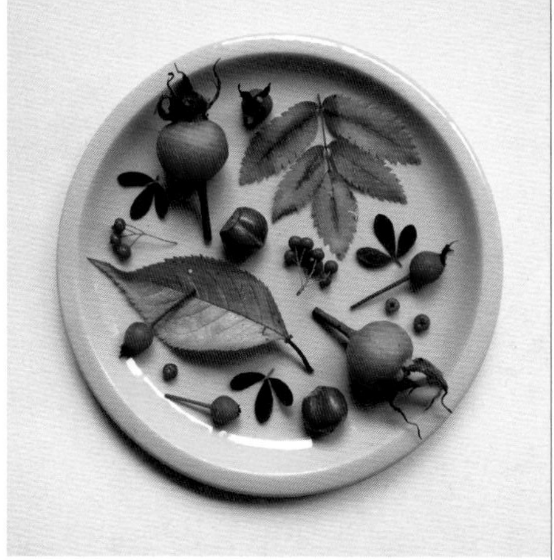

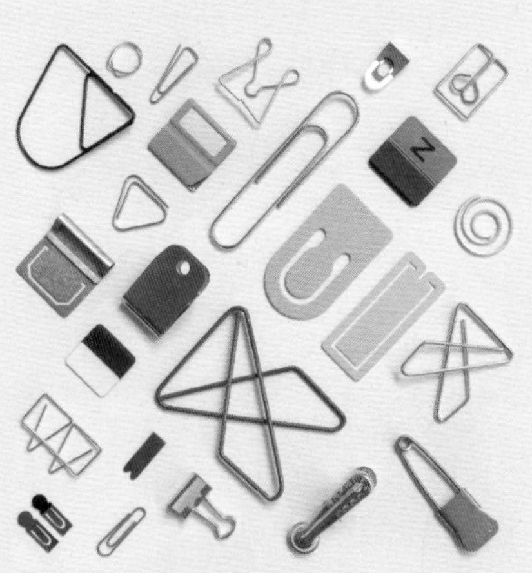

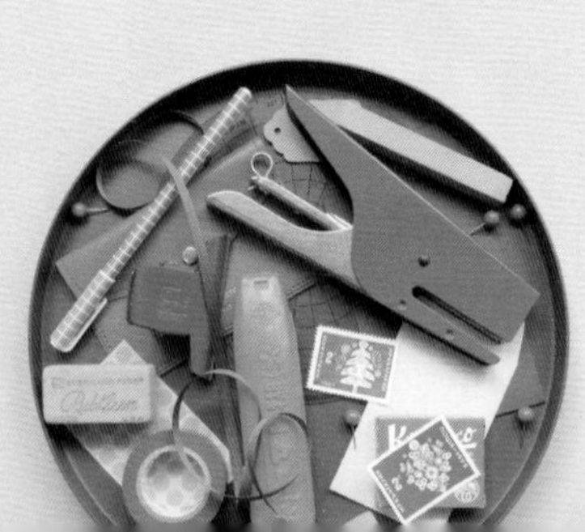

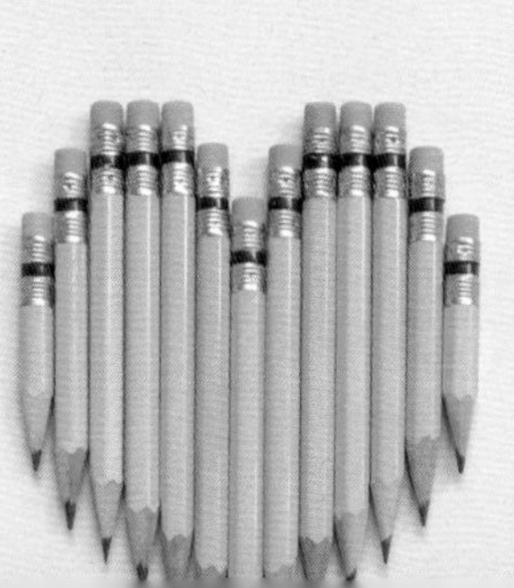

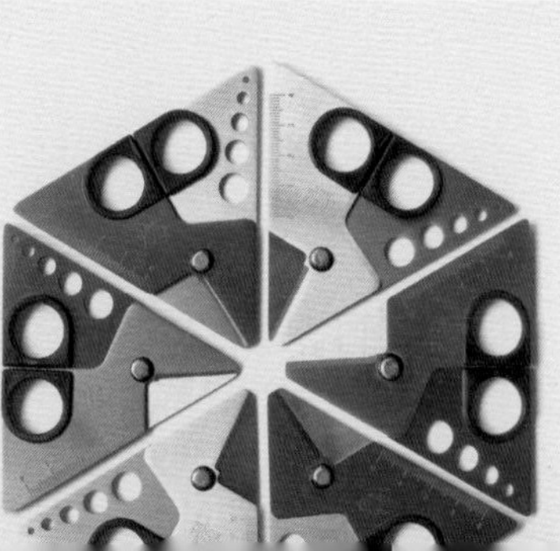

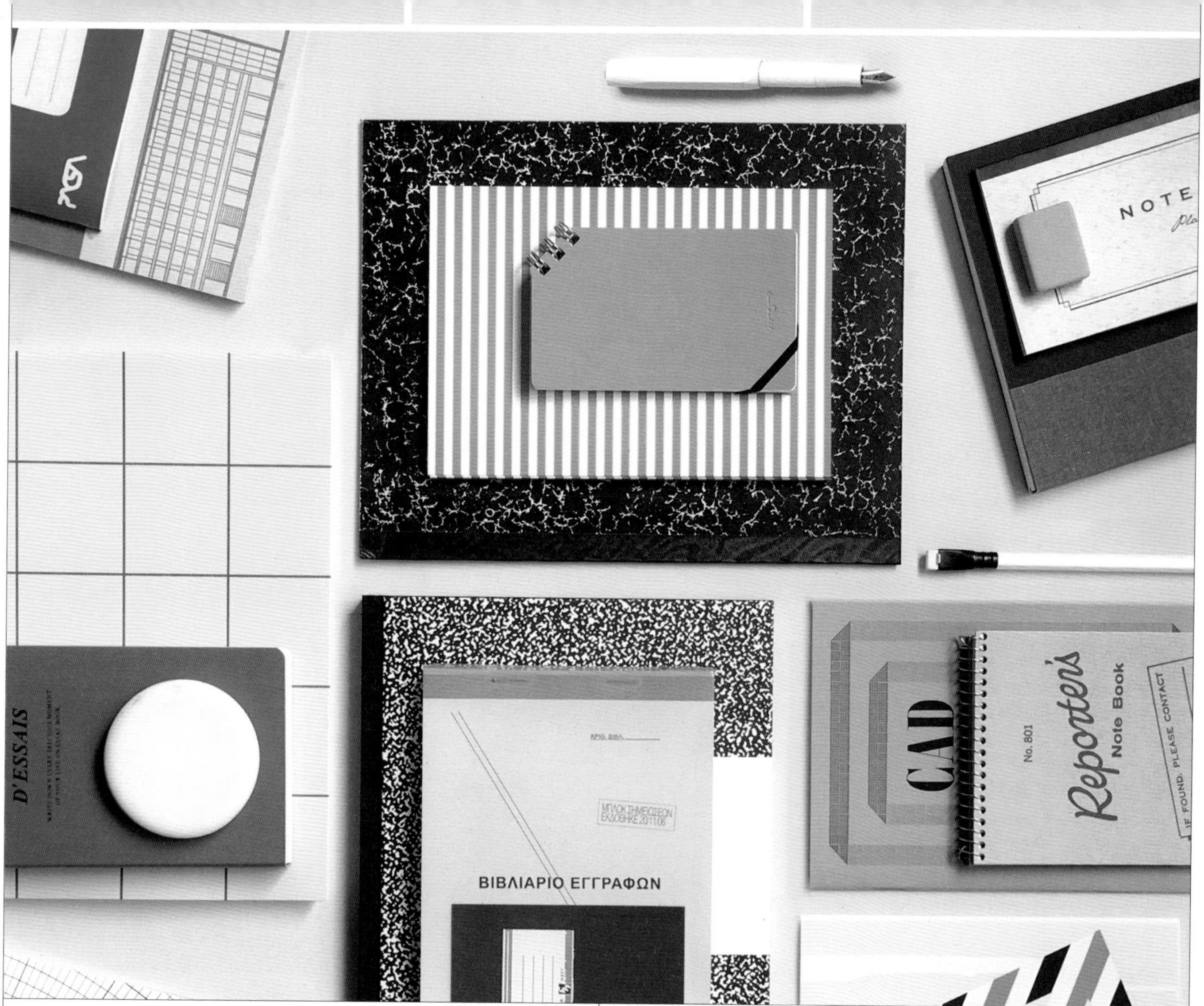

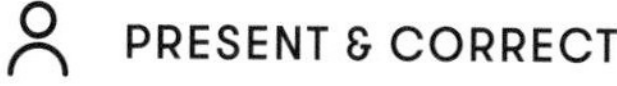

PRESENT & CORRECT

presentandcorrect

Present & Correct is the result of a long-term obsession with stationery. An ever-evolving store featuring its own designs and things the owners love by other designers from around the world, it aims to spark distant memories and make viewers smile.

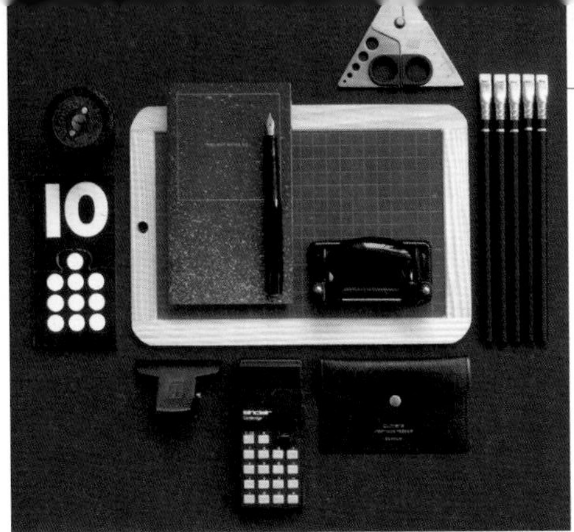

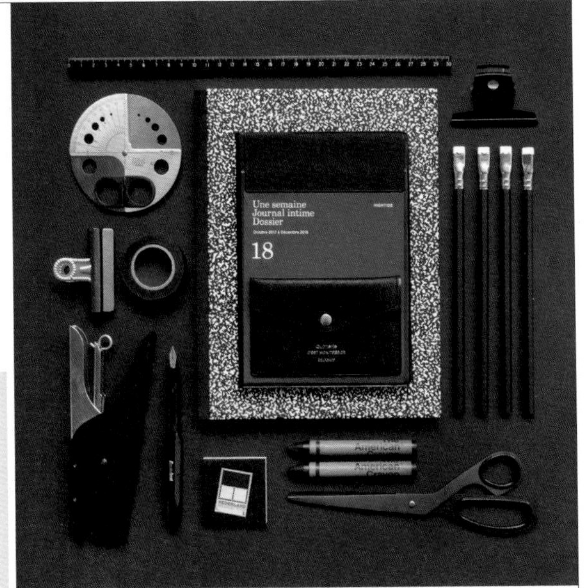

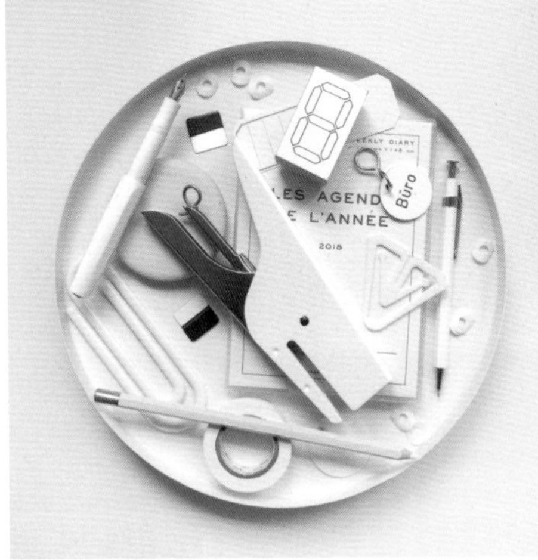

“I look at the Instagram grid as a layout, in that I try to balance the tone and types of images, so that when you see them all as a group, they still look nice.”

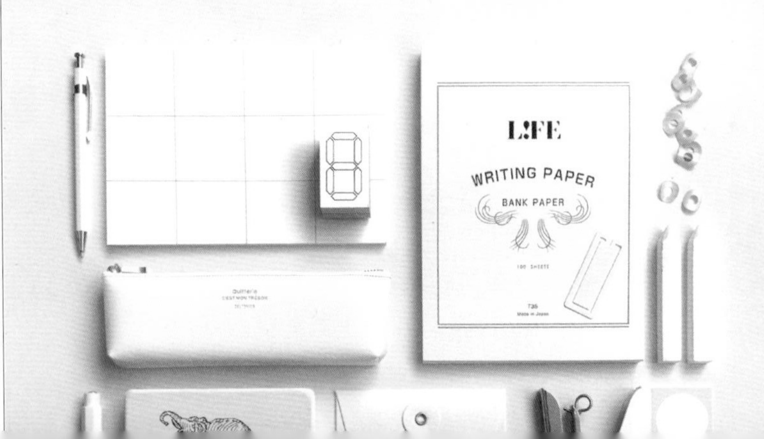

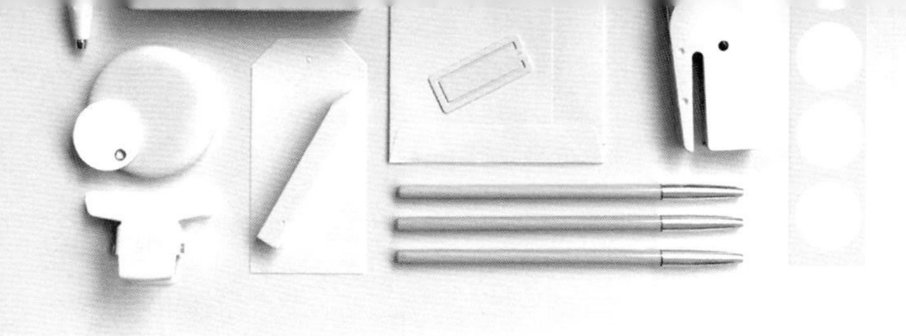

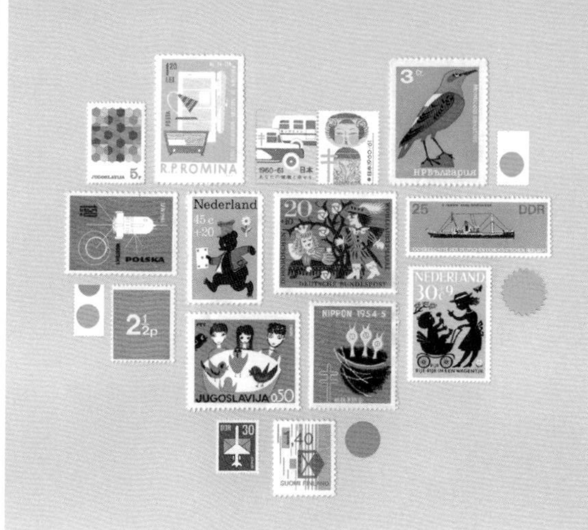

R.P.ROMINA
Nederland
POLSKA
DDR
NEDERLAND
NIPPON 1954-5
JUGOSLAVIJA

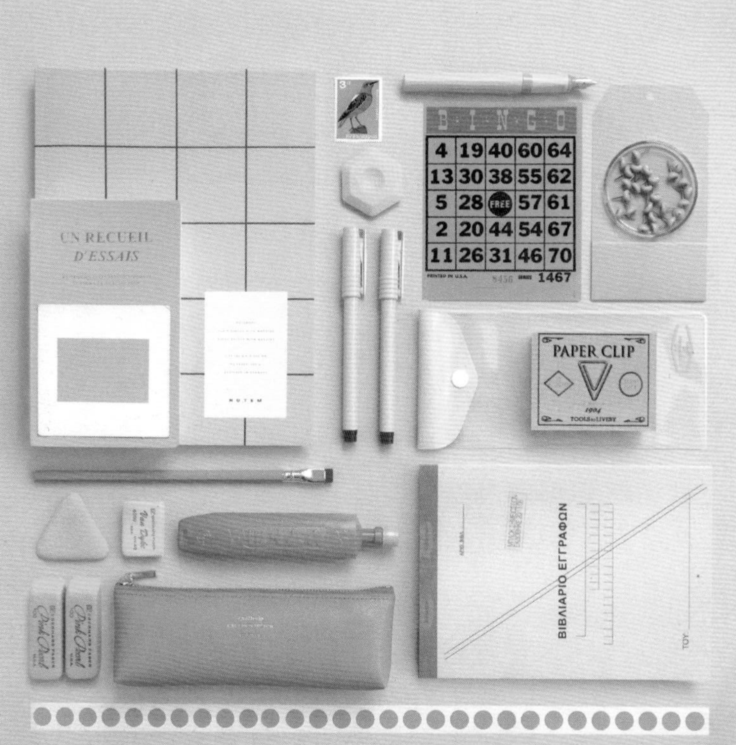

UN RECUEIL
D'ESSAIS
B I N G O
4 19 40 60 64
13 30 38 55 62
5 28 FREE 57 61
2 20 44 54 67
11 26 31 46 70
1467
PAPER CLIP
ΒΙΒΛΙΑΡΙΟ ΕΓΓΡΑΦΩΝ

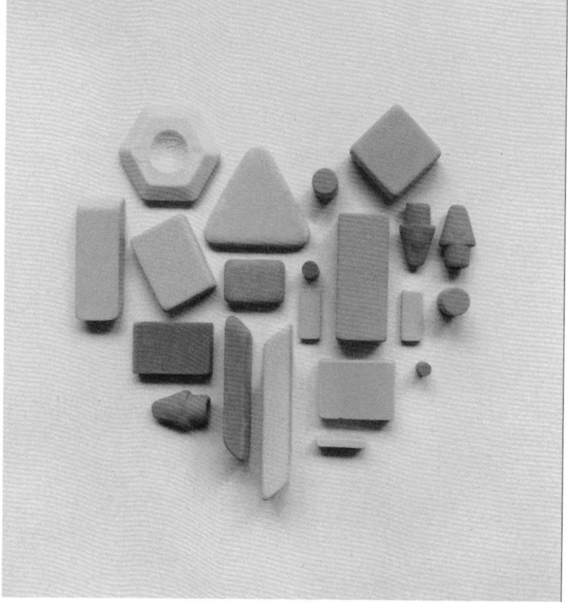

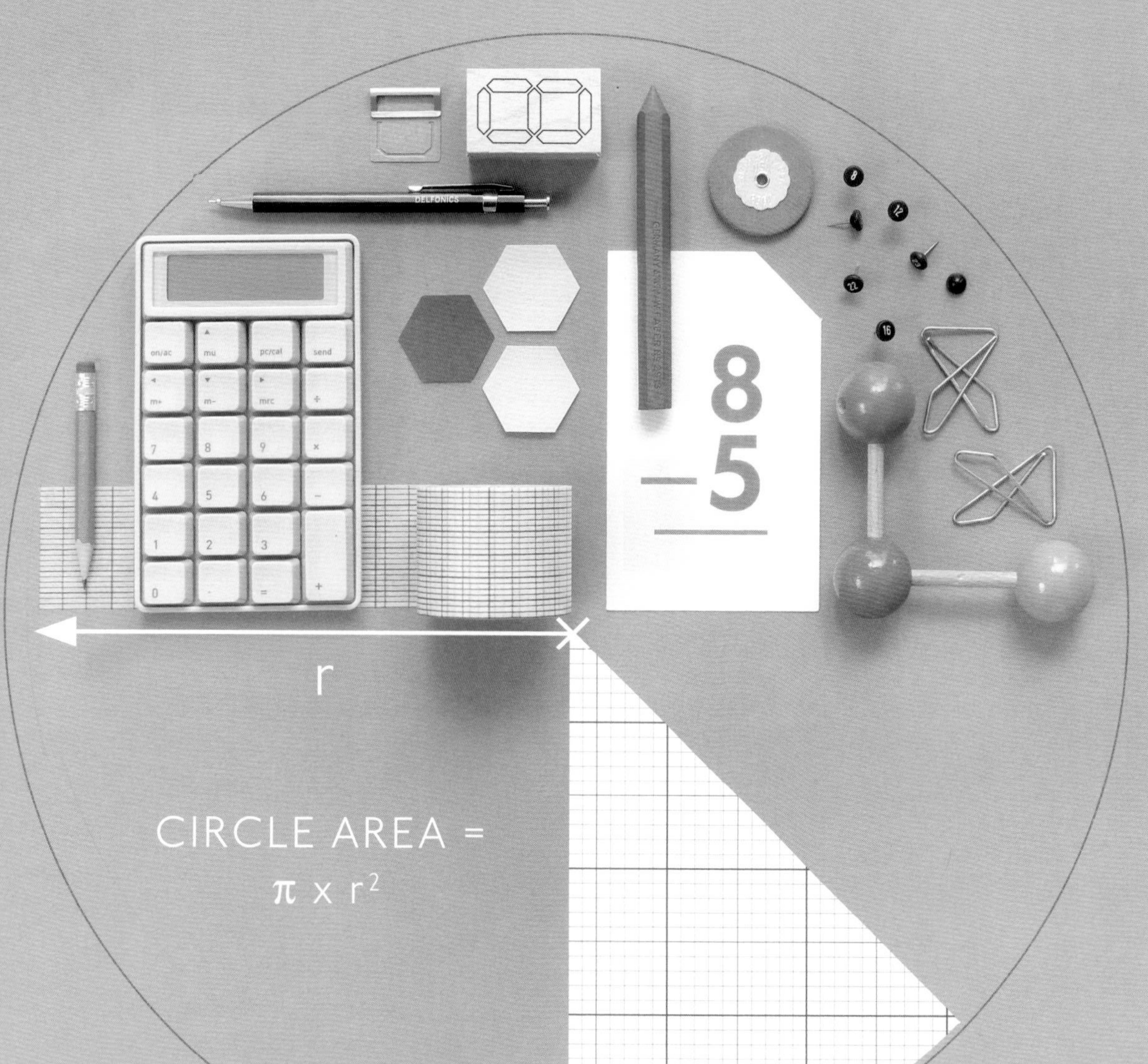

DELFONICS
8
−5
r
CIRCLE AREA =
$\pi \times r^2$

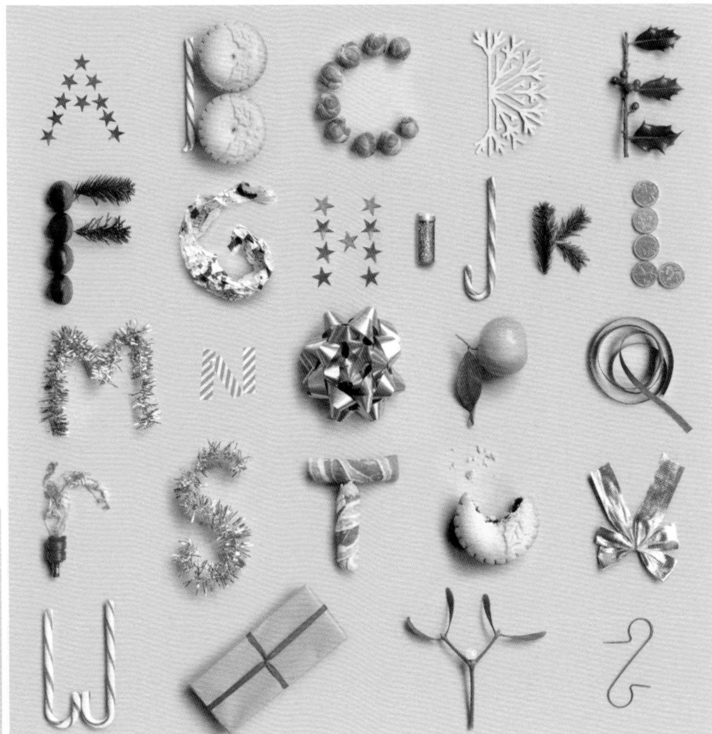

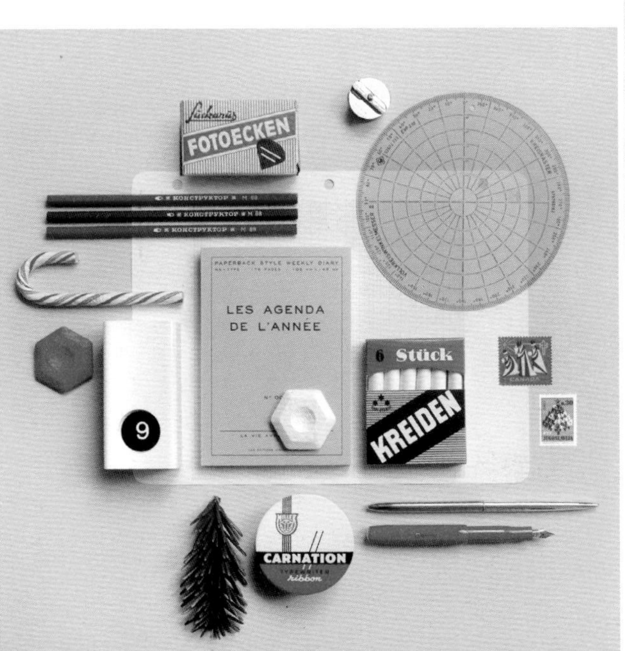

FOTOECKEN
PAPERBACK STYLE WEEKLY DIARY
LES AGENDA
DE L'ANNÉE
6 Stück
KREIDEN
9
CARNATION
ribbon

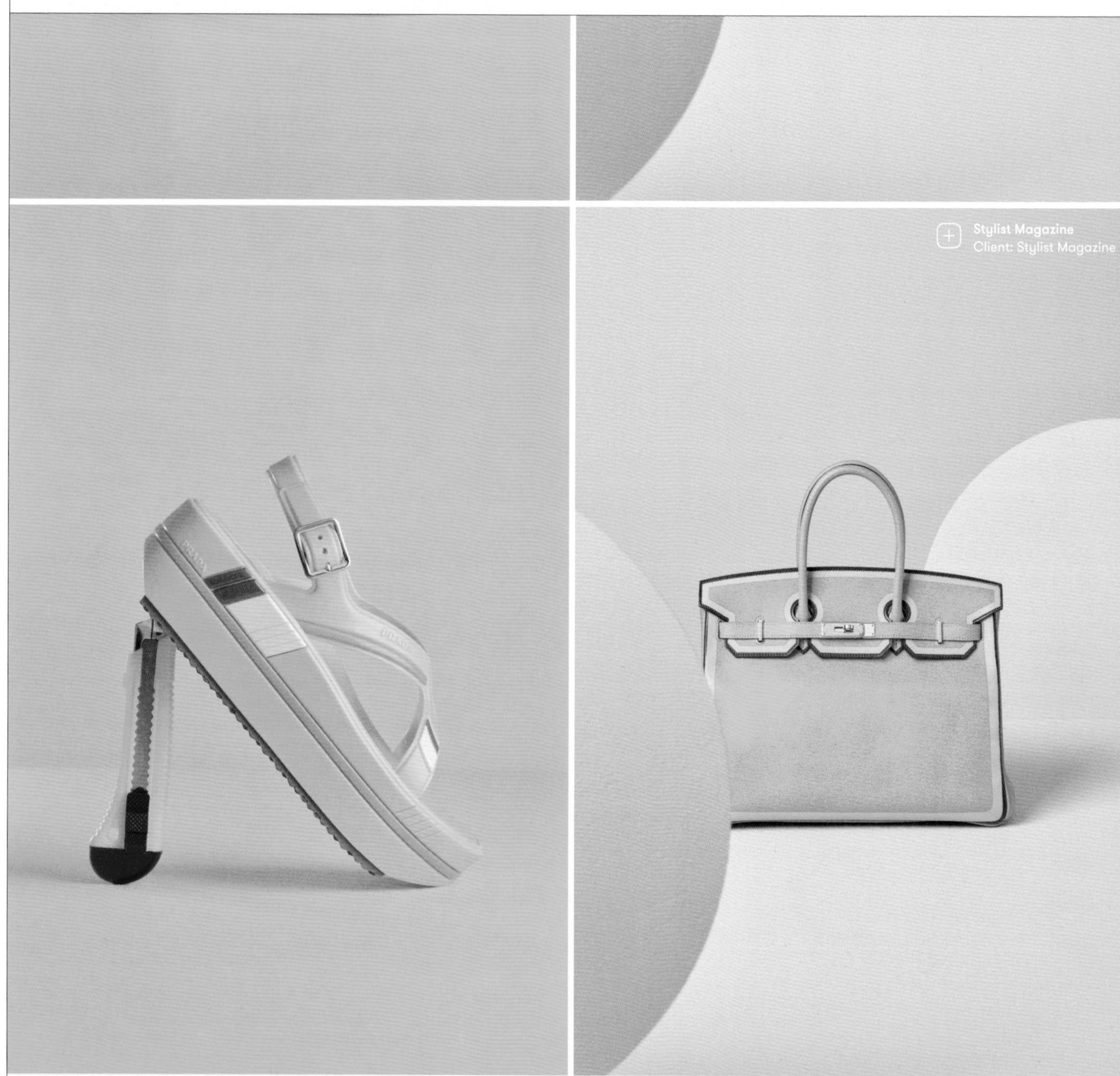

Stylist Magazine
Client: Stylist Magazine

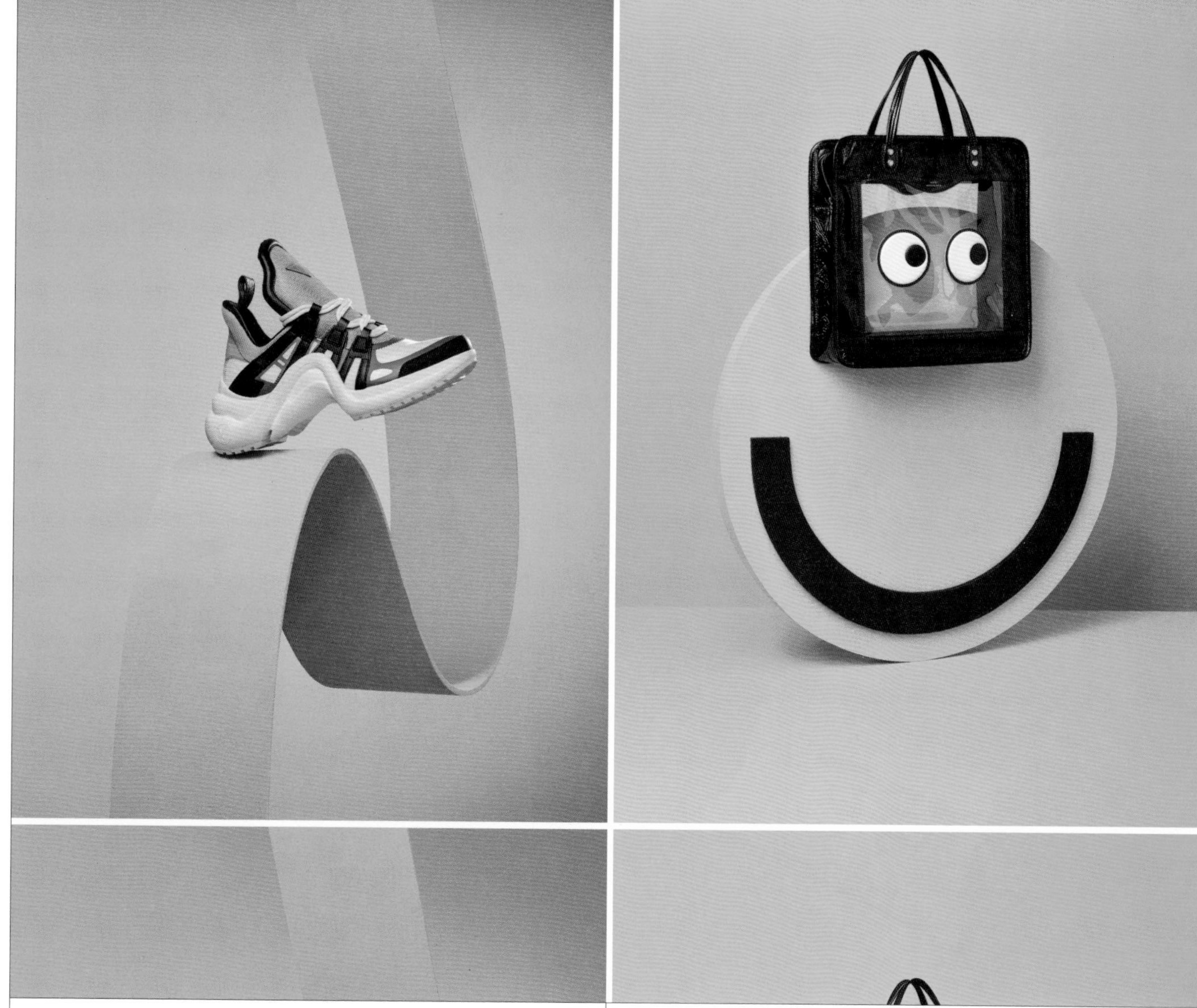

AKATRE

akatrestudio

Akatre is a creative studio that was founded by Valentin Abad, Julien Dhivert, and Sébastien Riveron. The trio express themselves through graphic design, photography, typography, videography, artistic installations, and music creation spanning the fields of art, fashion, culture, media, and luxury.

Stylist Magazine
Client: Stylist Magazine

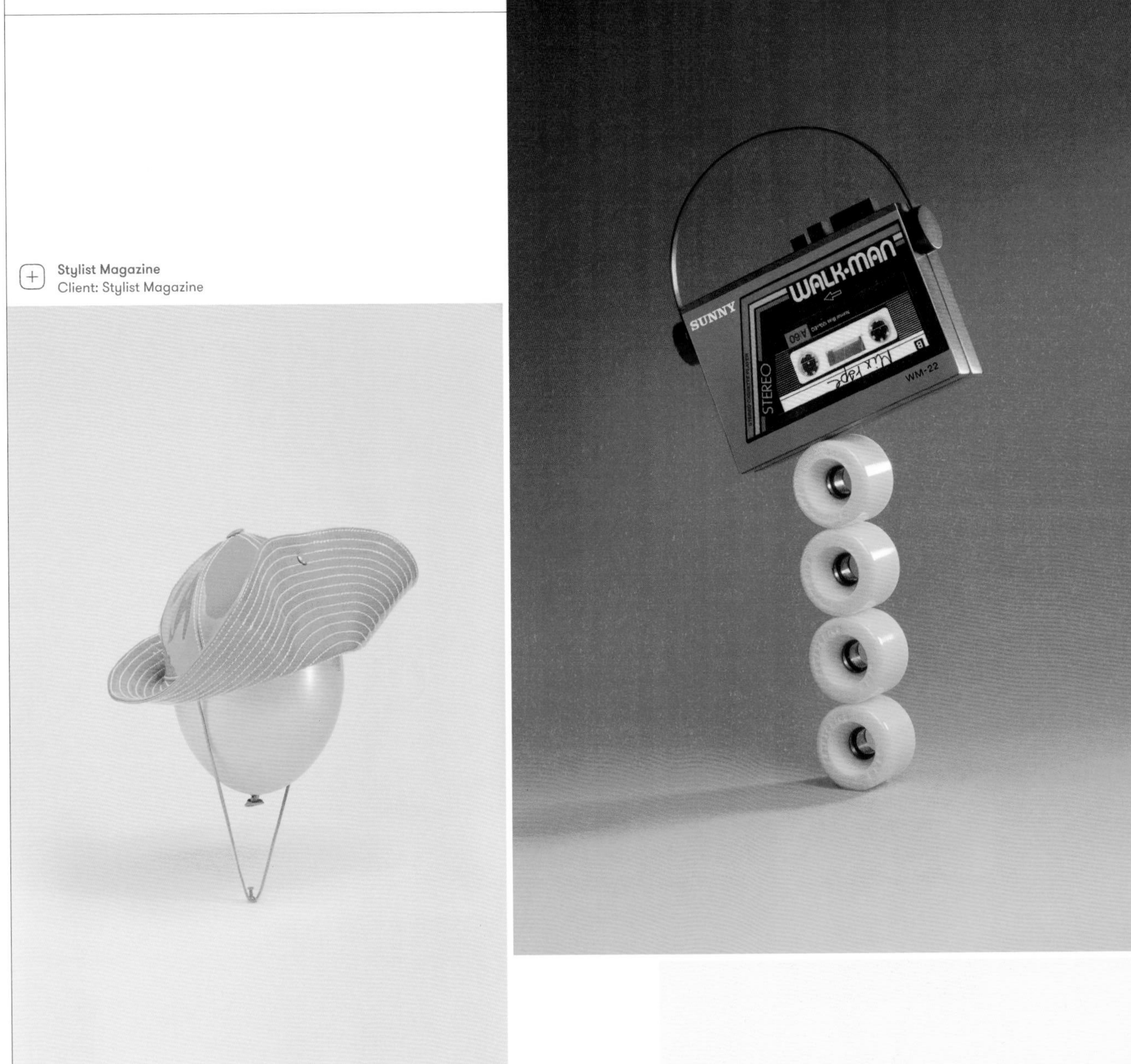

"The goal is to get an image, not a commercial."

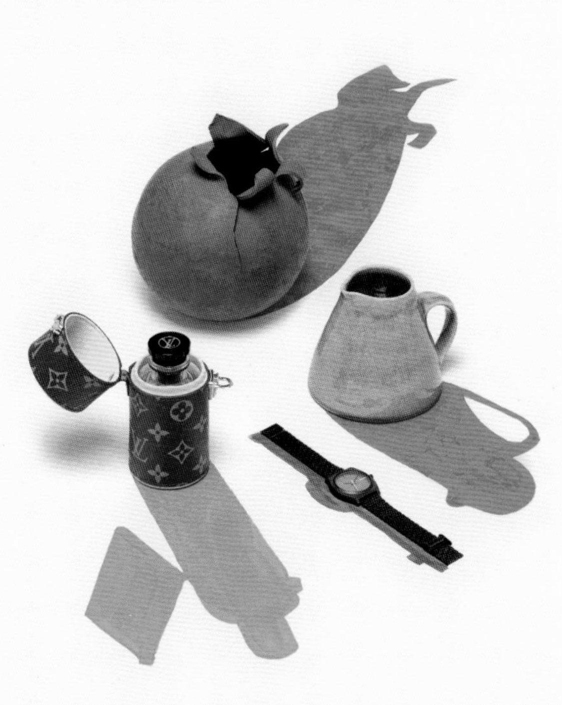

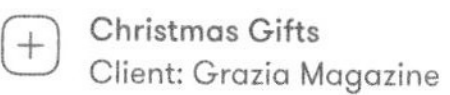

Christmas Gifts
Client: Grazia Magazine

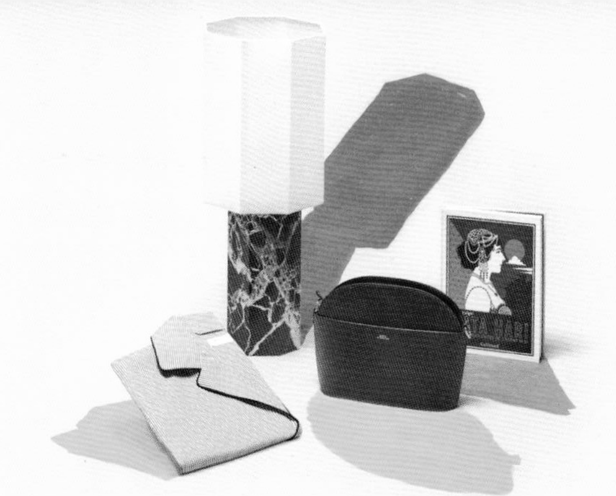

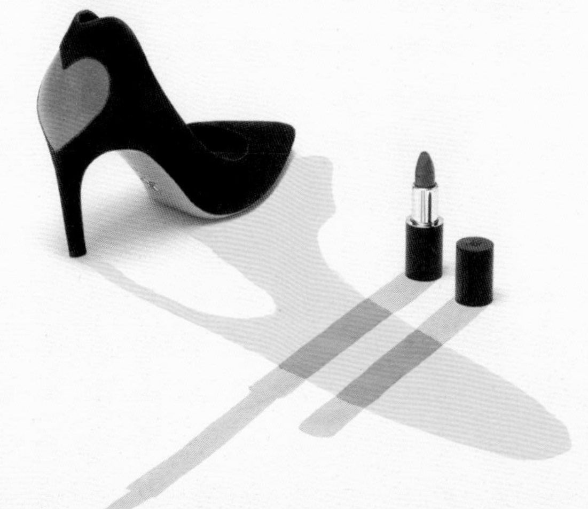

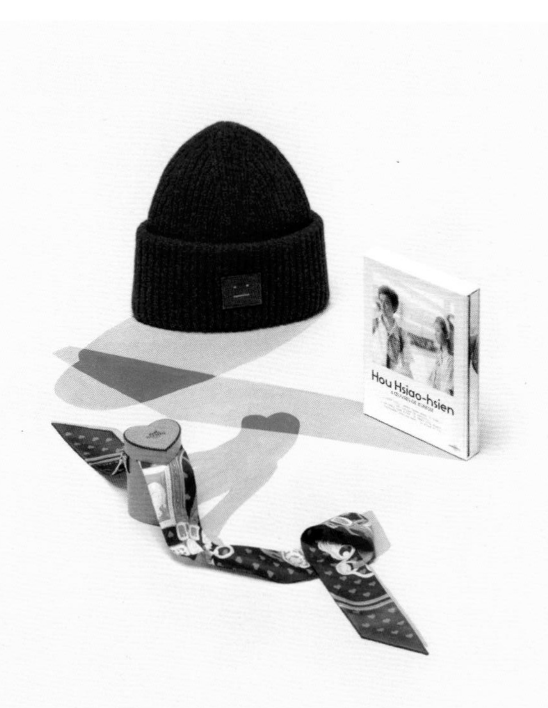

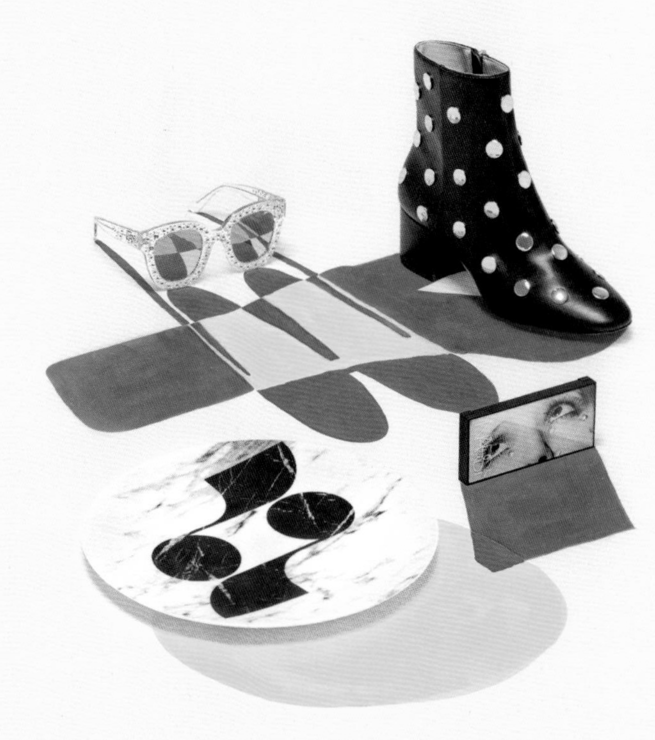

"When your idea turns real and is even better that what you drew, it is rewarding."

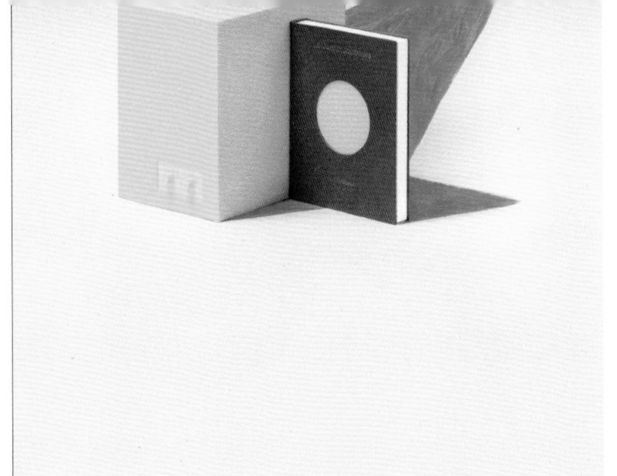

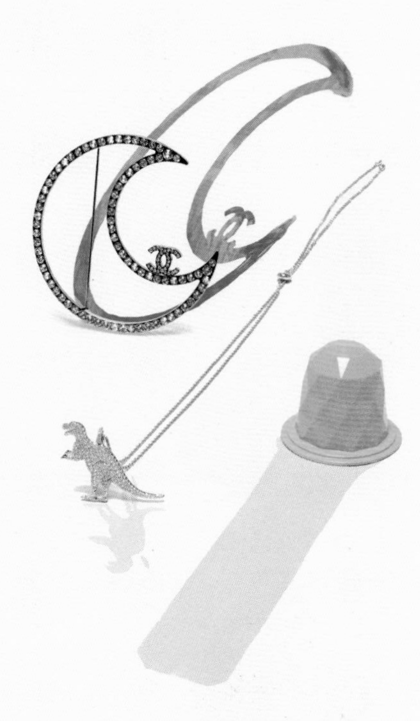

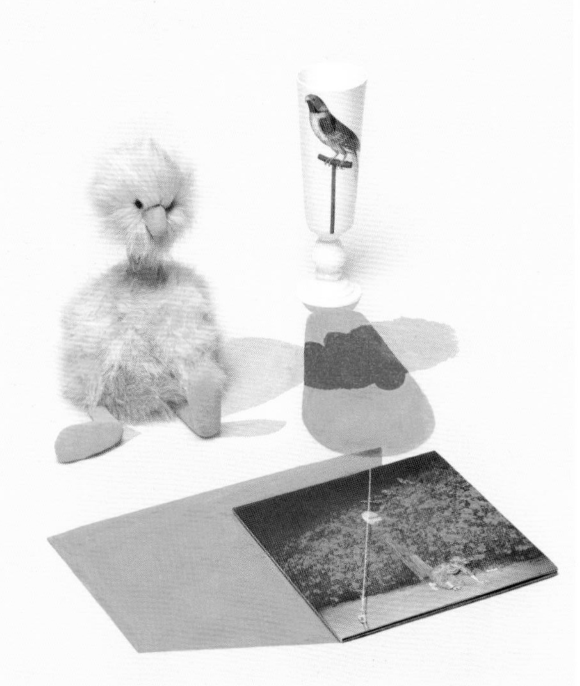

Christmas Gifts
Client: Grazia Magazine

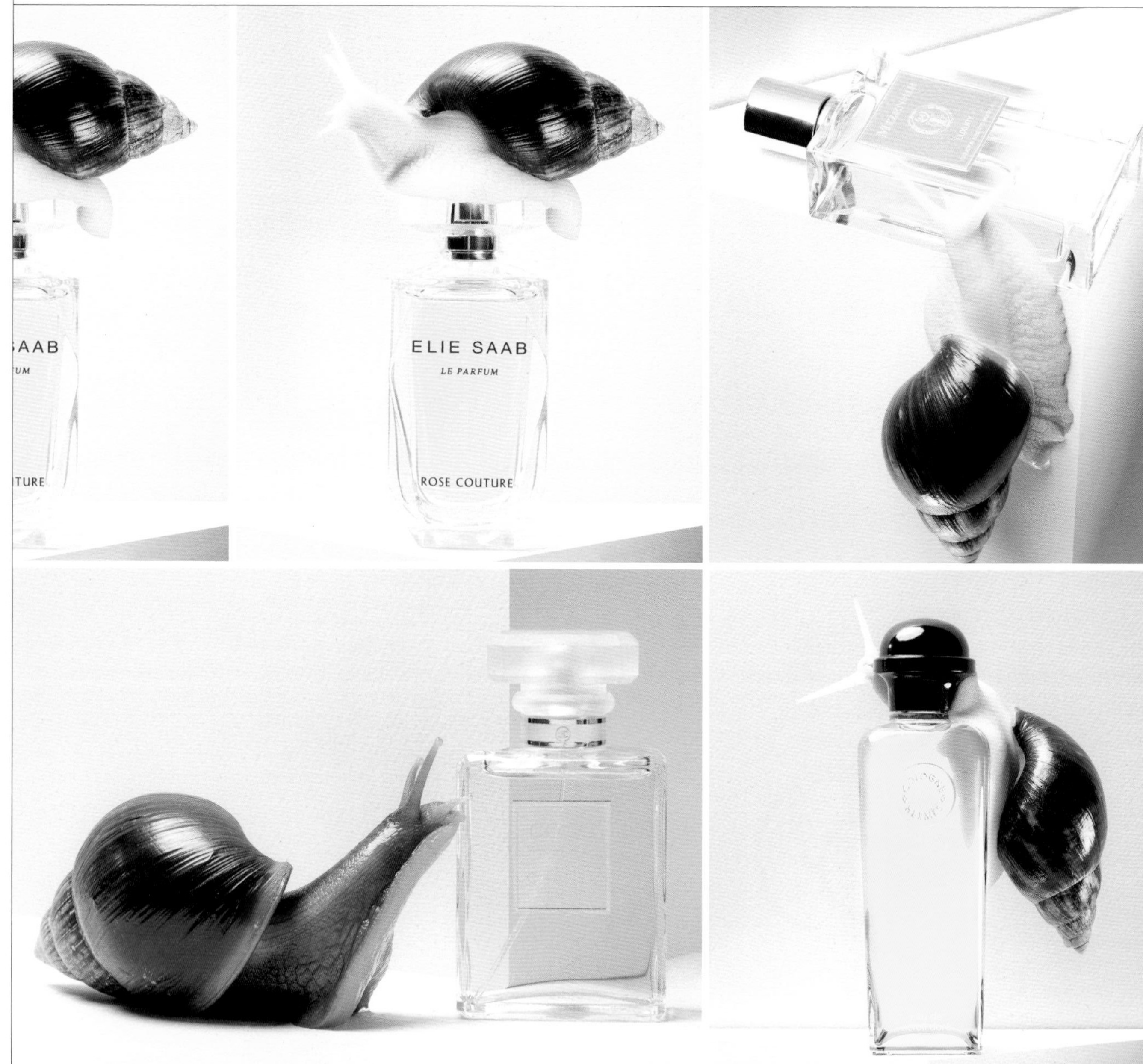
ELIE SAAB
LE PARFUM
ROSE COUTURE

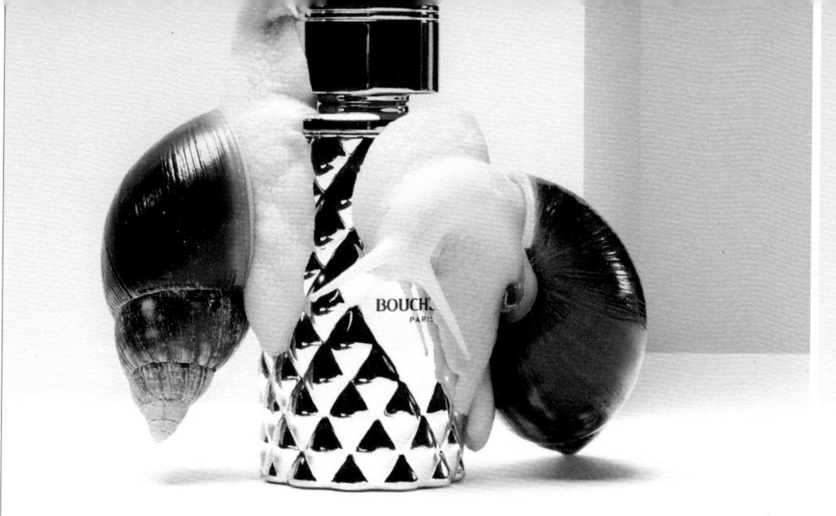

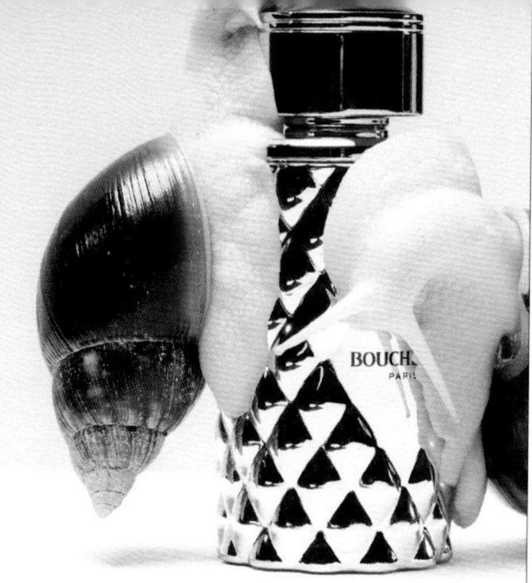

WEAREOSKAR

we.are.oskar

WEAREOSKAR are a pair of Brussels-based creatives, Thi-Thi and Arnaud, who specialise in still life photography using a playful and surrealistic approach. They are also involved in creative direction, set styling, and production.

Snail on Trail
A photo series that mixed luxurious and rigid perfume packaging with unusual and slimy creatures.

Client: Recto Verso Magazine

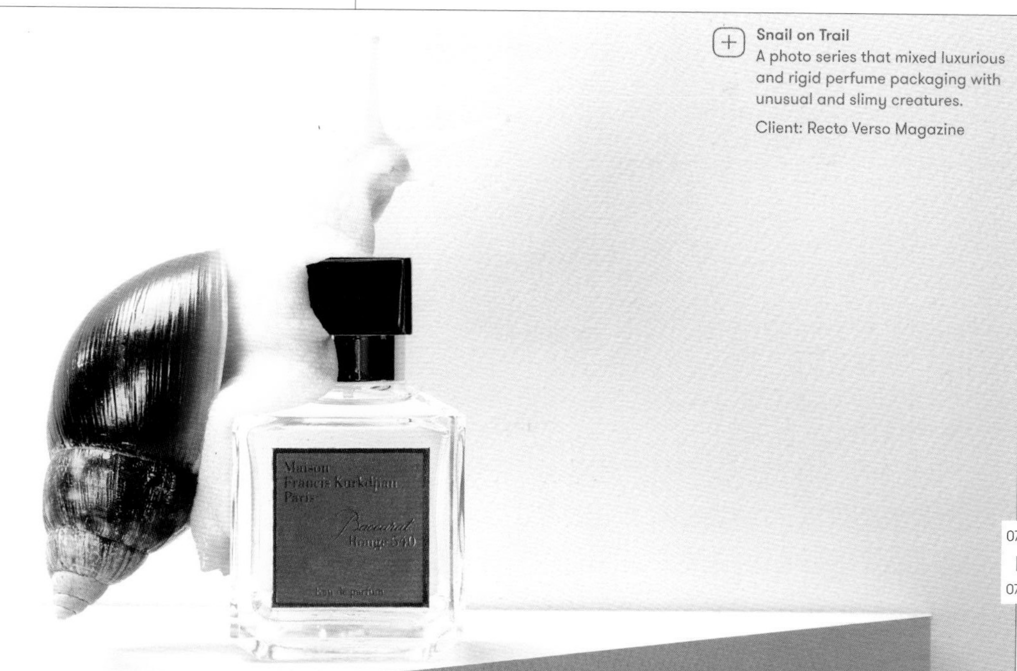

"Balance between the product and its backdrop is key. We always work step-by-step — pushing forward the product, millimetre by millimetre."

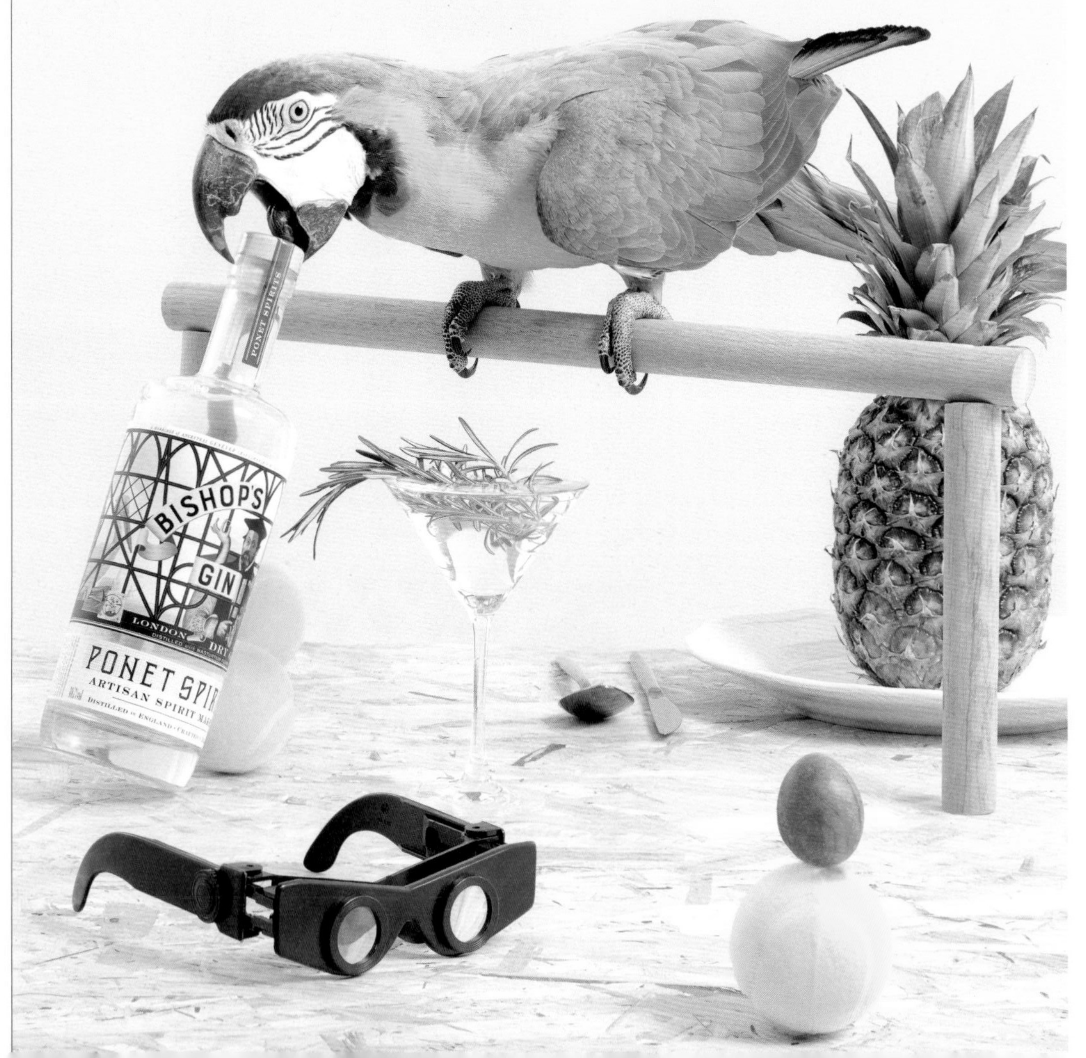

“The light is and will always be most important in the making of an image.”

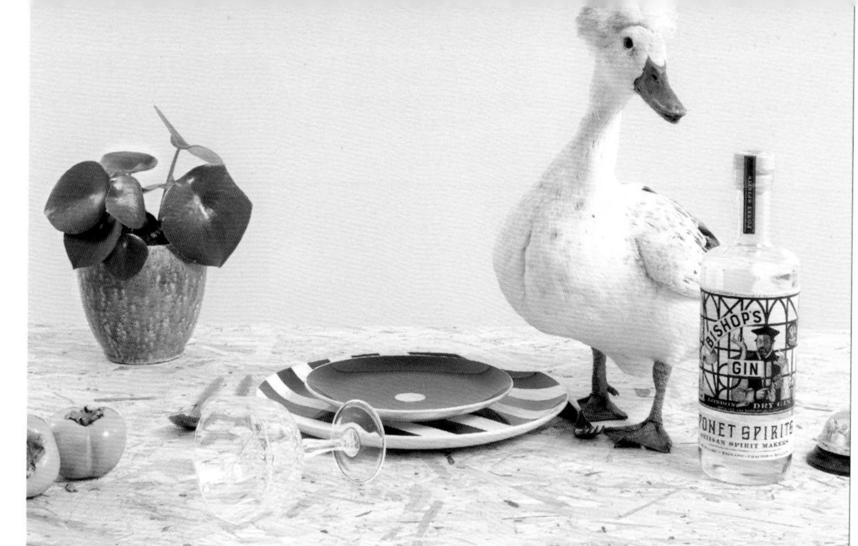

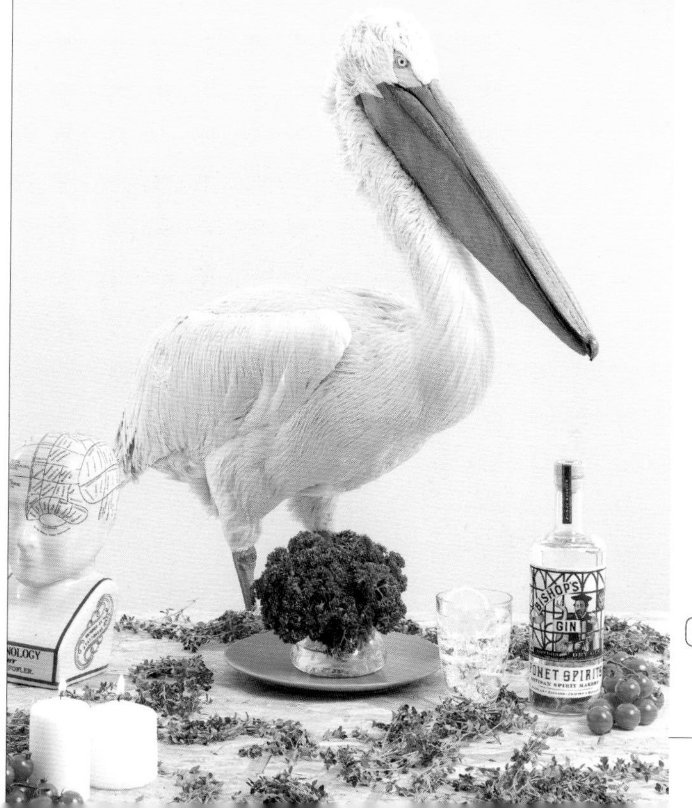

Bishop's Gin
A photo series that mixes the legacy of the 16th century English reformer Bishop John Ponet with today's culture.

Client: Ponet Spirits

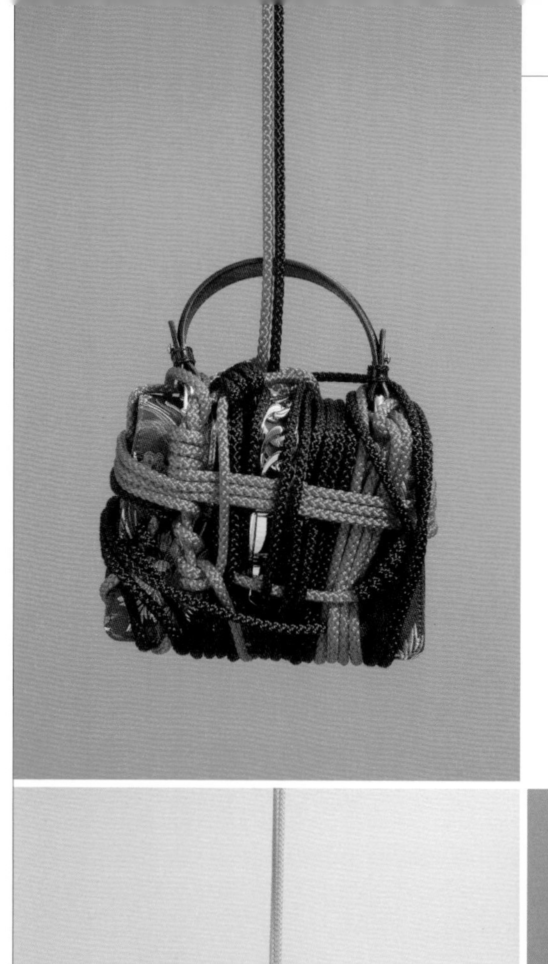

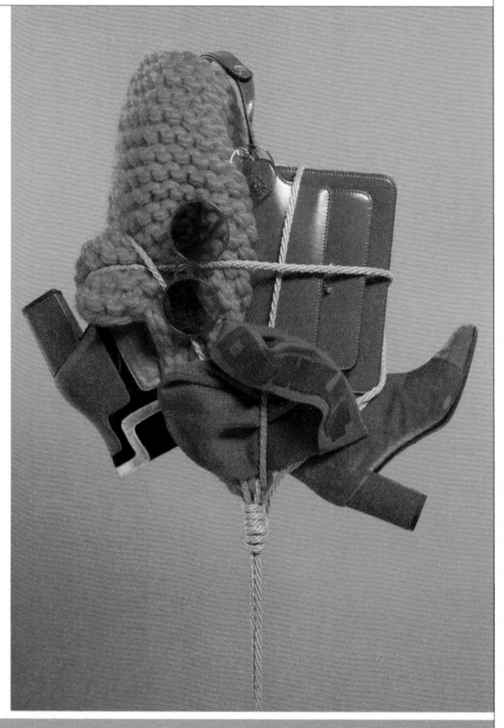

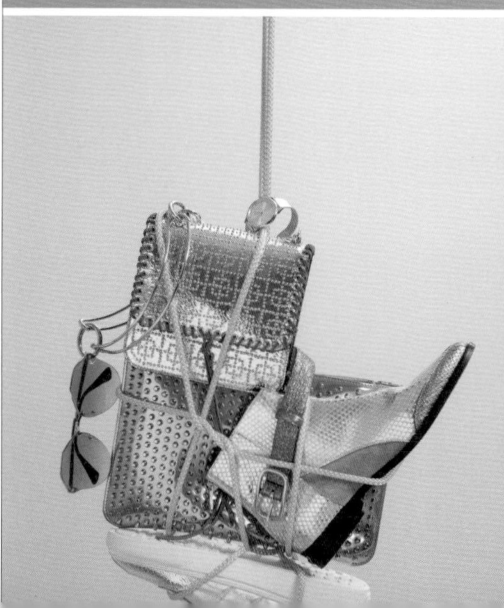

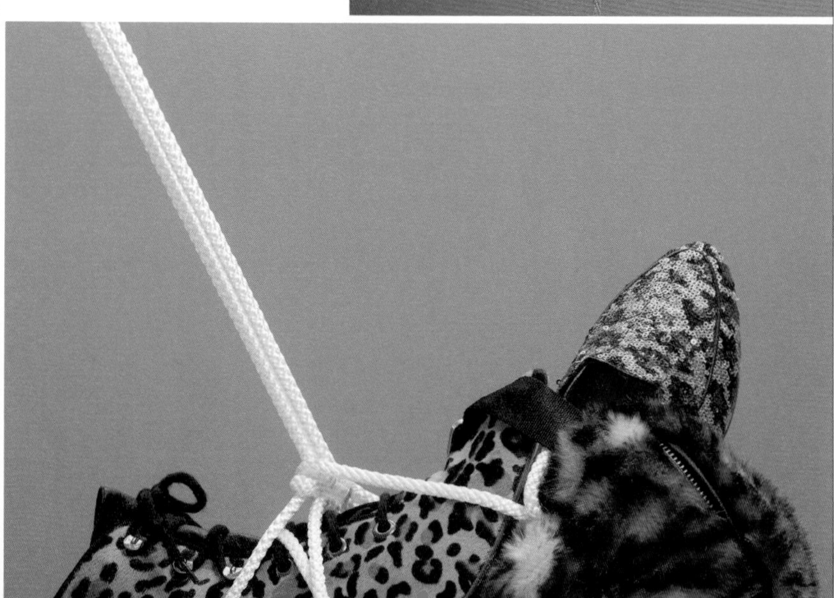

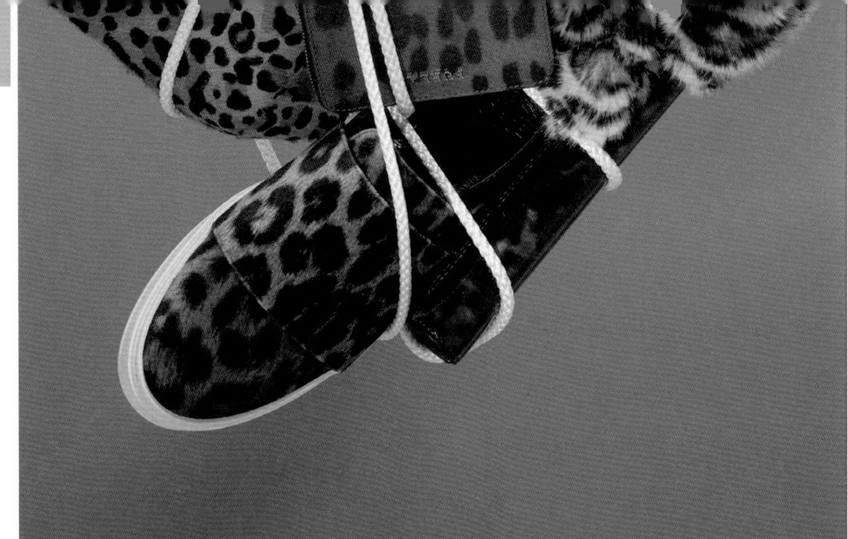

Fashion Bondage
The rope in this photo series is a reminder that accessories can be seen as fetishist objects.

Client: De Morgen Magazine / Fashion Accessories Styling: Lieve Gerrits

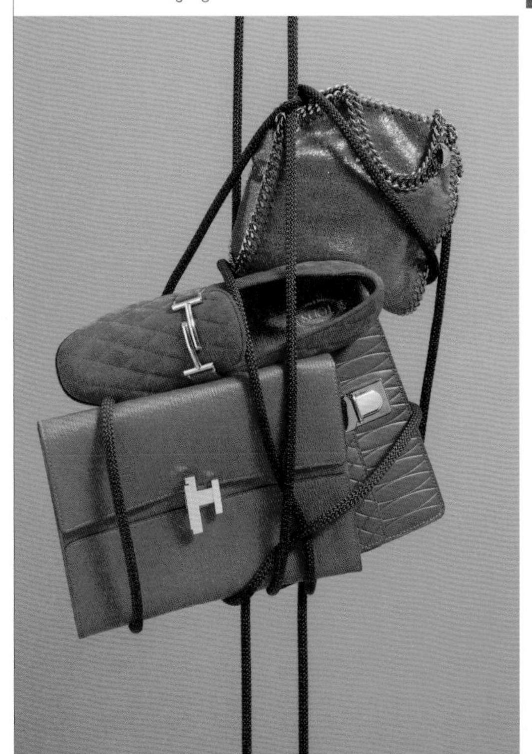

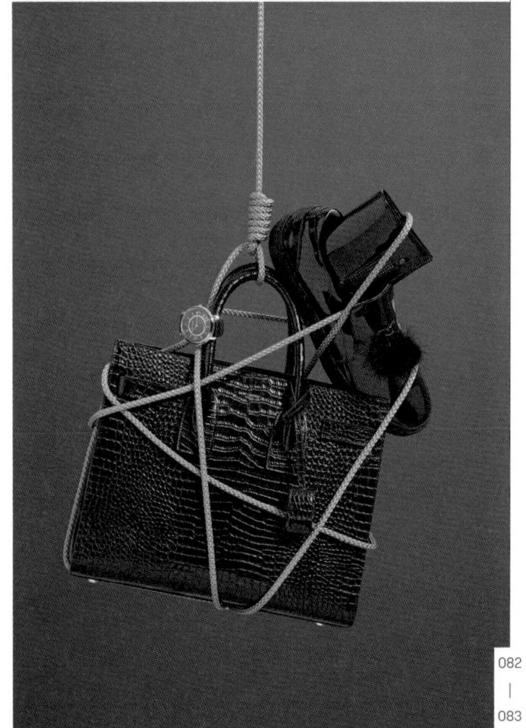

OLIVIA JECZMYK

oliviajeczmyk

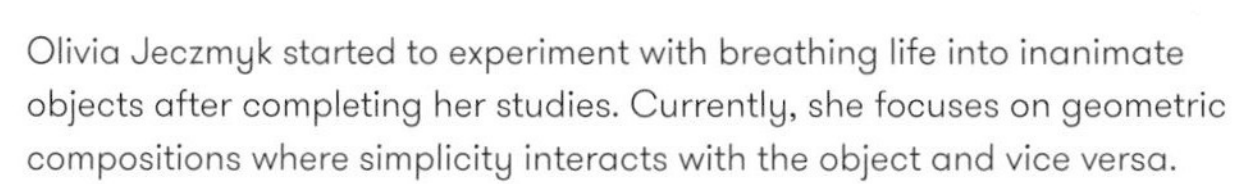

Olivia Jeczmyk started to experiment with breathing life into inanimate objects after completing her studies. Currently, she focuses on geometric compositions where simplicity interacts with the object and vice versa.

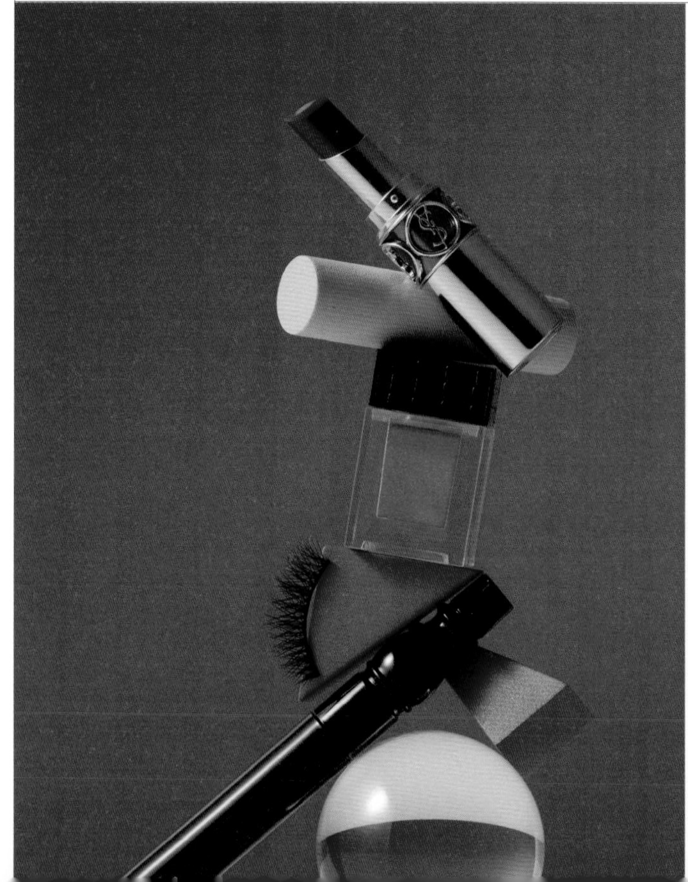

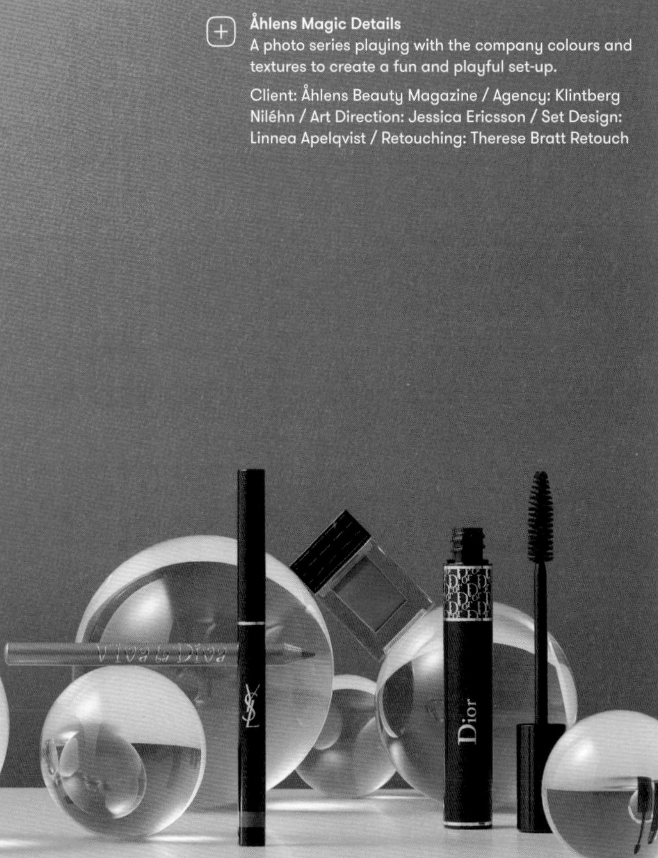

Åhlens Magic Details
A photo series playing with the company colours and textures to create a fun and playful set-up.

Client: Åhlens Beauty Magazine / Agency: Klintberg Niléhn / Art Direction: Jessica Ericsson / Set Design: Linnea Apelqvist / Retouching: Therese Bratt Retouch

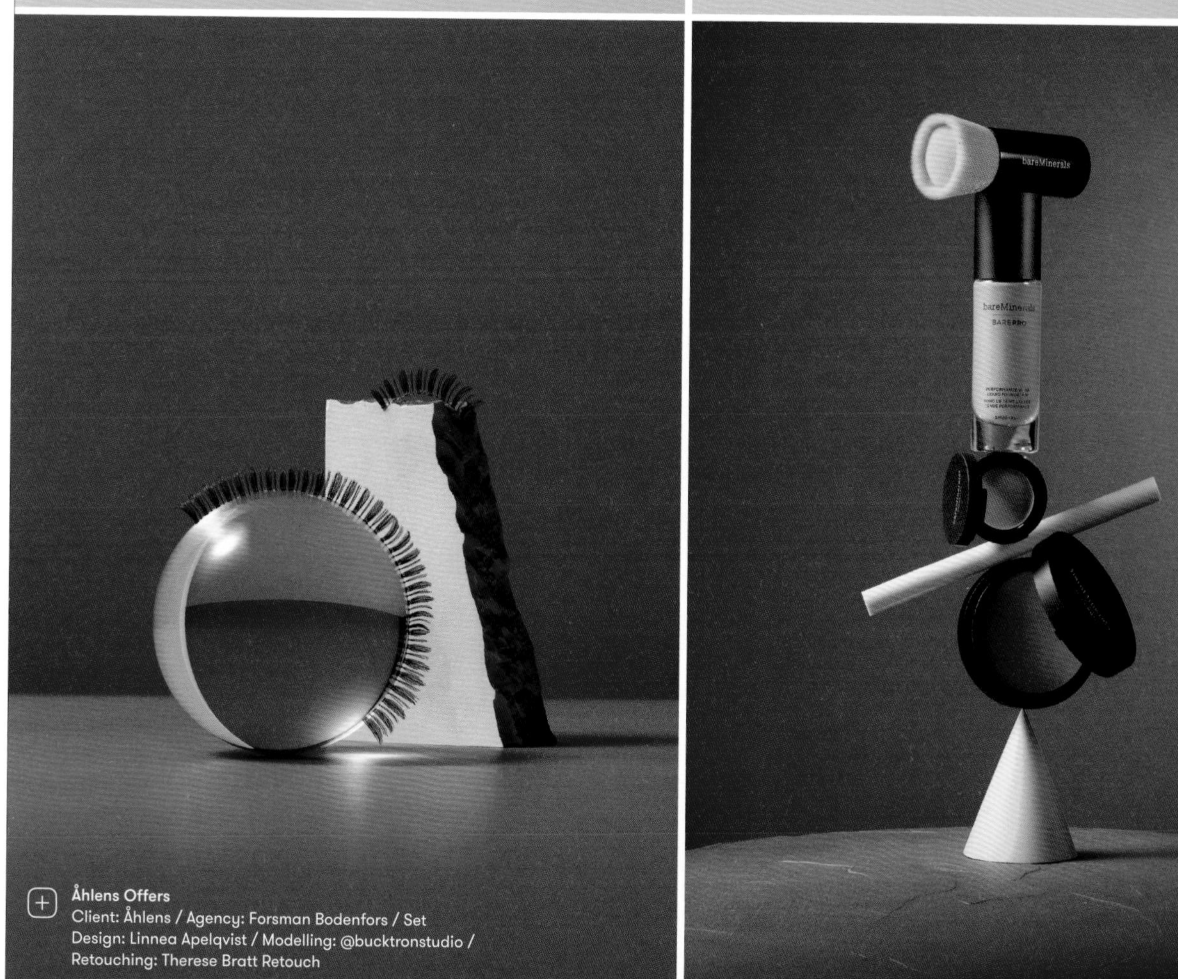

Åhlens Offers
Client: Åhlens / Agency: Forsman Bodenfors / Set Design: Linnea Apelqvist / Modelling: @bucktronstudio / Retouching: Therese Bratt Retouch

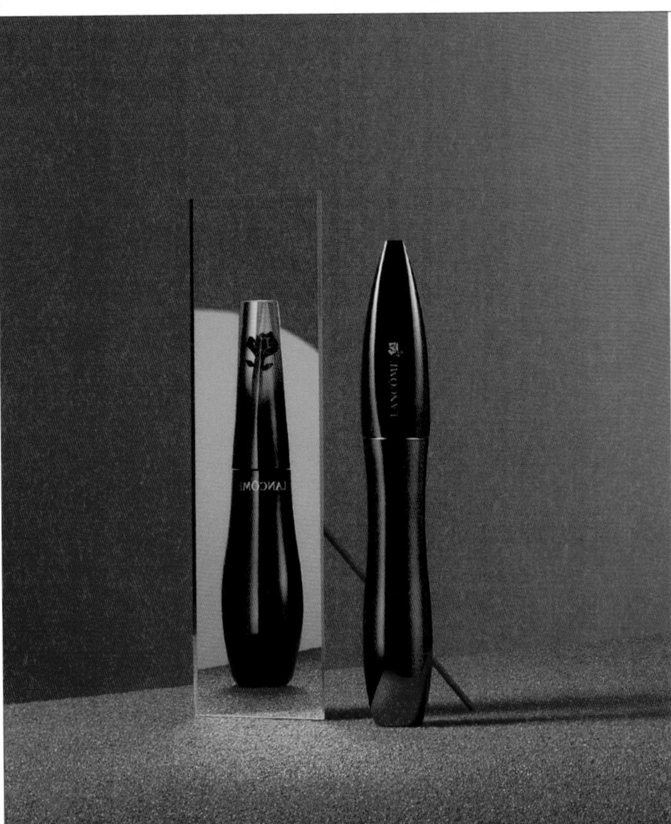

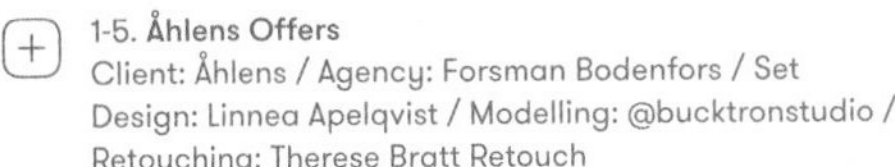

1-5. Åhlens Offers
Client: Åhlens / Agency: Forsman Bodenfors / Set Design: Linnea Apelqvist / Modelling: @bucktronstudio / Retouching: Therese Bratt Retouch

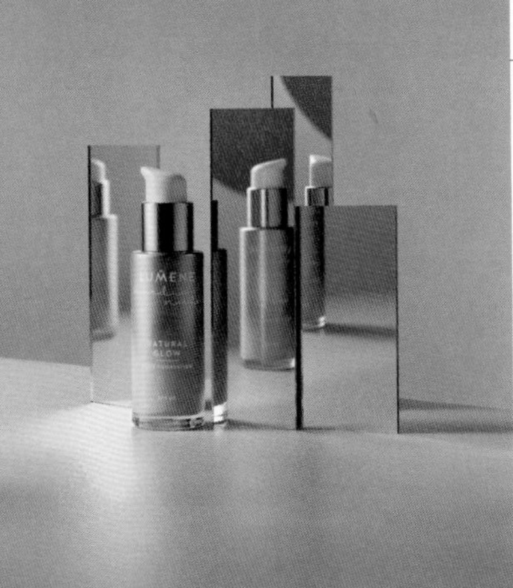

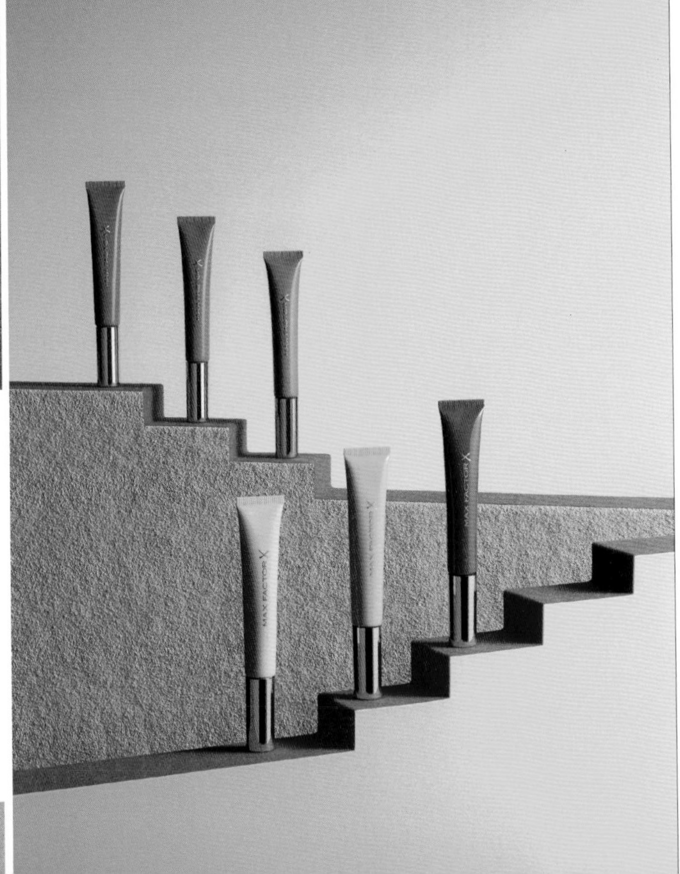

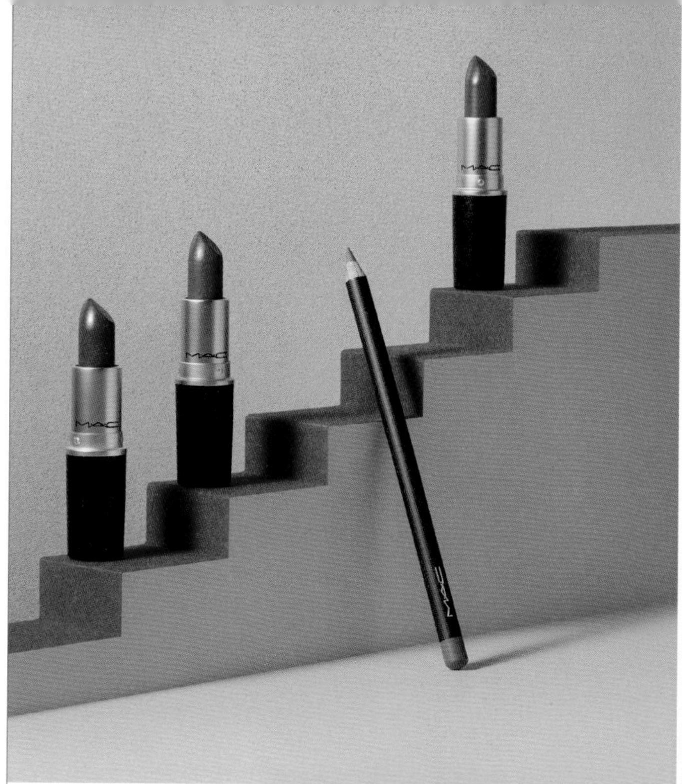

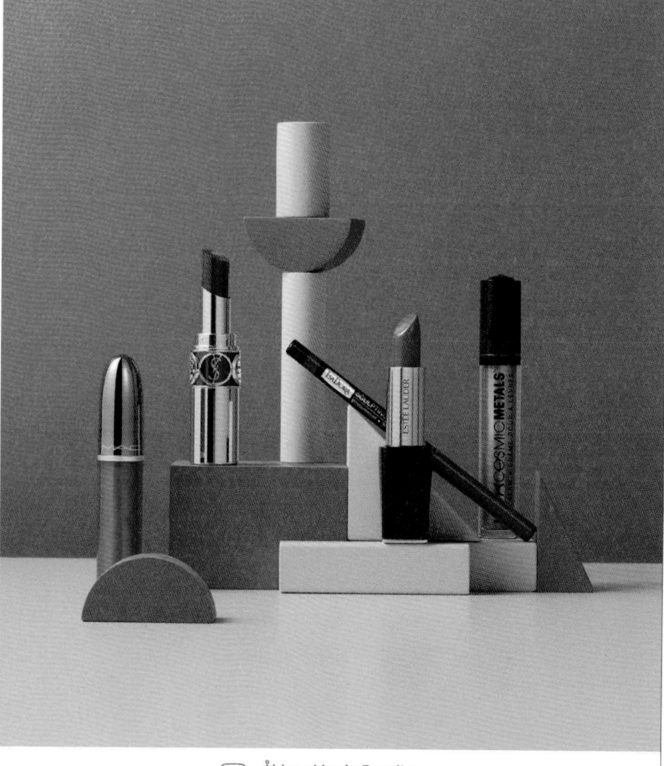

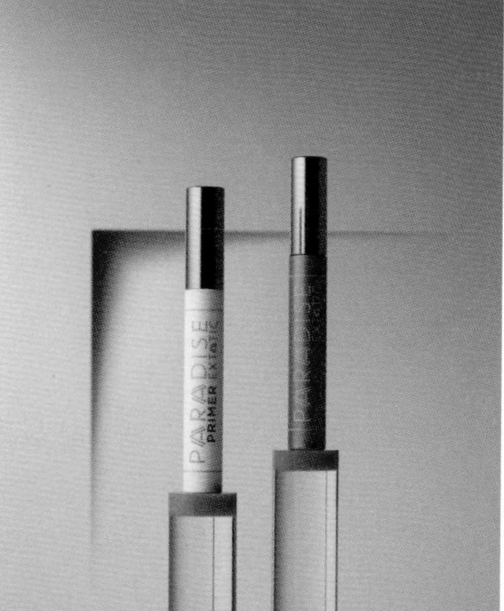

Åhlens Magic Details
Client: Åhlens Beauty Magazine / Agency: Klintberg Niléhn / Art Direction: Jessica Ericsson / Set Design: Linnea Apelqvist / Retouching: Therese Bratt Retouch

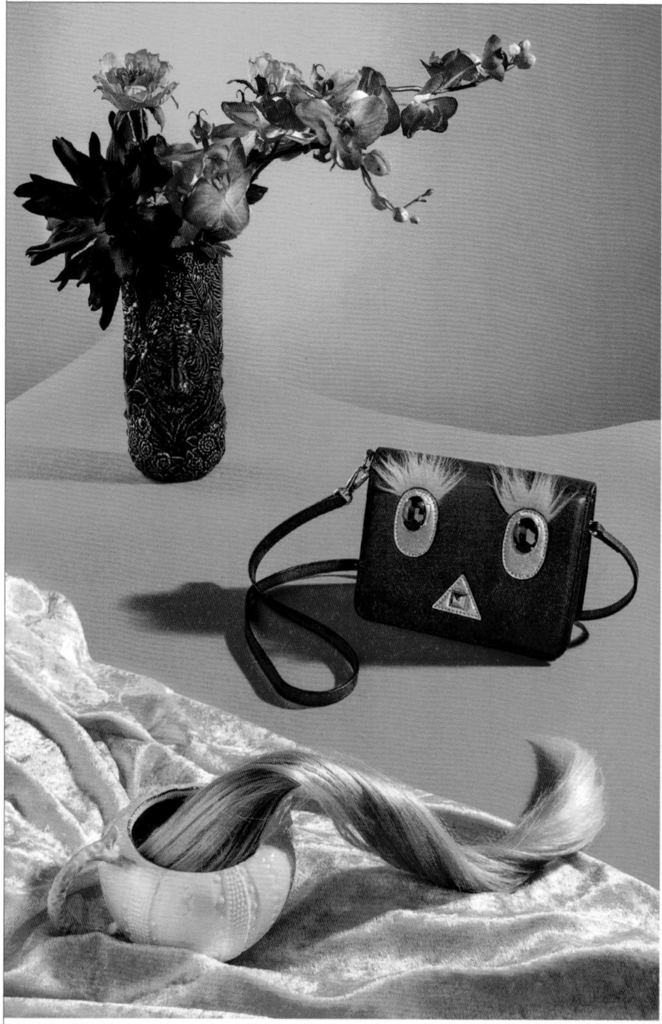

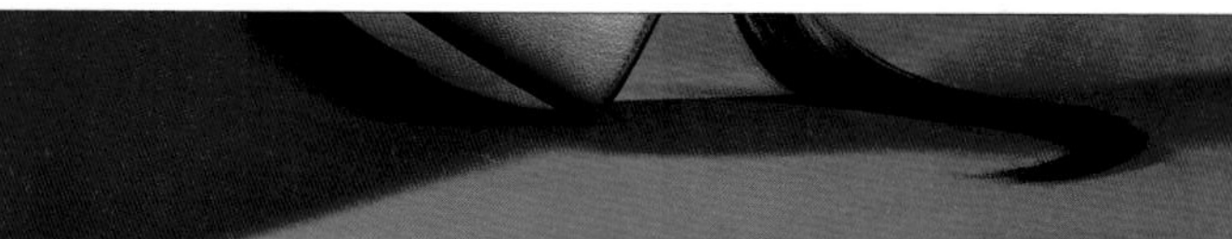

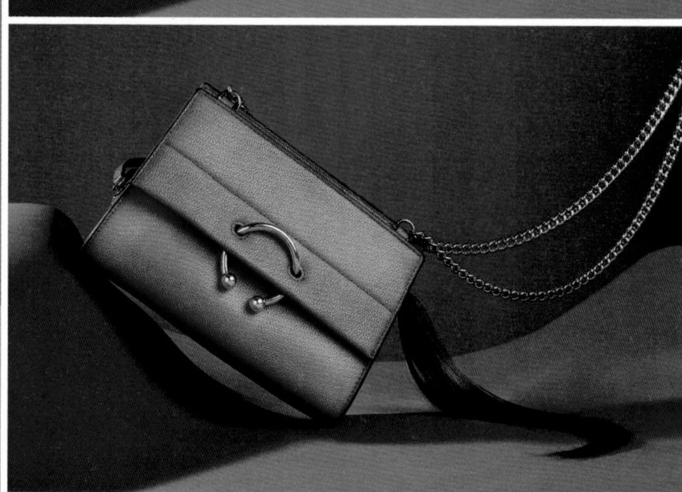

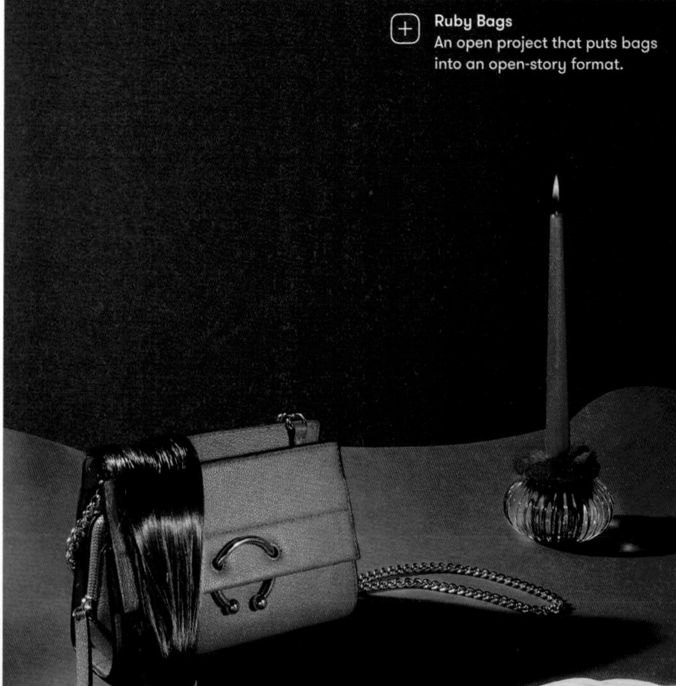

Ruby Bags
An open project that puts bags into an open-story format.

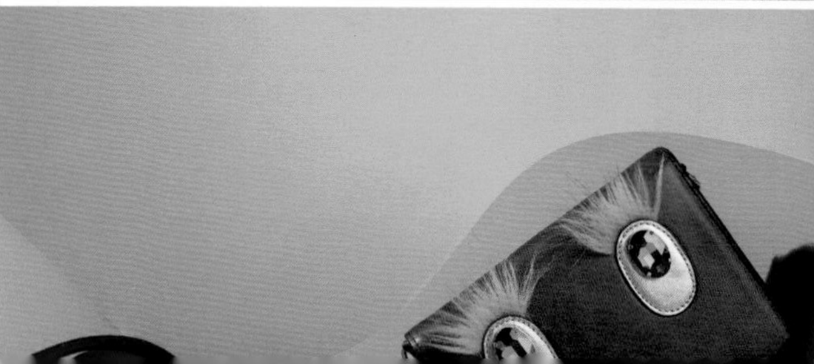

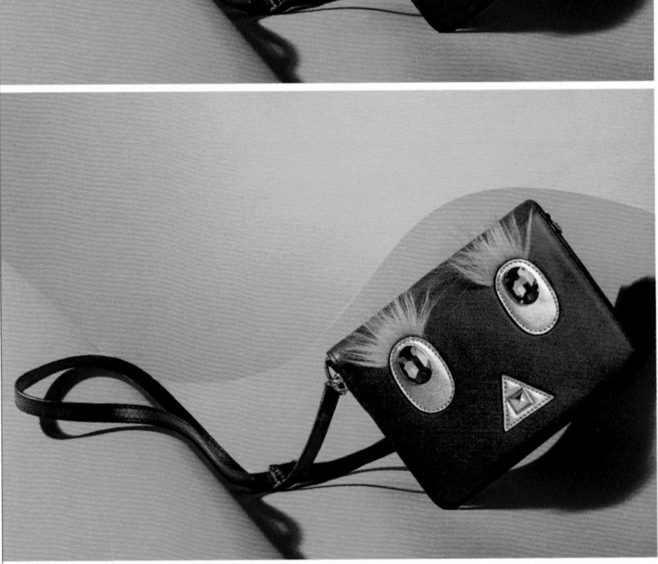

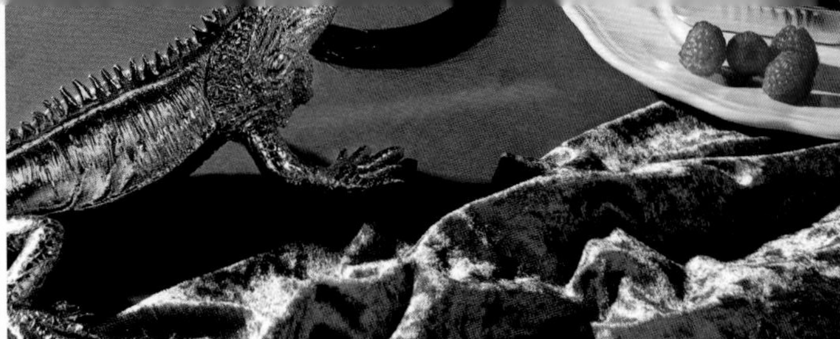

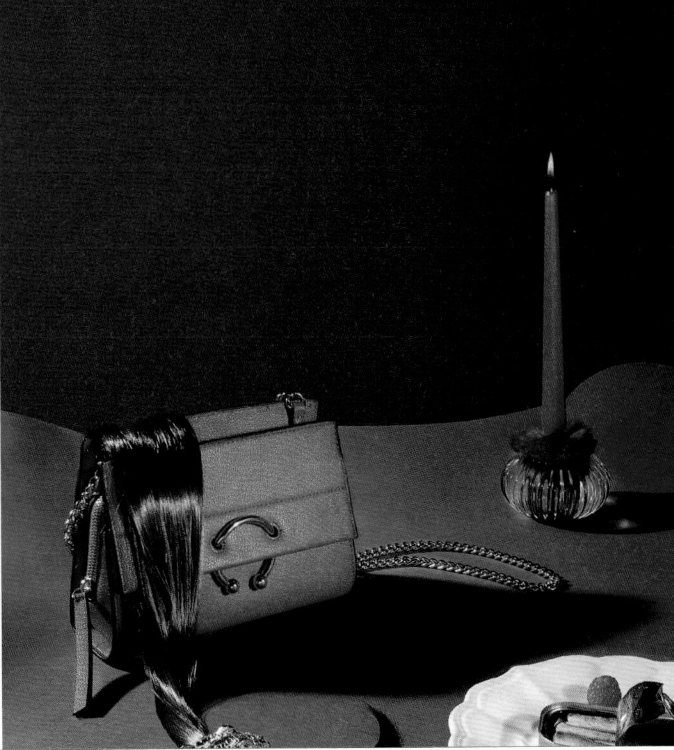

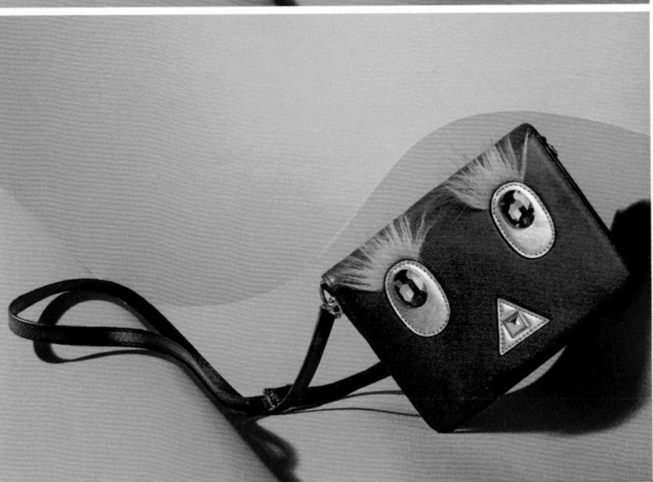

I'M BLUE I'M PINK

iamblueiampink

I'm Blue I'm Pink is an art direction, set design, and photography studio founded by two curious minds – brothers Pedro and Teo González. Armed with a passion for art and design, they help brands create their own personalities via editorial projects, artistic and cultural events, advertising campaigns, as well as look books.

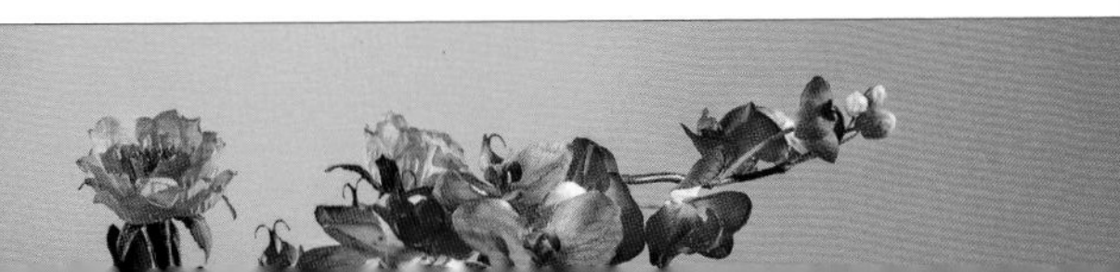

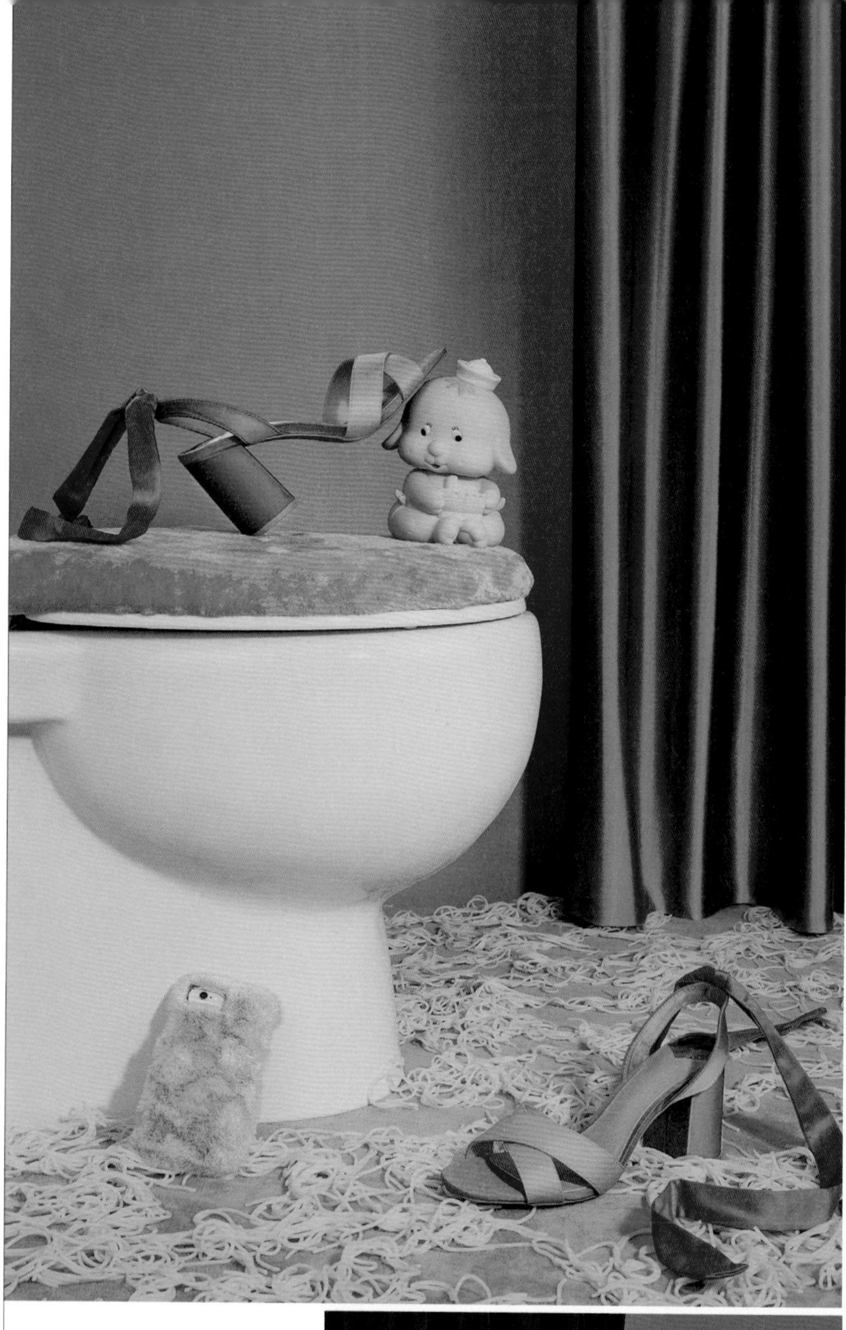

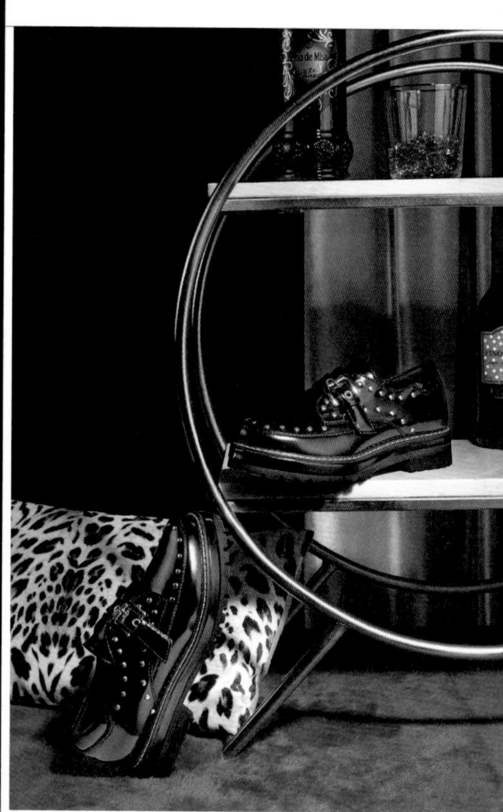

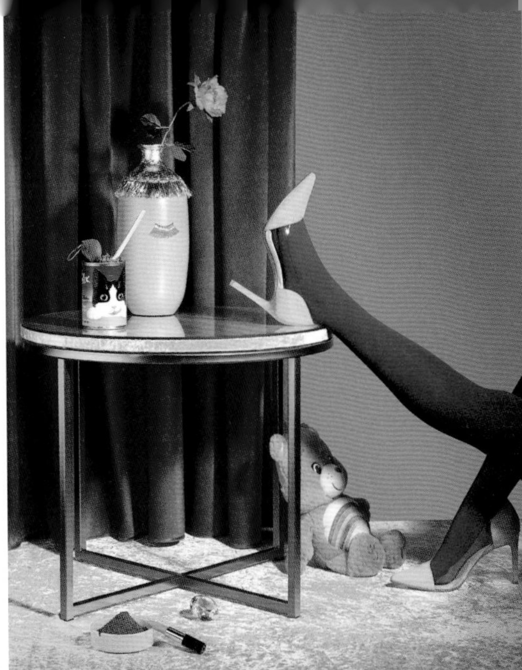

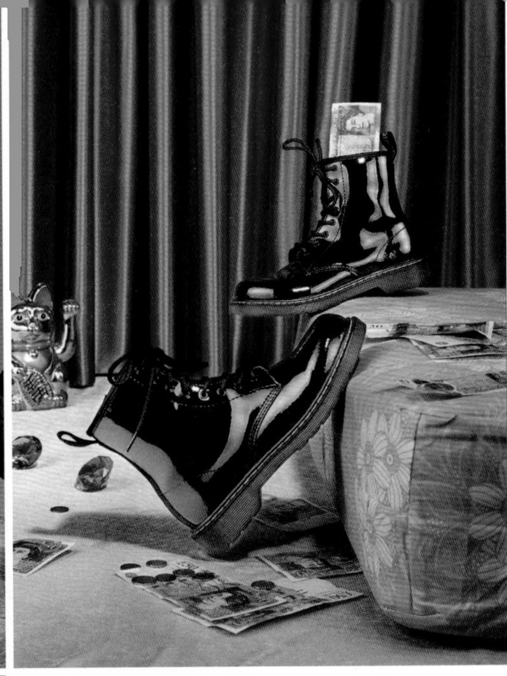

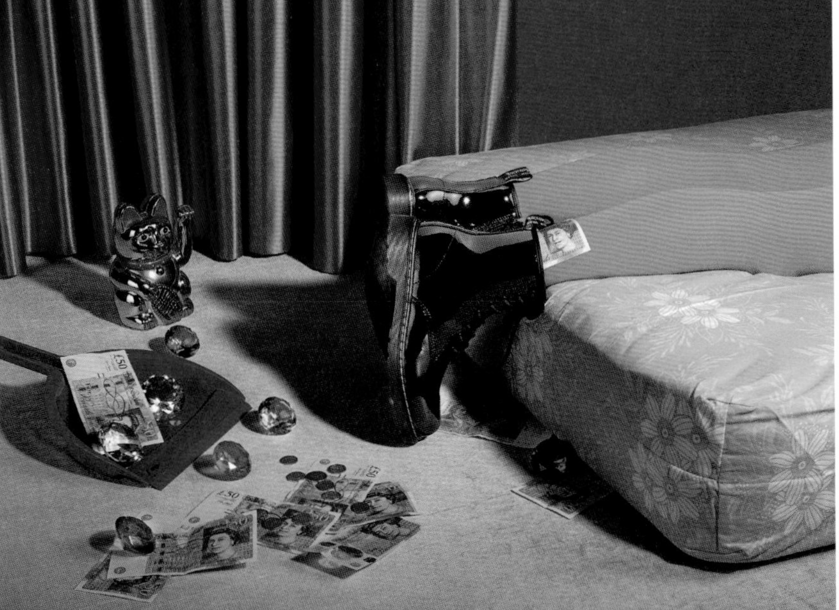

Diamond Shoes
An editorial project showcasing trendy shoes by picturing what might happen once women reach home.

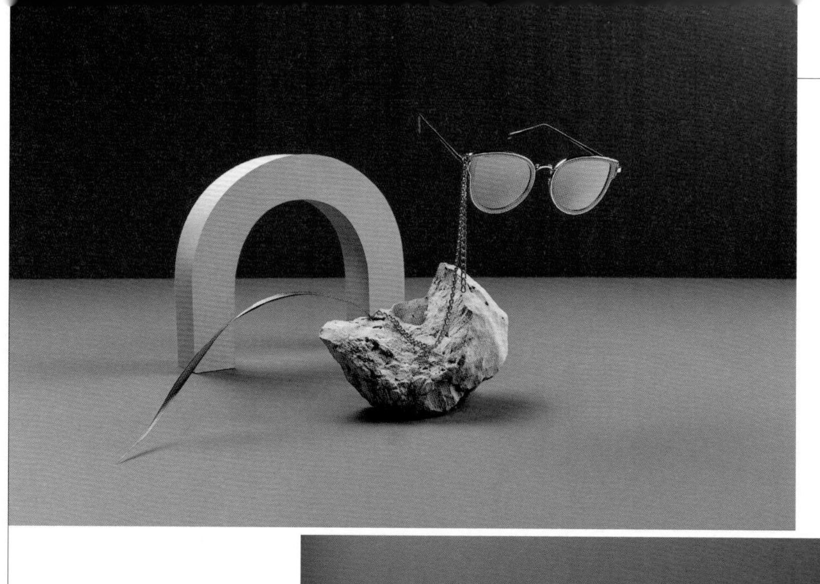

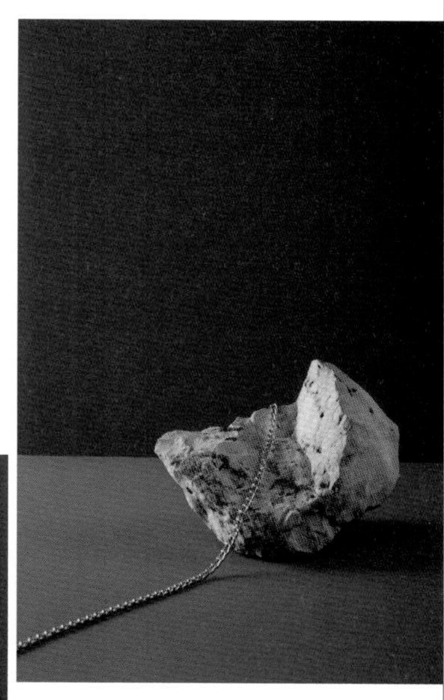

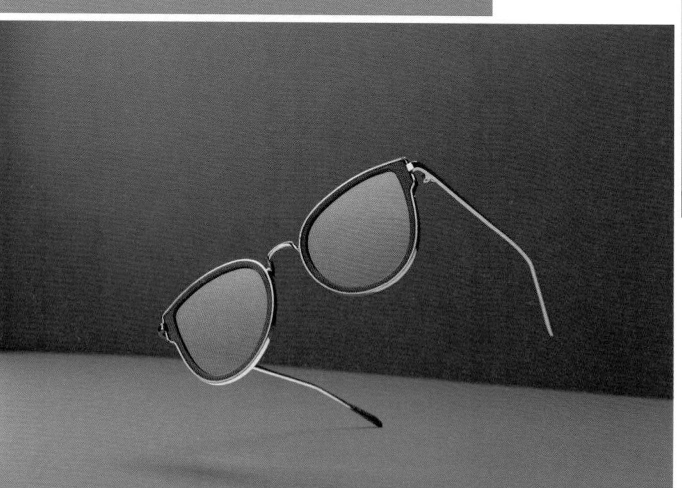

“For us, mixing products in a surreal set is a way to enhance history and visual impact.”

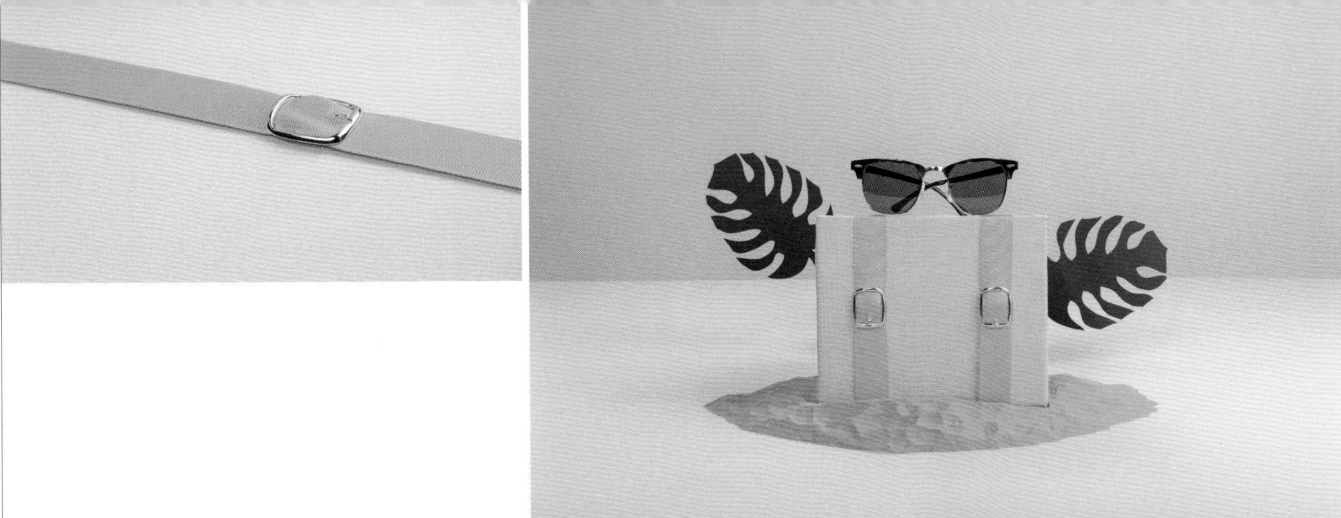

Sakura
A photo series linking eyewear to the concept of travelling around different spaces.

Client: SAKURA EYEWEAR

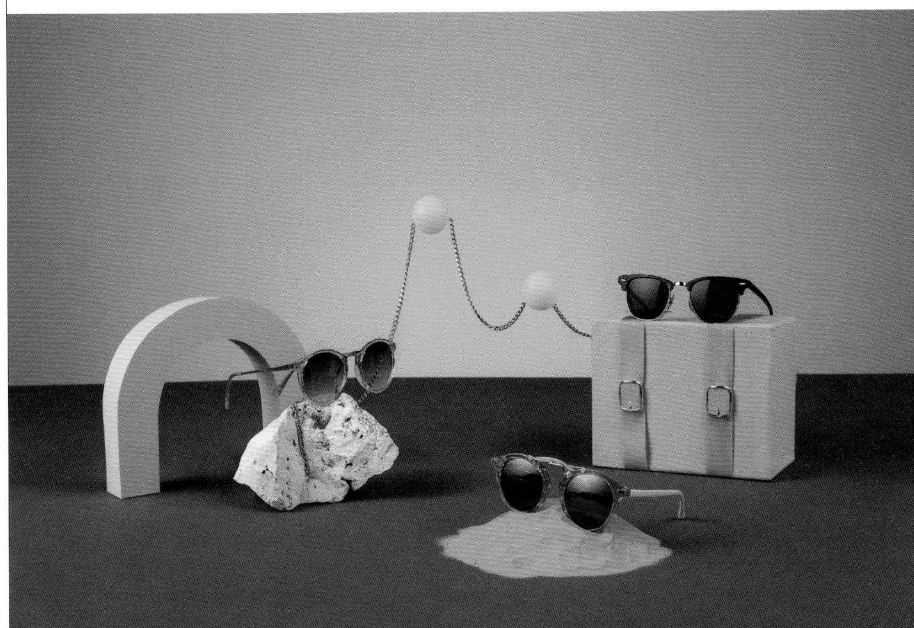

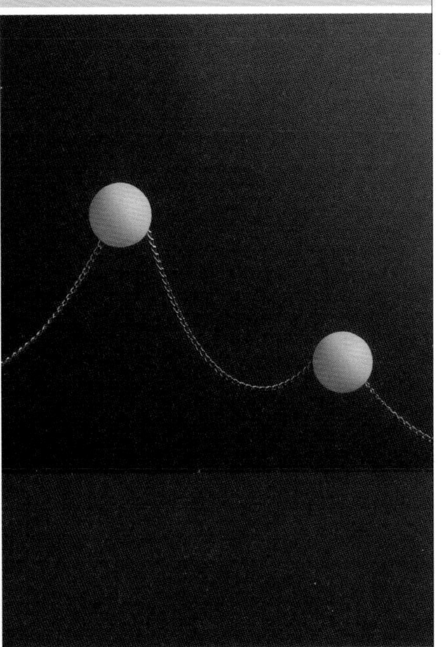

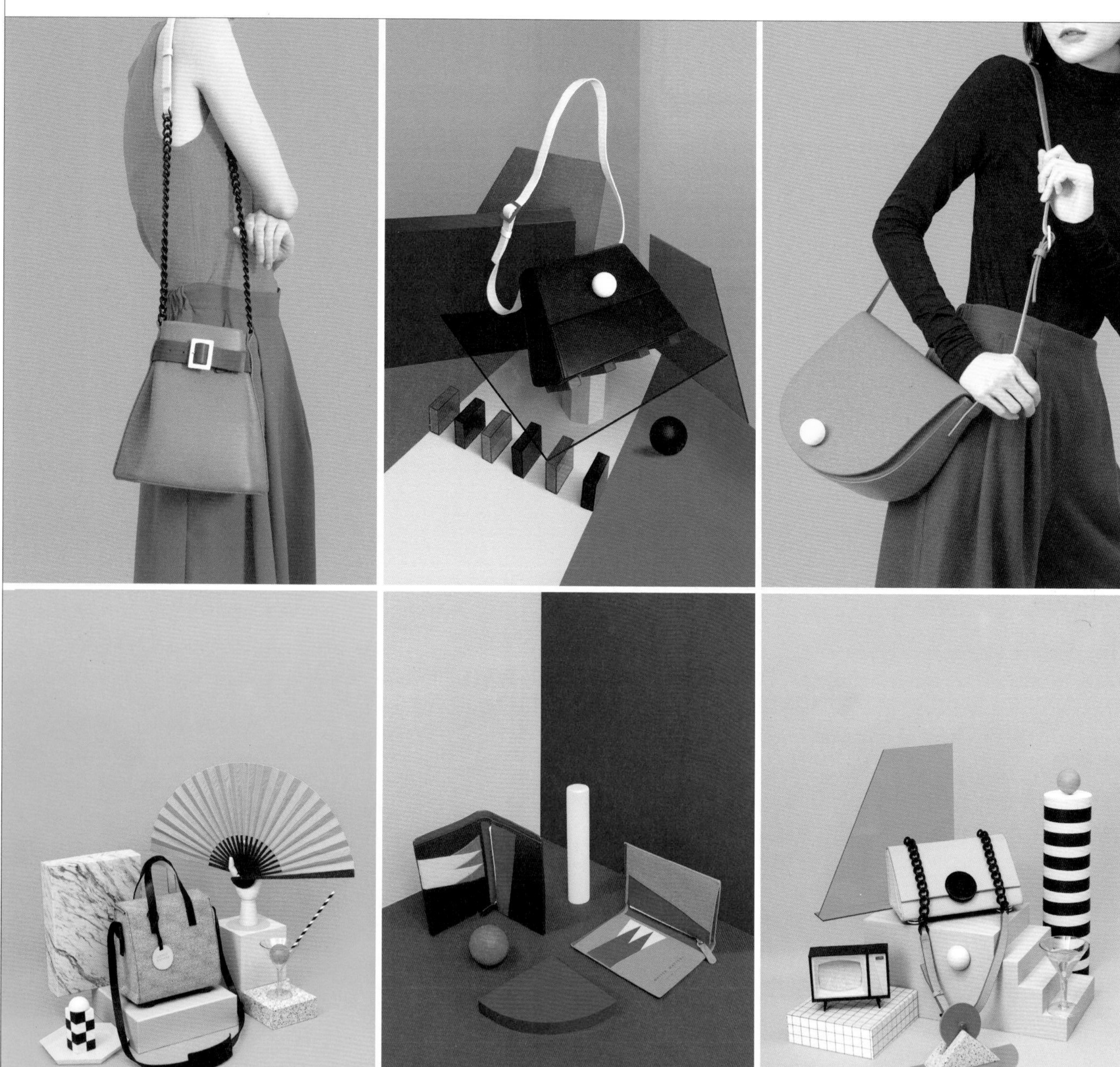

MATTER MATTERS

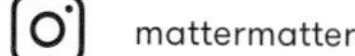

mattermatters

Matter Matters is a Hong Kong-based brand that was set up by designer Flora Leung. Its visual language is heavily influenced by art deco, Bauhaus and post-modernist aesthetics from 1980s Memphis.

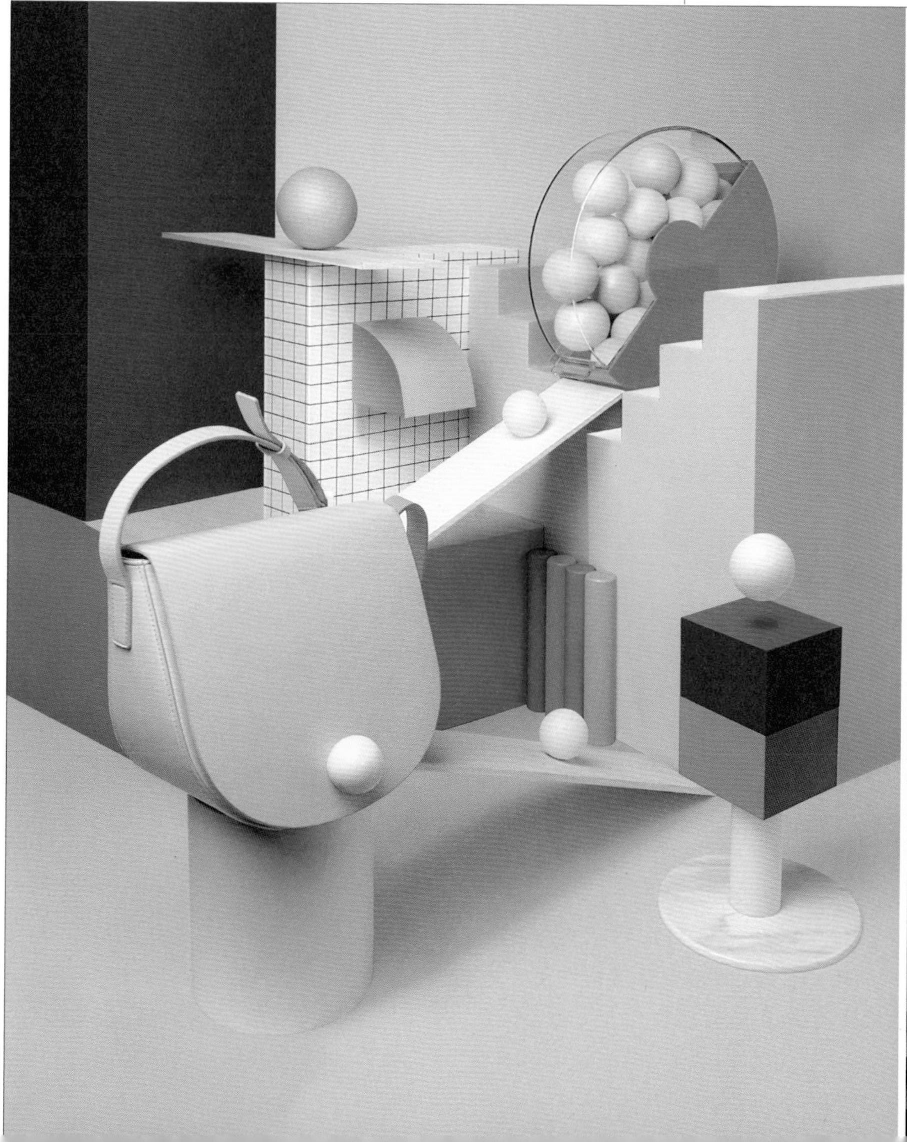

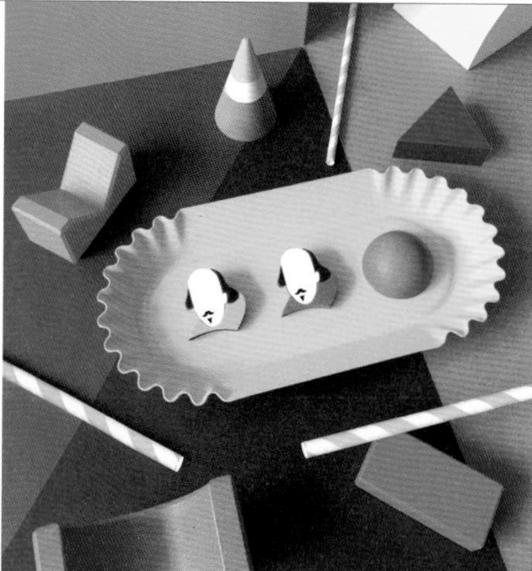

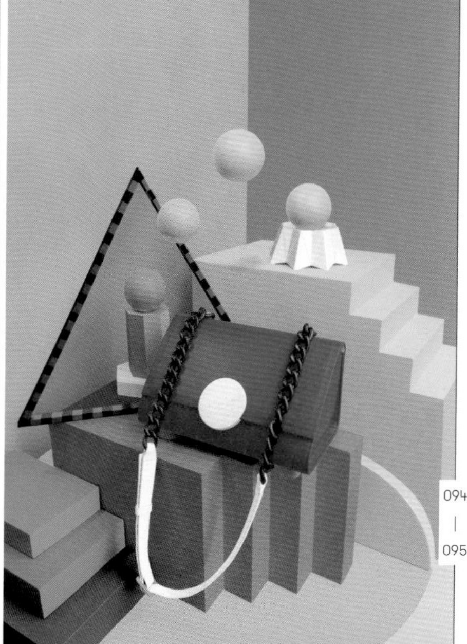

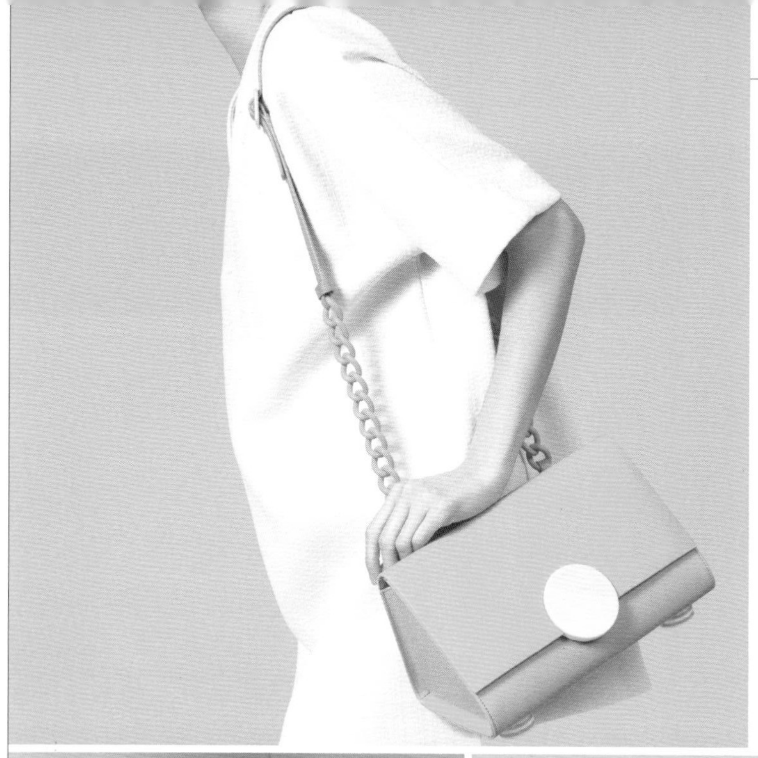

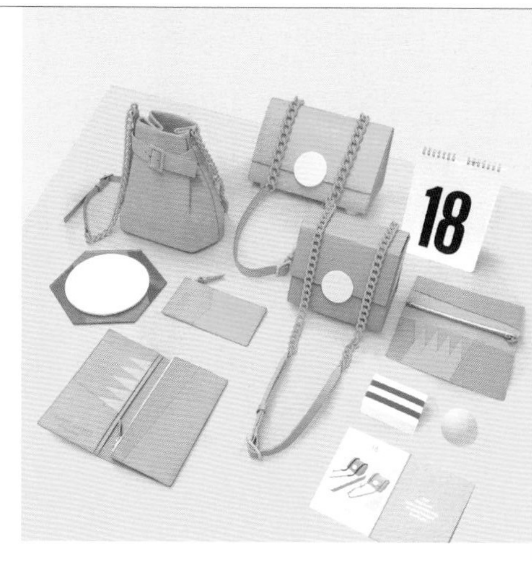

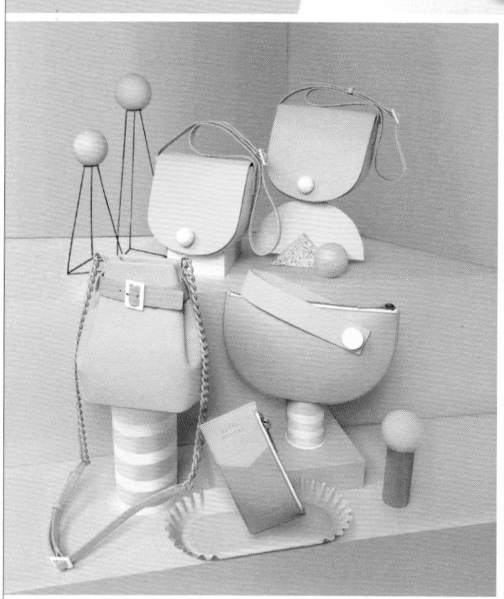

"Fashion photography for social media is closer to the taste of the general crowd – less preparation and more spontaneous."

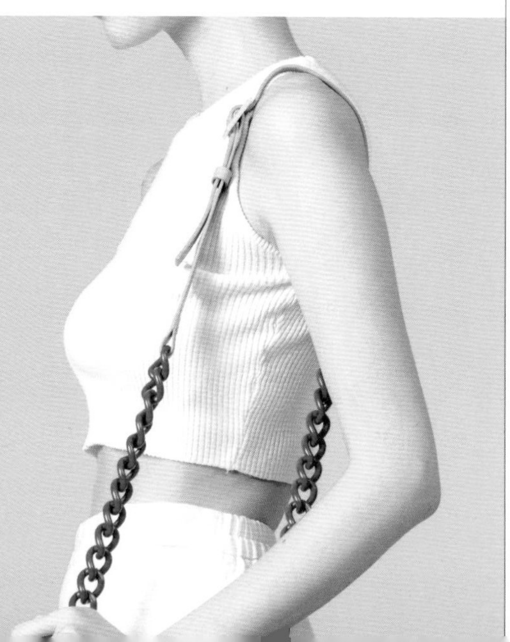

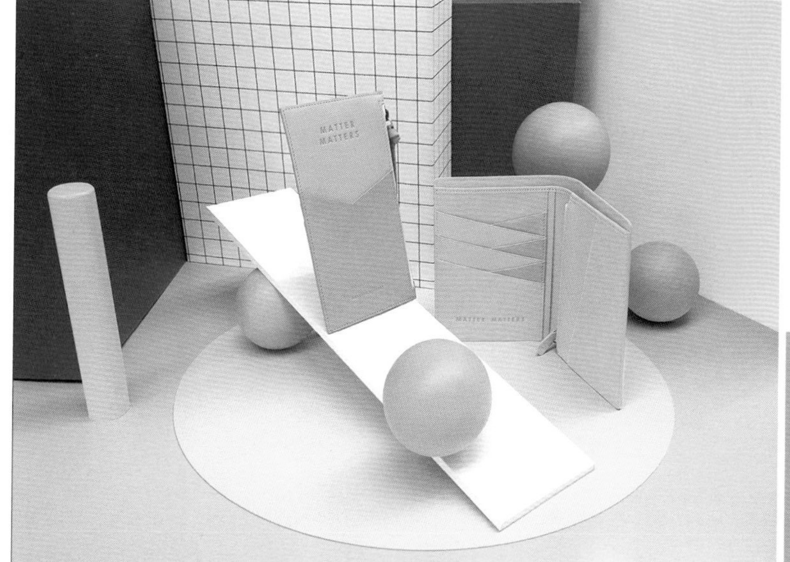
MATTER
MATTERS
MATTER MATTERS

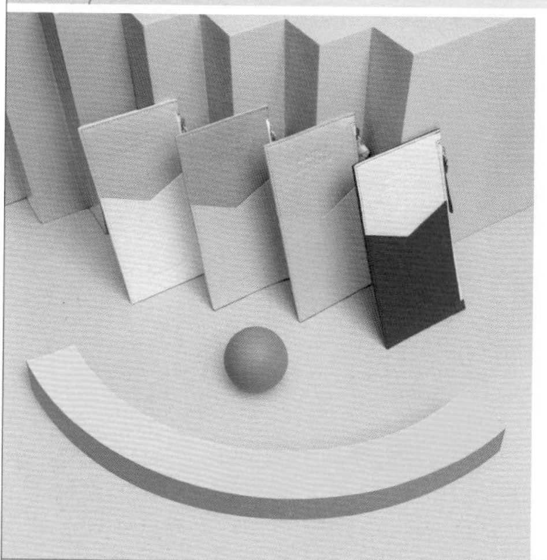

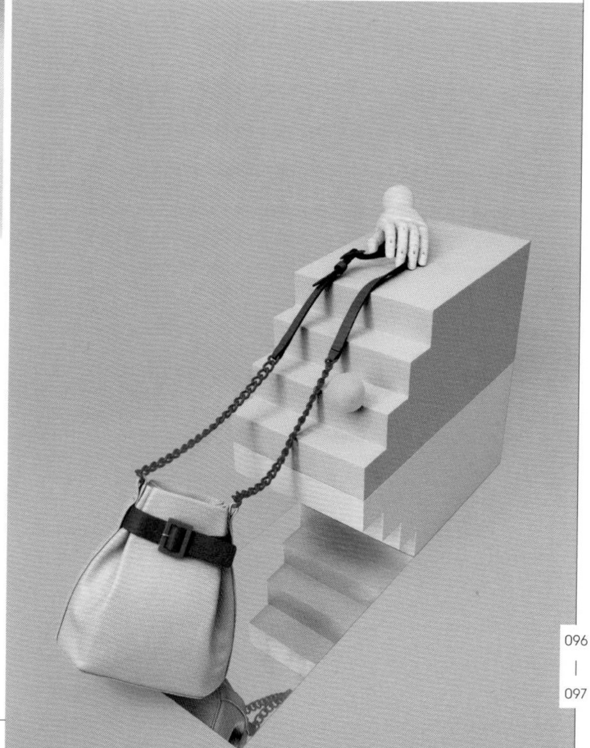

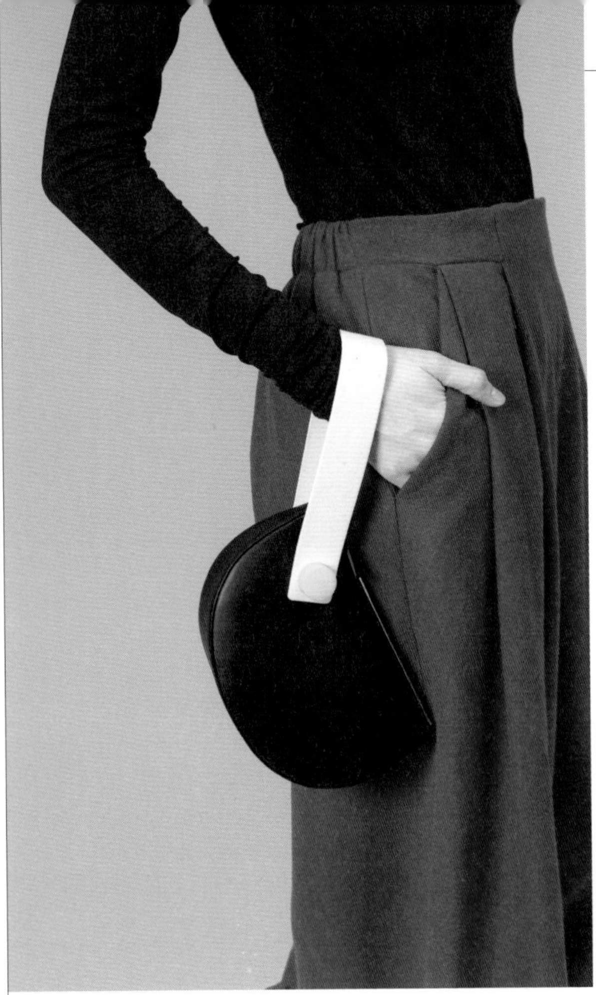

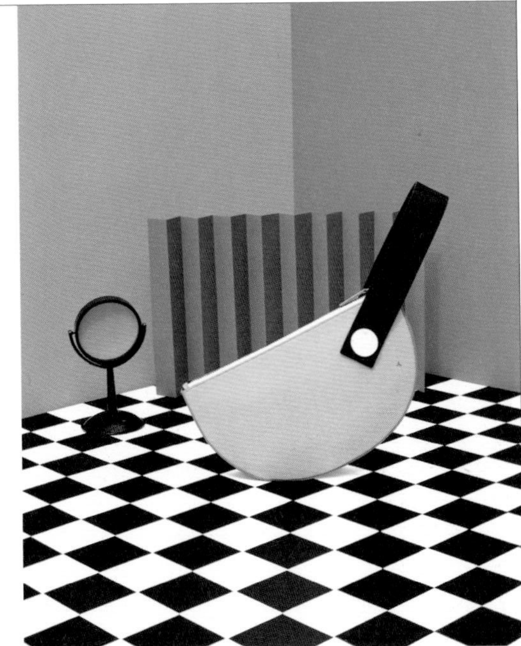

“To me, the biggest challenge is finding the perfect angle to make the core product the first thing to be noticed.”

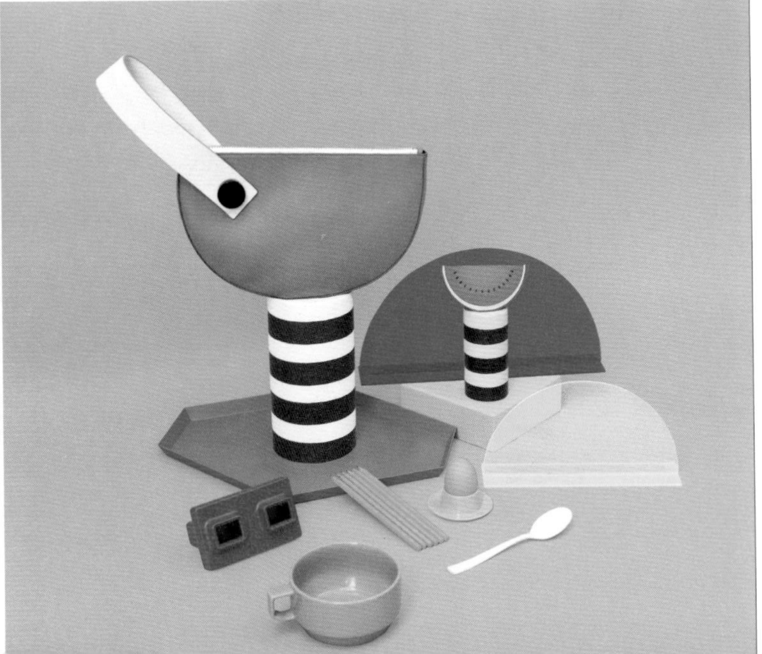

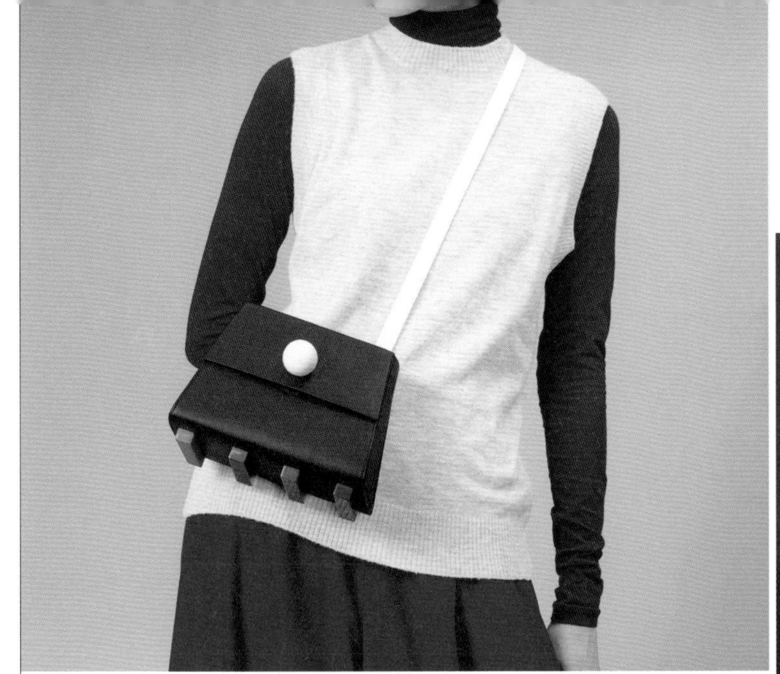

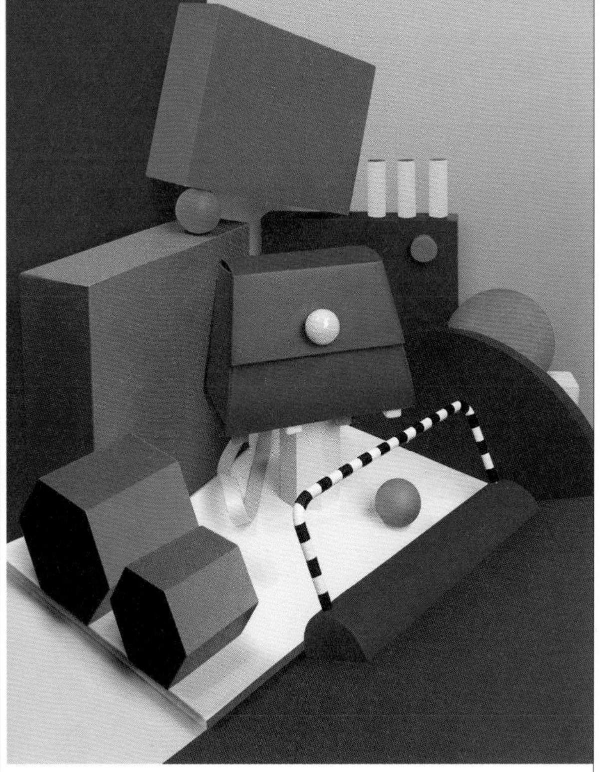

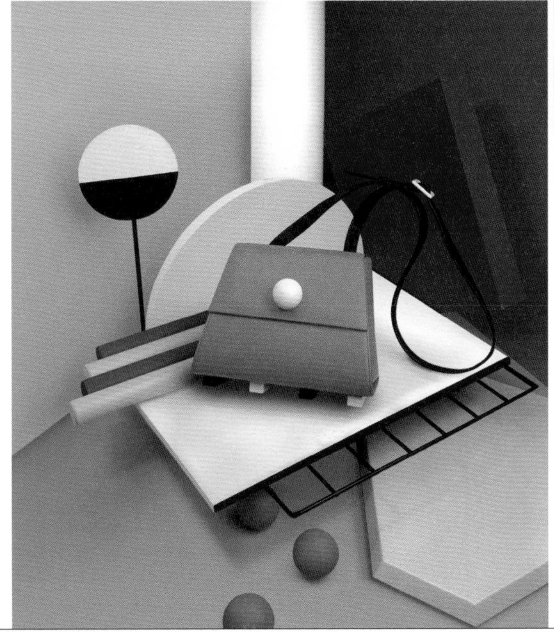

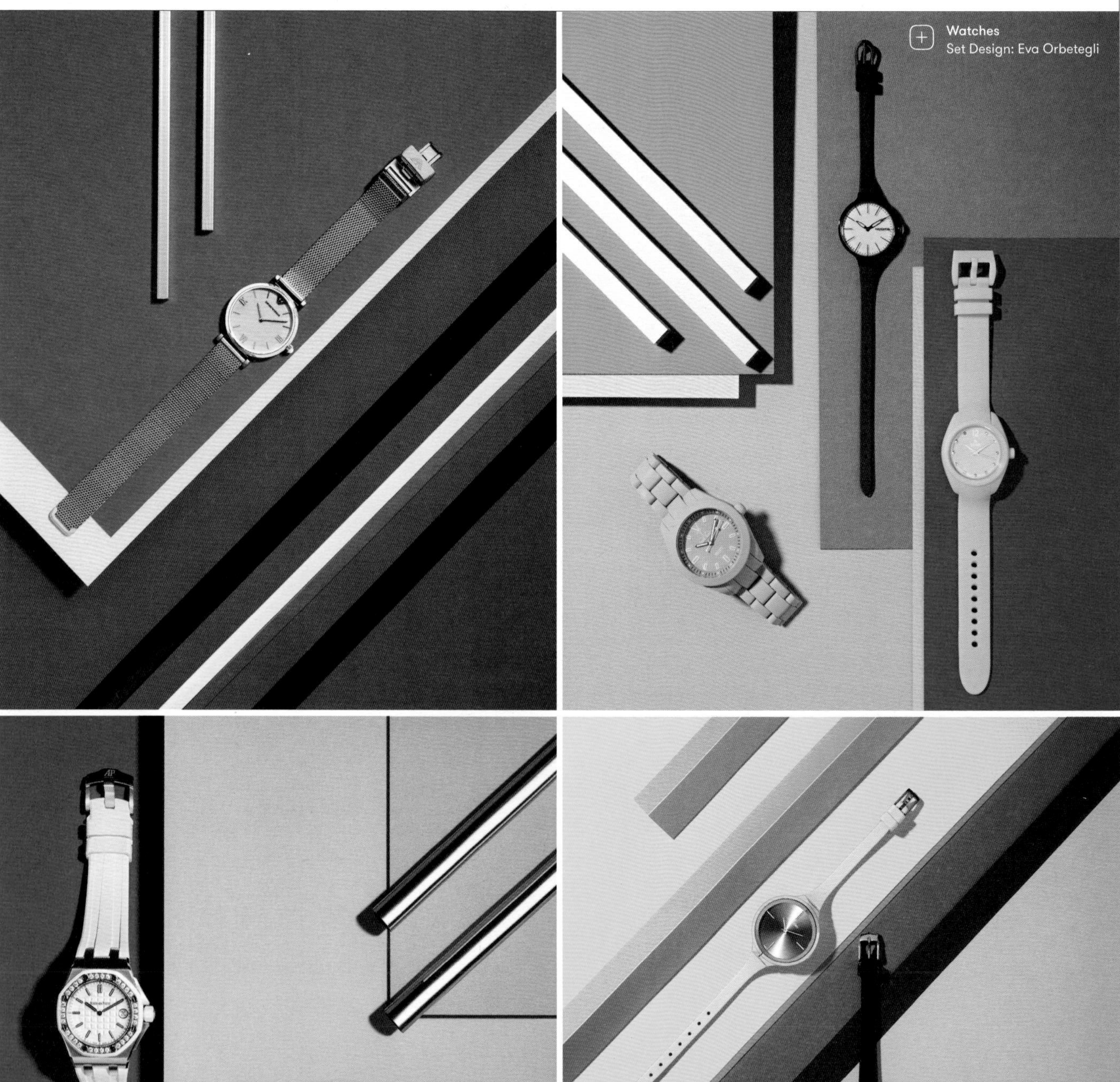
Watches
Set Design: Eva Orbetegli

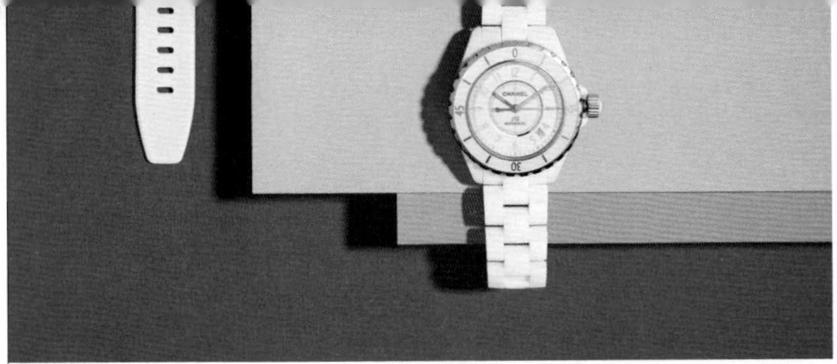

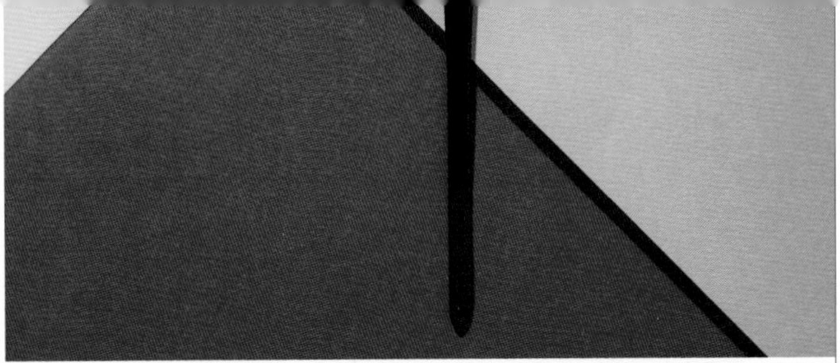

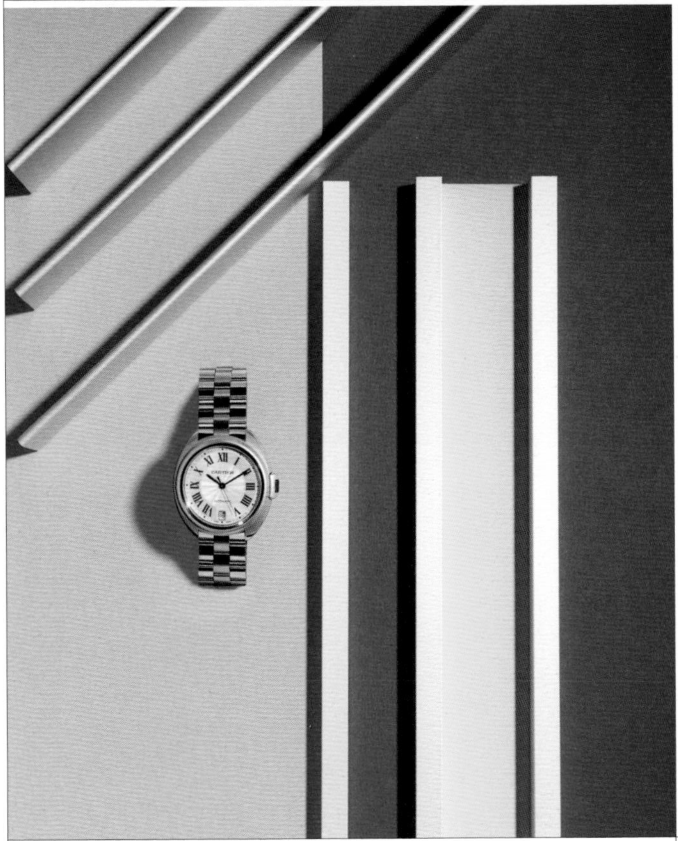

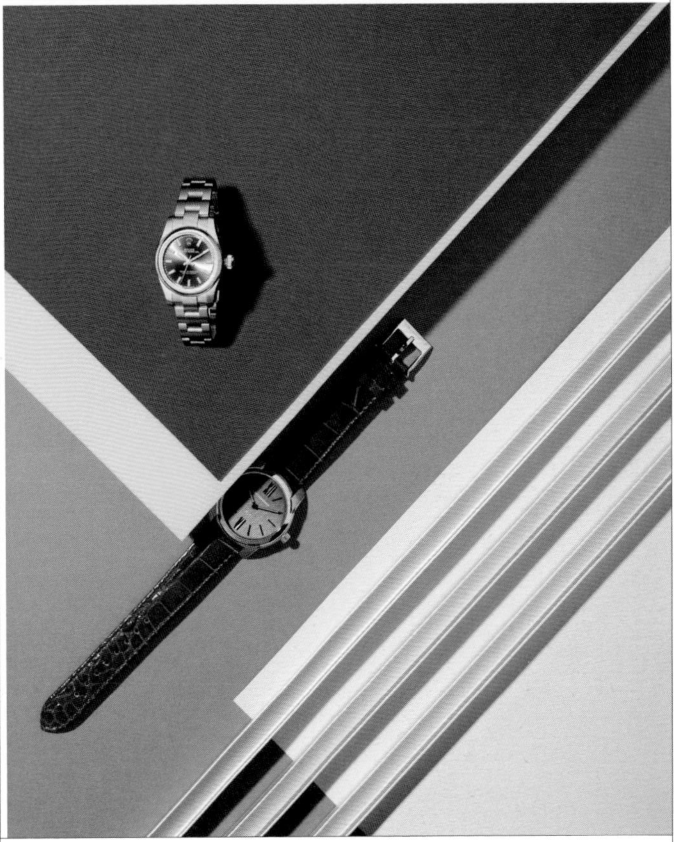

NICOLA GALLI

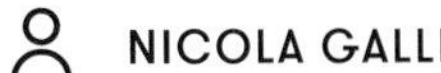

nicola_galli.studio

Nicola Galli is a still life photographer based in Milan. A perfectionist and an innovator, his images are characterised by the search for a combination of light and geometry, with particular attention paid towards the aesthetics of colour.

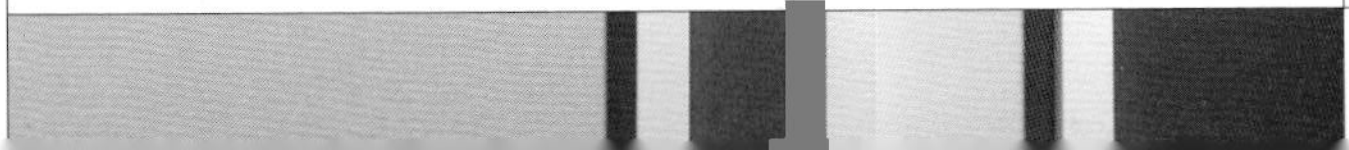

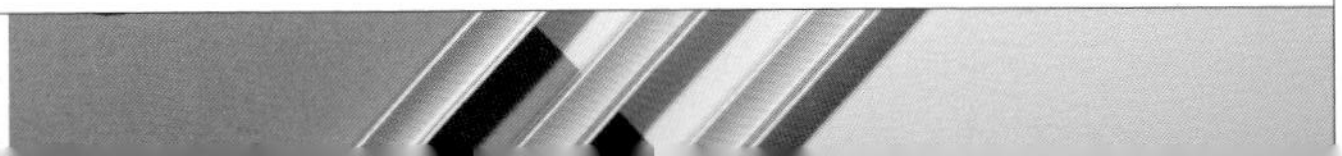

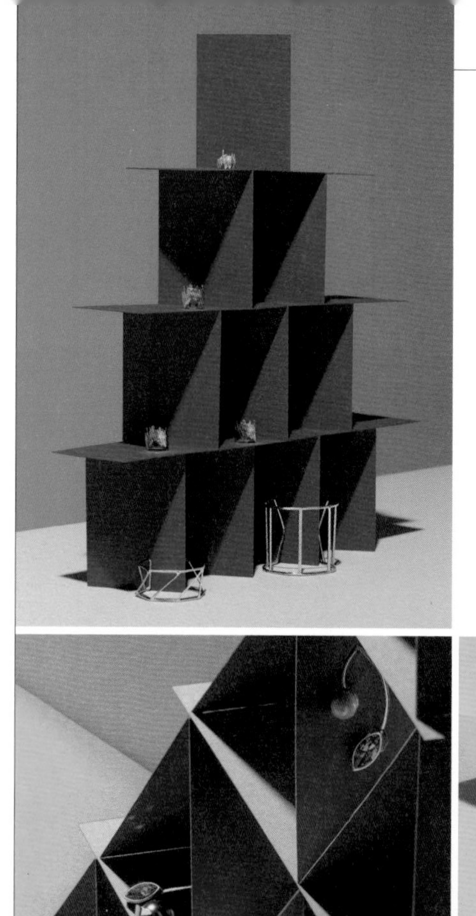
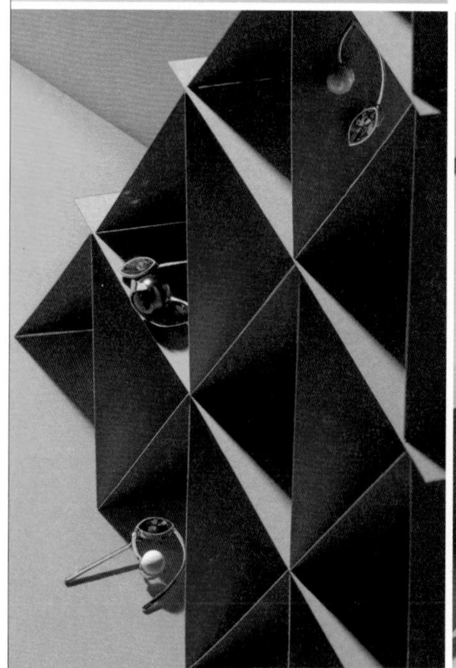
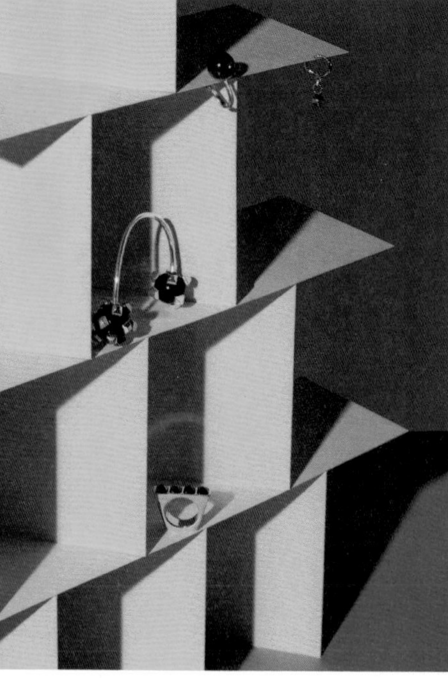
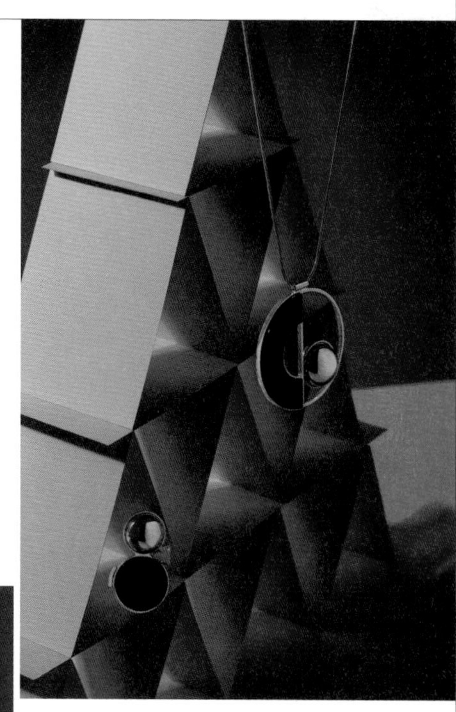
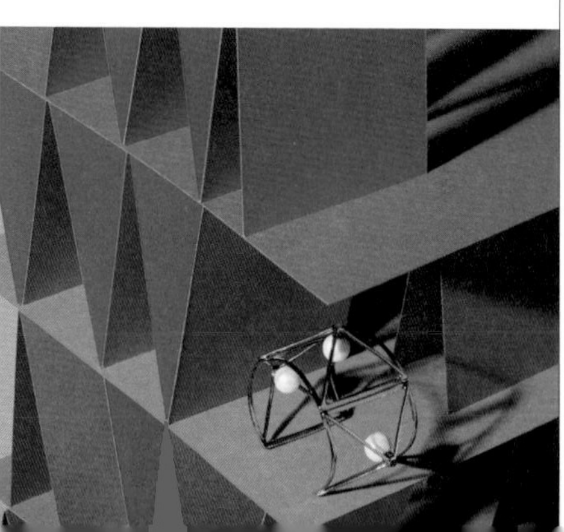

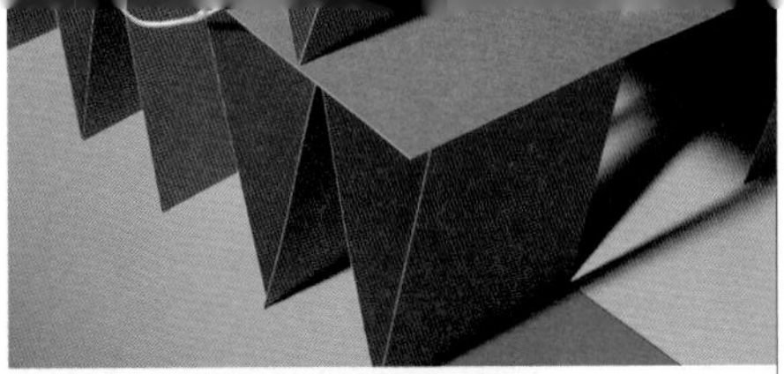

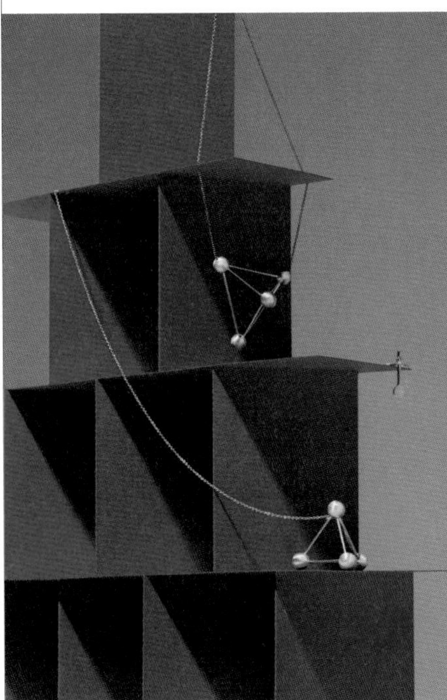

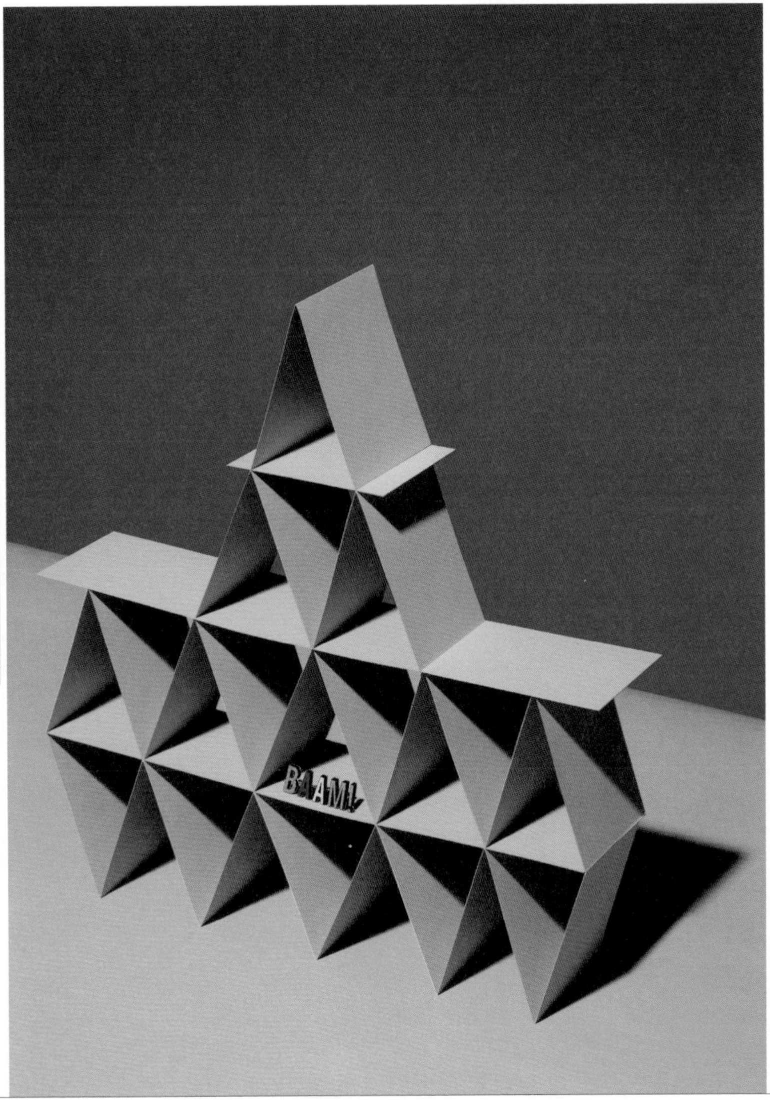

Castle of Cards
Styling: Rossana Mazza /
Set Design: Chiara Romano

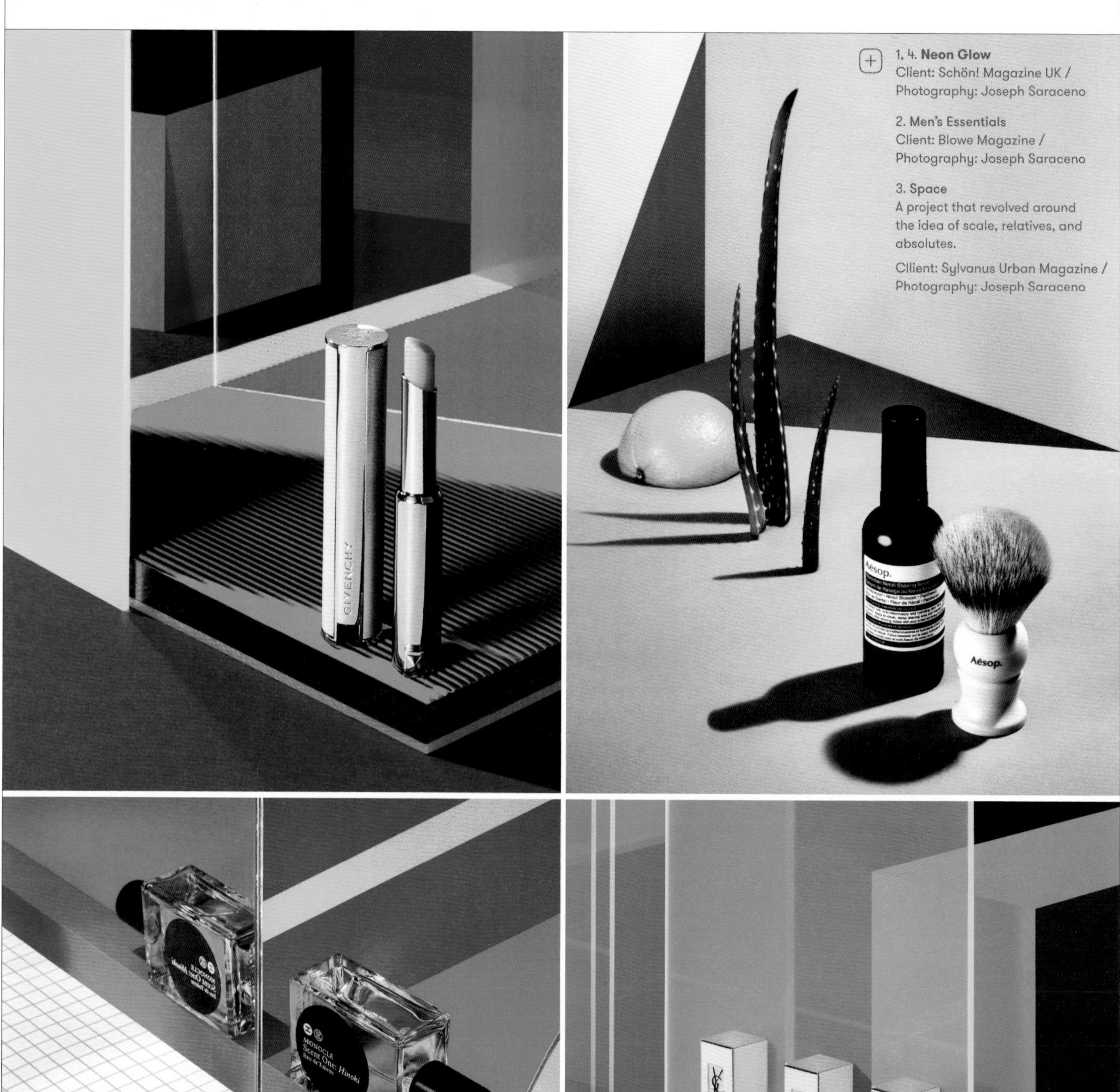

1, 4. **Neon Glow**
Client: Schön! Magazine UK / Photography: Joseph Saraceno

2. Men's Essentials
Client: Blowe Magazine / Photography: Joseph Saraceno

3. Space
A project that revolved around the idea of scale, relatives, and absolutes.

Cllient: Sylvanus Urban Magazine / Photography: Joseph Saraceno

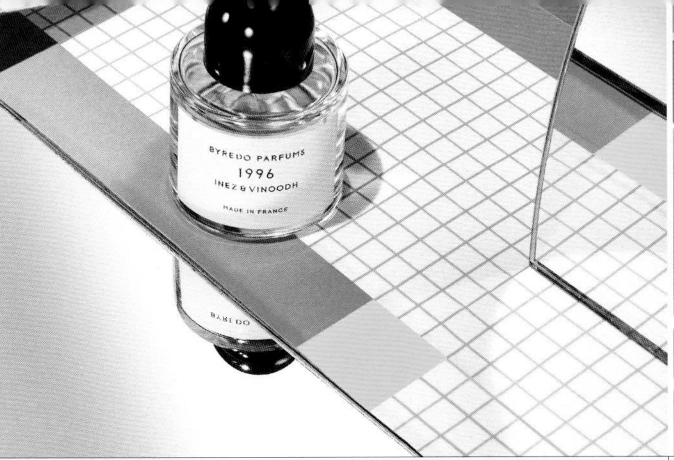

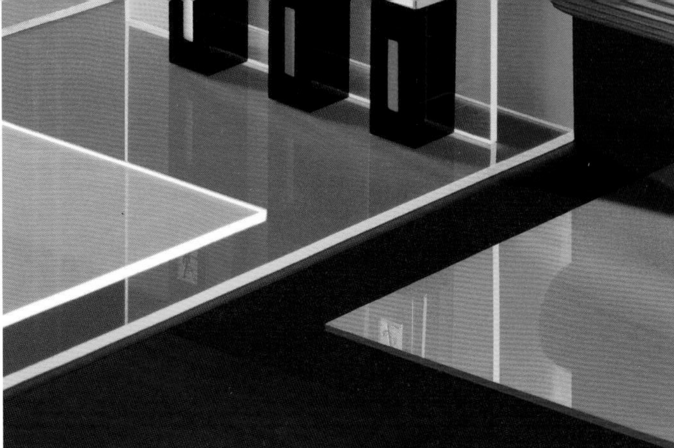

WILSON WONG

wilson_off_figure_styling

Wilson Wong is an award-winning still life product stylist and creative director based in Toronto who has a natural ability to fuse art into photography for visually impactful results. His passion lies in working with light, colours, and textures.

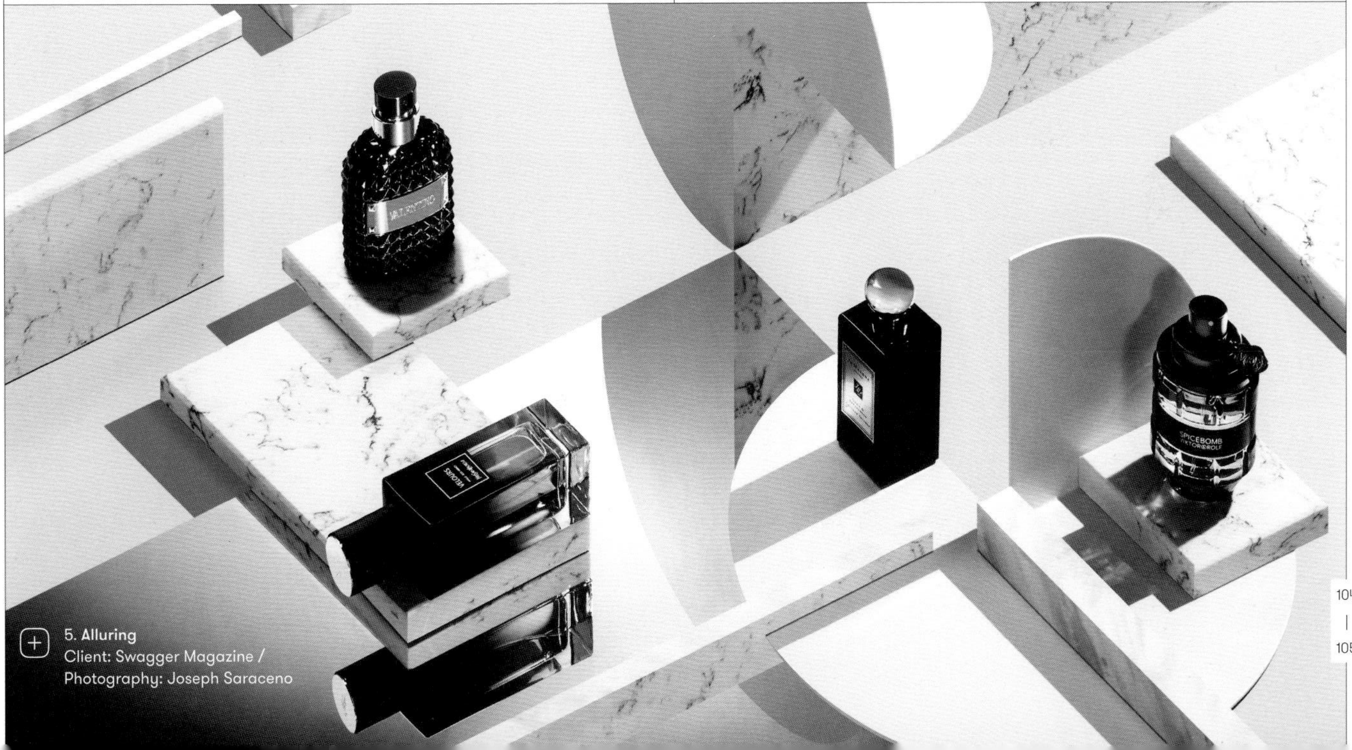

5. Alluring
Client: Swagger Magazine /
Photography: Joseph Saraceno

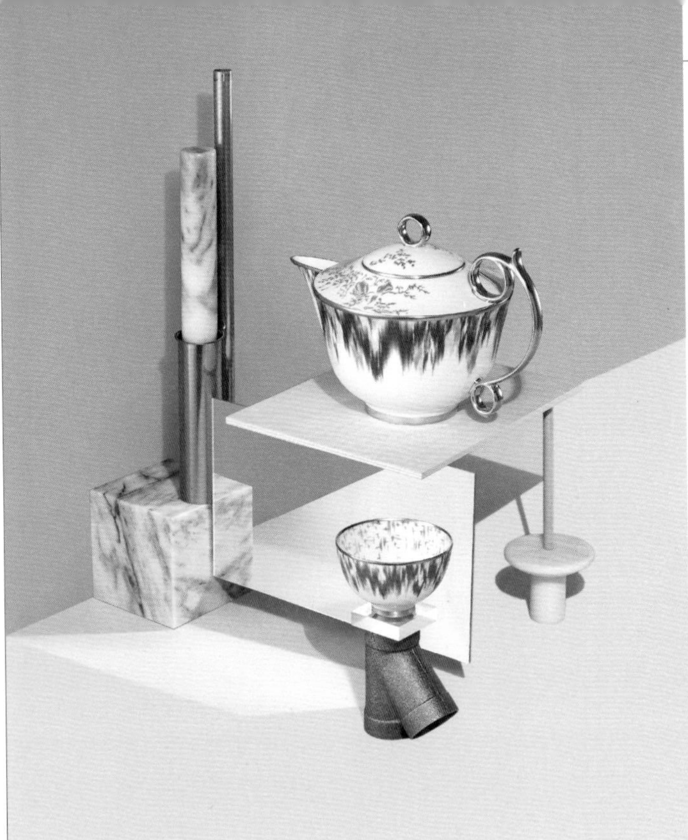

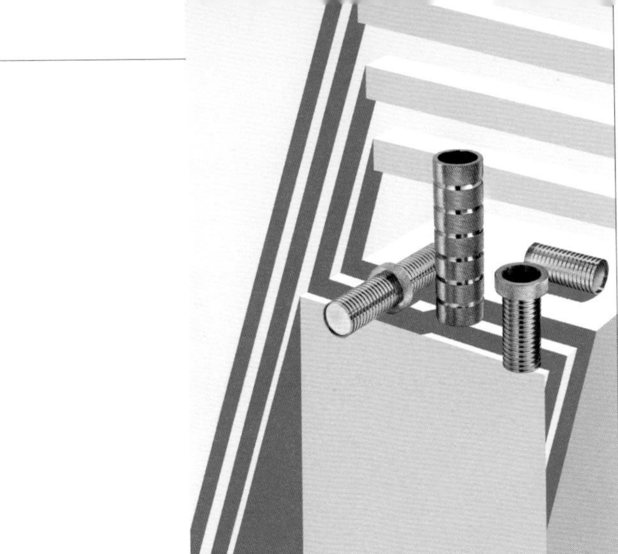

1, 3. **Jux.ta.po.si.tion**
A project that explored the tension between opulent objects and utilitarian products

Client: Metal Magazine Barcelona / Photography: Joseph Saraceno

2. **Details**
Client: Sylvanus Urban Magazine / Photography: Joseph Saraceno

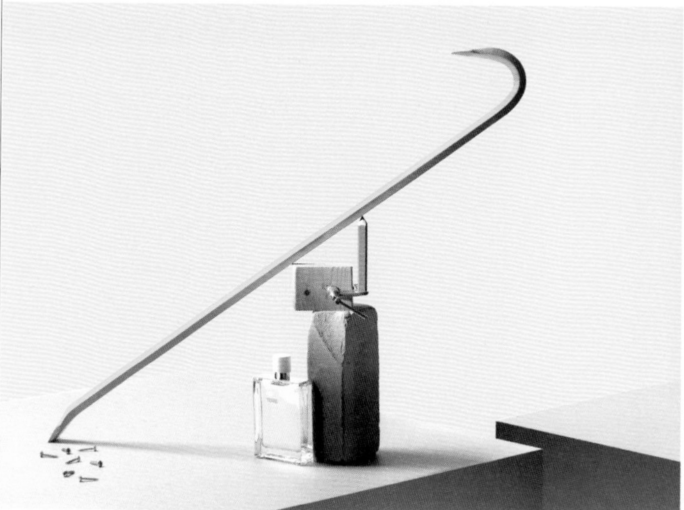

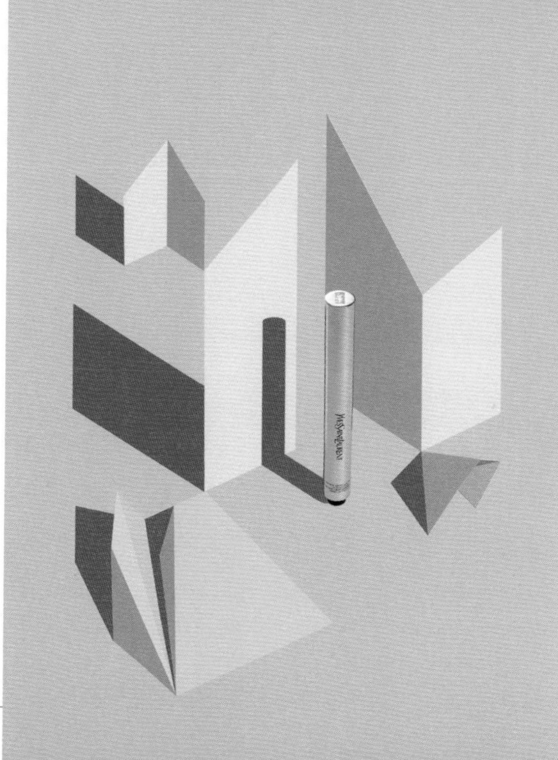

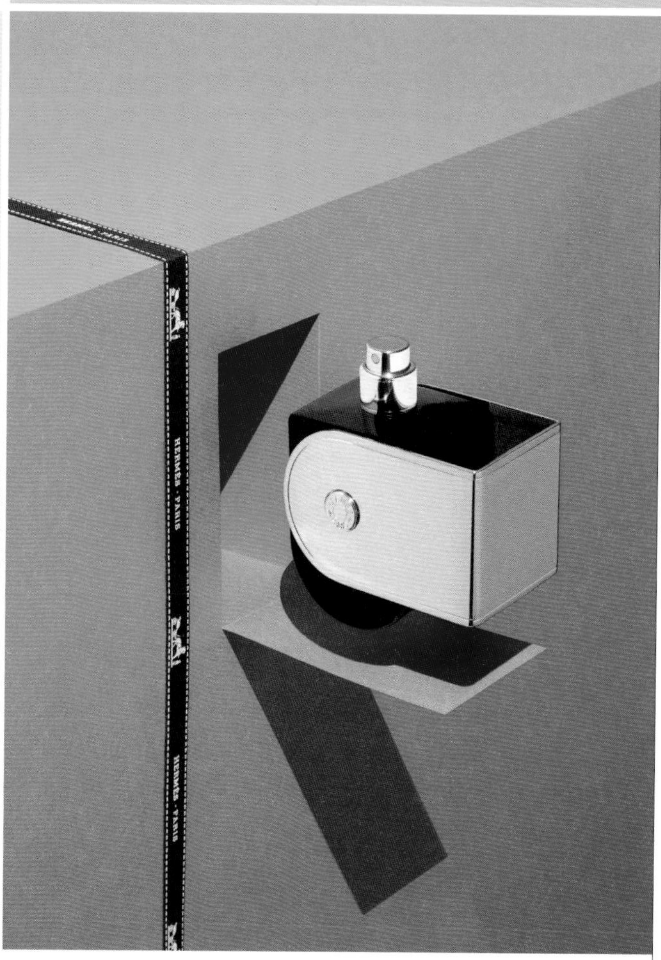

4-5. **Hermes Fragrance**
Photography: Andrew Grinton

6. **Paper Cuts**
Client: Atlas Magazine /
Photography: Joseph Saraceno

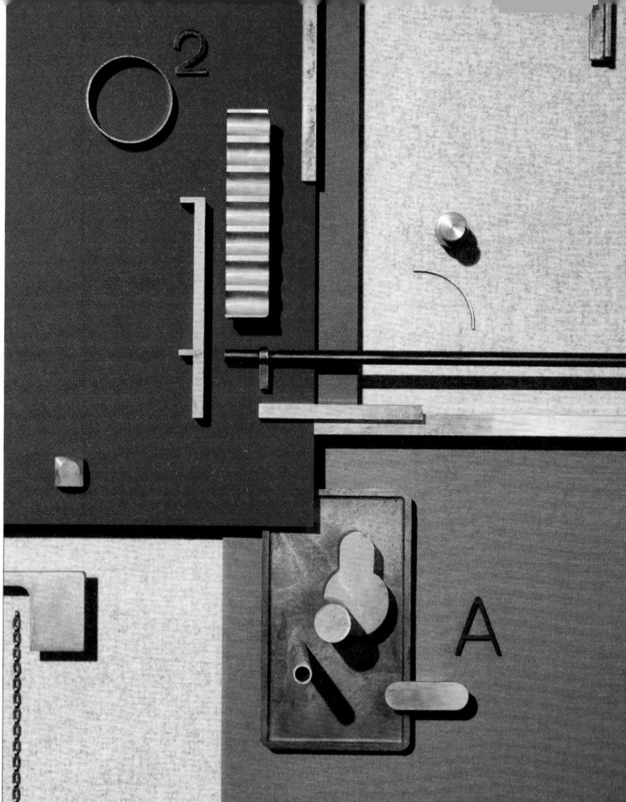

1. Constructivism
A project that was heavily inspired by the art movement of the same name, with ideas borrowed from its most influential artists.

Client: Filo Timo / Photography: Joseph Saraceno / Special Thanks: Amy Czettisch & Jill Redden (Redbox Creative), George Simionopoulos & Erica Pecoskie (Filo Timo)

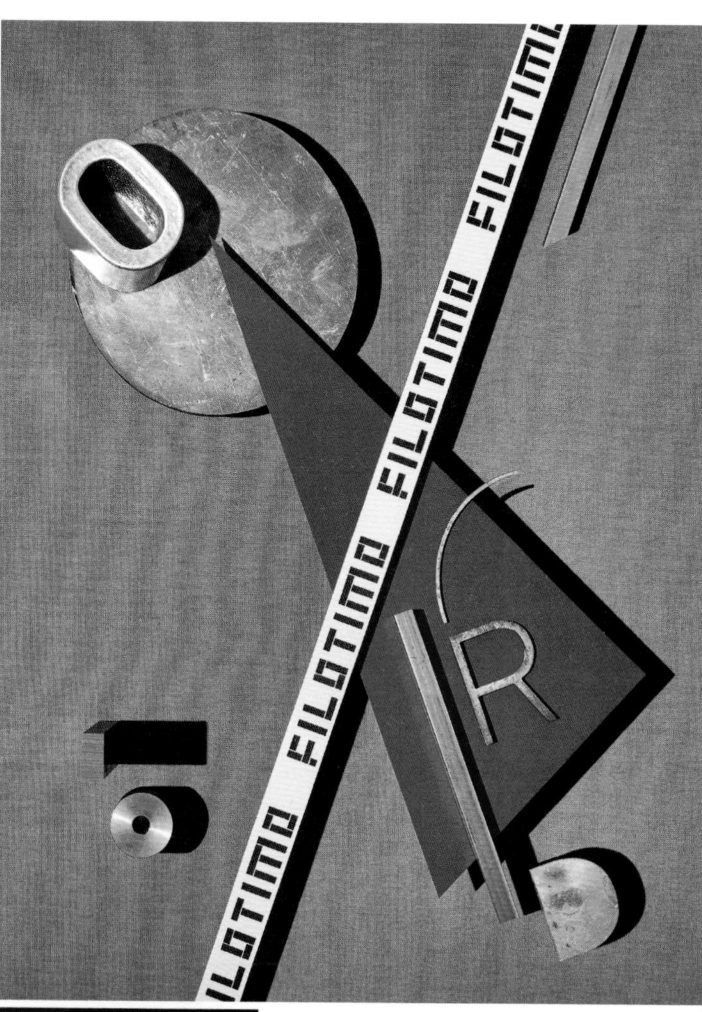

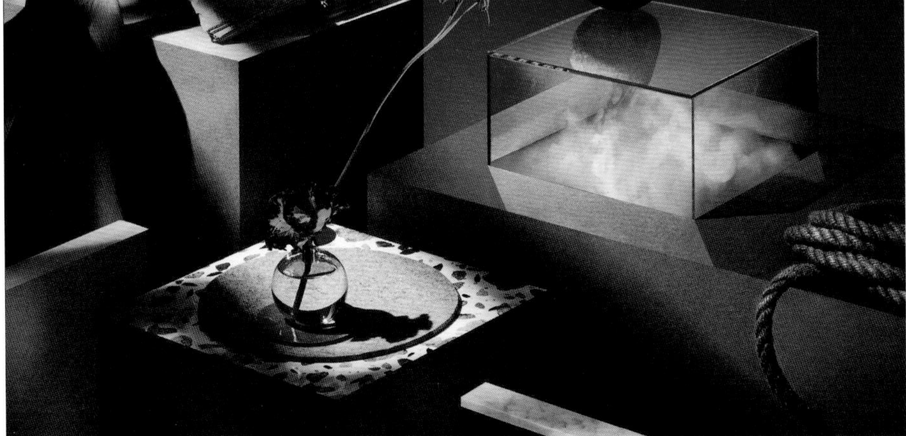

2. **Anachronism**
Client: DLTD-Scenes Magazine Stockholm / Photography: Joseph Saraceno / Flora: Lauren Sellen (Coyote Flowers)

3. **Edge**
Client: Sylvanus Urban Magazine / Photography: Joseph Saraceno / Props: Suzanne Campos, Lumicrest

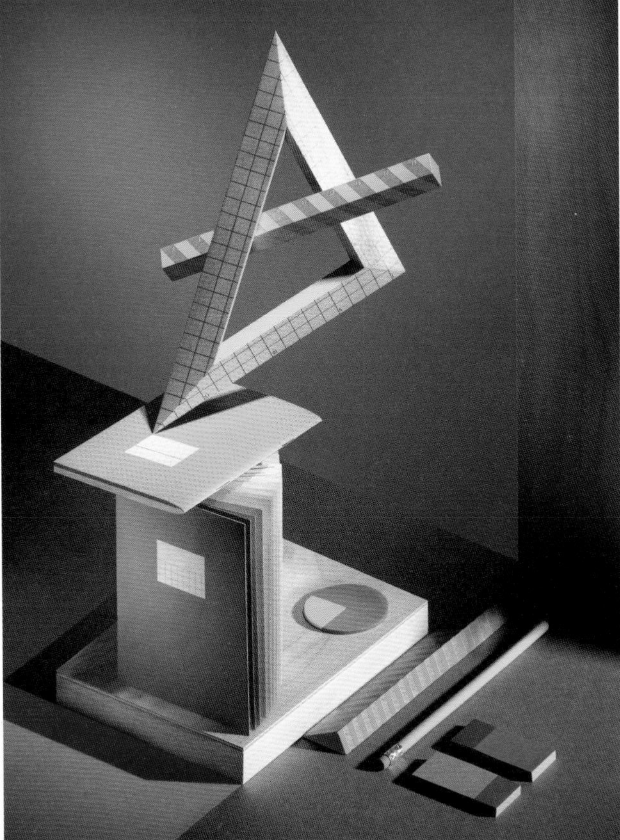

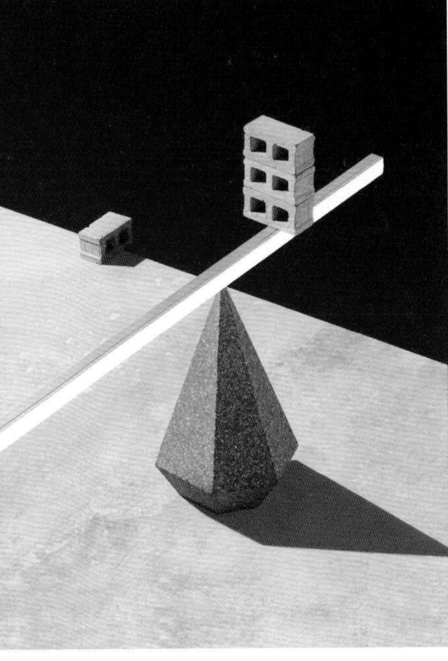

4. **Balancing Act**
A project that sought to add character and personality to beautifully designed stationery.

Photography: Andrew Grinton

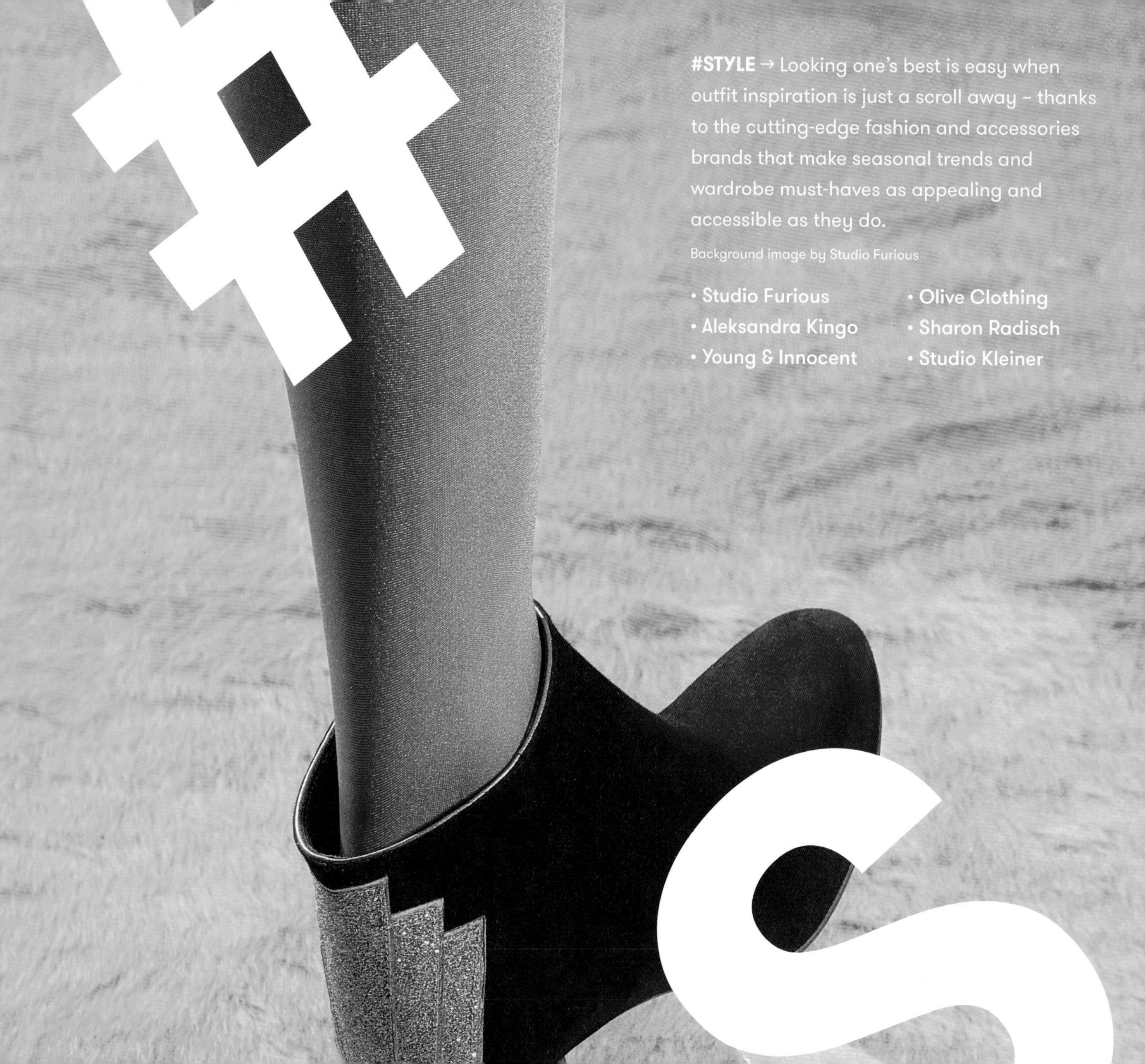

#STYLE → Looking one's best is easy when outfit inspiration is just a scroll away – thanks to the cutting-edge fashion and accessories brands that make seasonal trends and wardrobe must-haves as appealing and accessible as they do.

Background image by Studio Furious

- Studio Furious
- Aleksandra Kingo
- Young & Innocent
- Olive Clothing
- Sharon Radisch
- Studio Kleiner

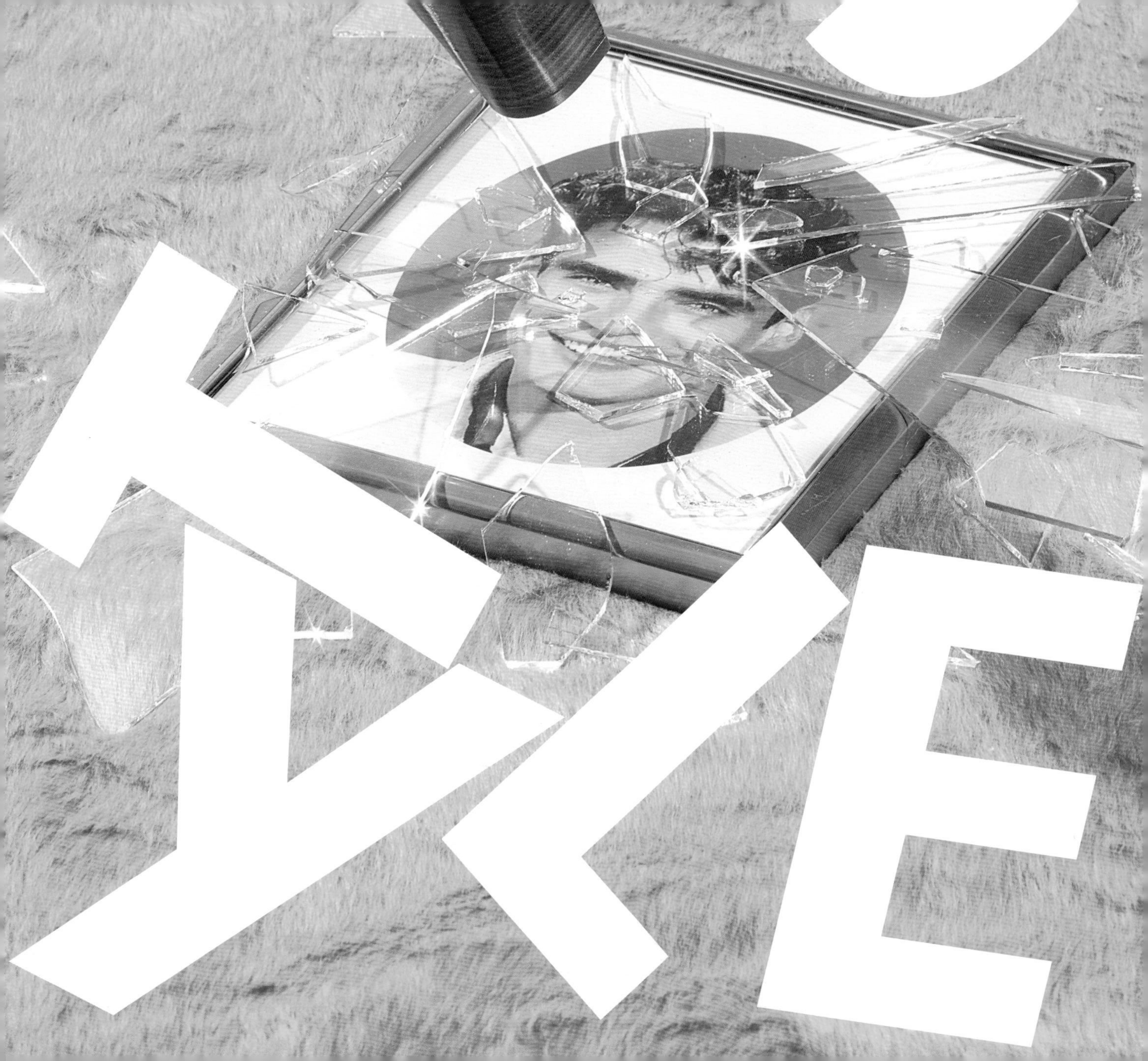

TIPS & TRICKS FOR FINDING YOUR OWN STYLE

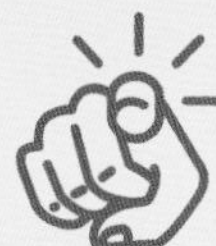

#47-69

GROW, GROW, GROW

In my opinion, studies and experience are not always sufficient. To grow your photography, you have to be able to find new ways and take risks.

— Nicola Galli

THINK OUTSIDE THE BOX

I do not consider myself a photographer – I just use photography as a way to create images, in the same way I have used painting, or collages, or digital tools such as Illustrator or Photoshop.

— Eloisa Iturbe

FREE YOUR IMAGINATION

For us, mixing products in a surreal setting is a way to enhance history and visual impact.

— I'm Blue I'm Pink

HAVE YOUR OWN PRINCIPLES

I think the best photography method varies from person to person. Everyone pursues different pictures. Personally, on a basic level, photos should be horizontal, objects should not be distorted if possible, white balance should be set correctly, and content should be logical.

— Chung-hui Shen

BE FEARLESS

Try, try, try.

— Akatre

DREAM BIG

We always try to think about a global artistic direction for each project we create.

— Studio Furious

START SOMEWHERE

Creating an image takes time and work. It is never good at the start.

— Paloma Rincón

SHOWCASE YOUR PERSONALITY

Go with your instincts. Shoot what makes you happy, what feels natural, and your style will develop over time.

— Present & Correct

EXPLORE DIFFERENT INTERESTS

I am very inspired by cubism and the modern art era, as well as architecture and the way hard sunlight shapes everything outside in an interesting way. Different textures and materials can also kick-start ideas that end up becoming a concept.

— Olivia Jeczmyk

STAND OUT

[The one mistake photographers often make is creating] the same images as others.

— Akatre

DON'T FORGET TO PLAY

I try to do at least one or two personal projects every year. This gives me the inspiration to create in a different way than when I am working on assignments where I have to take clients into consideration.

— Olivia Jeczmyk

MAINTAIN GOOD STANDARDS

I allow myself to do what I like and be more spontaneous, but then I take care of the final image so that it looks sharp and powerful.

— Eating Patterns / Vega Hernando

LIVE IN THE MOMENT

It does not have to be so polished – it can really be about the here and now. Being able to work on and capture an idea, then have it go live to our audience within minutes is really powerful.

— Olive Clothing

TRAIN YOUR DESIGN EYE

[Having a good eye for design] is definitely important because your product shots not only sell your items, but also your brand.

— Present & Correct

DON'T BE SLOPPY

Just make sure that your style is maintained, and your Instagram will look very special.

— Chung-hui Shen

BELIEVE IN YOURSELF

Follow your inner voice: it will guide you to create images that you will feel satisfied with.

— Olivia Jeczmyk

DO IT FOR YOURSELF

I try to think more about creating something that can be placed on the wall, rather than quickly consumed on social media or advertising.

— Olivia Jeczmyk

LEARN ABOUT YOURSELF

I think Instagram is a very visual way to understand your stuff, what you like to do, and what makes images work best for you.

— Daniel Rueda & Anna Devís

BE COHESIVE

[Some photographers make the mistake of] not having their own style, and not being consistent enough. I think consistency and cohesion are fundamental.

— Eloisa Iturbe

IMITATION IS NOT ALWAYS FLATTERY

Social media is awash with amazing reference points and influences for creative content. Taking inspiration from, but not imitating, is an important part of refining your practice.

— Olive Clothing

MIX & MATCH

I love mixing all my inspiration together to create a unique style of photography with humour and wit, and hope the photos always look interesting.

— Matter Matters

INNOVATION IS KEY

After all the references I have come across, I wish to create ad campaigns with styles I have never seen before.

— Matter Matters

STAY AUTHENTIC

As long as each image I share is representative of my style as a photographer, then I'm happy.

— Sharon Radisch

Lazy Panties, Stretching, Monday Mornings, Bootycall
Client: Jolie Culottes

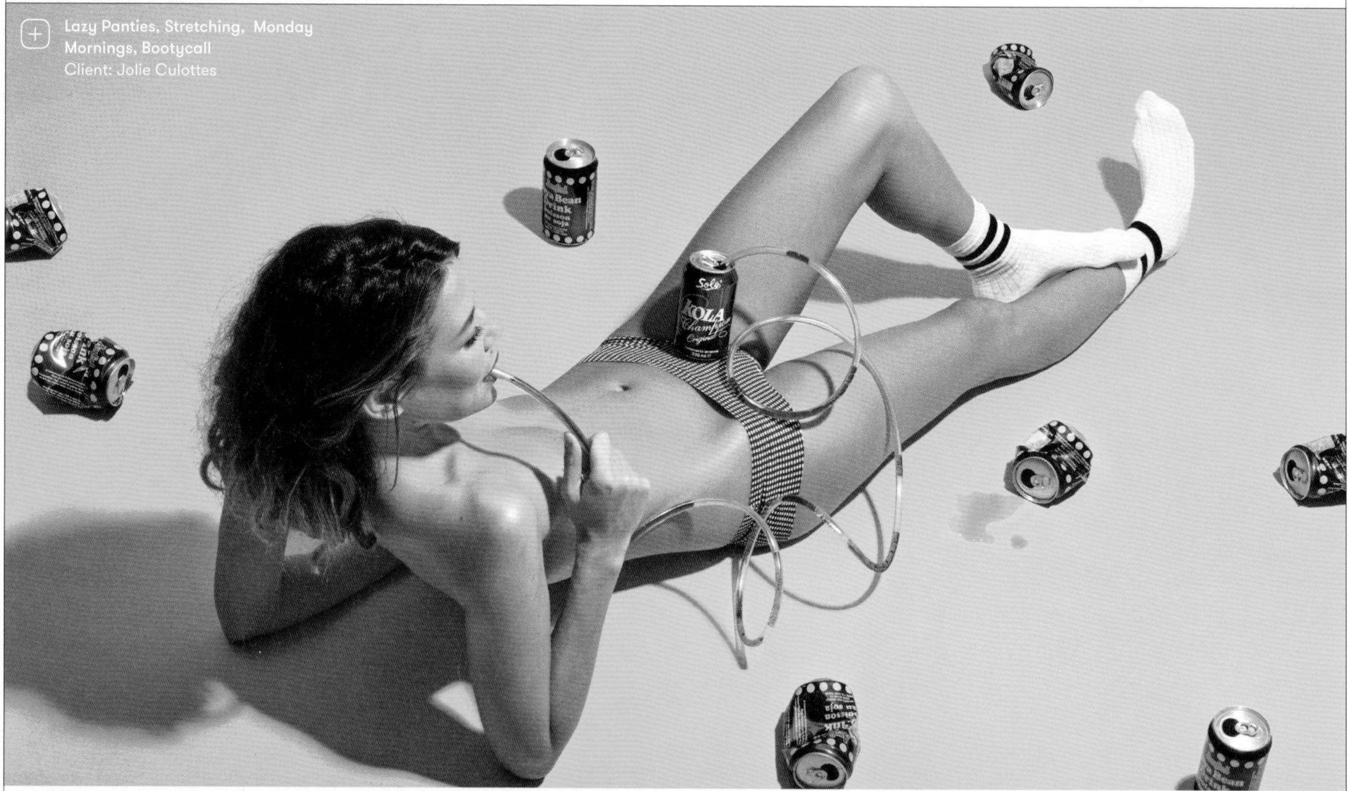

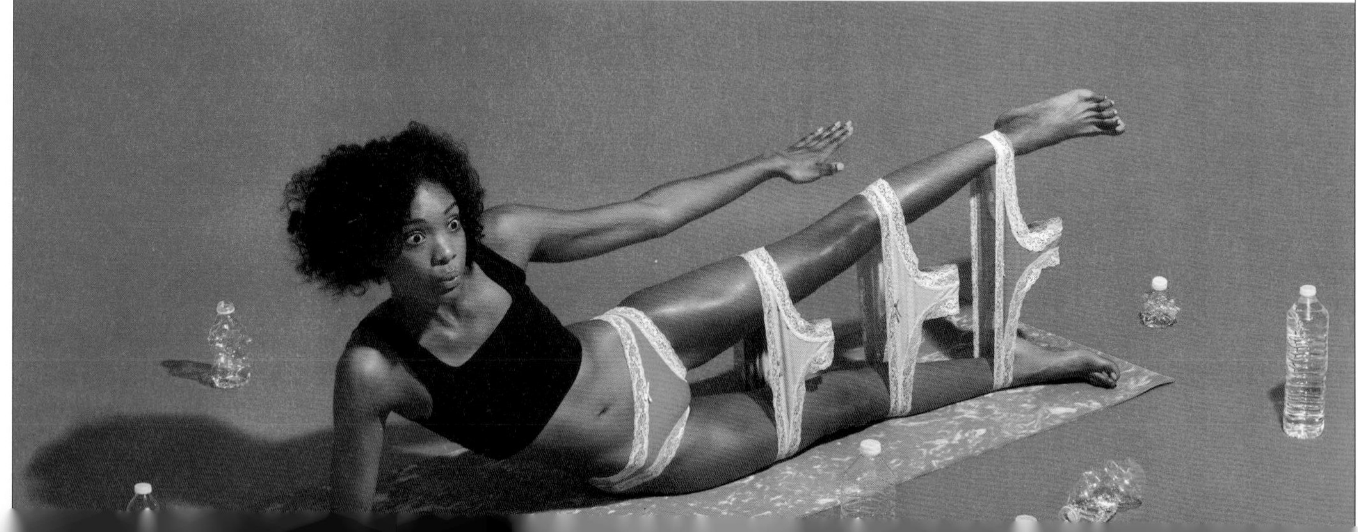

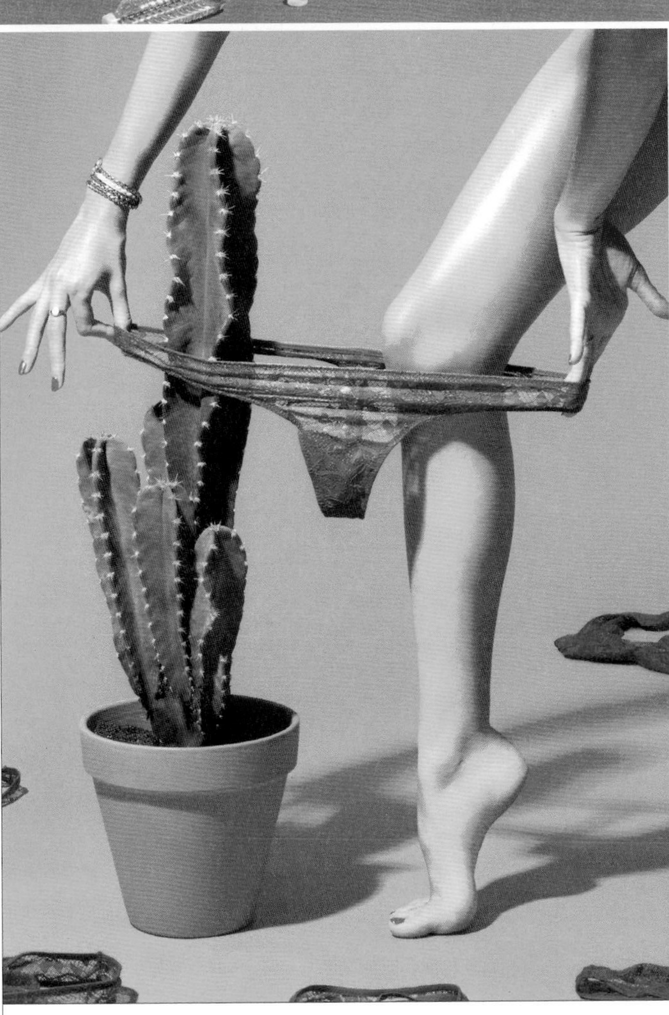

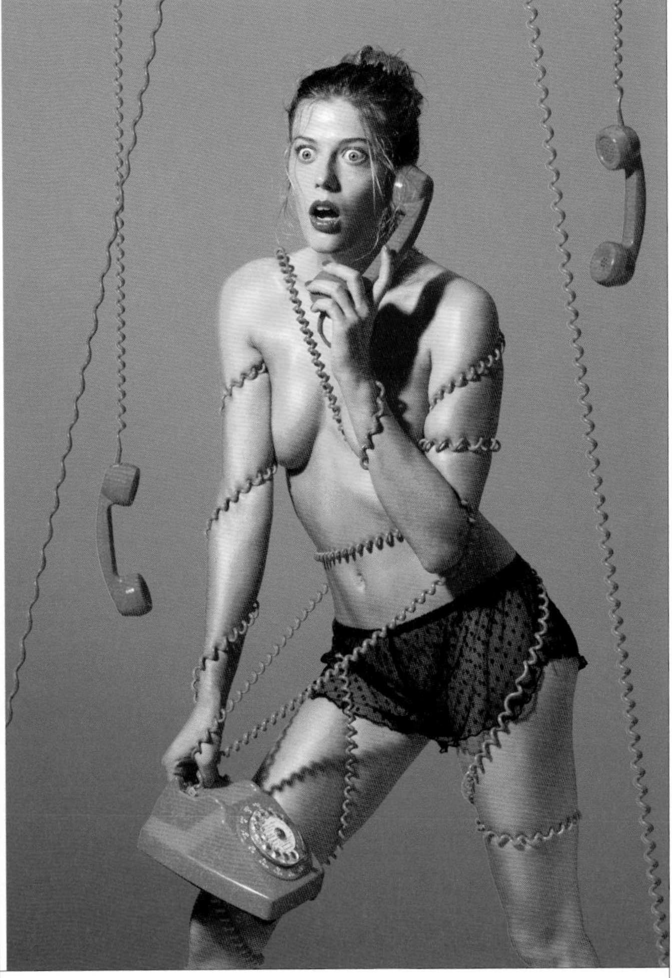

STUDIO FURIOUS

studiofurious

Studio Furious specialises in graphic design and art direction. It is involved in cooking up fashion, design, culture, food, and cosmetics projects.

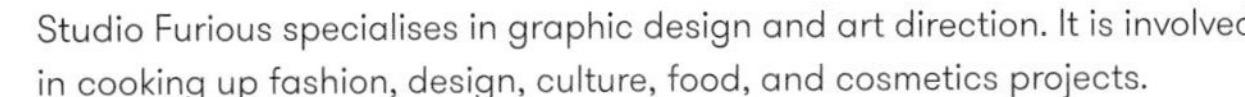

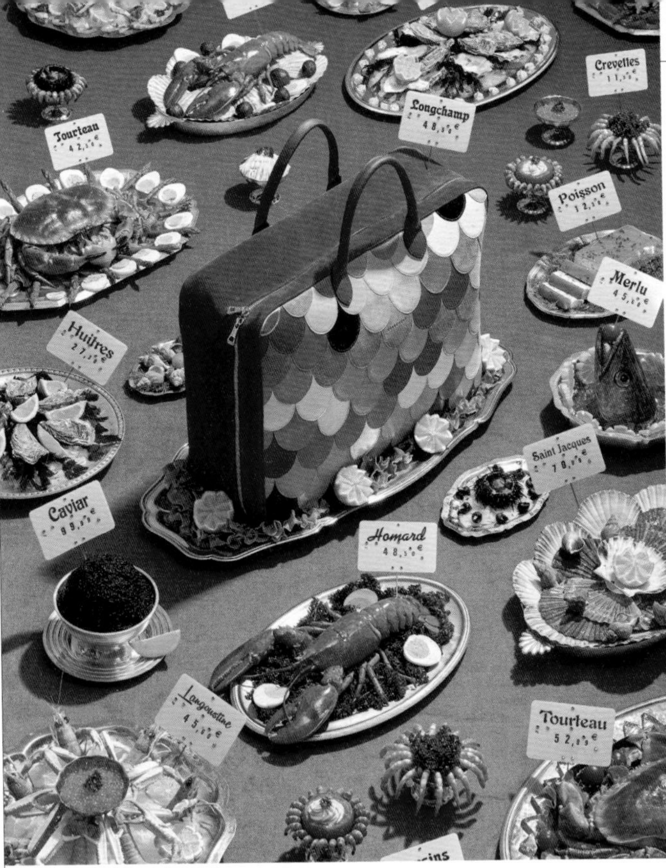

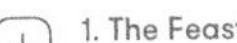

1. The Feast
Client: Longchamps and Grazia Magazine

2. The Bug
Client: MiuMiu and Grazia Magazine

3. Thievery
Client: BEAUROW

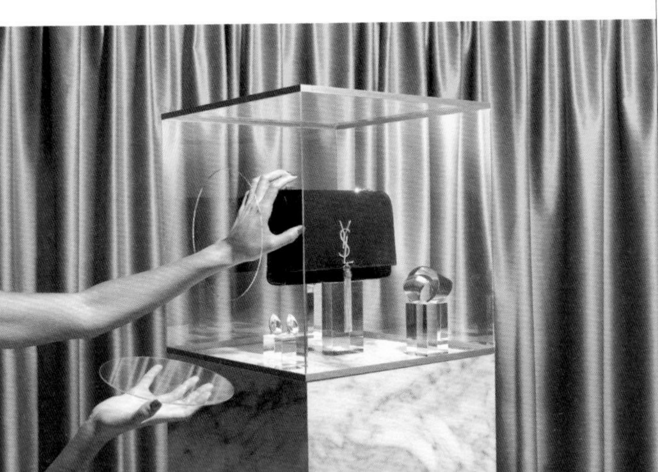

"We like to focus our work on ideas rather than look for a specific style..."

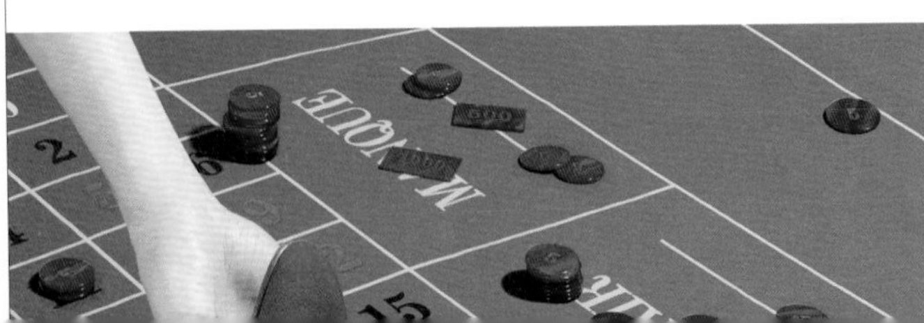

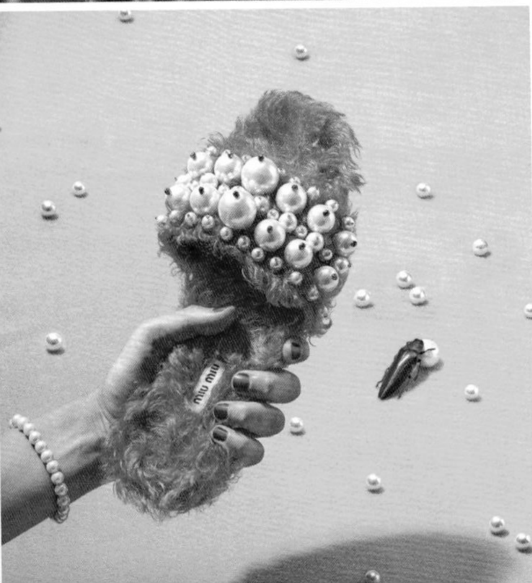

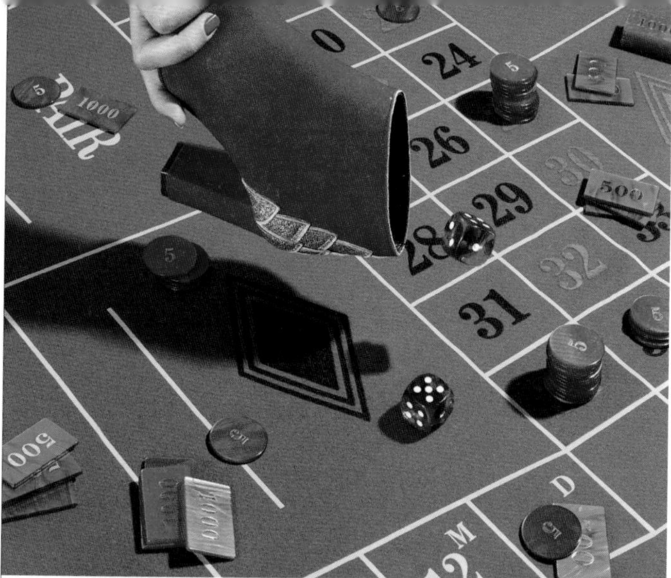

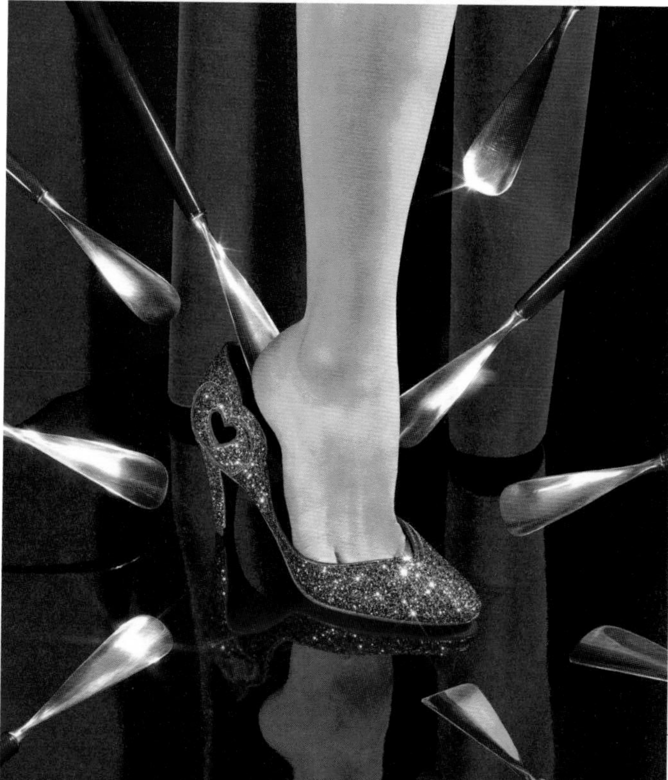

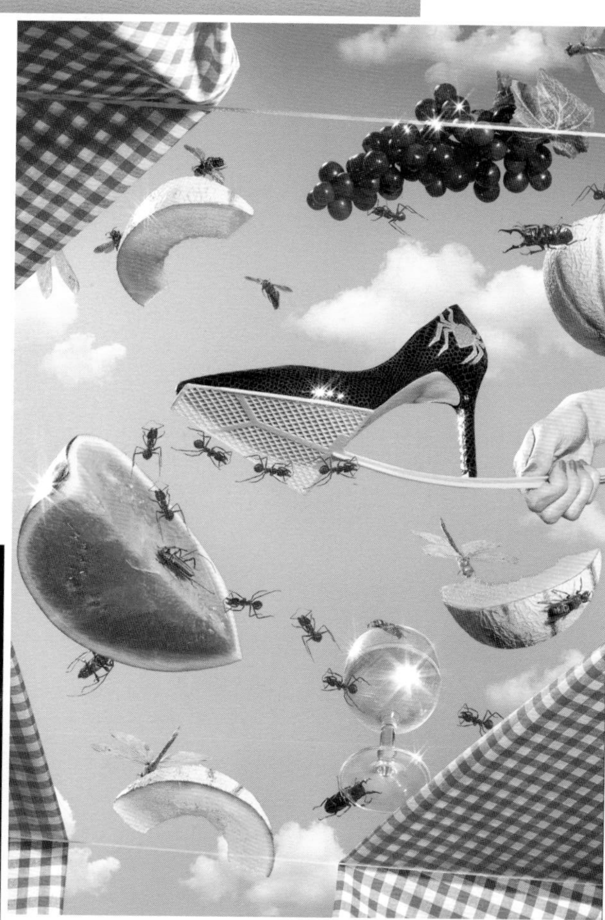

4-6. **The Casino, The Swatter, and The Shoehorns**
Visuals for FW 18/19 Collection Campaign
Client: Patricia Blanchet

The Balls, The Bobbins, The Bricks, and The Mirrors
Client: Delveaux

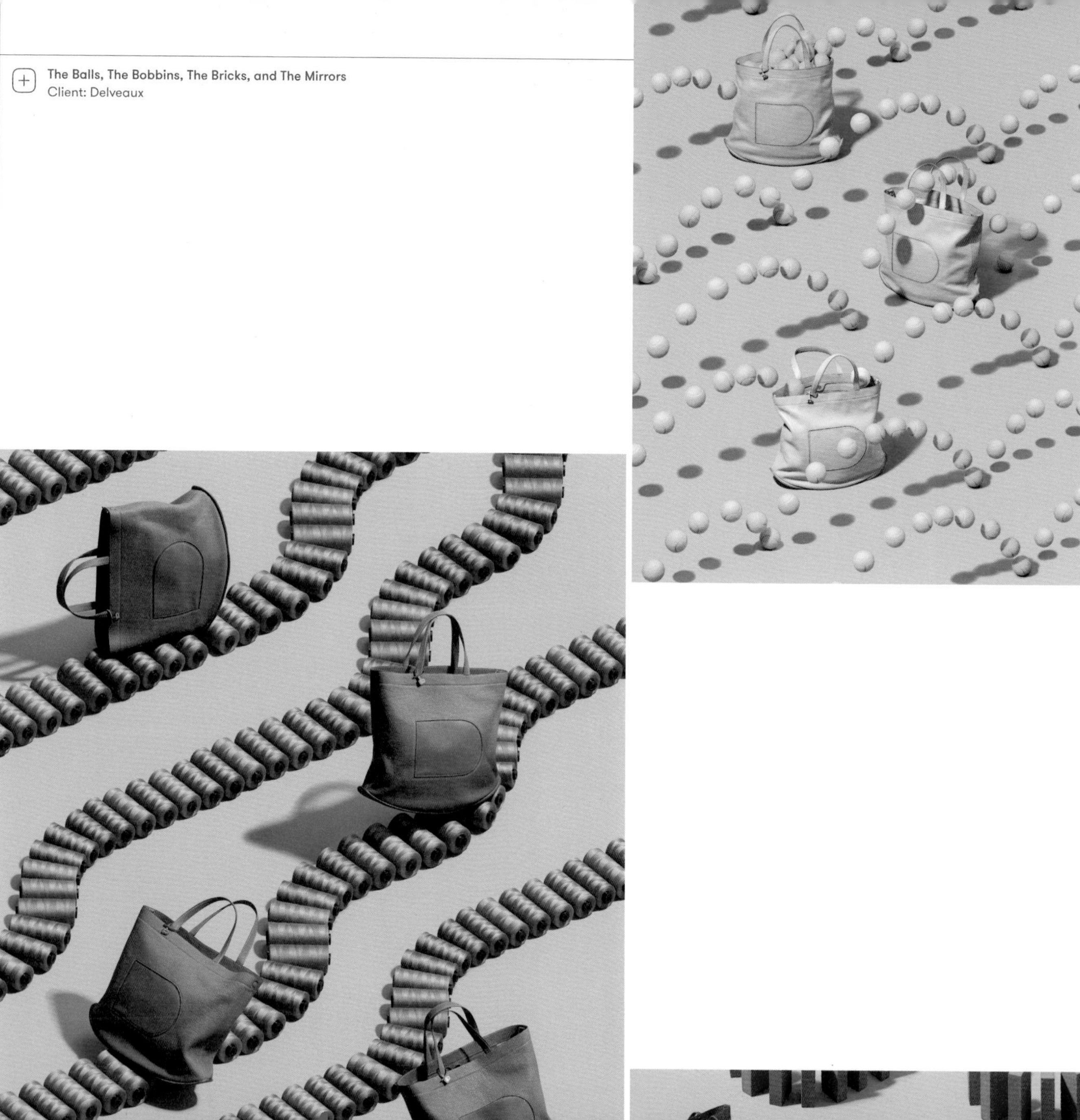

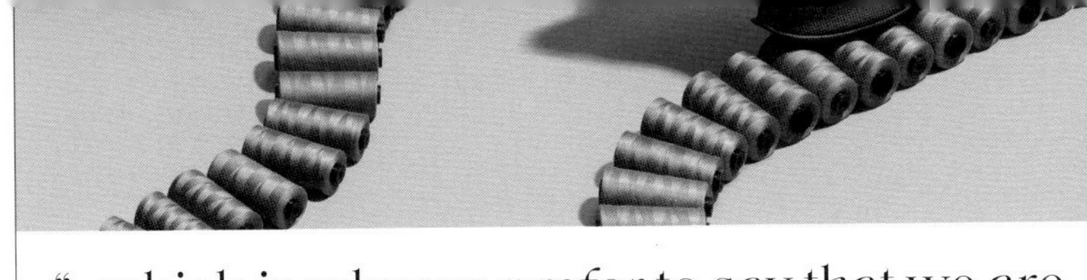

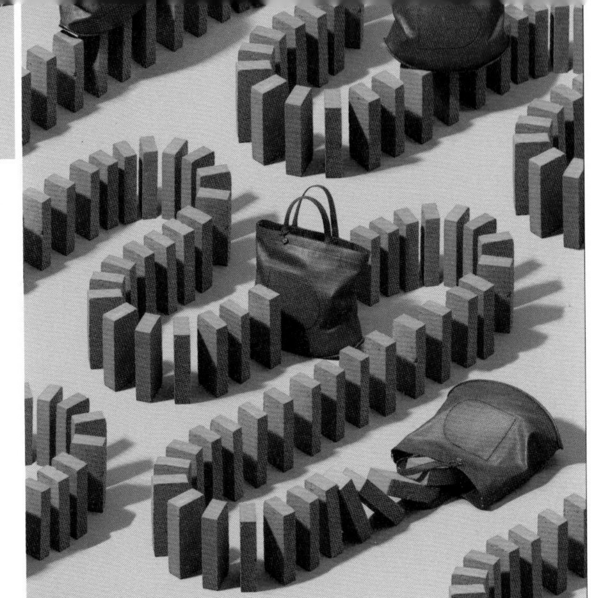

"...which is why we prefer to say that we are artistic directors and image makers rather than photographers."

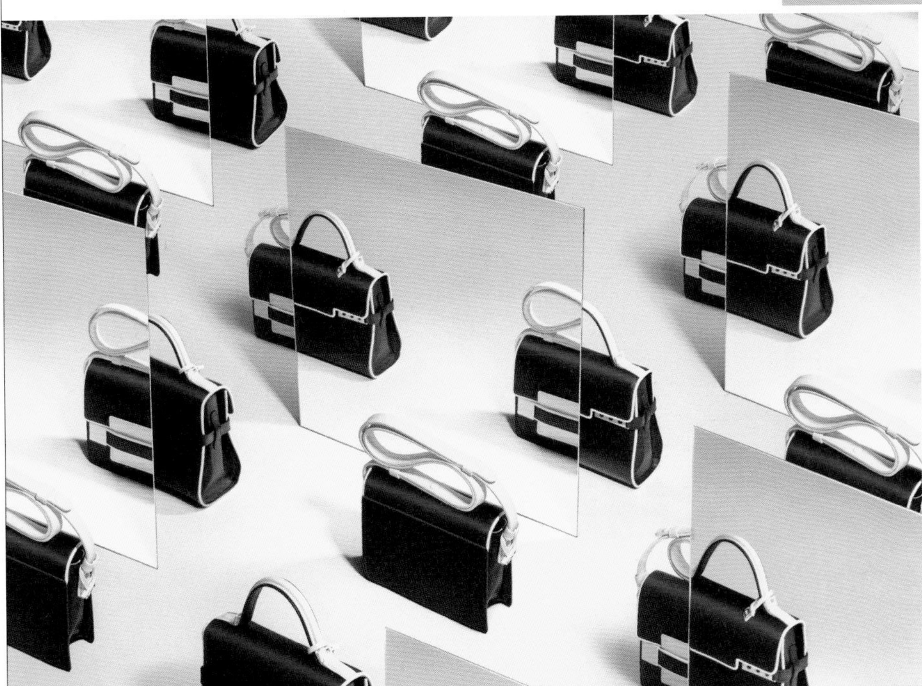

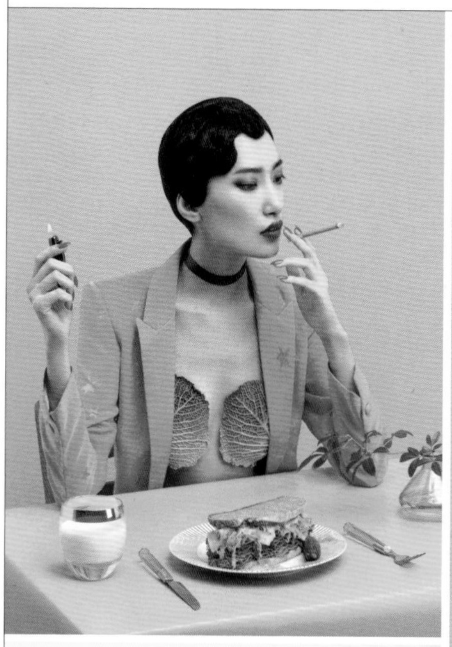

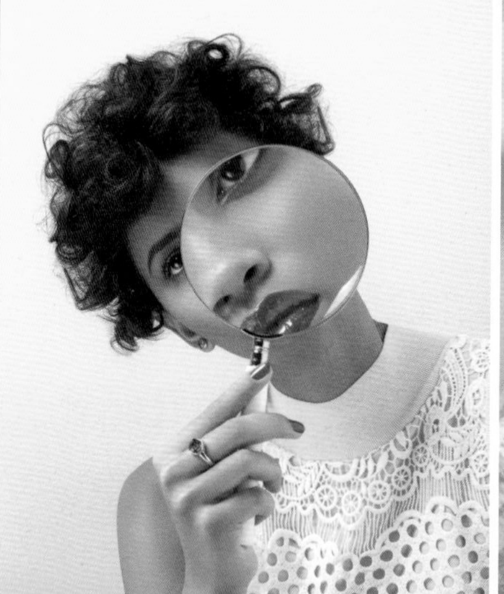

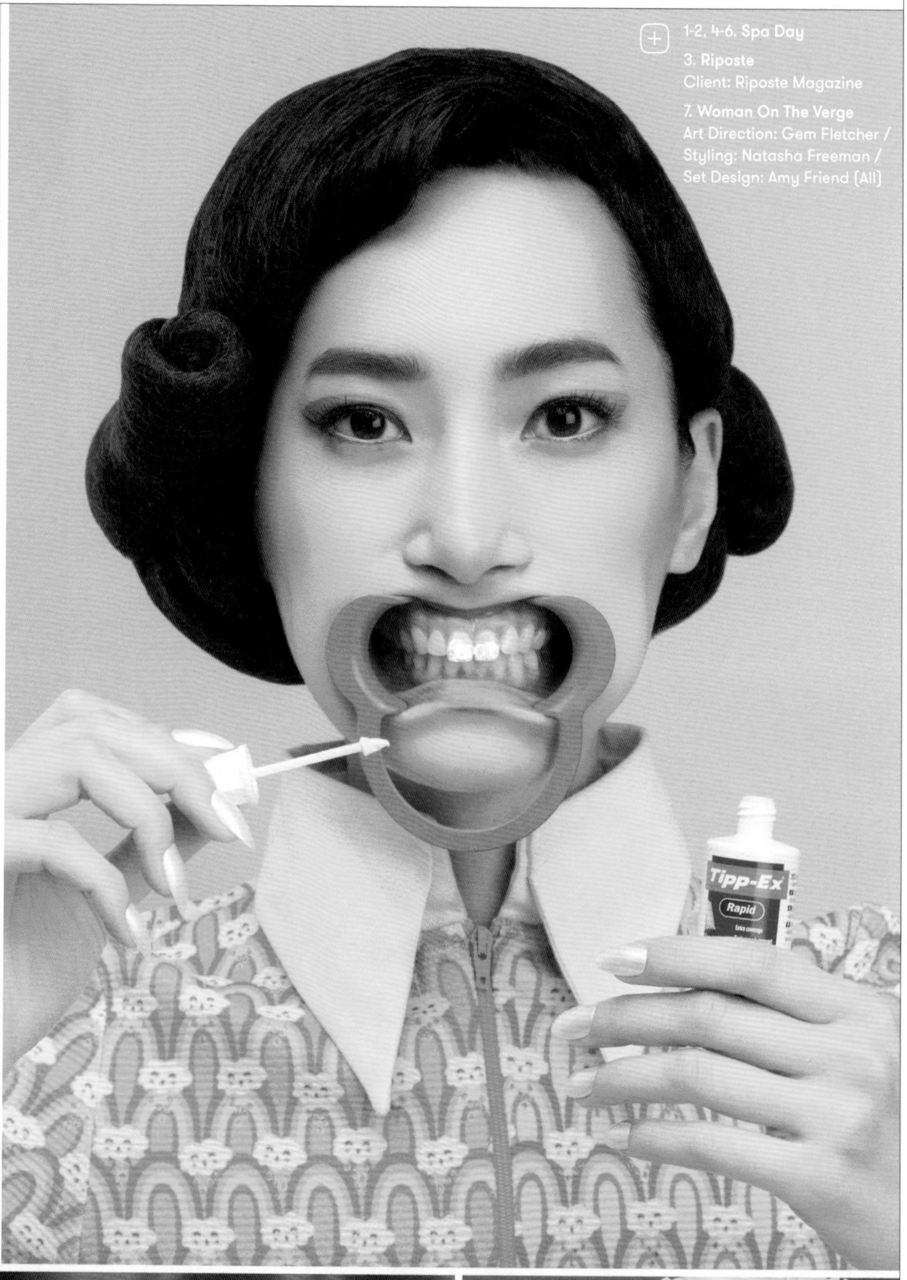

1-2, 4-6. Spa Day

3. Riposte
Client: Riposte Magazine

7. Woman On The Verge
Art Direction: Gem Fletcher / Styling: Natasha Freeman / Set Design: Amy Friend (All)

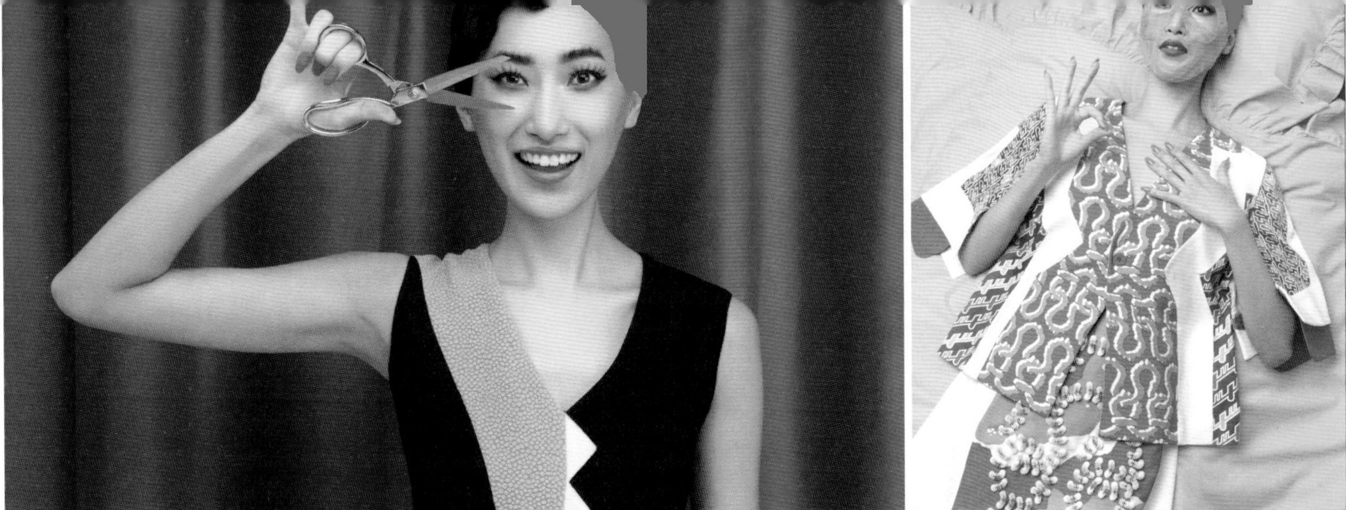

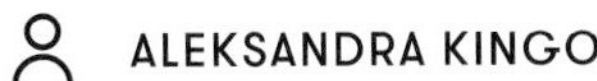

ALEKSANDRA KINGO

aleksandrakingo

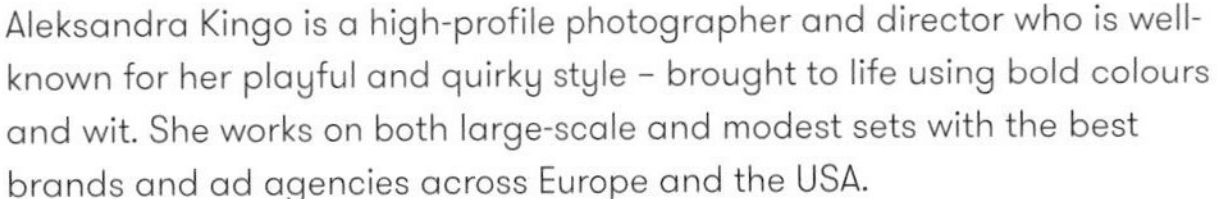

Aleksandra Kingo is a high-profile photographer and director who is well-known for her playful and quirky style – brought to life using bold colours and wit. She works on both large-scale and modest sets with the best brands and ad agencies across Europe and the USA.

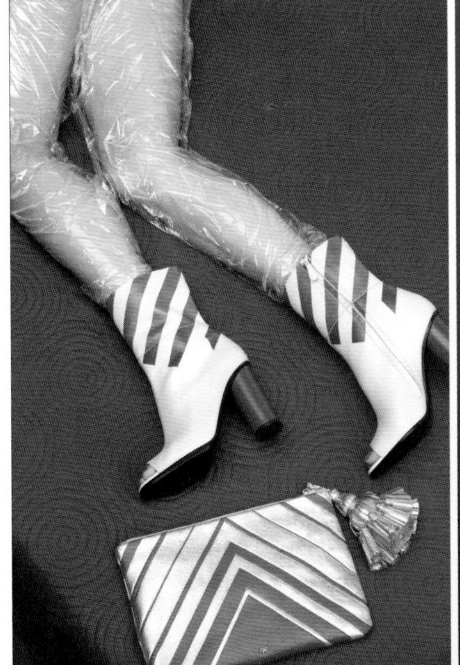

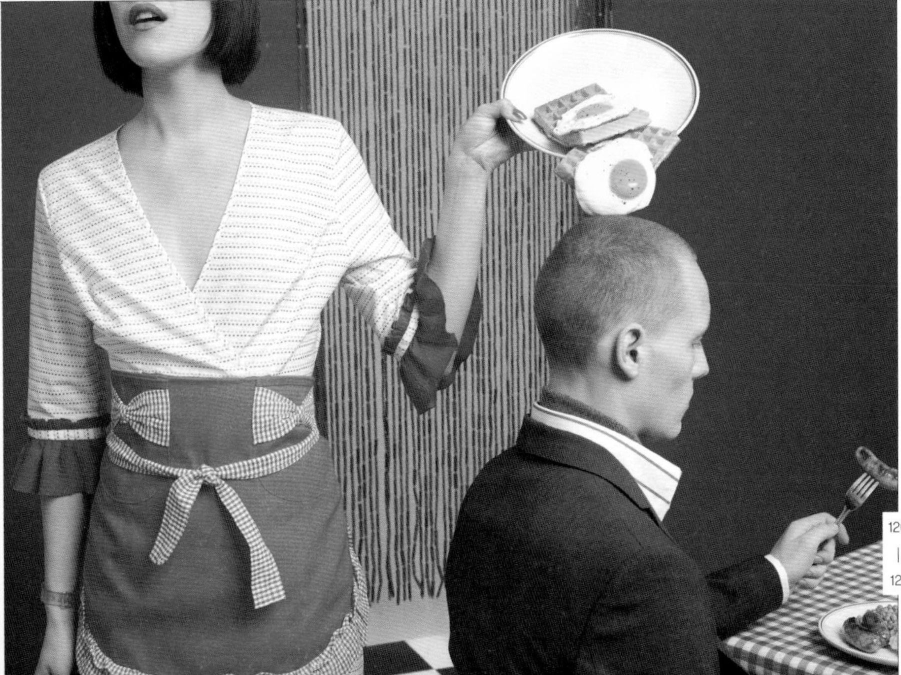

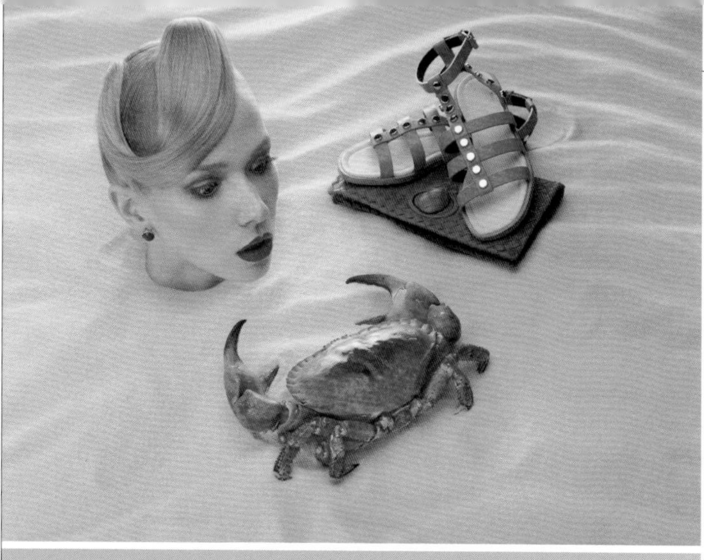

1. **Aishti**
Client: Aishti / Creative Direction: Jessica Walsh / Styling: Natasha Freeman / Set Design: Amy Friend

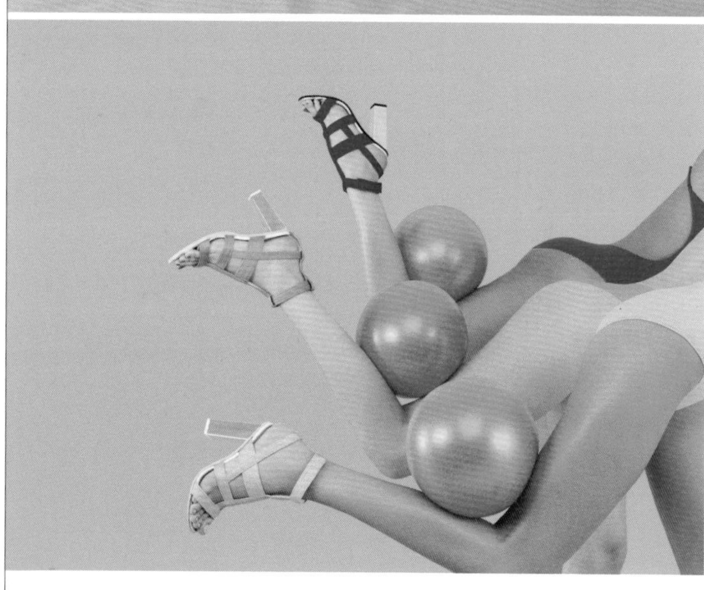

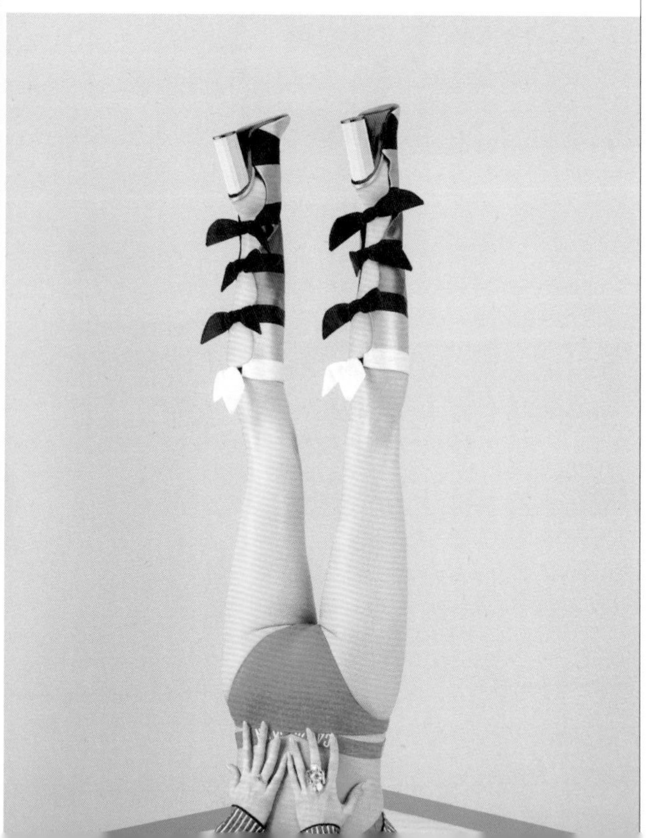

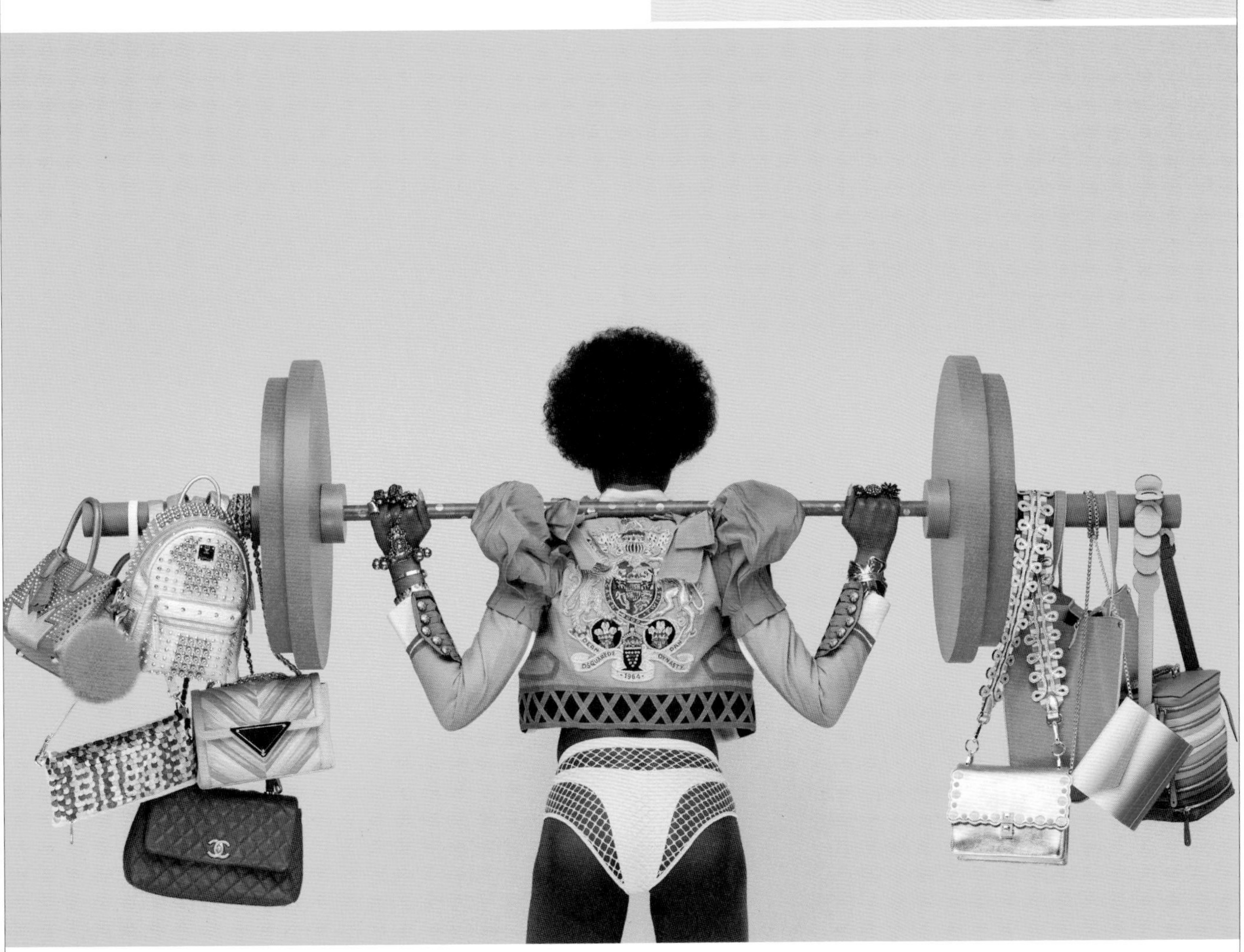

2-4. Lets Get Physical
Client: Hunger Magazine / Art Direction: Vicky Lawton /
Styling: Kim Howells / Set Design: Amy Friend

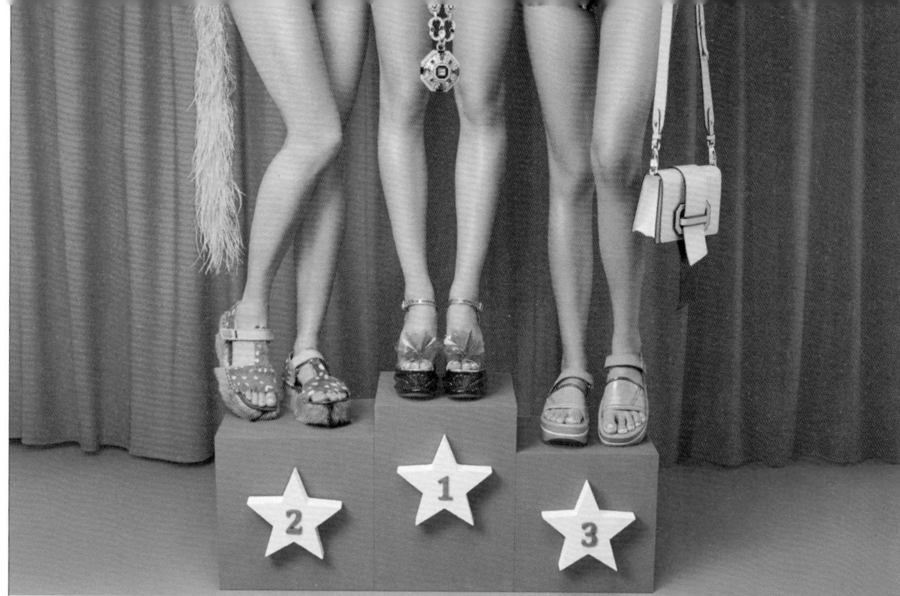

1-2. **Lets Get Physical**
Client: Hunger Magazine / Art Direction: Vicky Lawton / Styling: Kim Howells / Set Design: Amy Friend

3-4. **Spa Day**
Art Direction: Gem Fletcher / Styling: Natasha Freeman / Set Design: Amy Friend

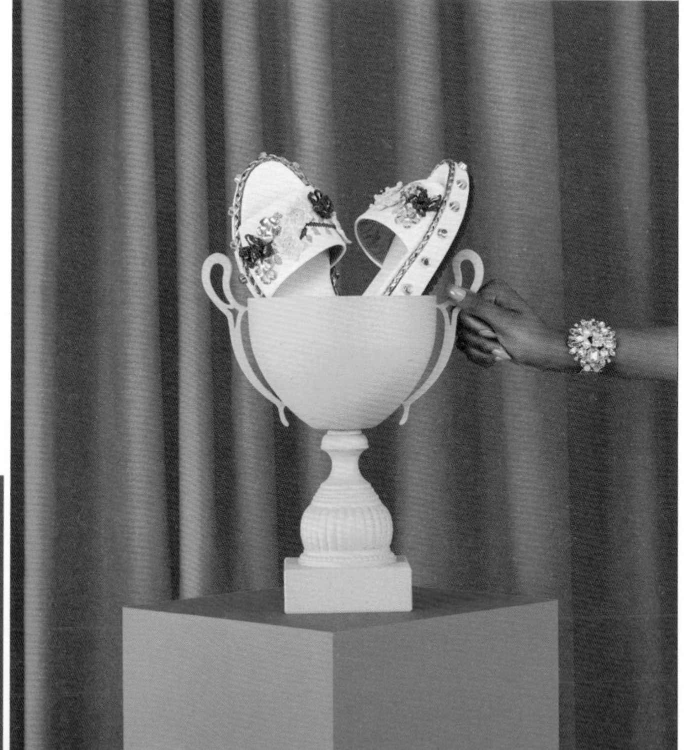

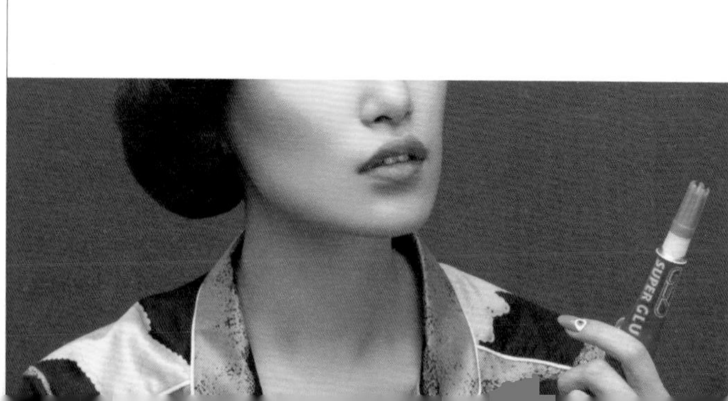

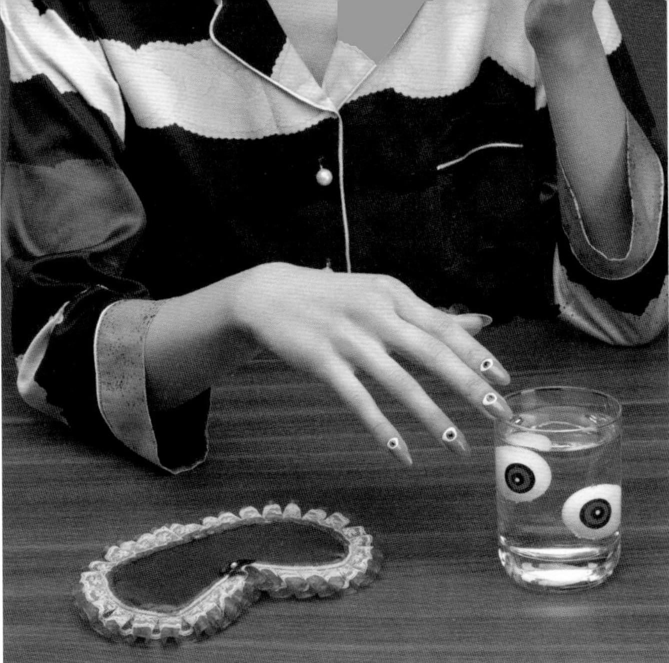

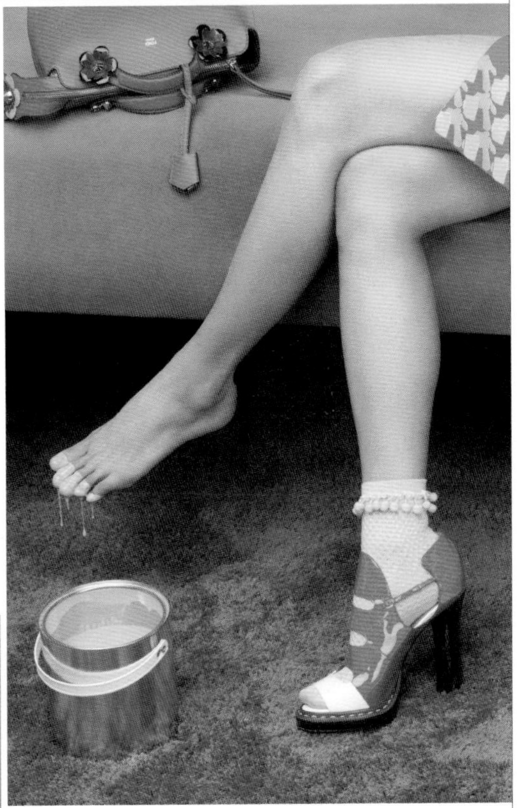

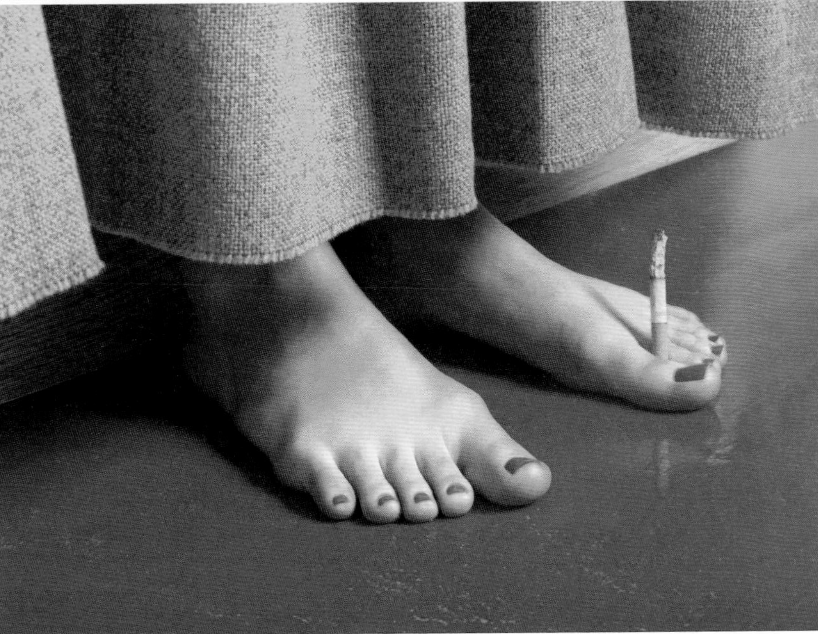

5. La Monda
Client: La Monda Magazine /
Set Design: Camille Boyer

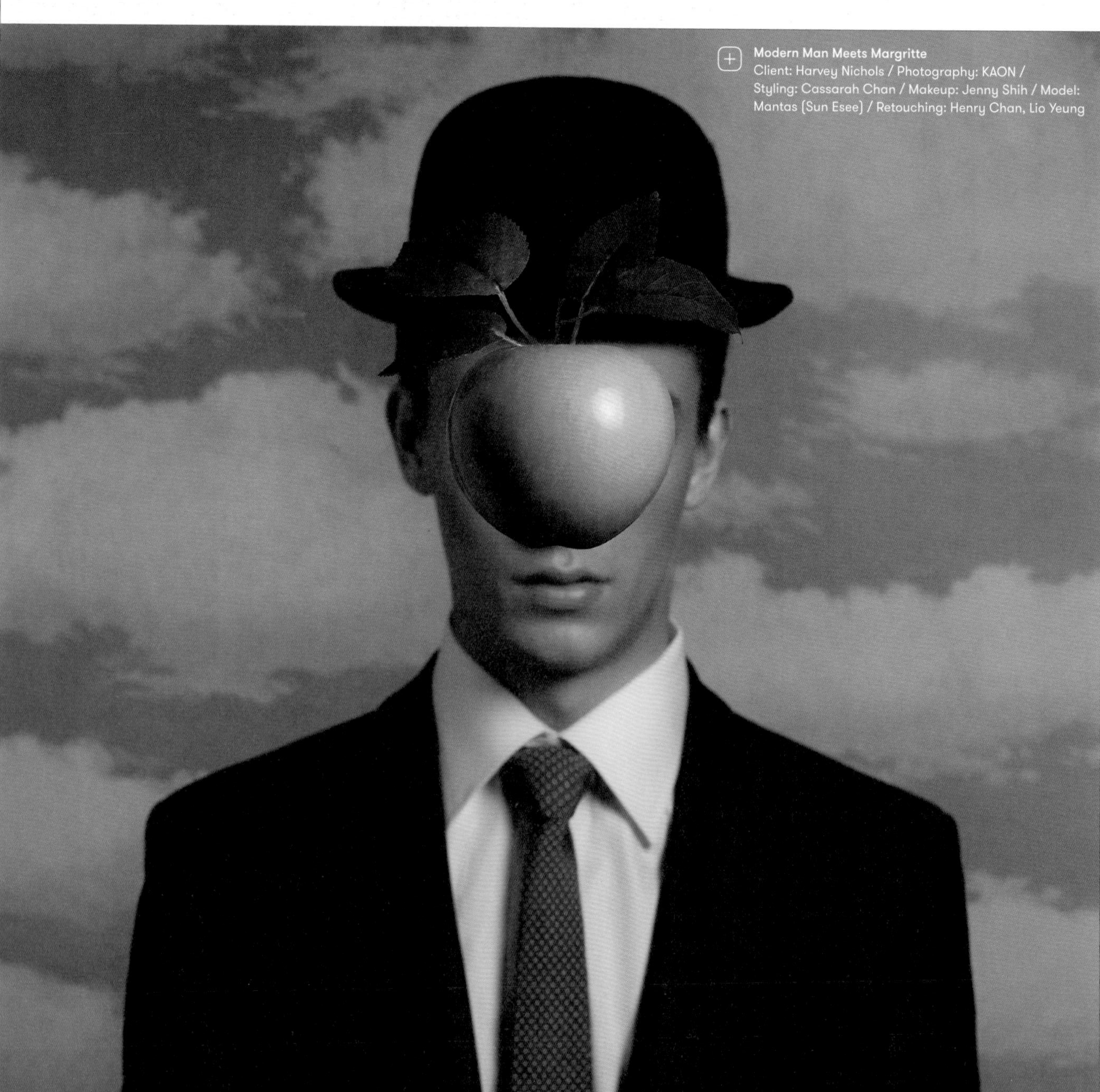

Modern Man Meets Margritte
Client: Harvey Nichols / Photography: KAON / Styling: Cassarah Chan / Makeup: Jenny Shih / Model: Mantas (Sun Esee) / Retouching: Henry Chan, Lio Yeung

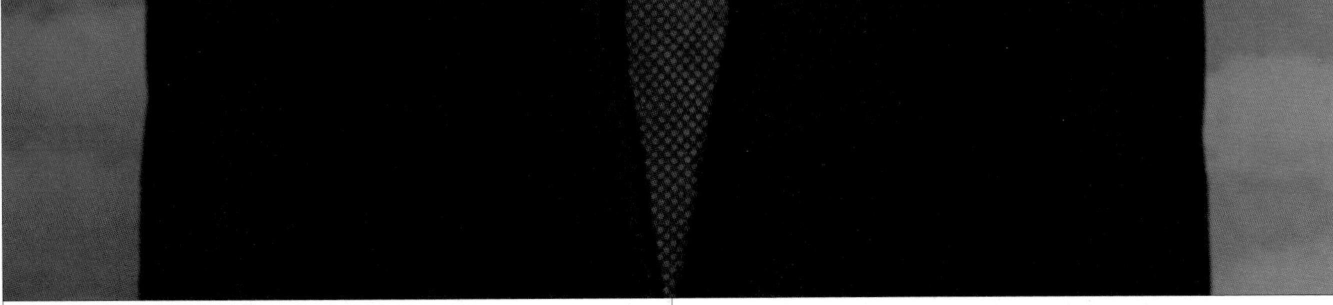

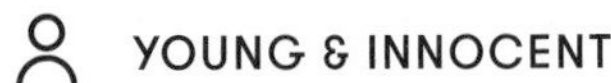

YOUNG & INNOCENT

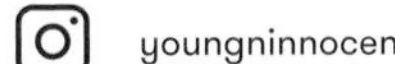

youngninnocent

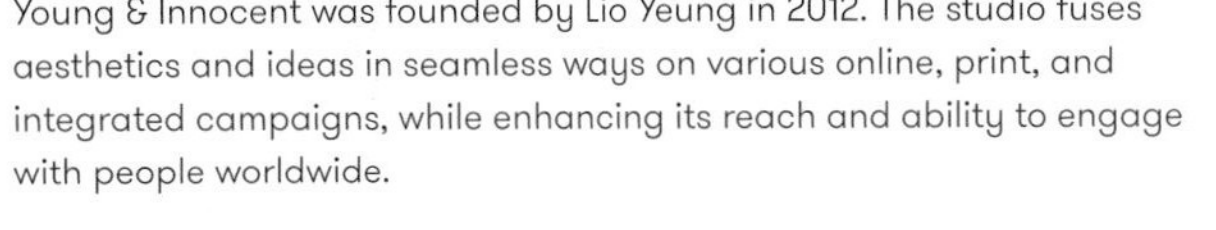

Young & Innocent was founded by Lio Yeung in 2012. The studio fuses aesthetics and ideas in seamless ways on various online, print, and integrated campaigns, while enhancing its reach and ability to engage with people worldwide.

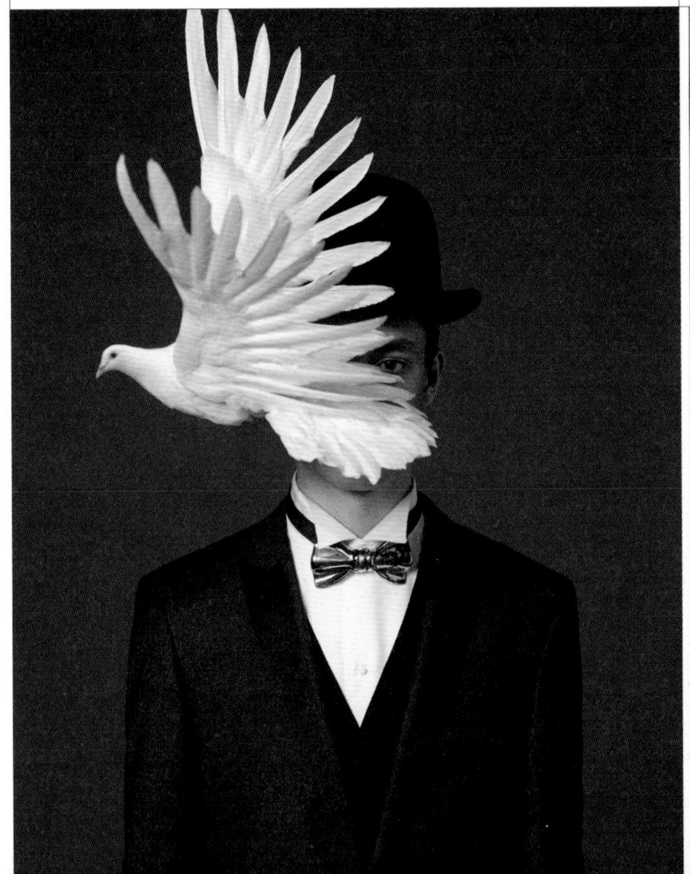

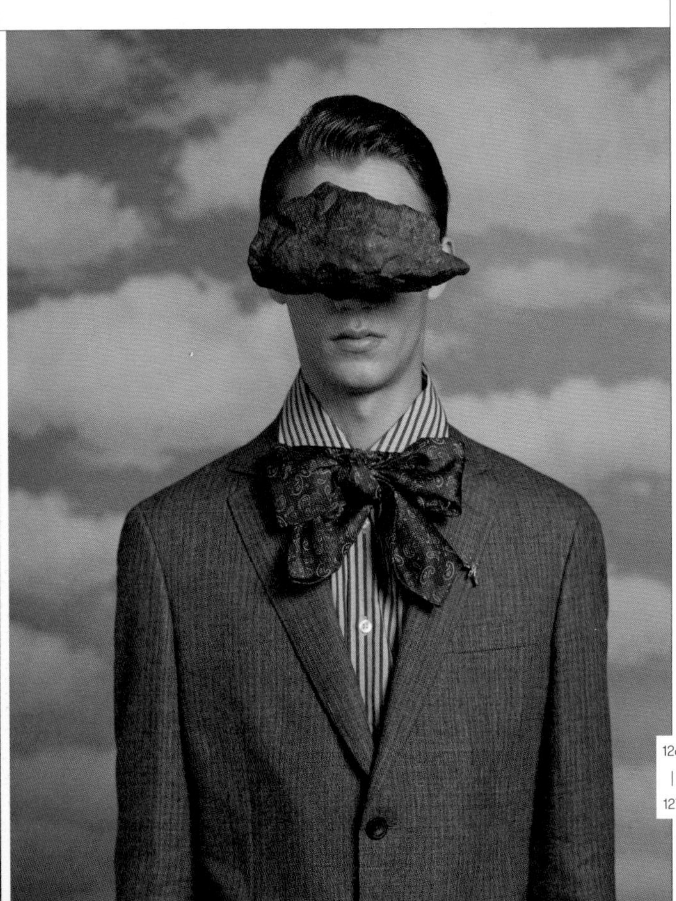

"The best photograph is often the outcome of great teamwork between the photographer, stylist, and make-up/hair artist with a polished idea or concept. None of them can work alone without each other."

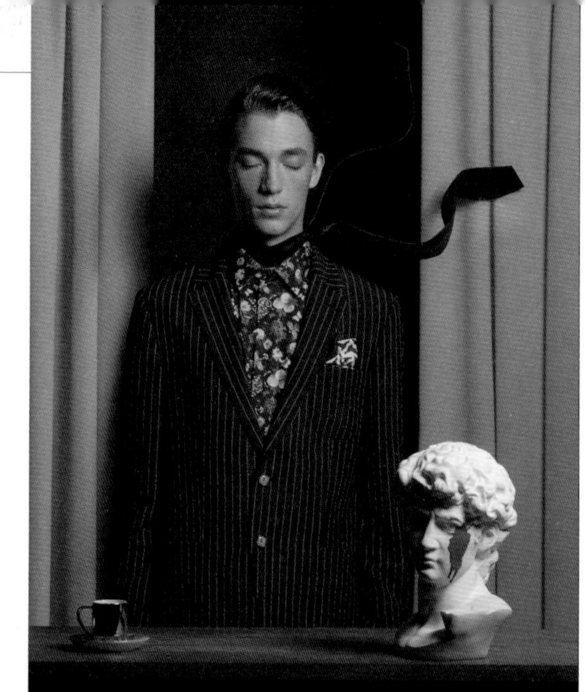

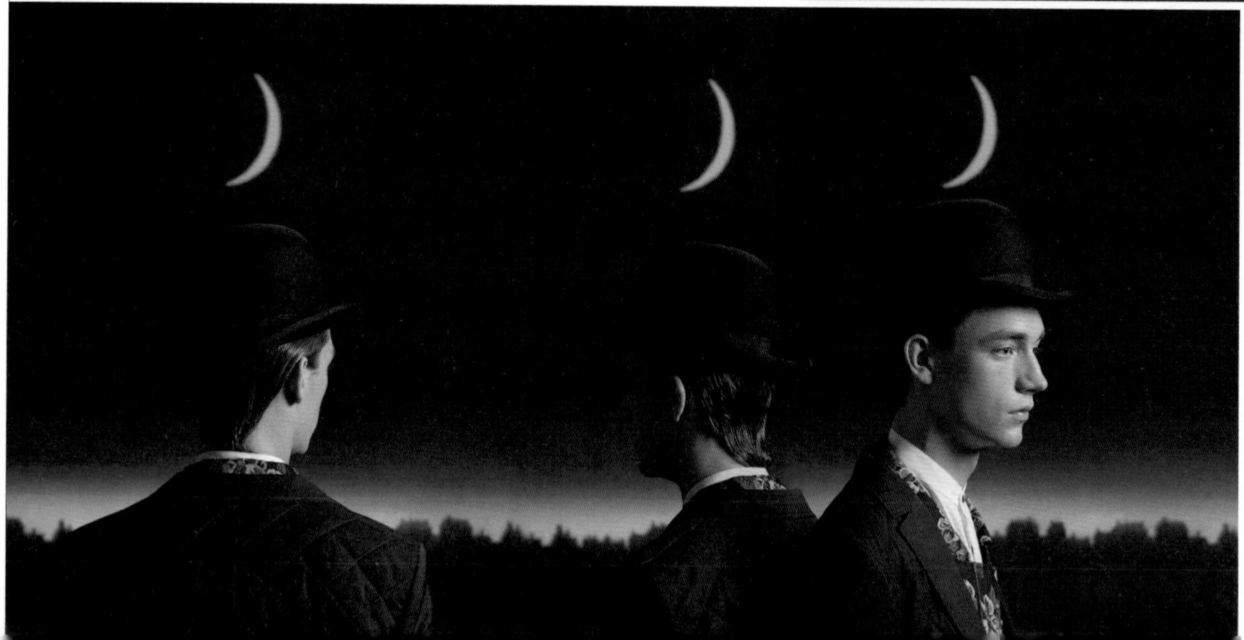

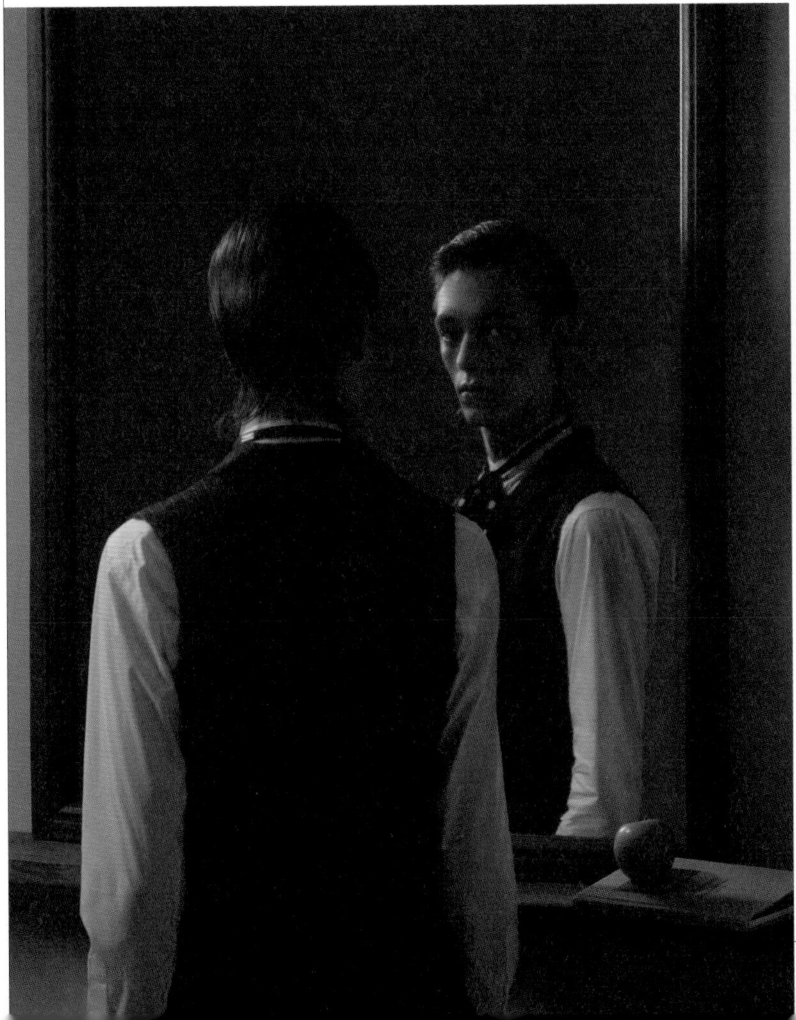

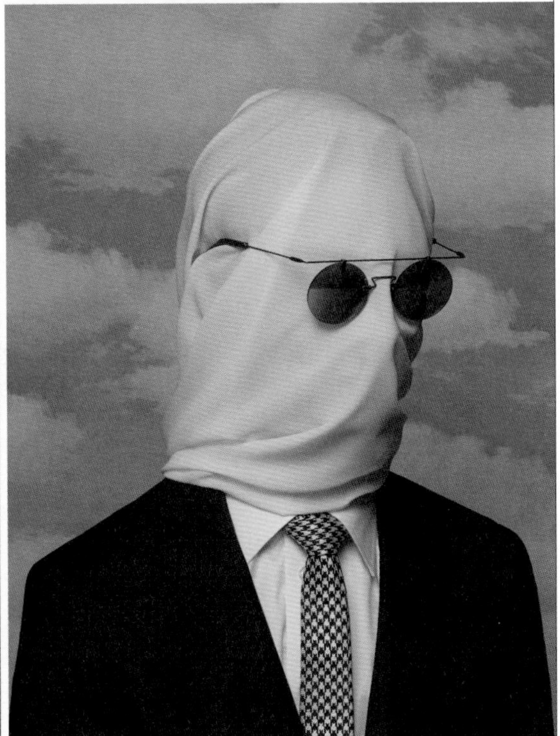

"We believe that a good photo can be everlasting, and overcome the passage of time."

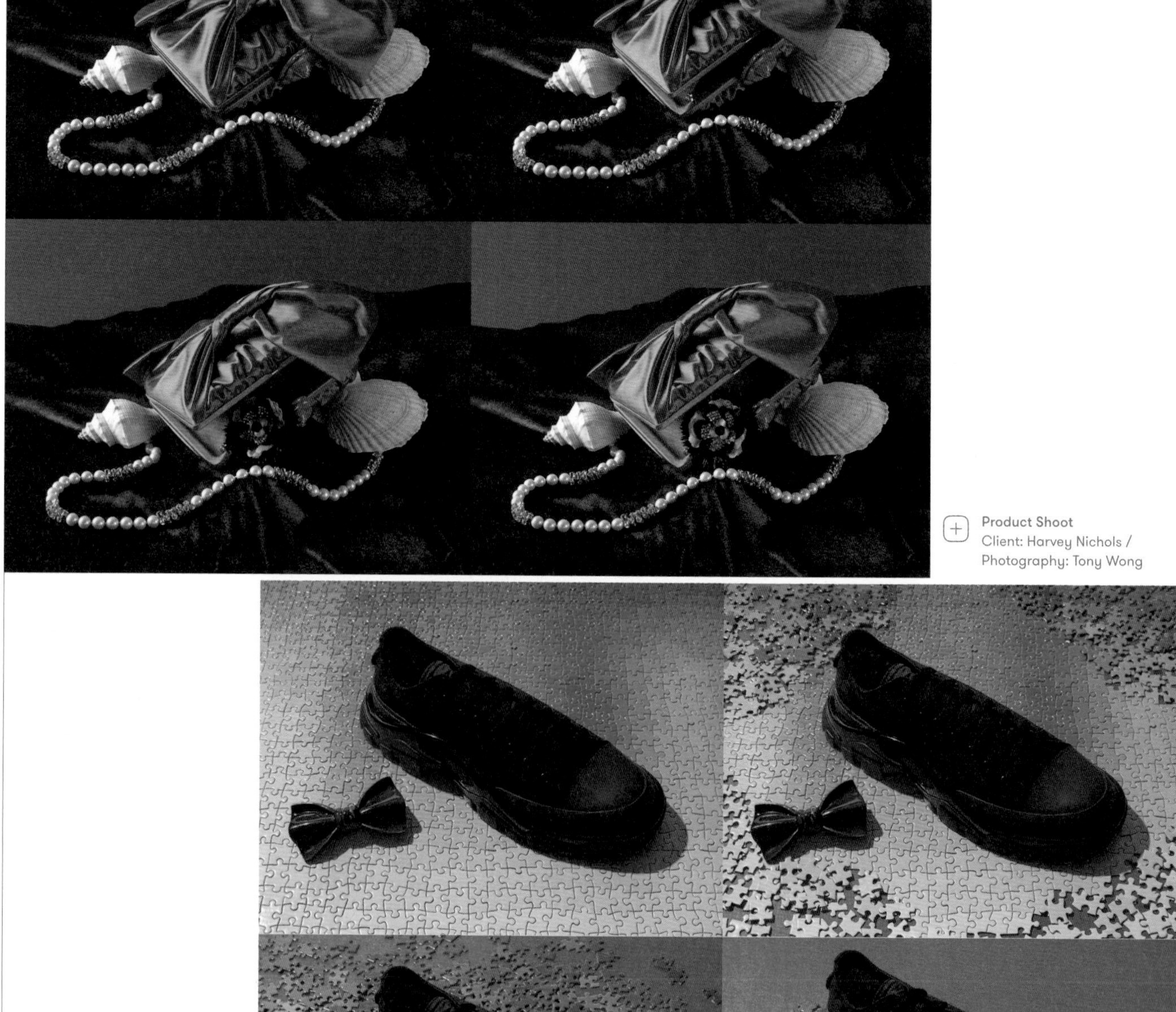

Product Shoot
Client: Harvey Nichols /
Photography: Tony Wong

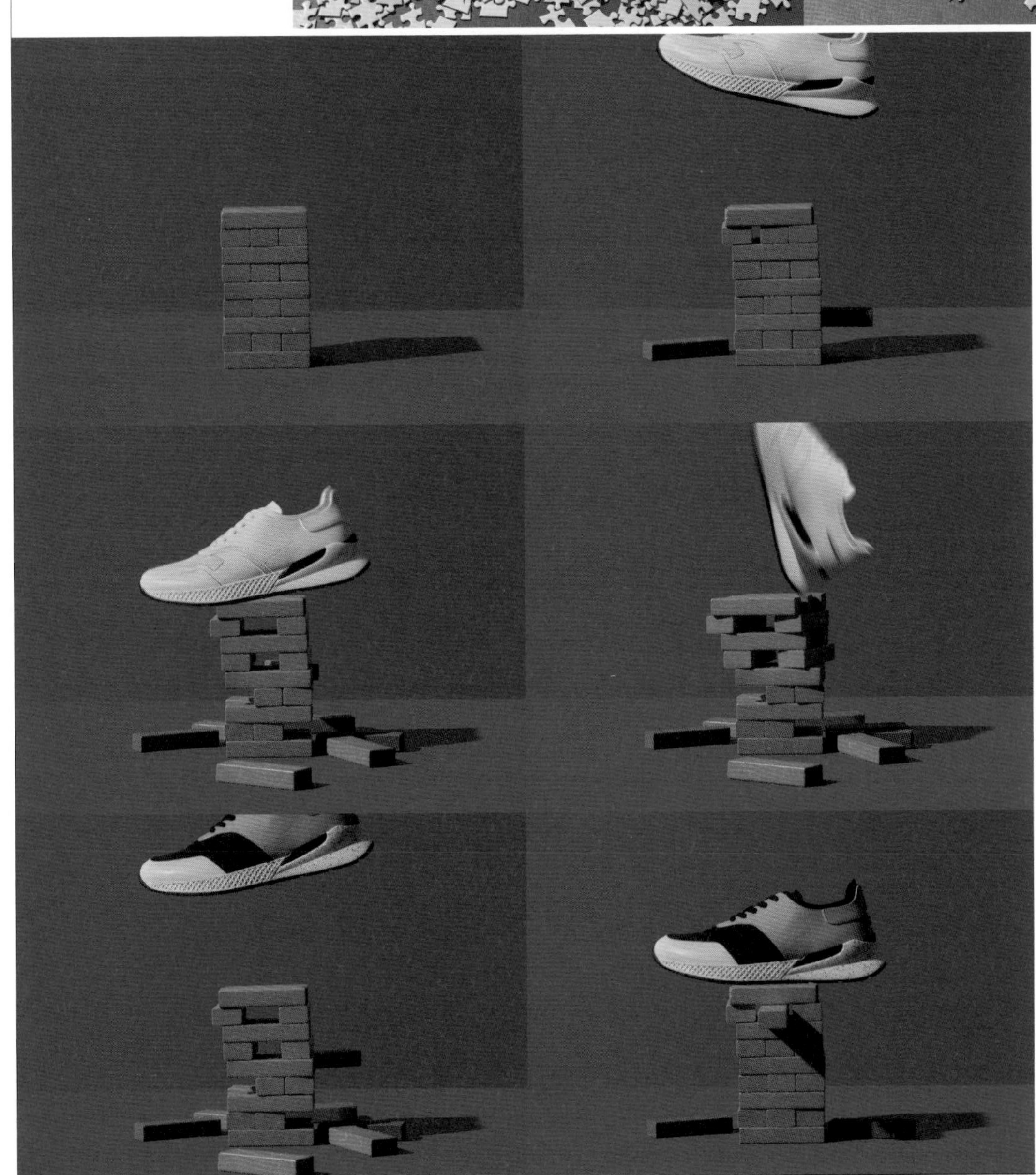

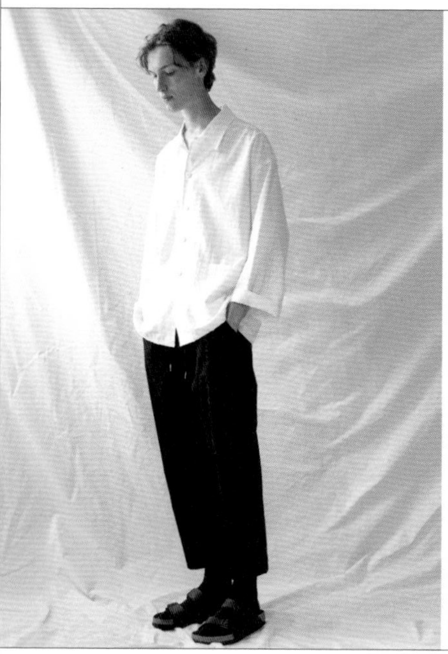

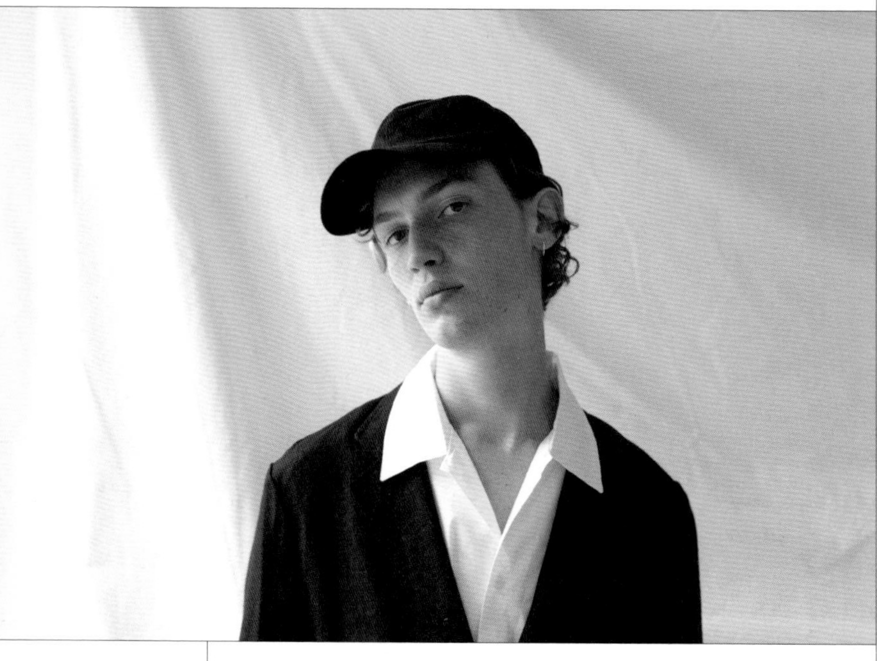

OLIVE CLOTHING

oliveclothing

Olive is a British contemporary clothing brand that combines heritage with modernity, simplicity with playfulness, as well as street style with understated elegance. It enjoys a vibrant, international customer community, and is sensitive to ethical considerations relating to the production process.

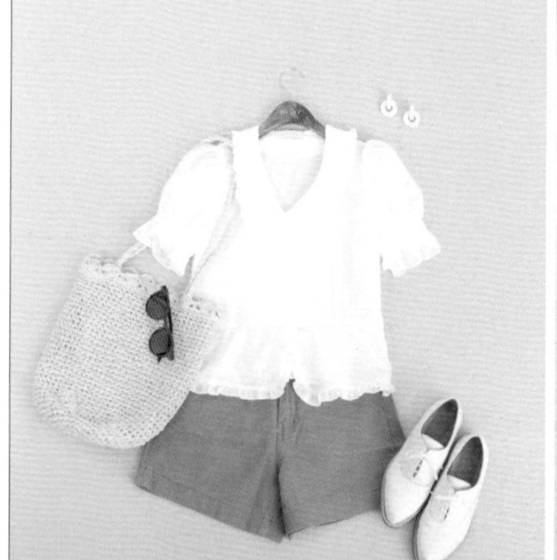

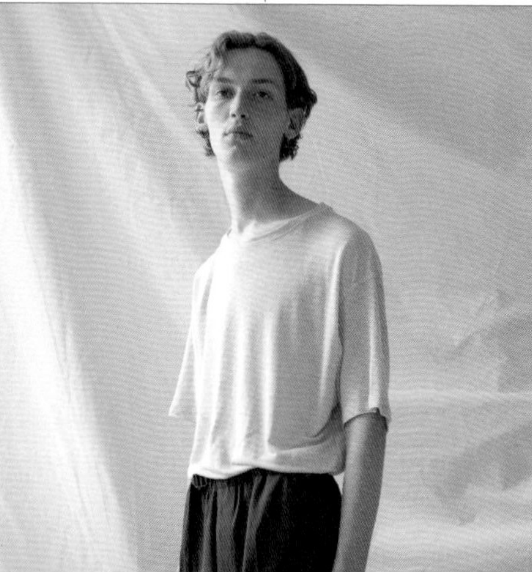

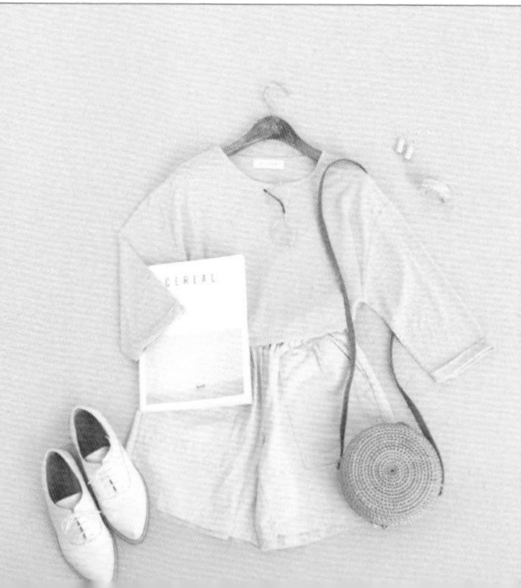

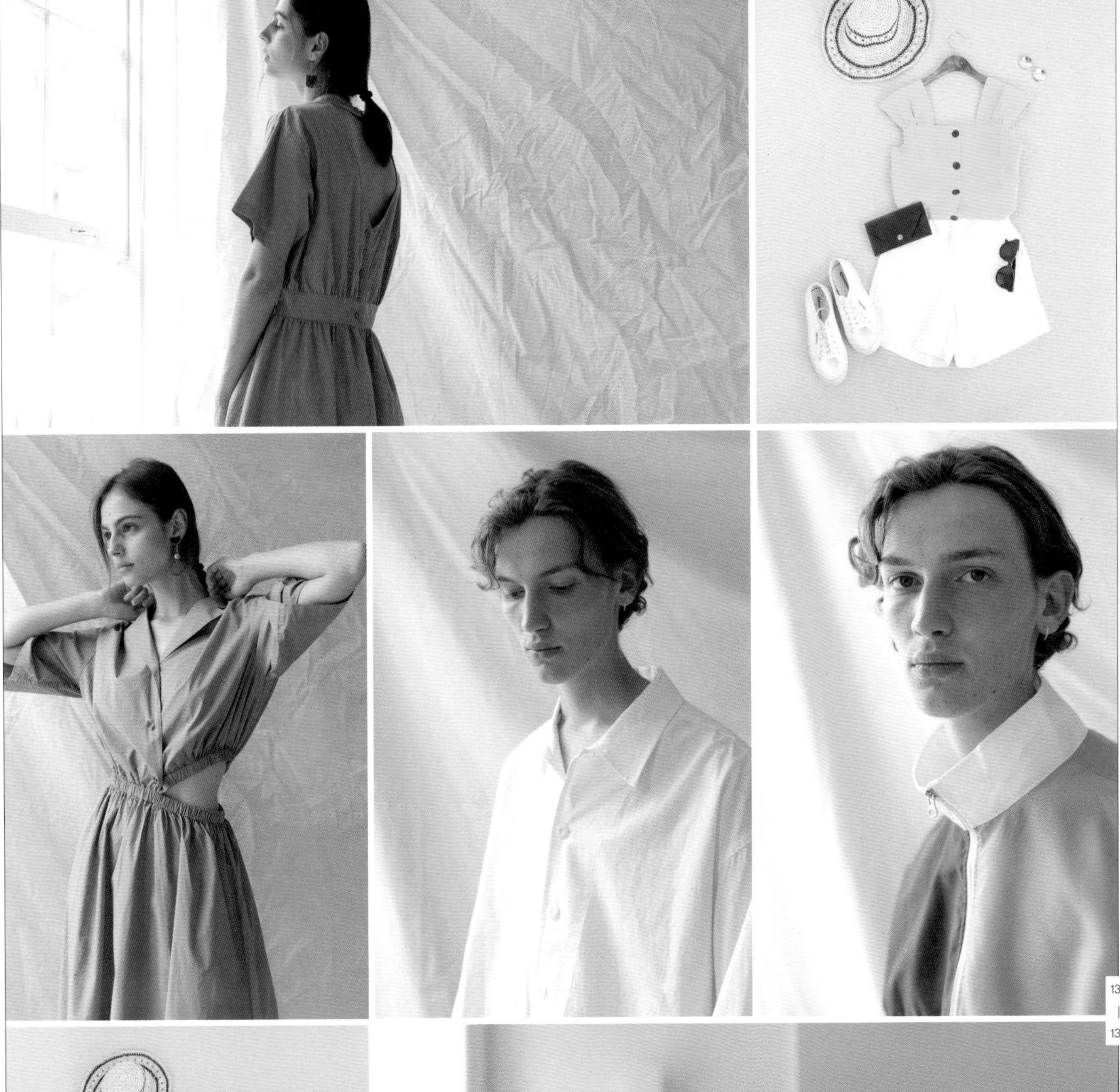

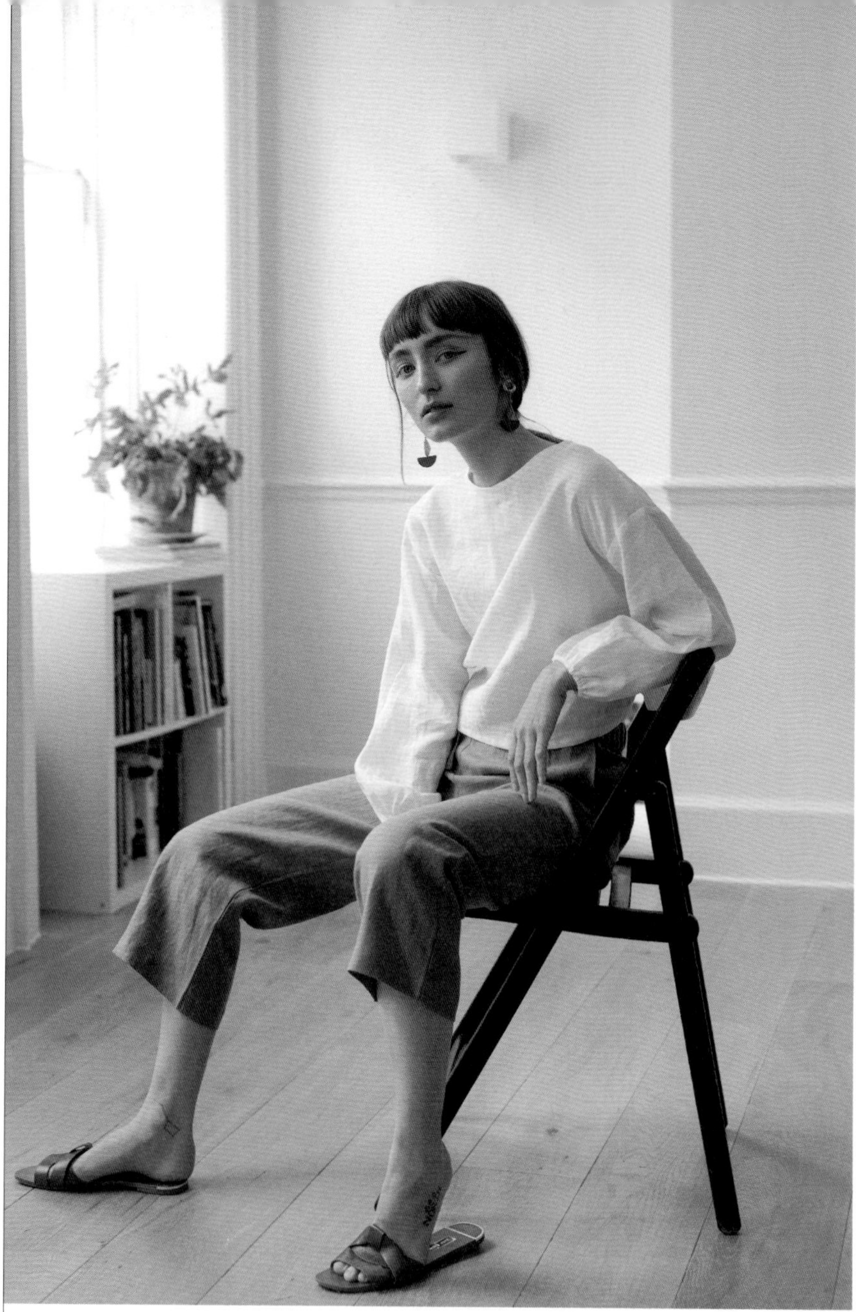

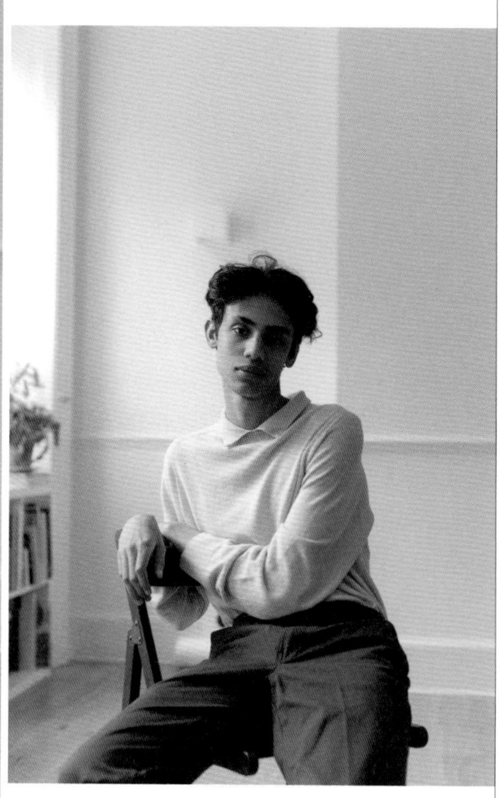

"We want to create the impression that our images extend beyond what the lens sees."

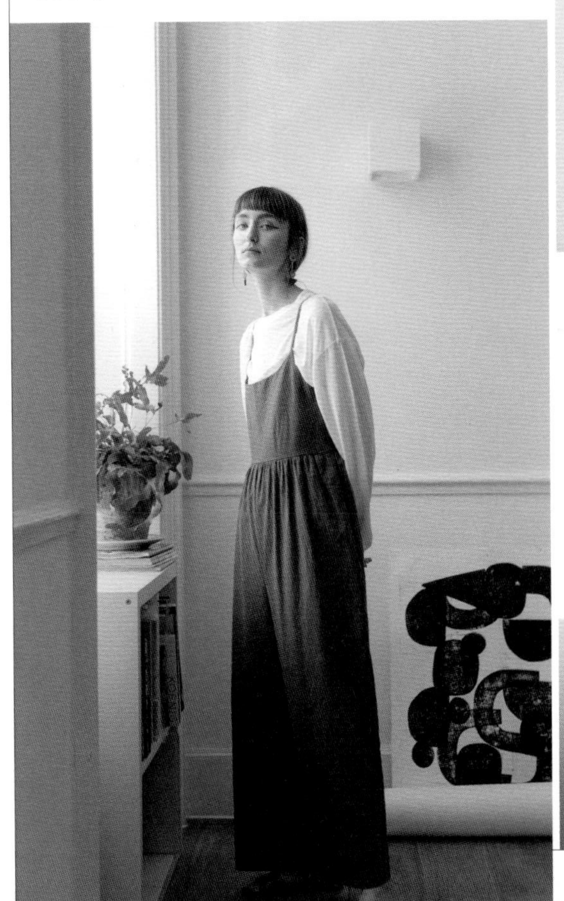

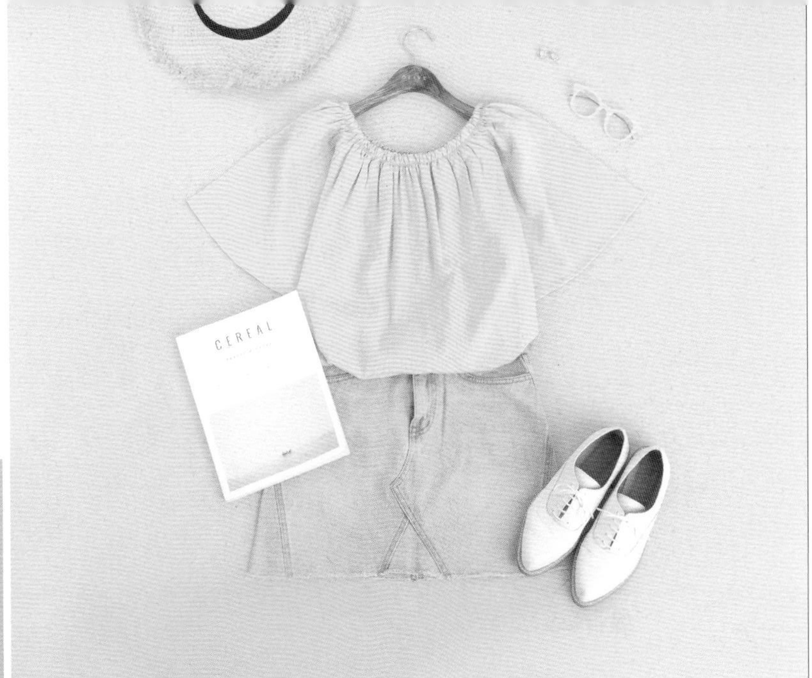

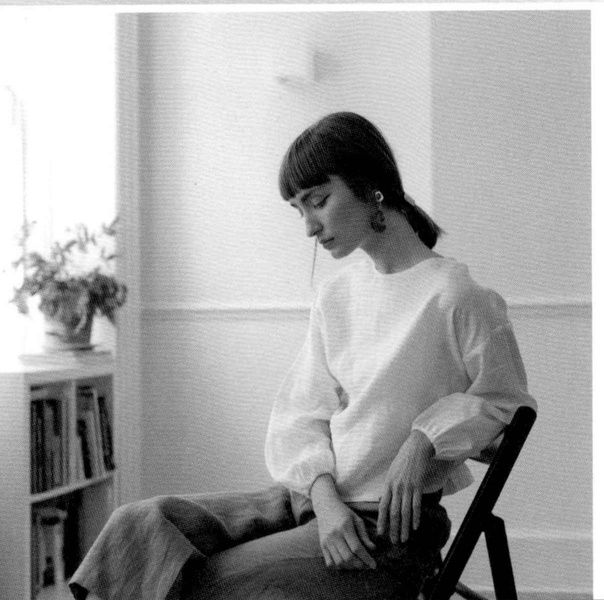

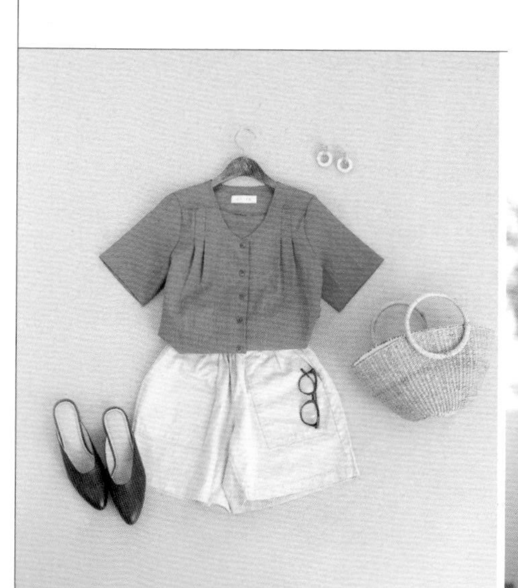
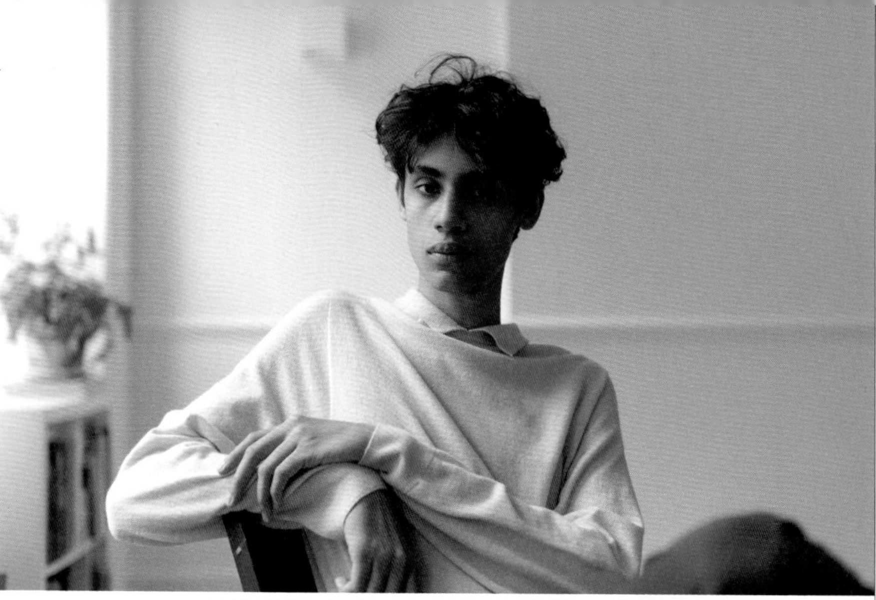
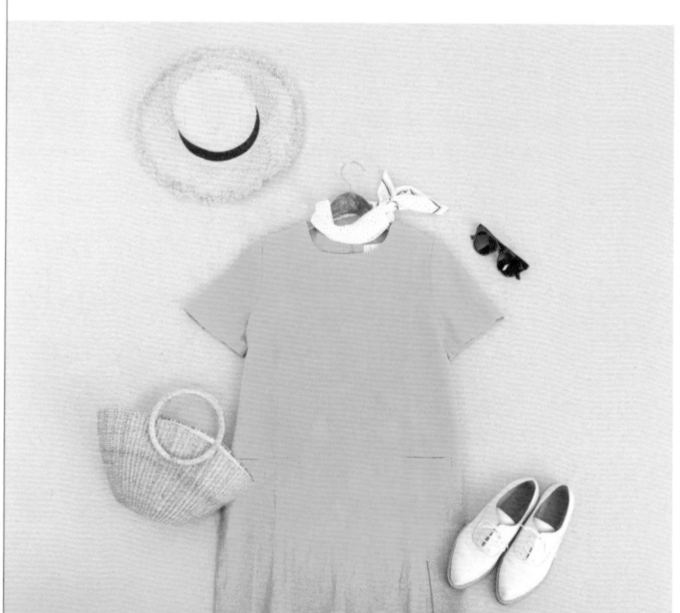
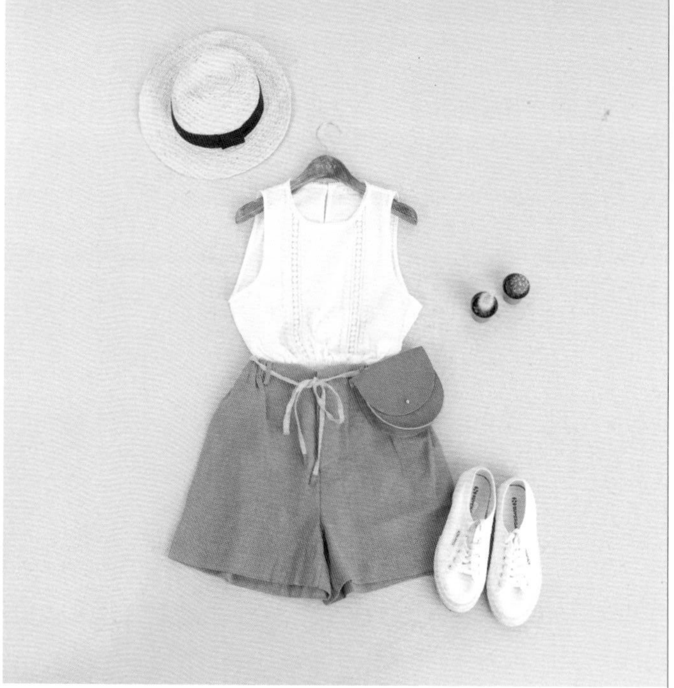

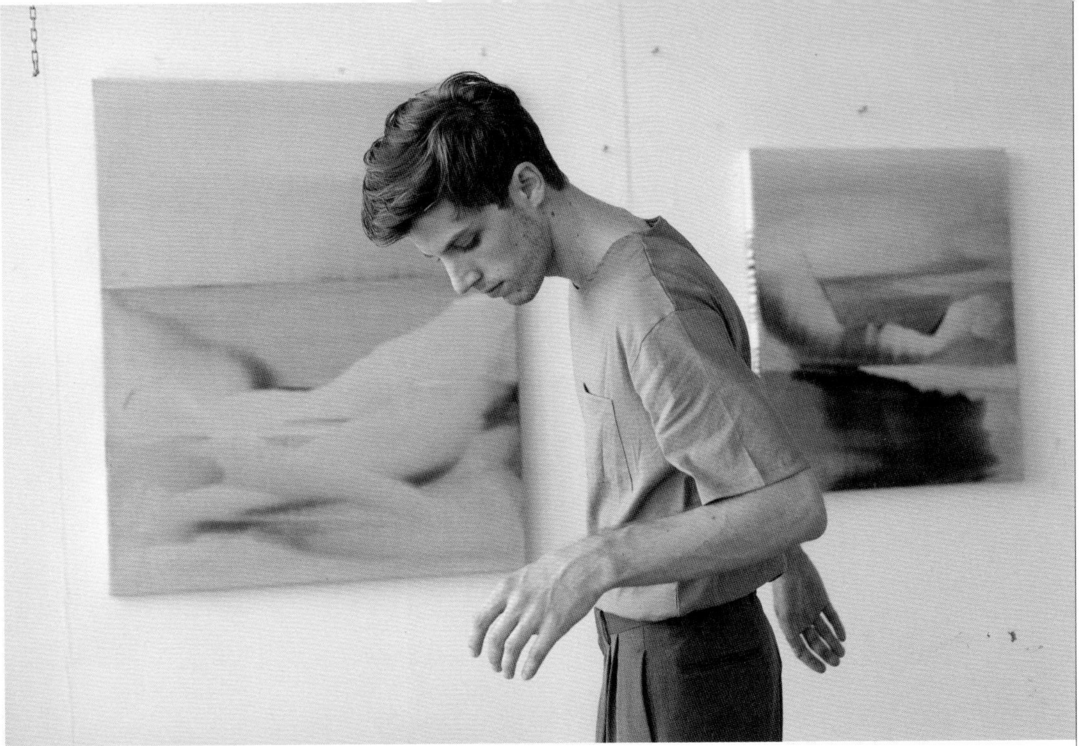

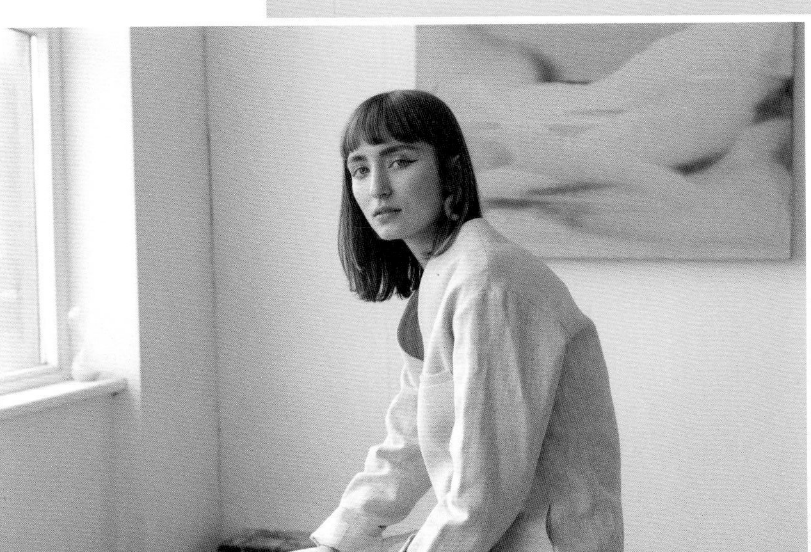

"Moments captured should feel open-ended, not finite – as if the models are in the midst of a conversation with us."

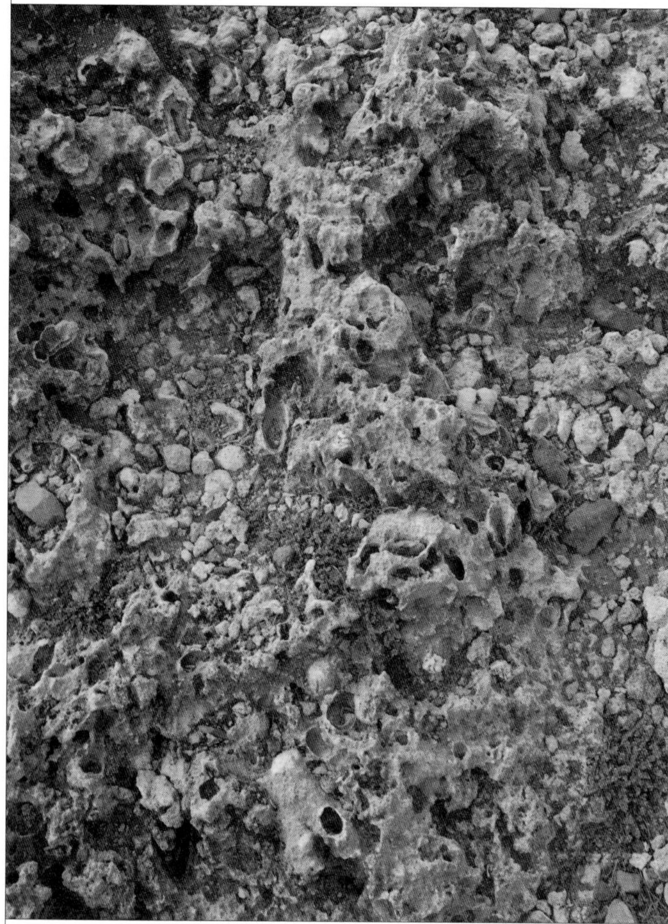

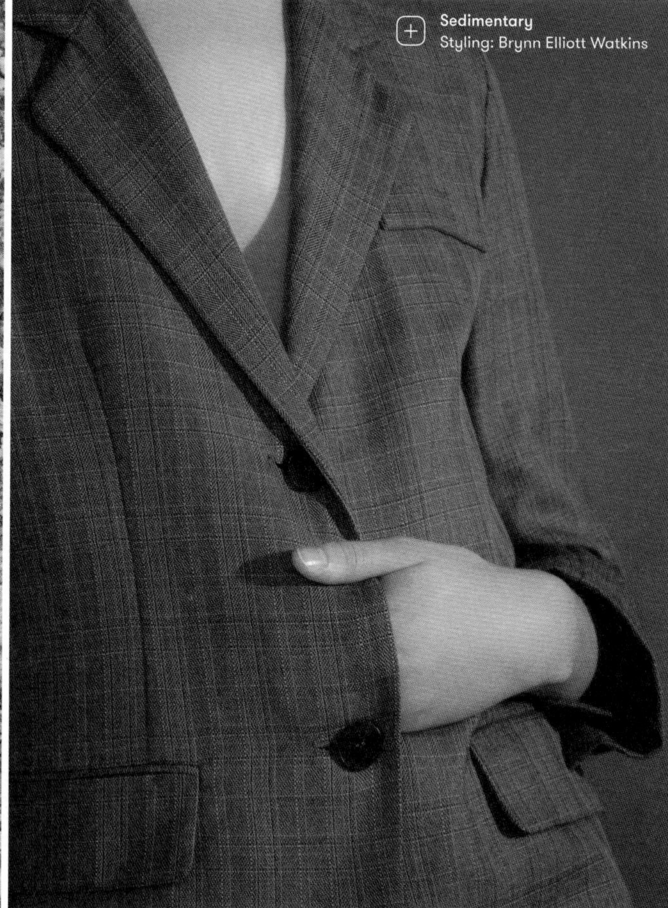

Sedimentary
Styling: Brynn Elliott Watkins

SHARON RADISCH

sharonradisch

Sharon Radisch is a New York-based photographer who specialises in still life, fashion, travel, and interiors. Although she currently lives in the USA, she has travelled extensively throughout Europe, South America, and Asia. In her past life, she worked in the medical research field with a Master's Degree in Biology.

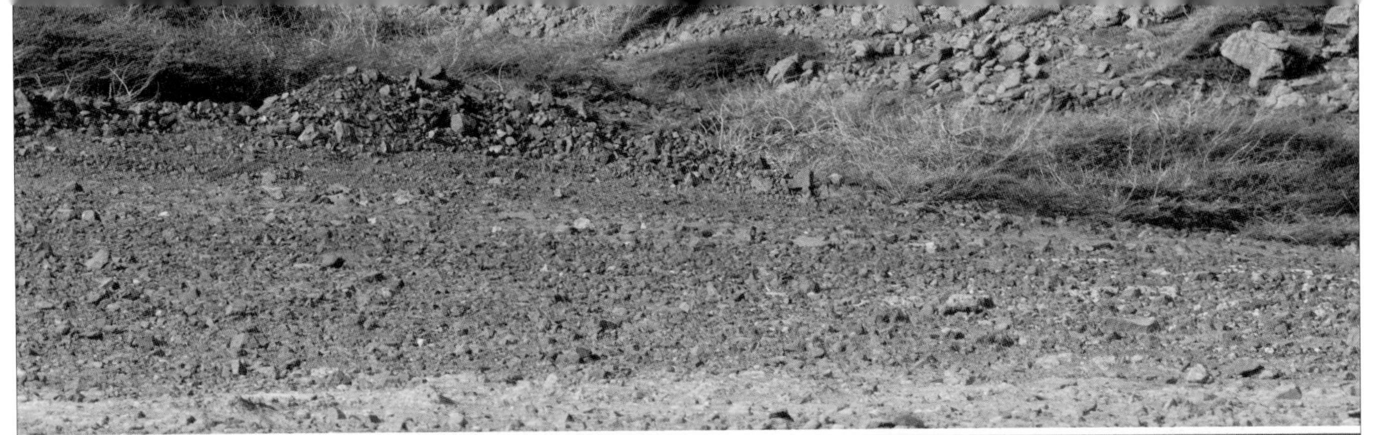

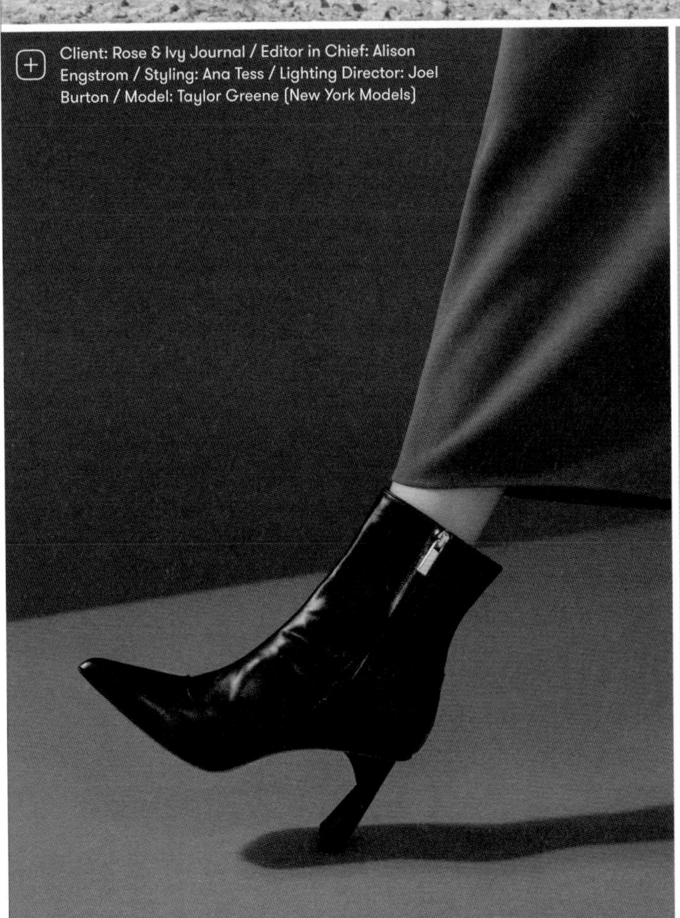

Client: Rose & Ivy Journal / Editor in Chief: Alison Engstrom / Styling: Ana Tess / Lighting Director: Joel Burton / Model: Taylor Greene (New York Models)

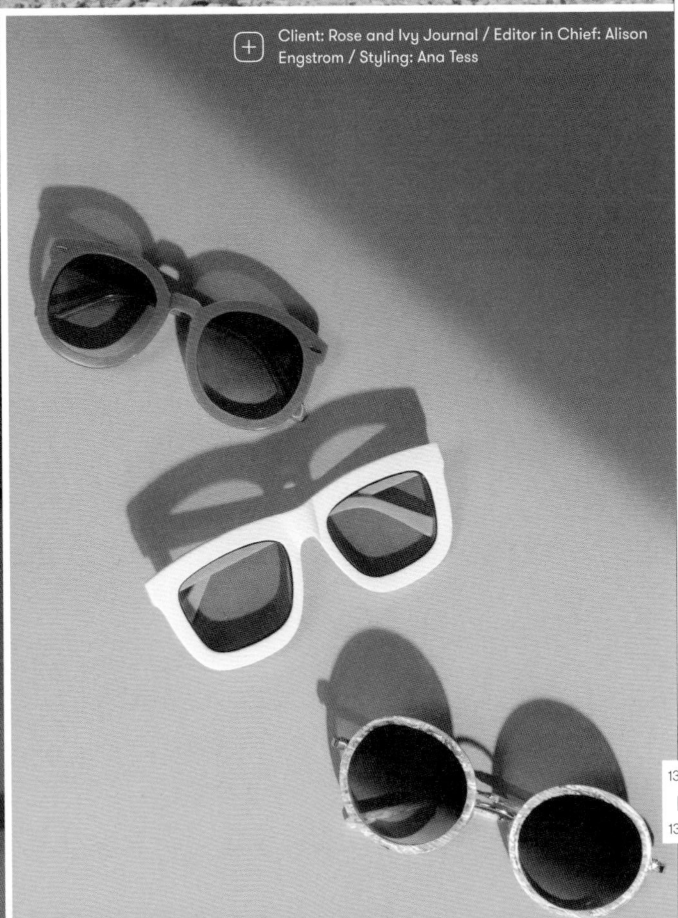

Client: Rose and Ivy Journal / Editor in Chief: Alison Engstrom / Styling: Ana Tess

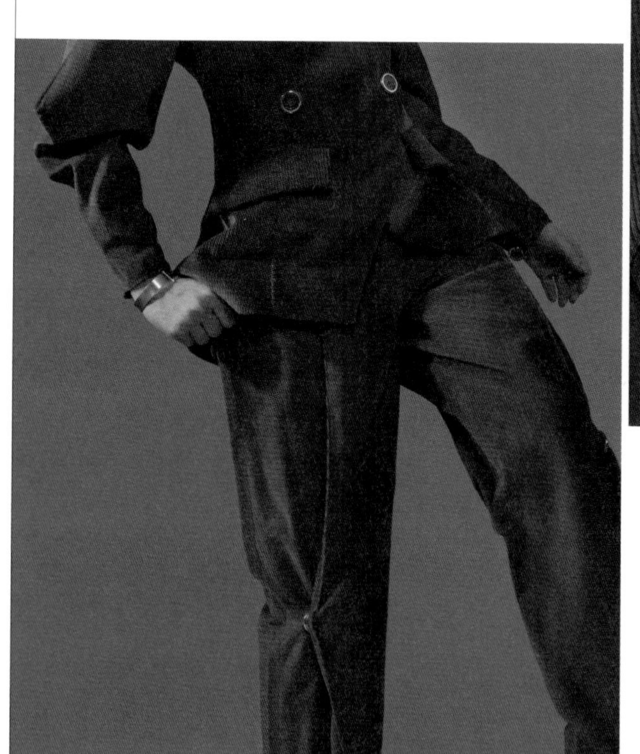

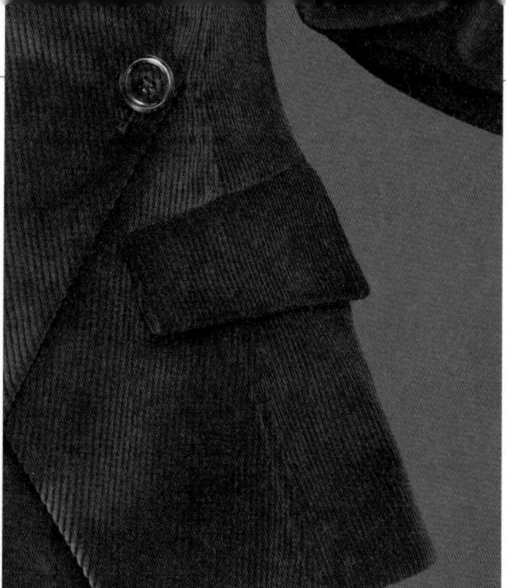

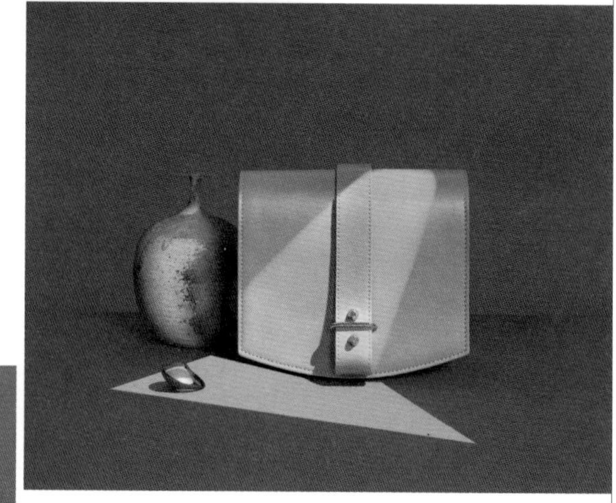

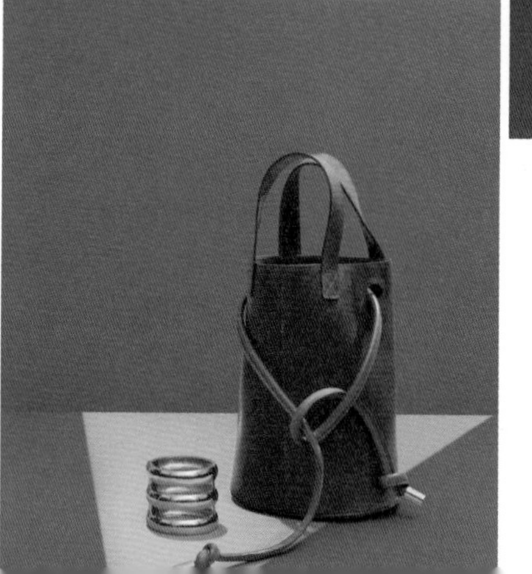

"With social media, there is only one chance, one image to tell the story."

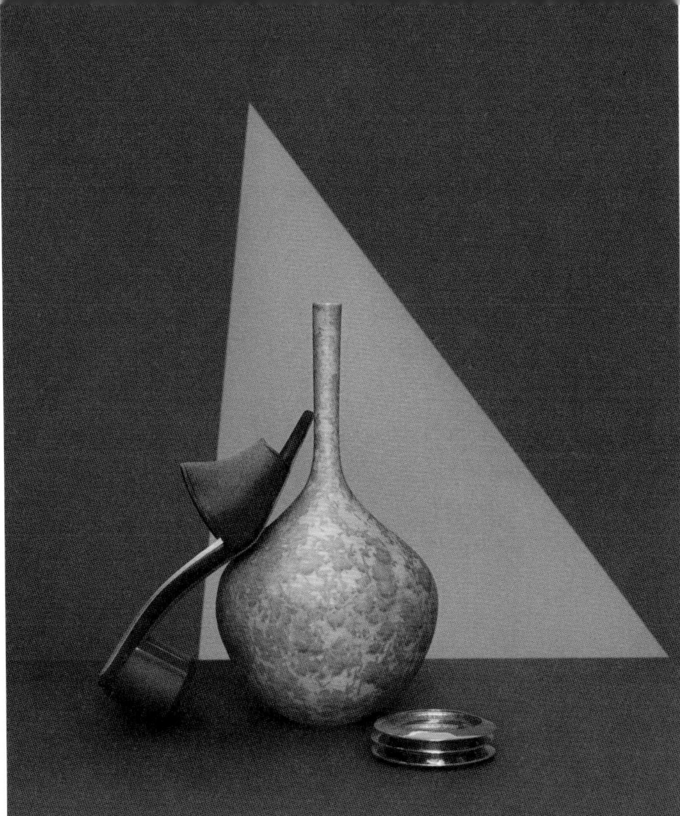

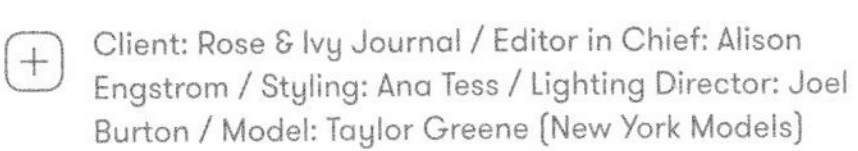

Client: Rose & Ivy Journal / Editor in Chief: Alison Engstrom / Styling: Ana Tess / Lighting Director: Joel Burton / Model: Taylor Greene (New York Models)

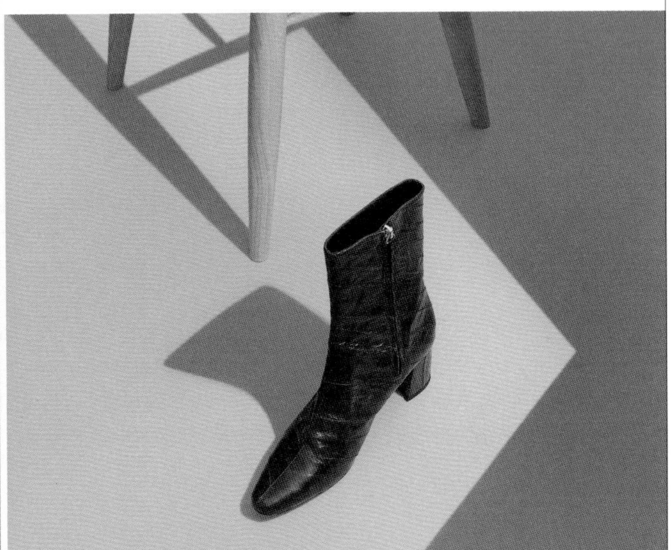

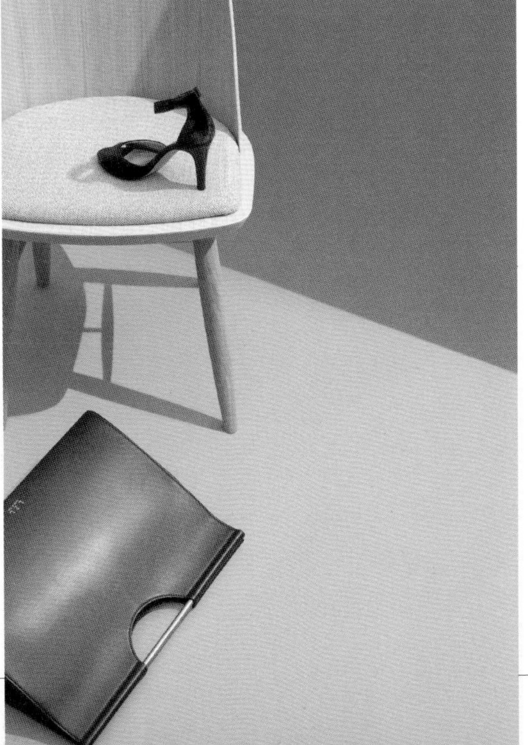

"Fashion photography on social media seems to be more about fashion as it represents a moment. It is more personal, relatable, and perhaps, even a bit more intimate."

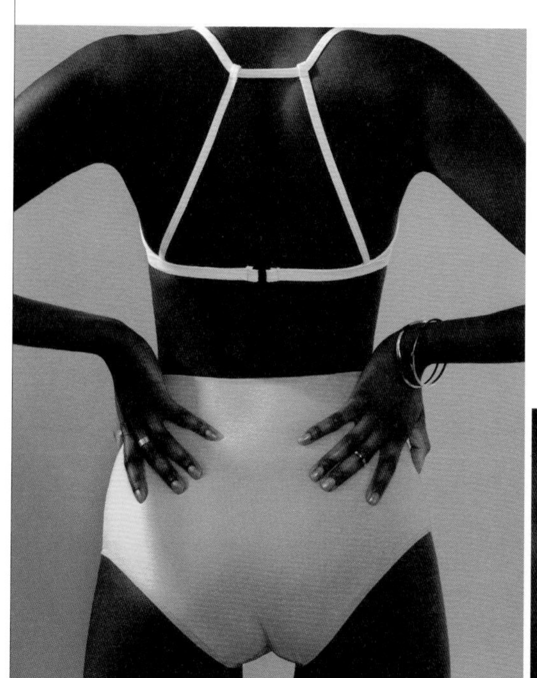

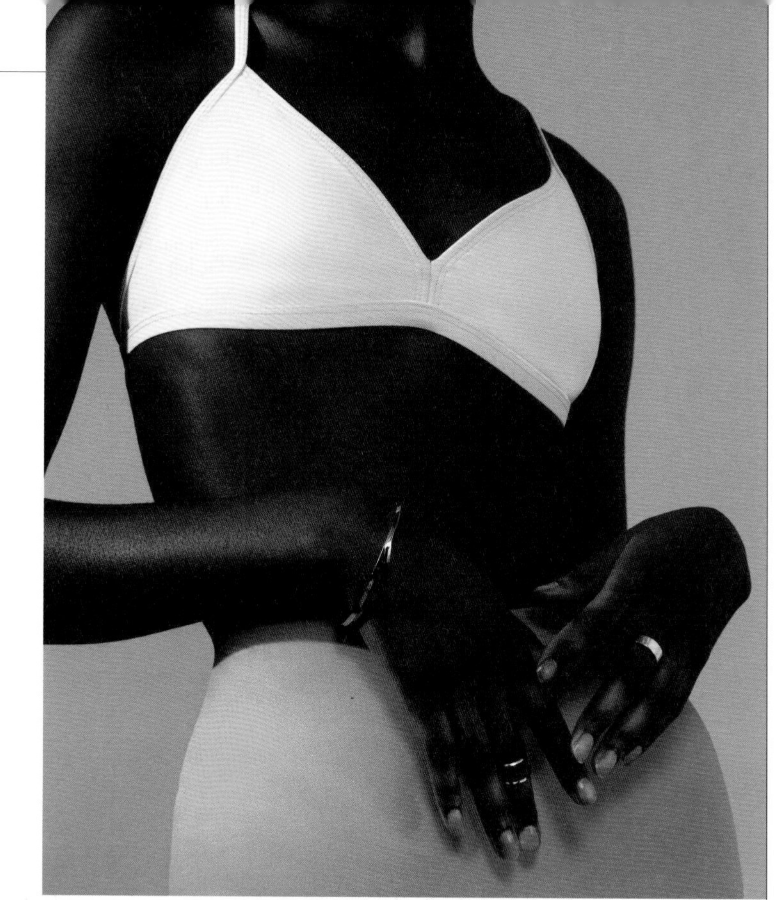

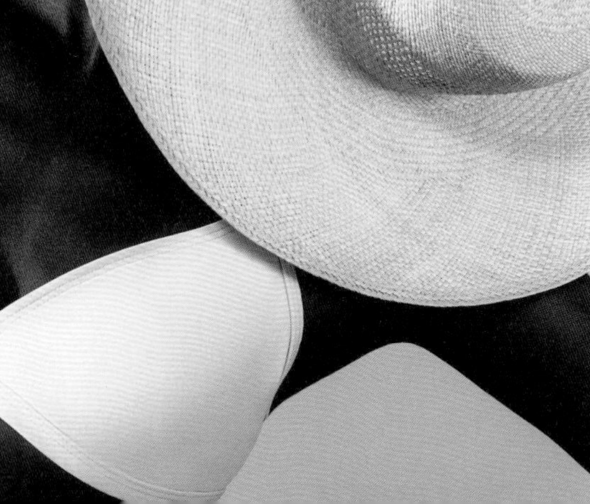

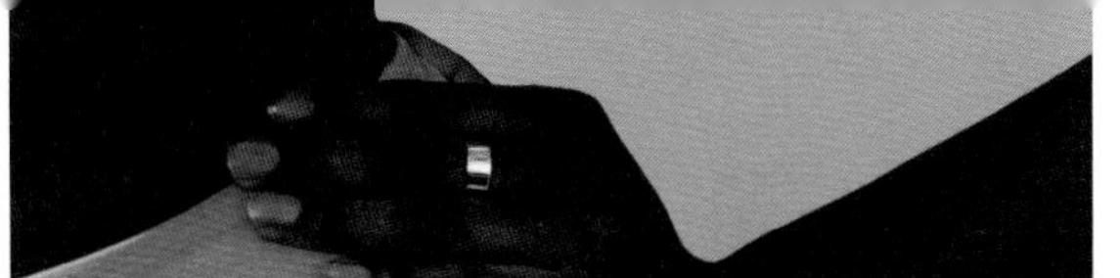

Client: Rose and Ivy Journal / Editor in Chief: Alison Engstrom / Styling: Ana Tess / Makeup & Hair: James Milligan (Rose and Ivy) / Model: Kayla Clark (Marilyn Agency)

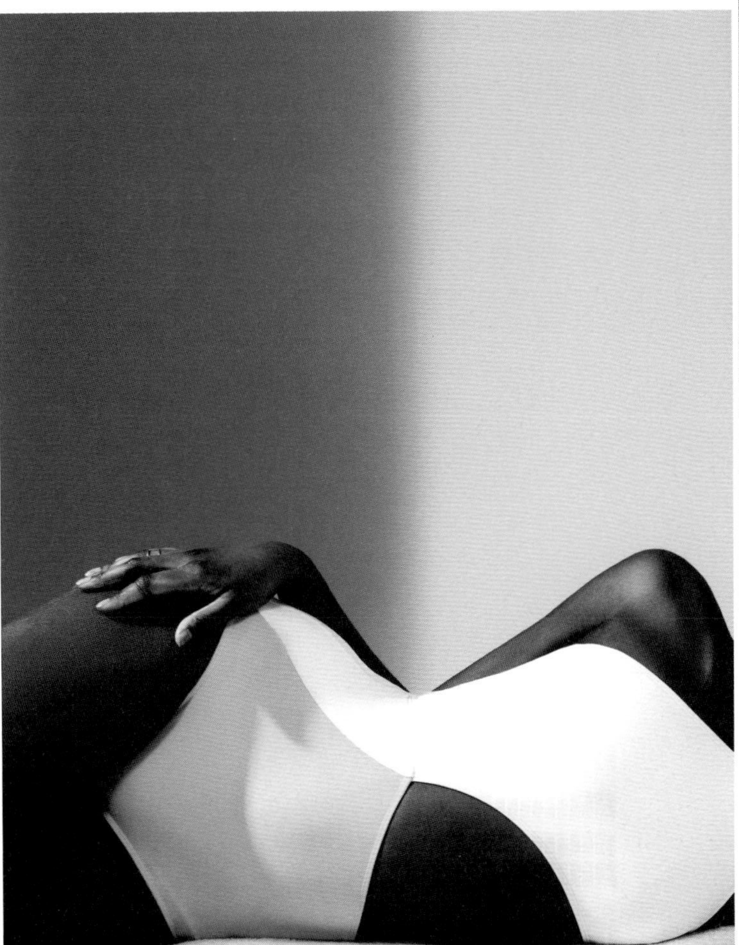

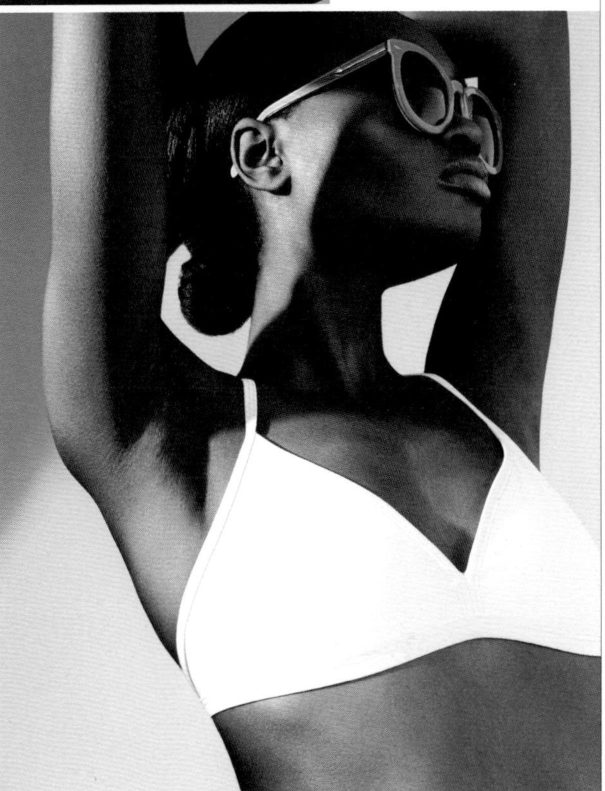

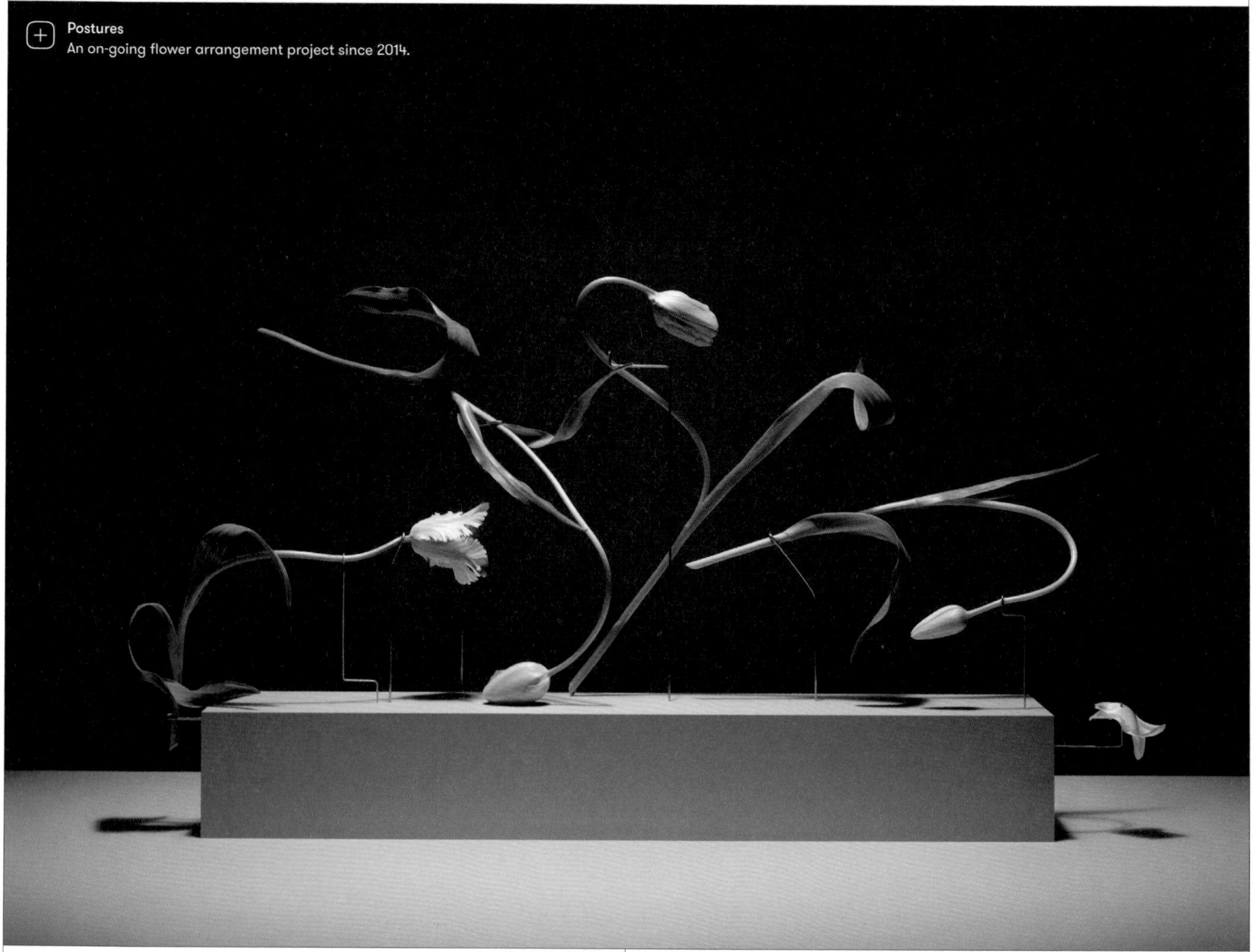

Postures
An on-going flower arrangement project since 2014.

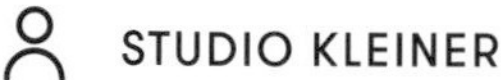

STUDIO KLEINER

carlkleiner

Carl Kleiner is a Swedish image maker who often works in close collaboration with his wife, Evelina. They photograph still life, portraits, as well as fashion and lifestyle products. Their visual language is playful and imaginative, where they often tell stories through colour, geometry, composition, and their sets.

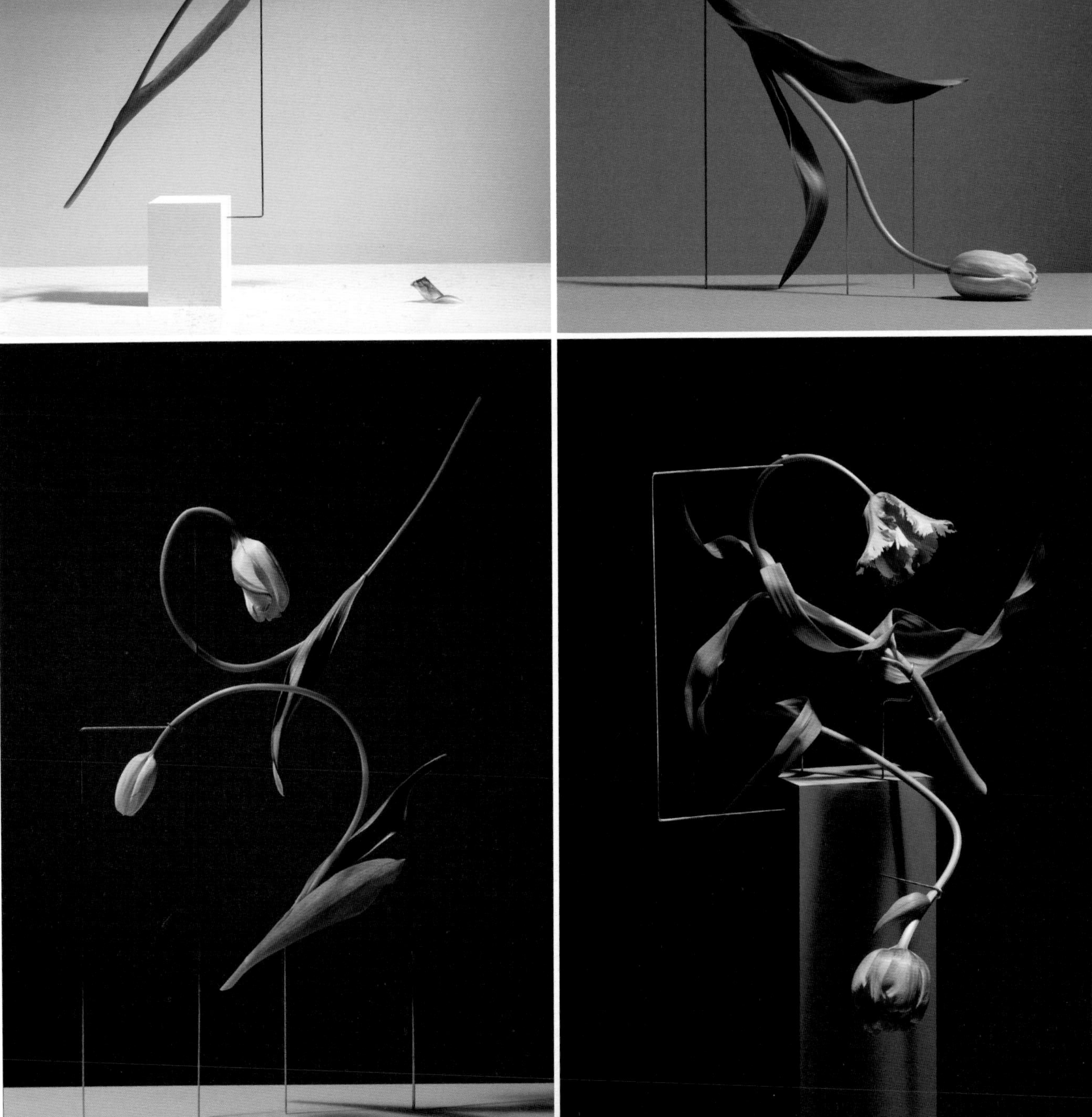

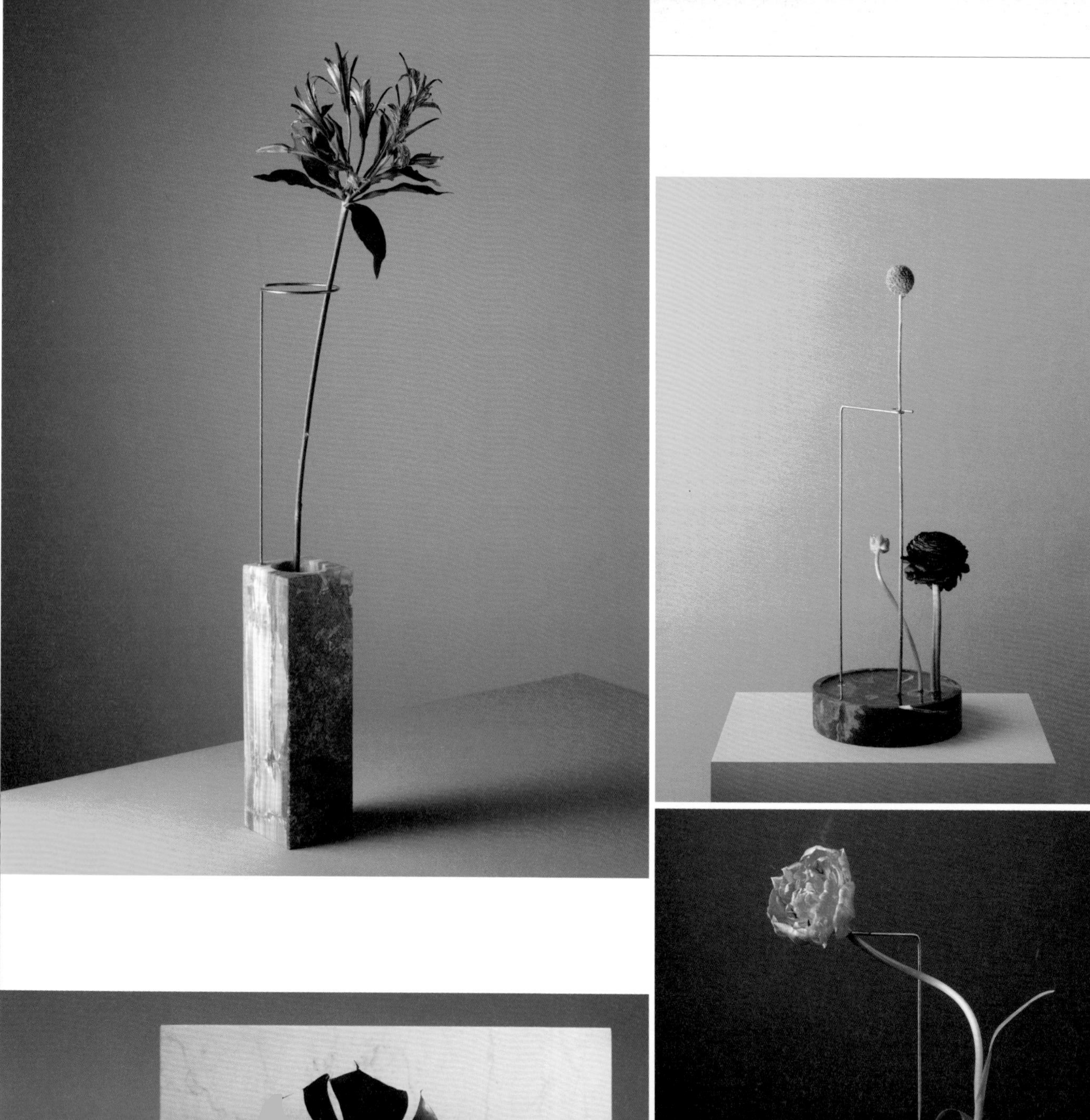

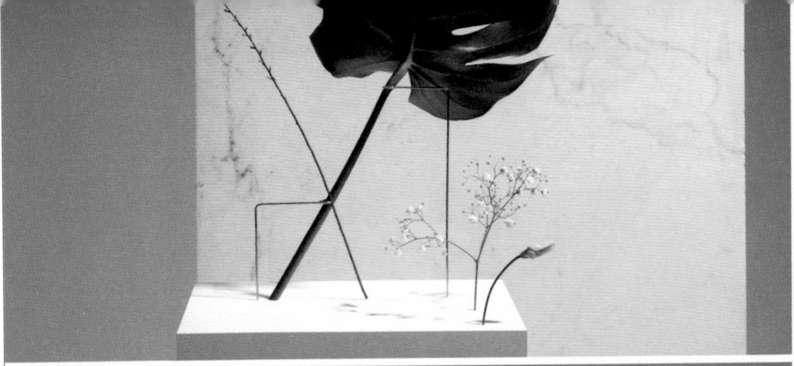

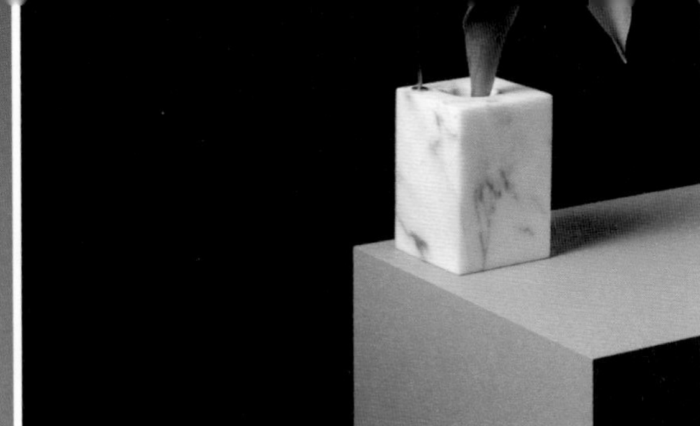

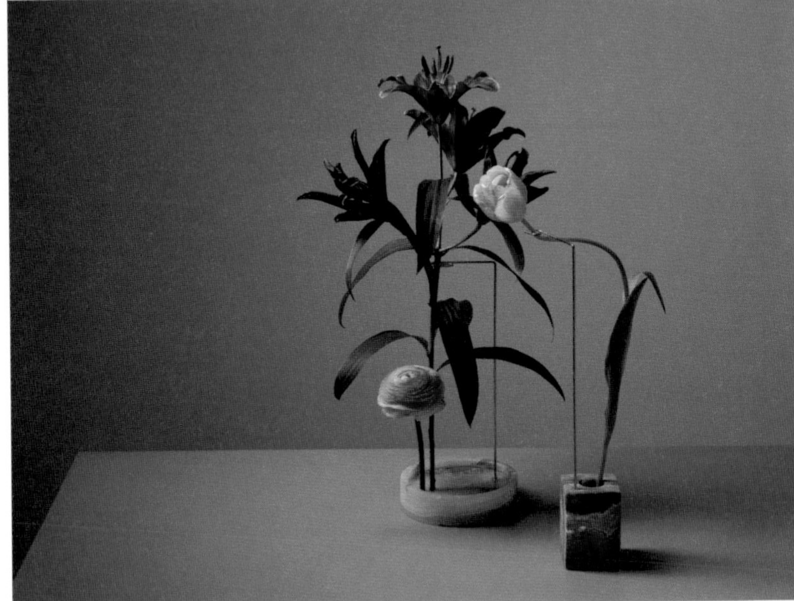

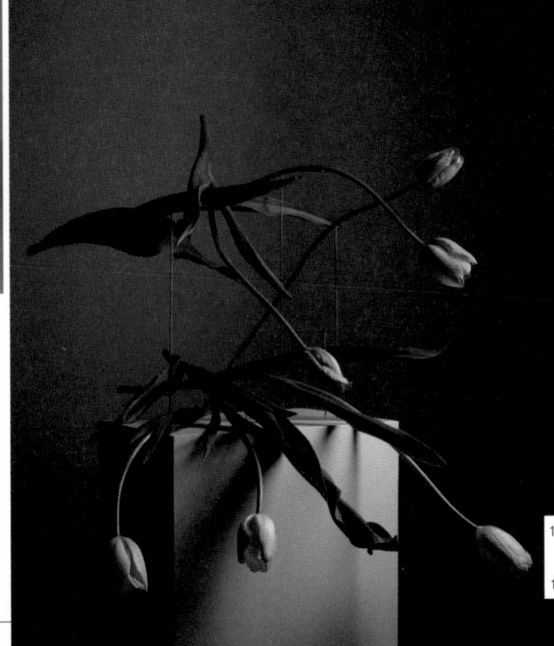

1-3, 5. **Postures Vases**
A 2017 project inspired by Studio Kleiner's 2014 'Postures' series.

Client & Collaborative Partner: Bloc Studios

4, 6. **Postures**
A series that explores the complexities of working with flowers.

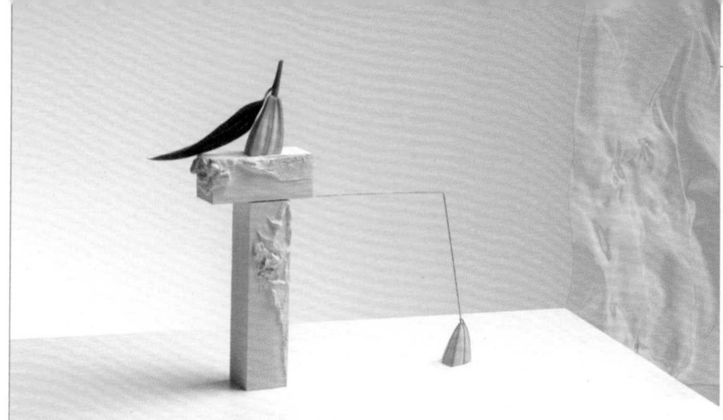

"Inspiration can come from anything. I find most of my ideas grasping for attention when I shower in the morning."

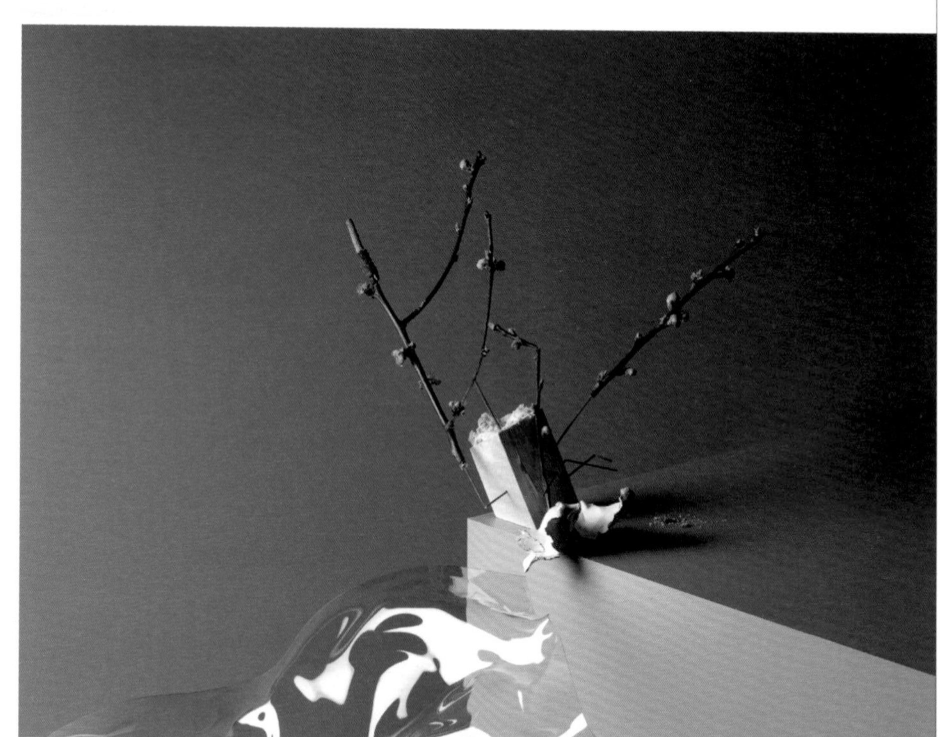

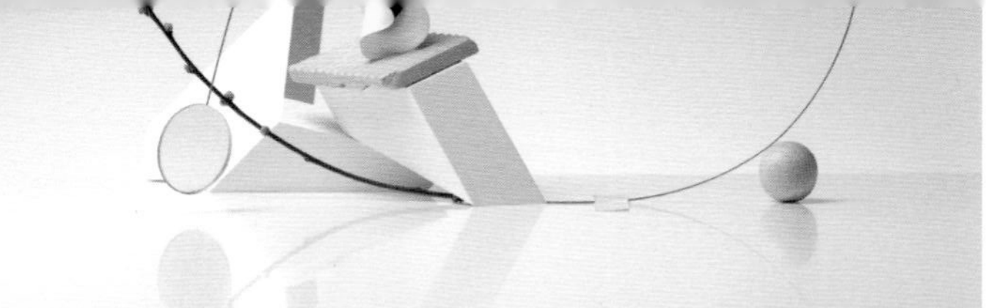

Studies From Spring
A 2014 project encompassing an abstract study of spring.

Collaborative Partner: Andrew Stellitano

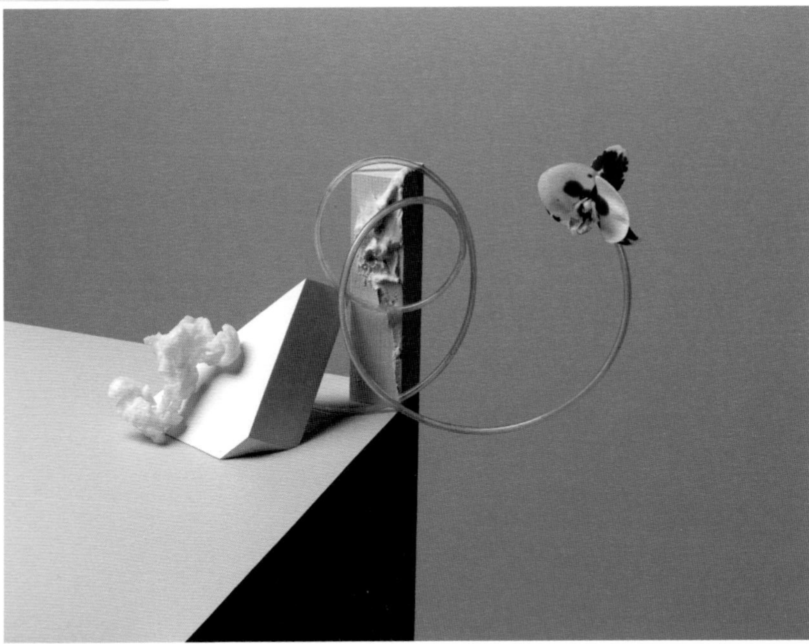

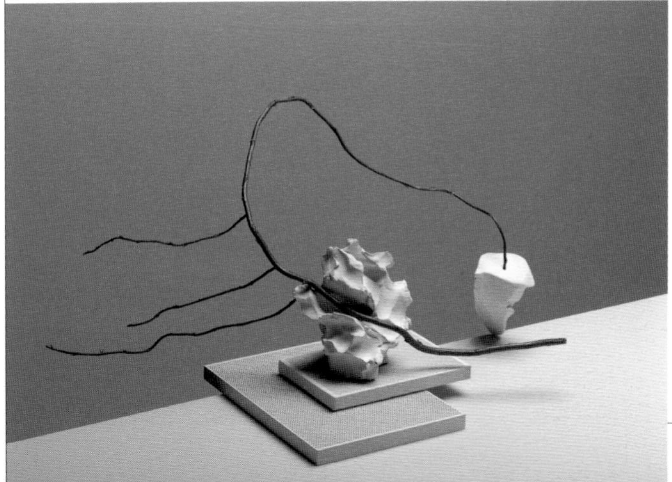

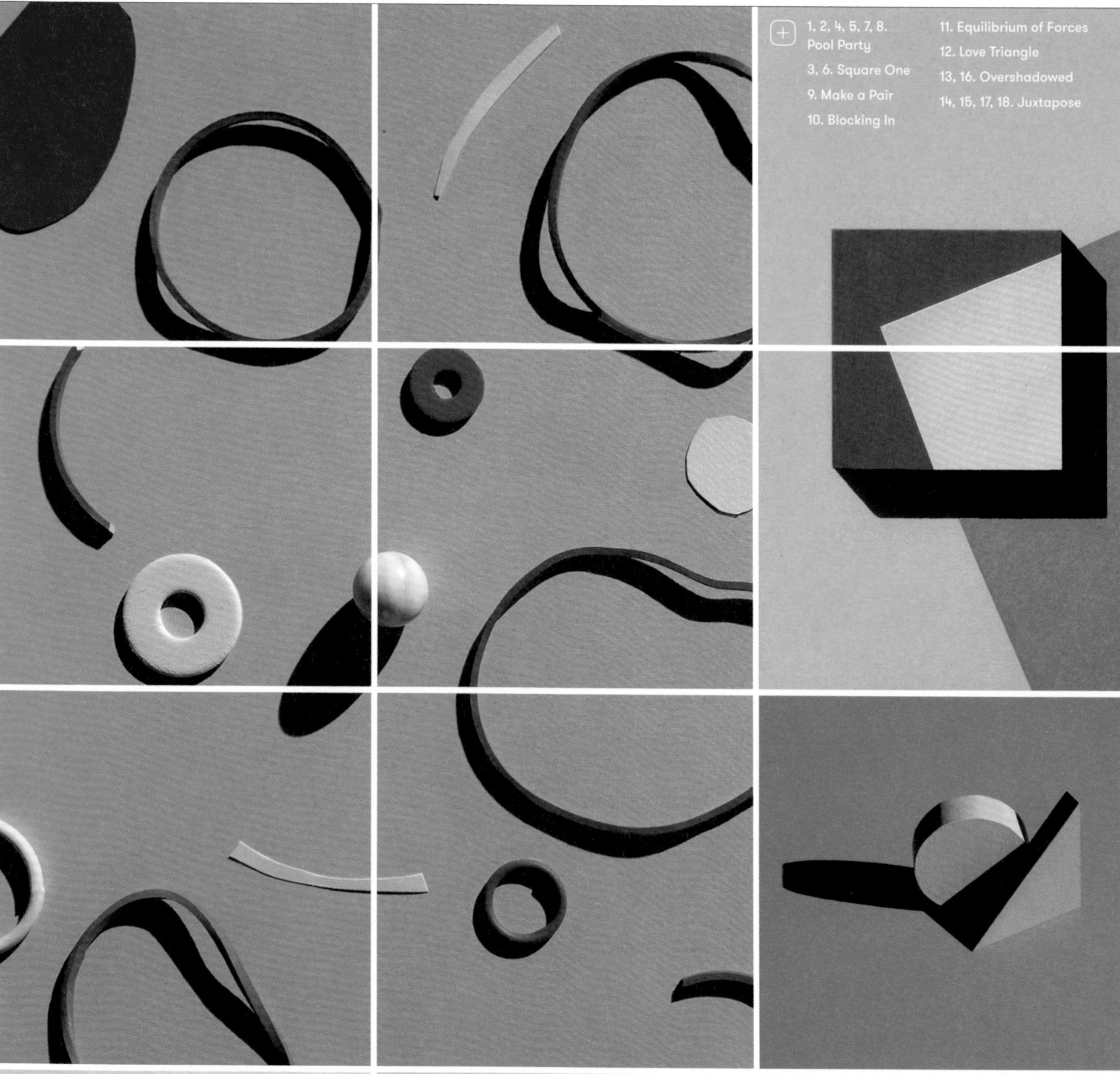

1, 2, 4, 5, 7, 8. Pool Party
3, 6. Square One
9. Make a Pair
10. Blocking In
11. Equilibrium of Forces
12. Love Triangle
13, 16. Overshadowed
14, 15, 17, 18. Juxtapose

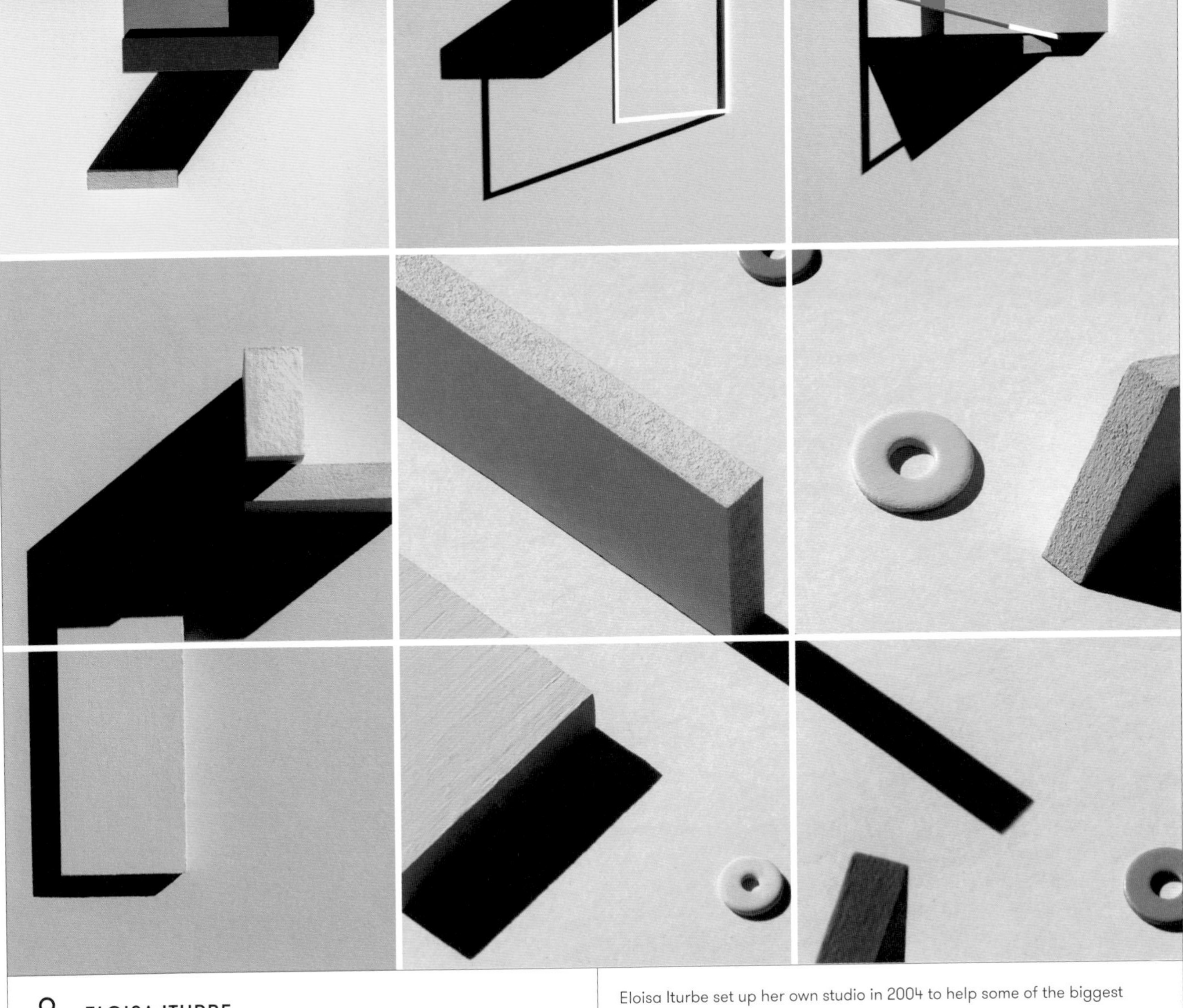

ELOISA ITURBE

elo_____

Eloisa Iturbe set up her own studio in 2004 to help some of the biggest TV networks worldwide bring their brands to life. Her Instagram account contains visual experiments focused on some of her interests besides work and functions as inspiration that fuels her day-to-day job.

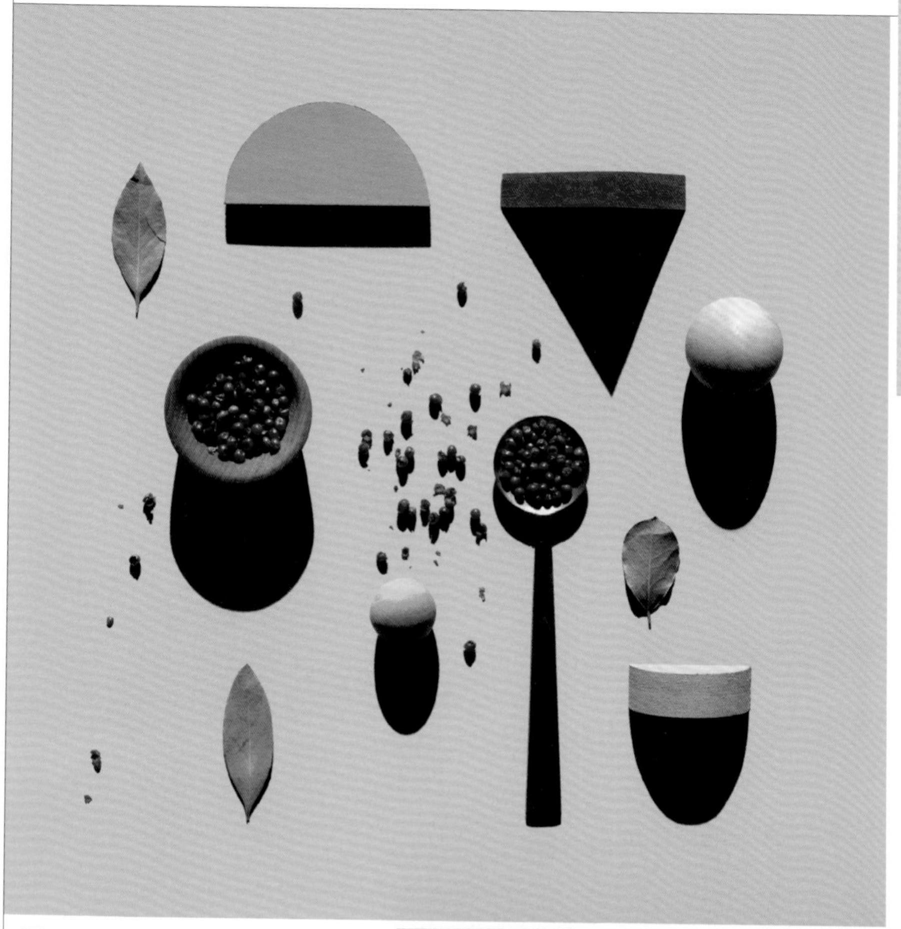

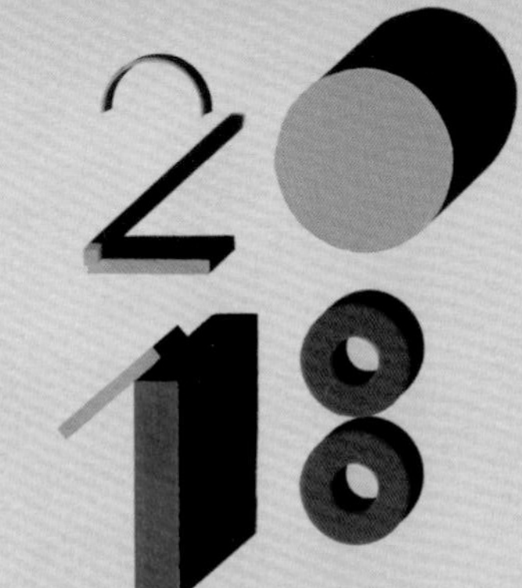

1. Add Some Pepper
2. Twenty-Eighteen
3. Stir It Up
4. Cooking by Colors

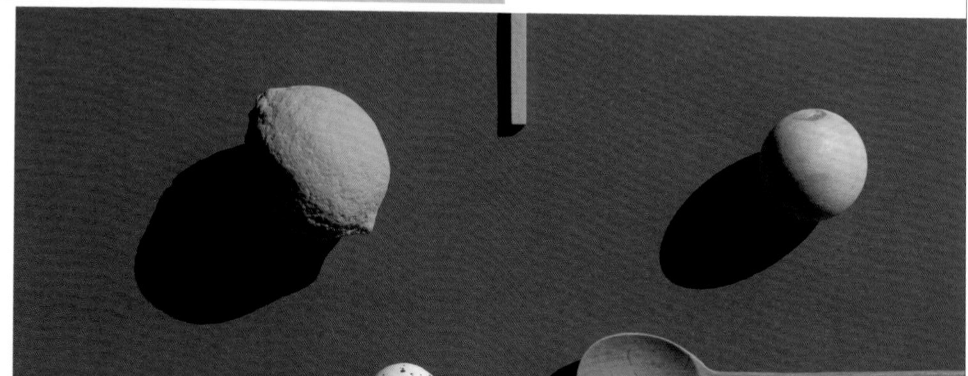

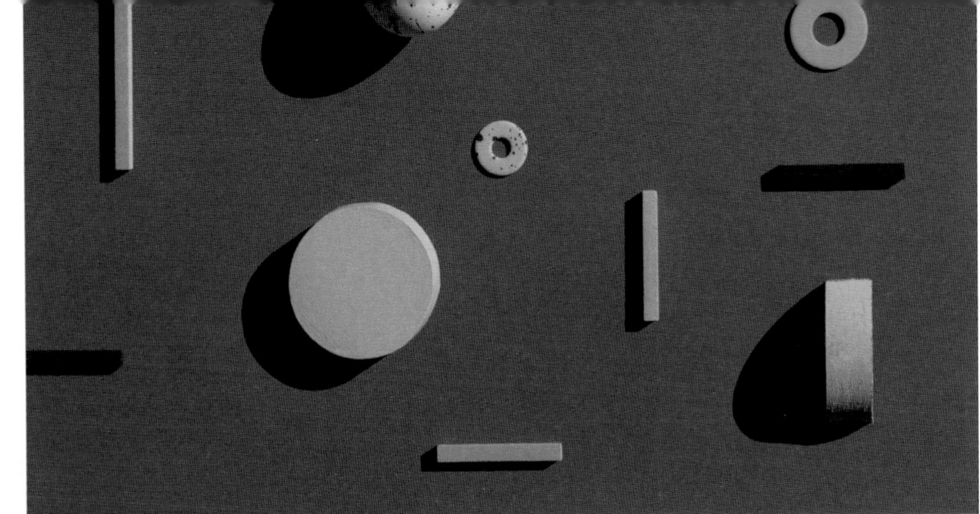

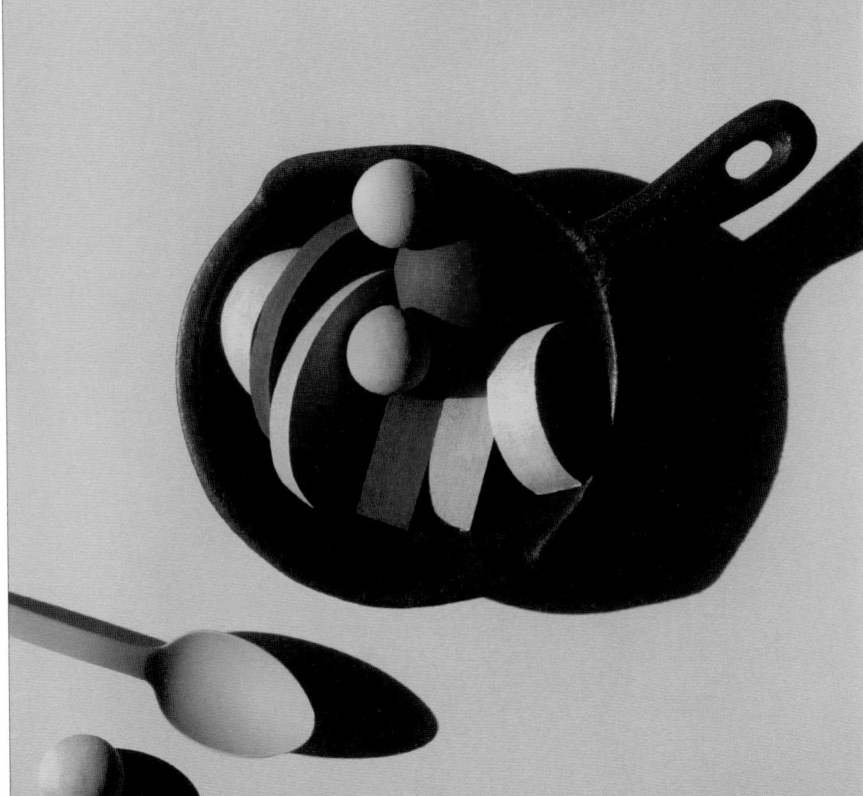

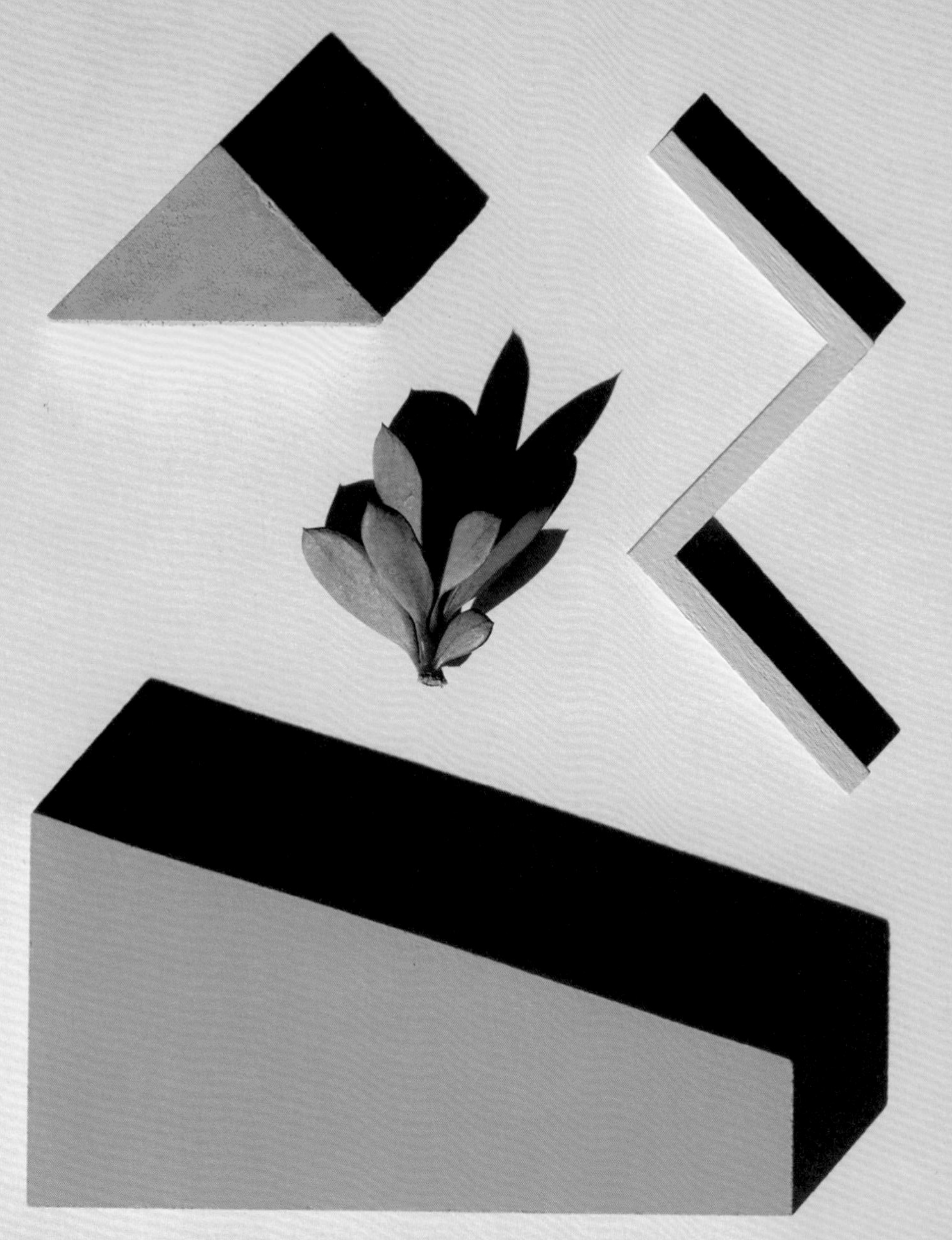

"I don't actually feature the products [themselves]. I create a little set that could be considered as a backdrop on which to display them."

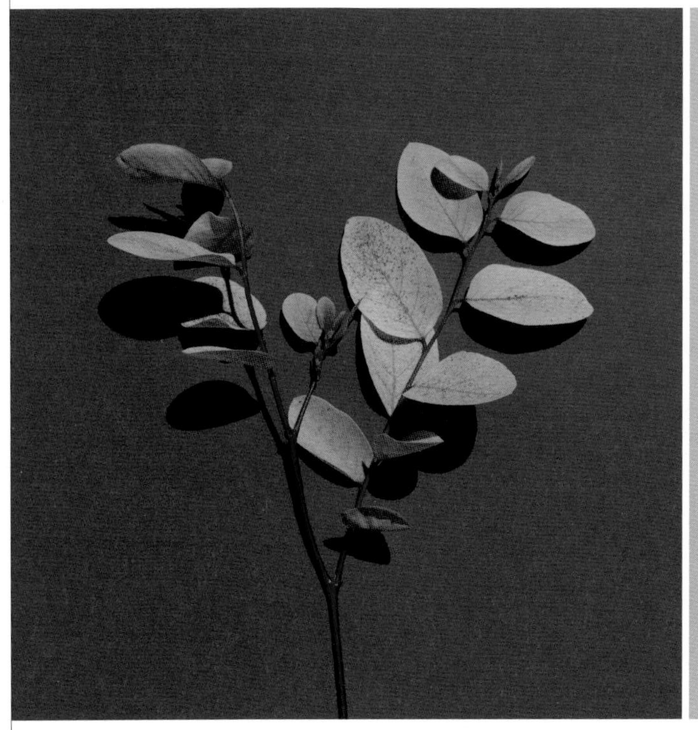

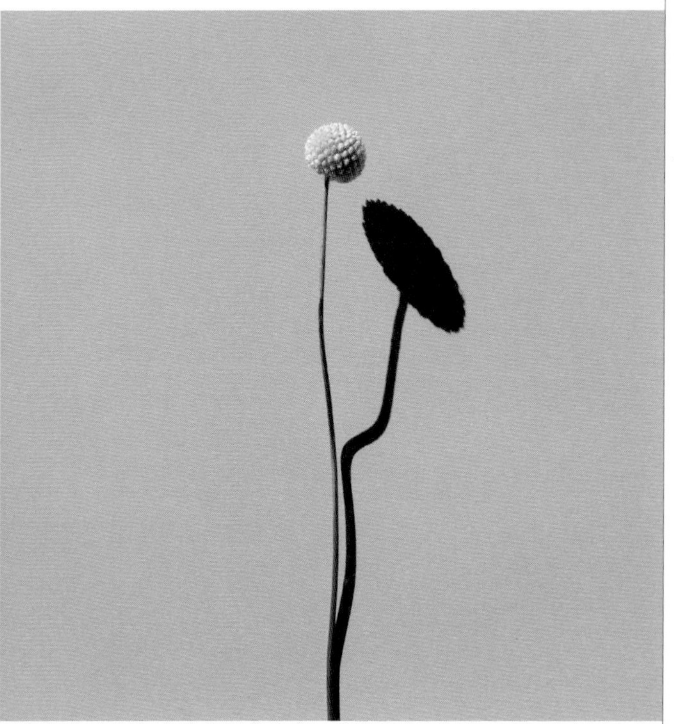

1. Succulence
2. Snow Bush
3. Billy Button

#GET ARTSY! → Whether they are thought-provoking or awe-inspiring, social media is the modern digital canvas for creative expressions, where those who enjoy experimenting or sharing their passions can connect with the like-minded through the beauty in every day.

Background image by Ice Cream Books / Ben Denzer

- Daniel Rueda & Anna Devís
- Serge Najjar
- Salvage Design
- Compendium Design Store
- Ice Cream Books / Ben Deezer

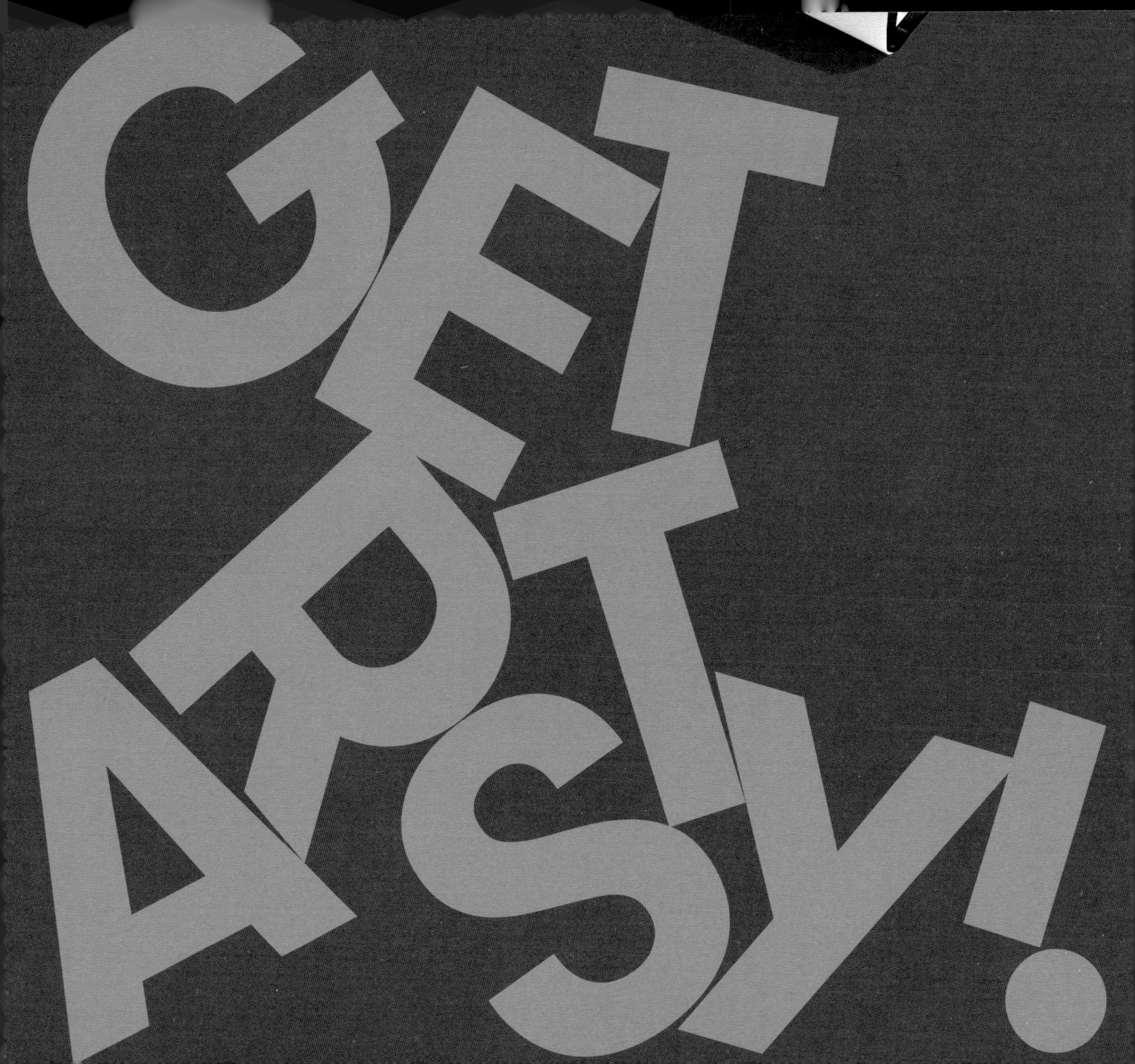
GET ARTSY!

THINK BEYOND YOUR SOFTWARE

Design decisions come more naturally when you are not constrained by the trappings of the Adobe Suite.

— Ice Cream Books / Ben Deezer

GET COLOURFUL!

The more minimalist and colourful [an image] is, the more it strikes attention.

— rvrbr studio

KEEP THINGS FRESH

We started out with regular product shots on a white background, and over time, evolved onto the isometric perspective – allowing us to keep the feed dynamic and move products around to create endless fresh layouts.

— Compendium Design Store

NATURAL CAN BE BEST

I do not use flashes or artificial lights – everything is lit by the sun. I love the quality and sharpness I get with it.

— Eloisa Iturbe

CREATE GOOD VIBES

Try to capture a vibe where modelled images extend beyond what the lens has captured at that exact moment, like there is a story that comes before and after.

— Olive Clothing

CONSISTENCY IS KEY

We work with a consistent background colour. We believe this ties everything together and helps fans recognise our new posts in their feed. We allow ourselves to play with that colour over time.

— Compendium Design Store

DON'T BE PLAIN

Be as graphic as possible.

— Akatre

SIMPLIFY THE MESSAGE

[Just have] one idea per image.

— Akatre

SIMPLIFY THE PALETTE

Use one, two or three colours maximum per image.

— Akatre

BE DYNAMIC YET STATIC

I use the dynamic sense of a picture as well as the static sense created by lights and shadows to pursue the picture that makes both of them co-exist.

— Chung-hui Shen

EXPERIMENT WITH SETTINGS

Sometimes, we take more than one picture of a setting, and change it by taking elements out of it until it becomes a whole new picture.

— Espacio Crudo

SIZES + ANGLES MATTER

The way a picture is cropped can really change how people respond to it.

— Present & Correct

IMPROVE AT IMPROVISING

Something that works very well is to have Porexpan plates as reflectors – they are cheap, manageable, and can soften the shadows very well.

— Eating Patterns / Vega Hernando

TAKE IT SLOW

[Photographers sometimes make the mistake of] rushing it.

— Compendium Design Store

BE PICKY ABOUT PRECISION

I am very careful to make sure that my images are always straight. I do not like wonky shots!

— Present & Correct

KNOW WHEN TO IGNORE ADVICE

We have never received good tips about photography. Maybe that is a good thing :)

— Lililoveme & Dmitry Buko

KEEP IT REAL

Try to get your final image with minimum retouching.

— I'm Blue I'm Pink

FOCUS FIRST

Sometimes, I realise that my edges are slightly out of focus only when I see the image on a computer screen. I hate it, because I like to get a clear effect on the whole image.

— Eating Patterns / Vega Hernando

COMPOSITION ISN'T EVERYTHING

When I first started, my main focus was in composition and the set. Now, it also includes lighting, which to me is my main consideration when shooting.

— Olivia Jeczmyk

IT'S NOT ABOUT YOUR EQUIPMENT

An image is not better or worse because of the camera, but the amount of idea and thought you put into it.

— Daniel Rueda & Anna Devís

FIND A BALANCE

Balancing the objects and creating an appealing composition are the best, as well as the most fun parts of the whole process. It can be challenging at times, and is definitely time consuming and labour-intensive – but that is what it takes to create beautiful still life images. The end results are well worth the energy and effort.

— Wilson Wong

PLAY AROUND WITH TECHNIQUES

Zoom in, then zoom out.

— Serge Najjar

THINK LIKE A DIRECTOR

I work to give every image that I produce a story that supports it; a set designed to outline a precise environment that evokes a small world, a stage where there is a protagonist and a scene that tells the whole story.

— Nicola Galli

FOCUS ON THE FOREGROUND

Some photographers tend to focus on side objects/the background and neglect the 'core', because they might not have a very clear story to tell in a visual.

—Matter Matters

TIPS & TRICKS FOR MAKING YOUR PHOTOS ROCK!

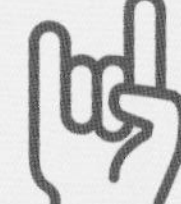

#70-93

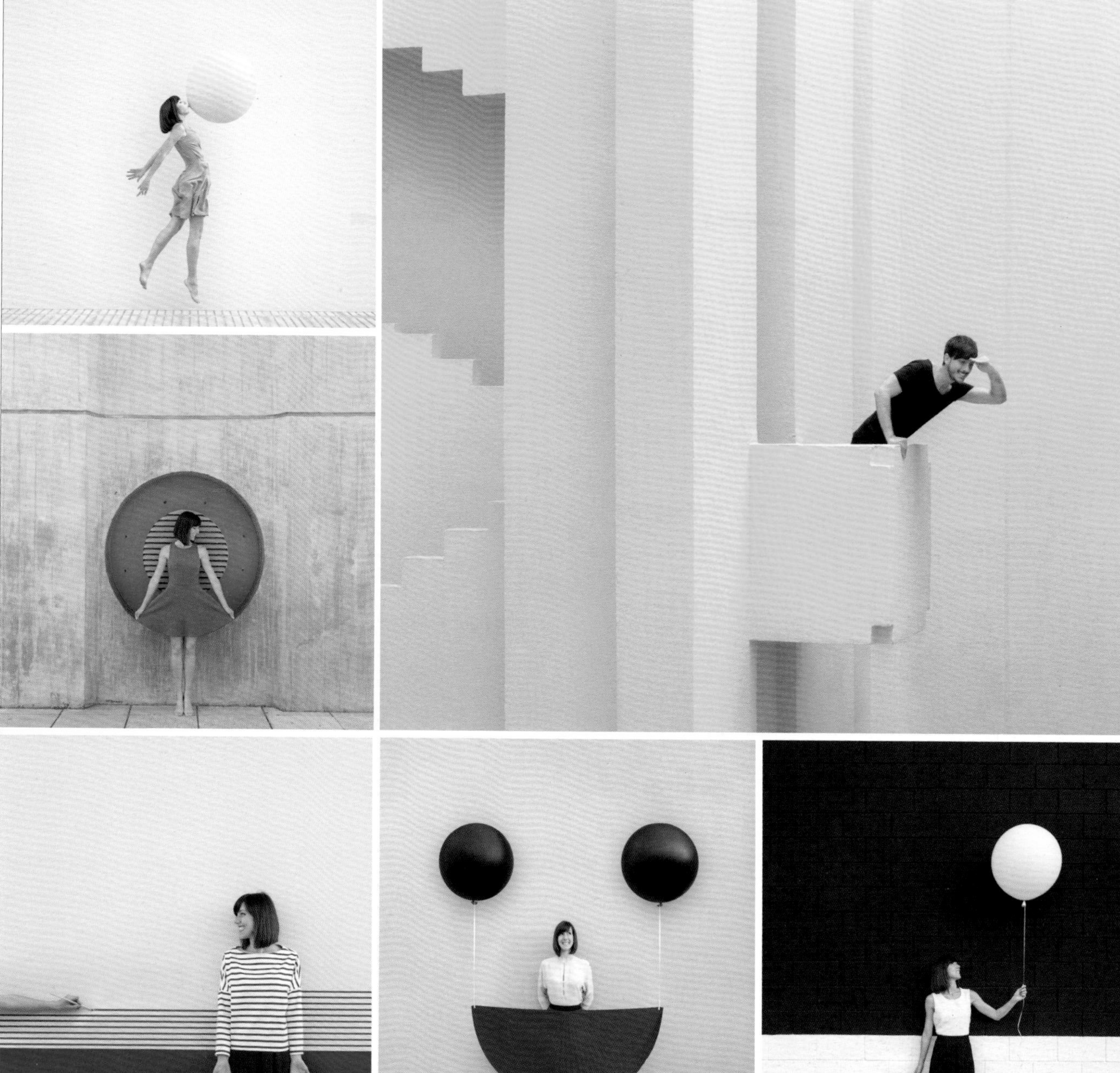

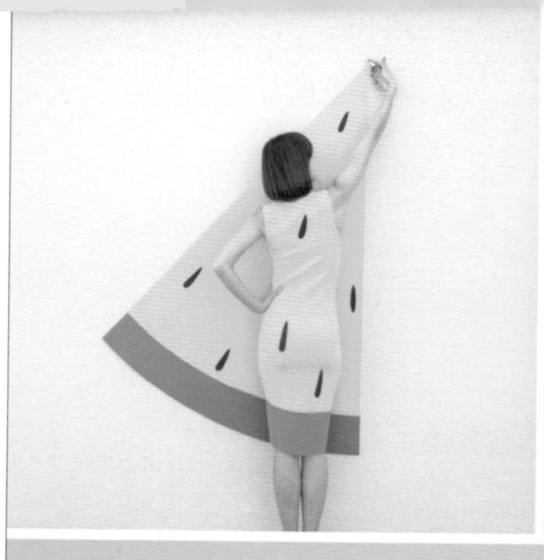

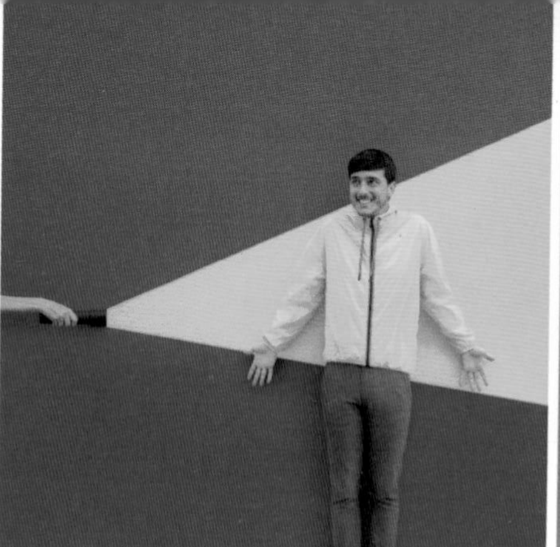

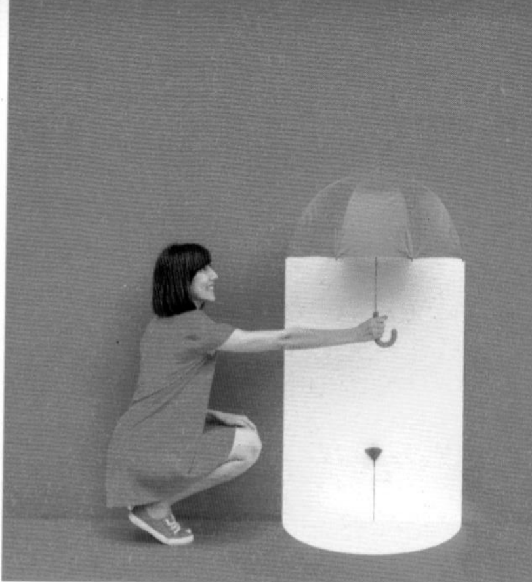

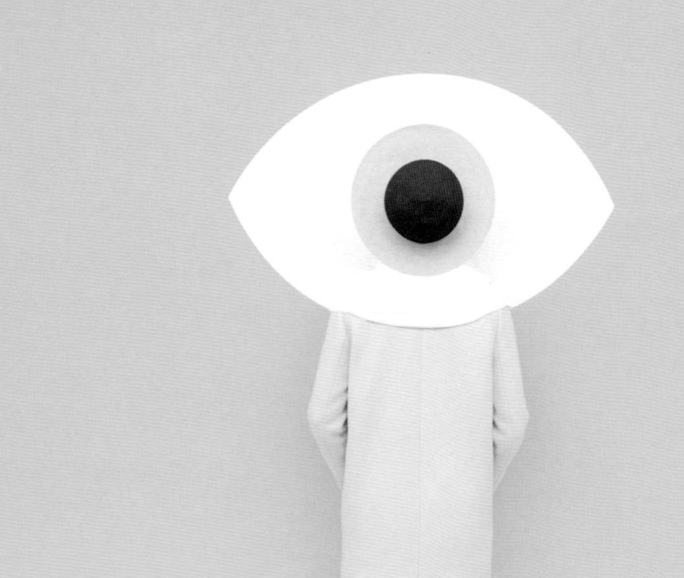

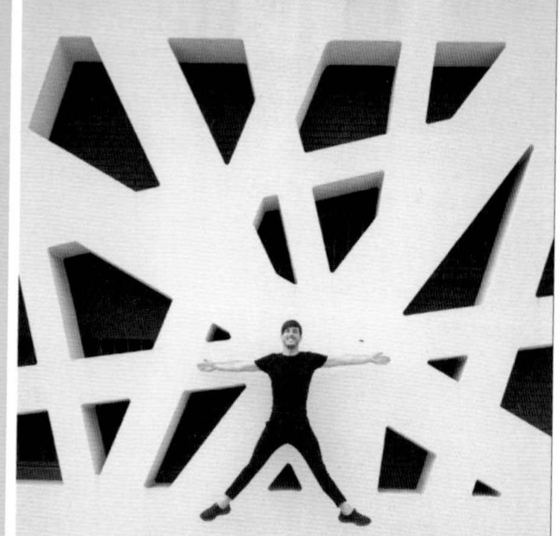

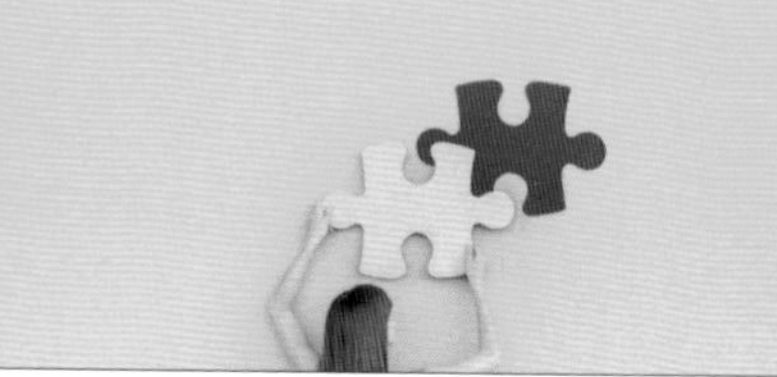

DANIEL RUEDA & ANNA DEVÍS

drcuerda / anniset

Daniel Rueda and Anna Devís are a Spanish duo who use creative photography to tell visual stories that capture their love for architecture through clever art direction, playful compositions, and witty captions.

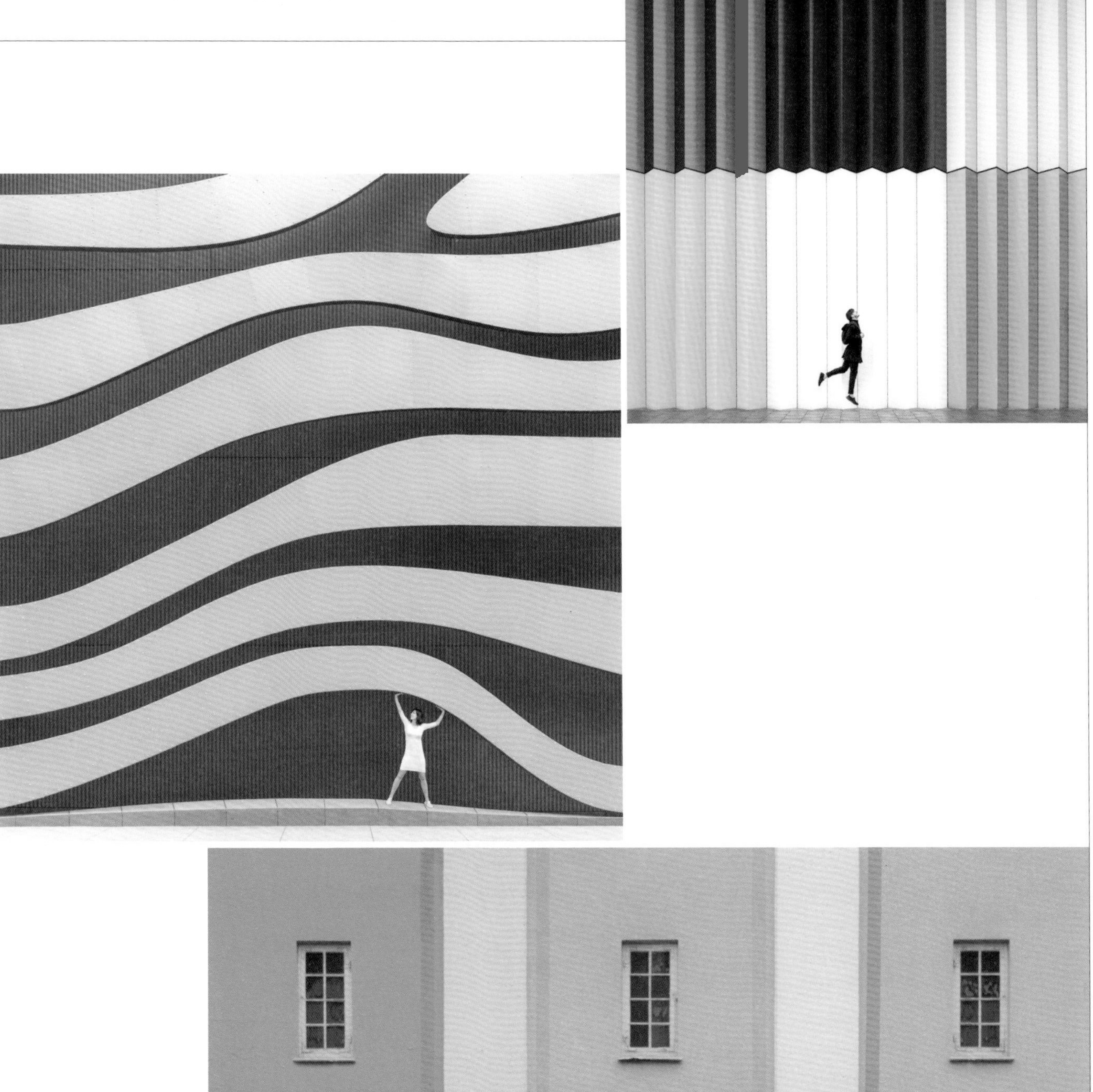

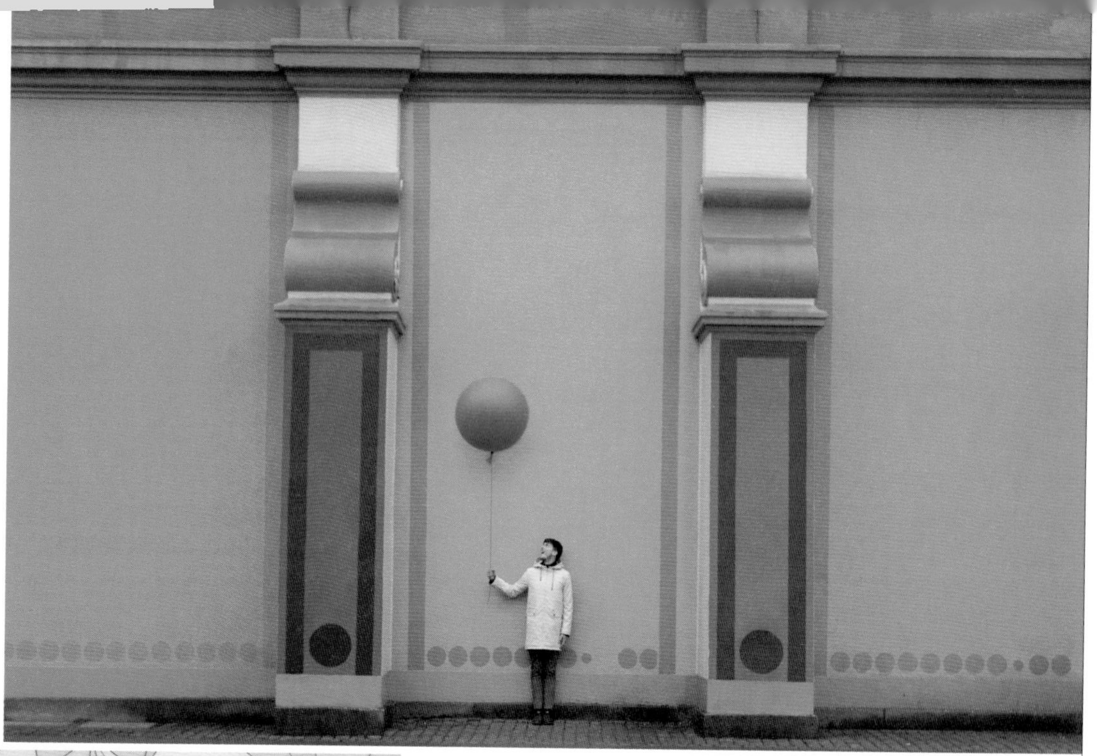

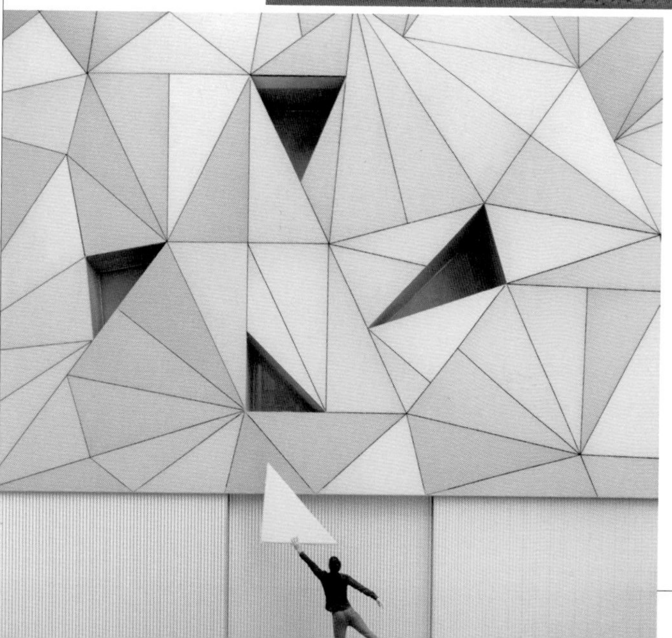

"[Our] utilisation of bright colours and meticulously composed props turn ideas into some very joyful and uplifting pieces of art."

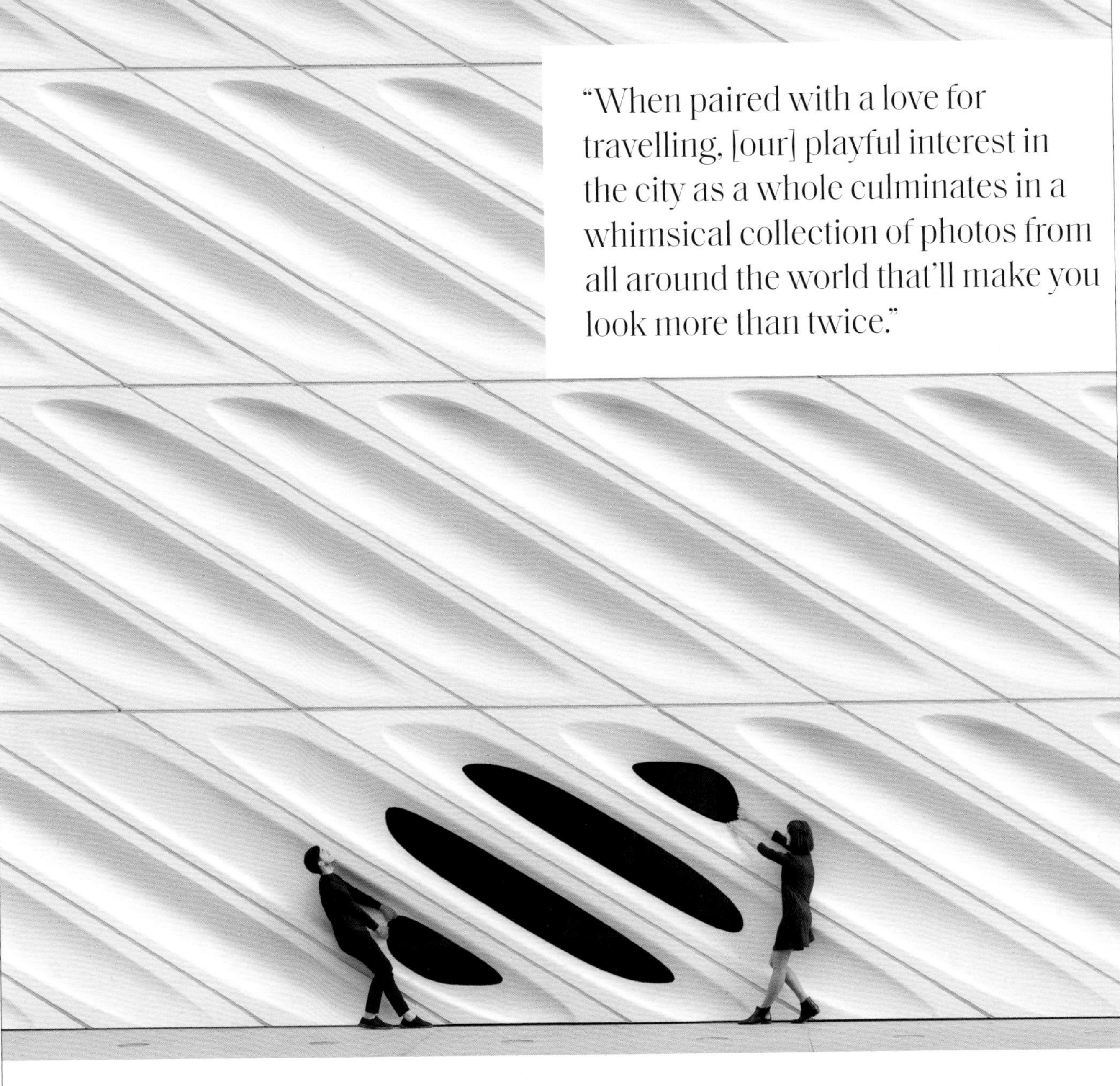

"When paired with a love for travelling, [our] playful interest in the city as a whole culminates in a whimsical collection of photos from all around the world that'll make you look more than twice."

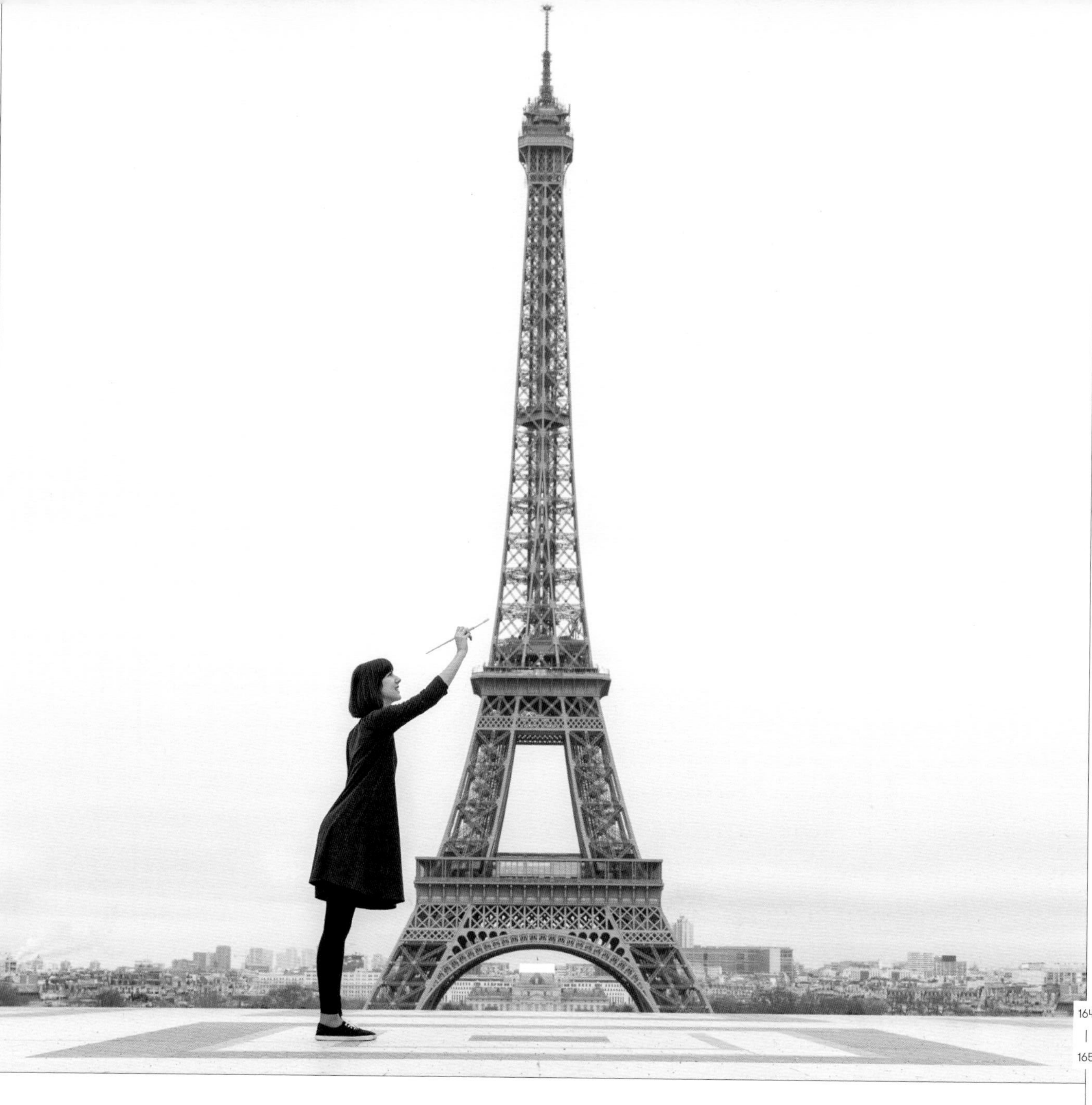

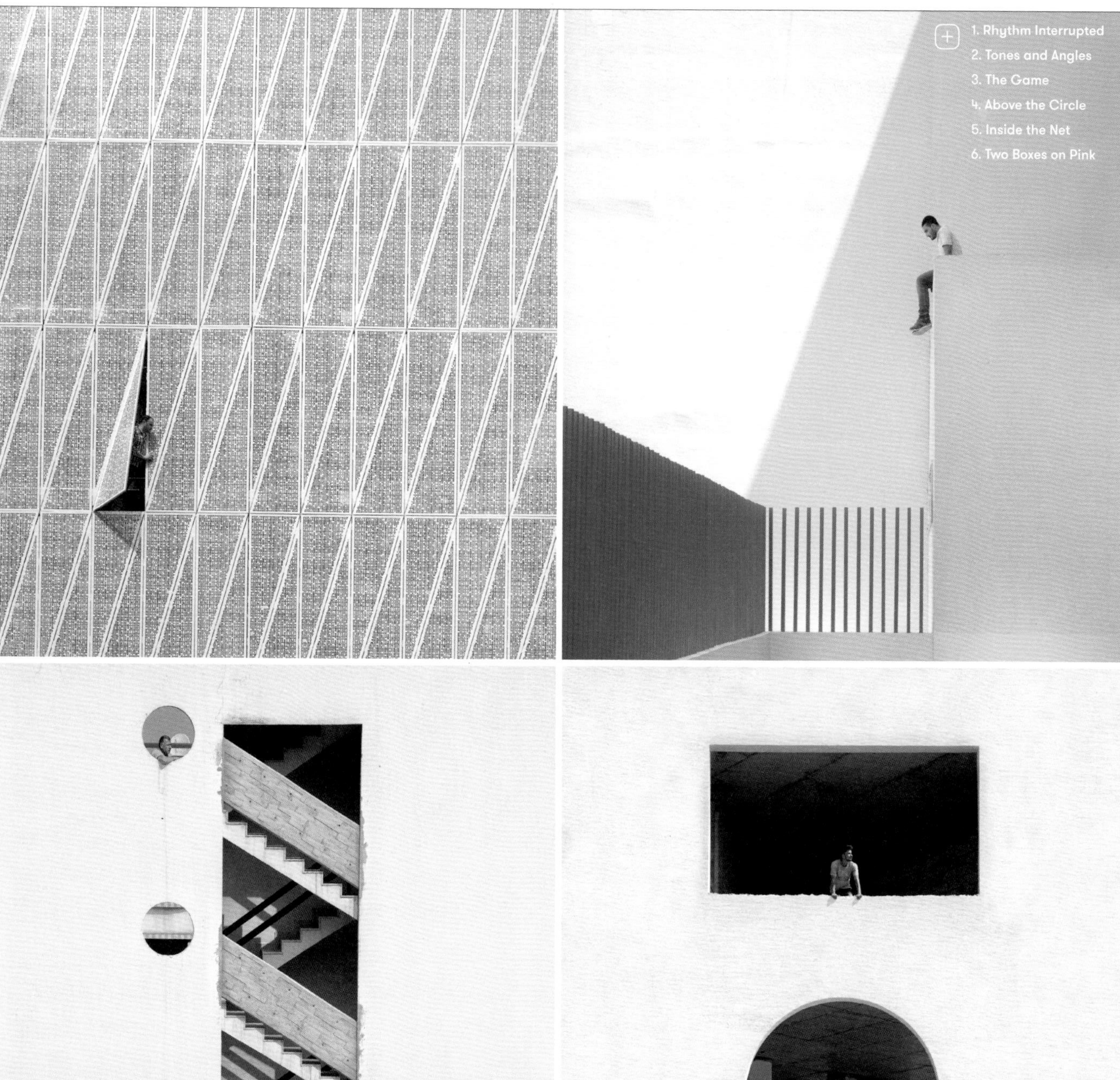

1. Rhythm Interrupted
2. Tones and Angles
3. The Game
4. Above the Circle
5. Inside the Net
6. Two Boxes on Pink

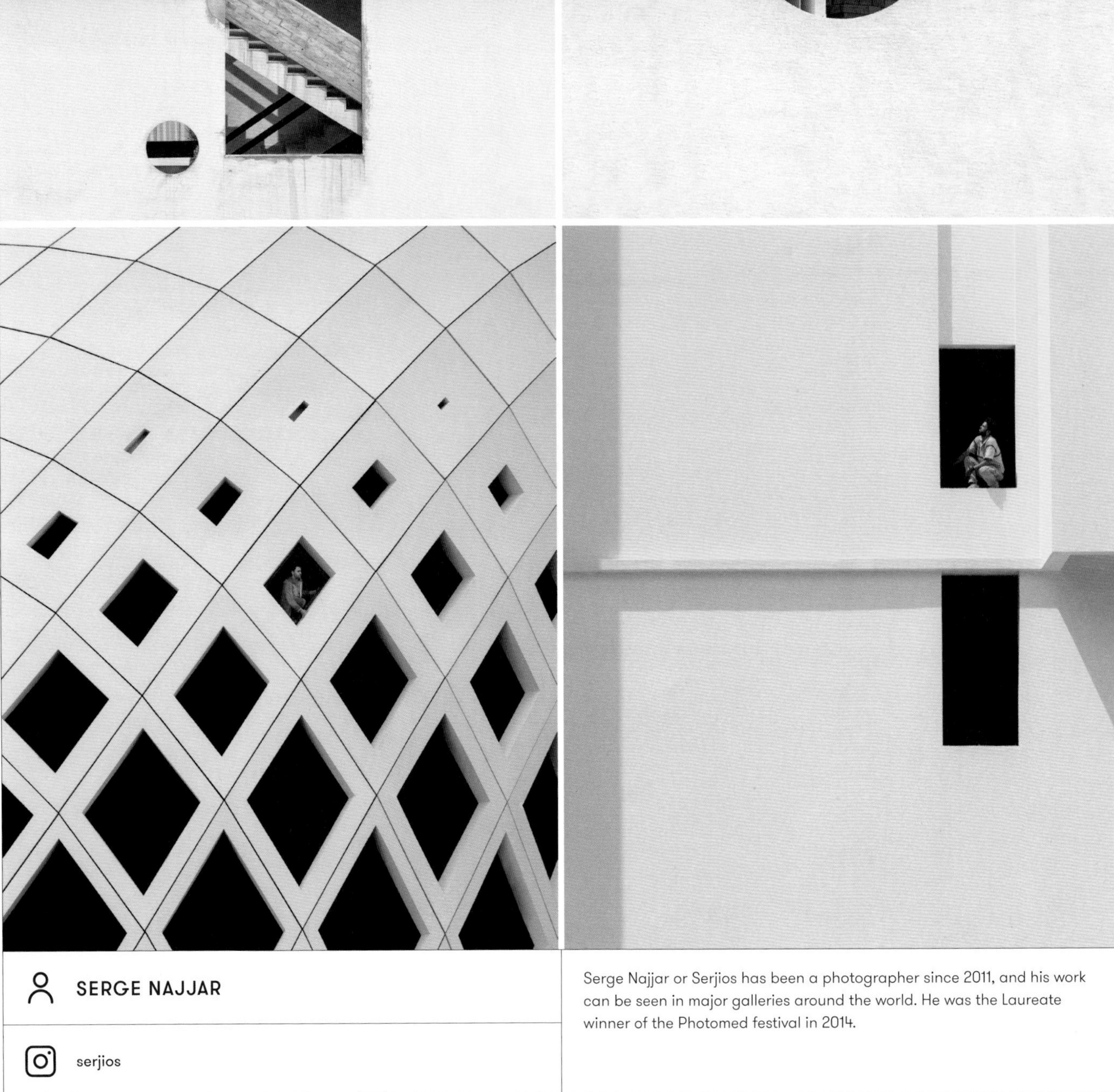

SERGE NAJJAR

serjios

Serge Najjar or Serjios has been a photographer since 2011, and his work can be seen in major galleries around the world. He was the Laureate winner of the Photomed festival in 2014.

"My challenge is to show how thin the line between art and (real-life) photography is."

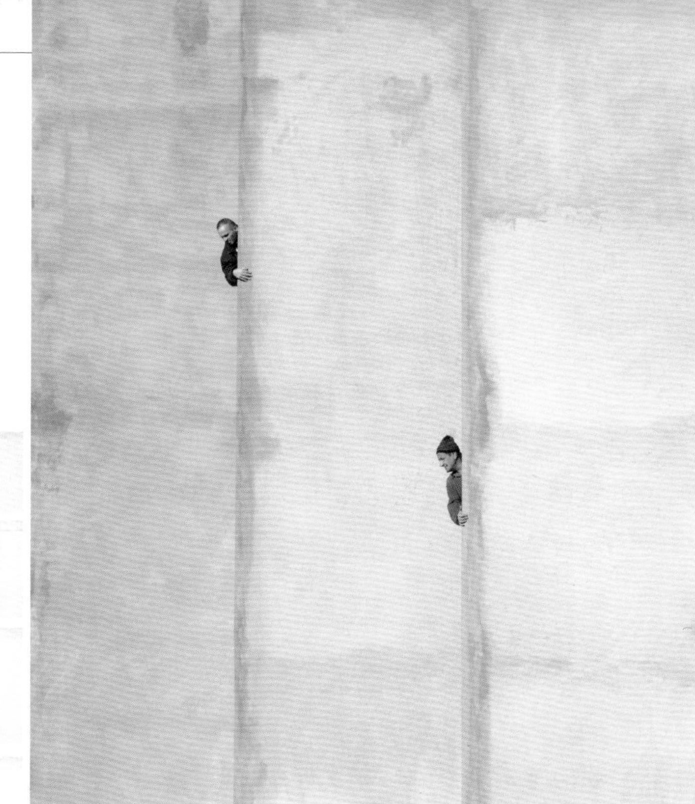

1. Two Commas
2. White Split
3. Reaching Out
4. The Optical Box
5. Turning my back on Light II
6. Shadow Box

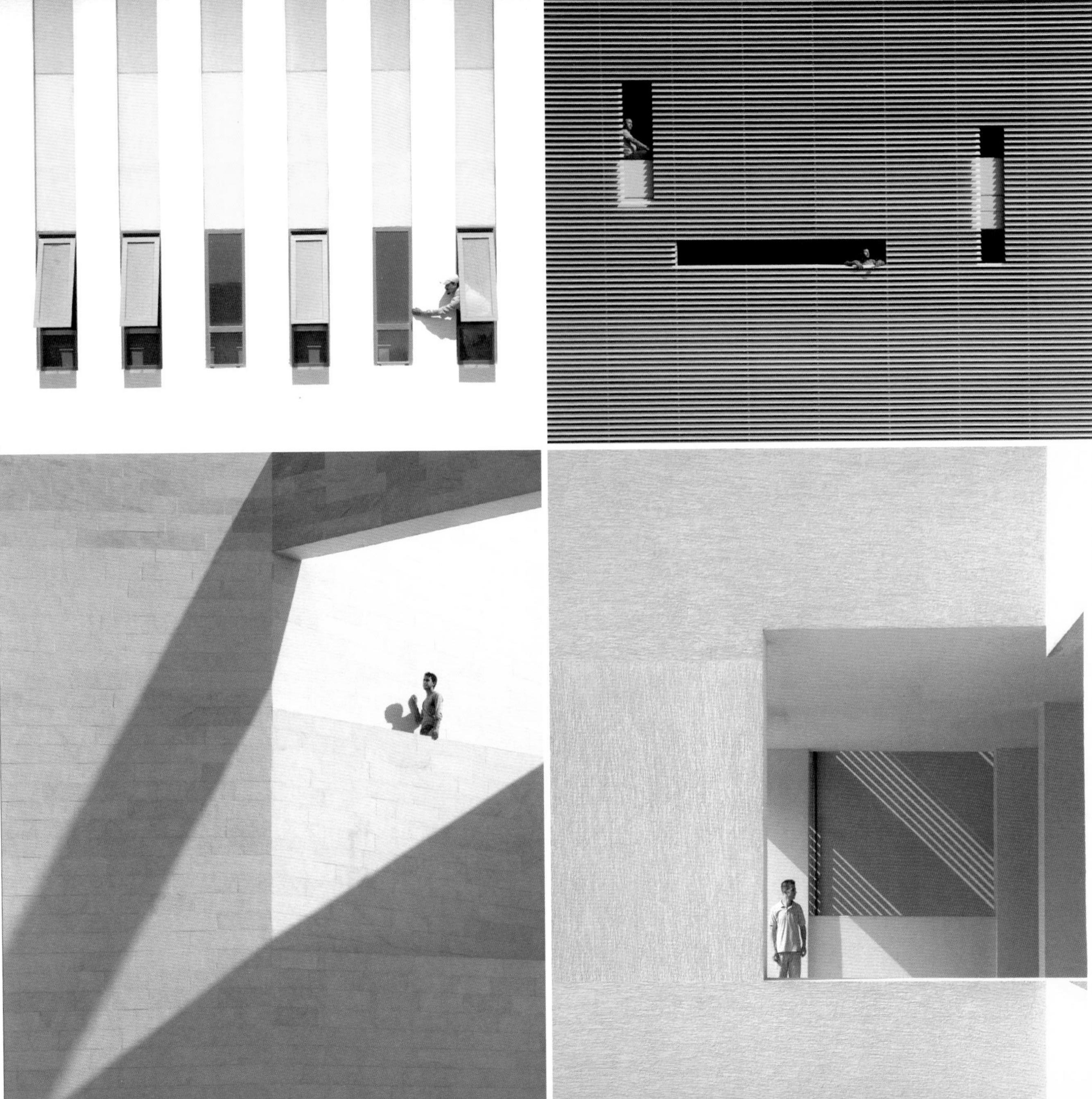

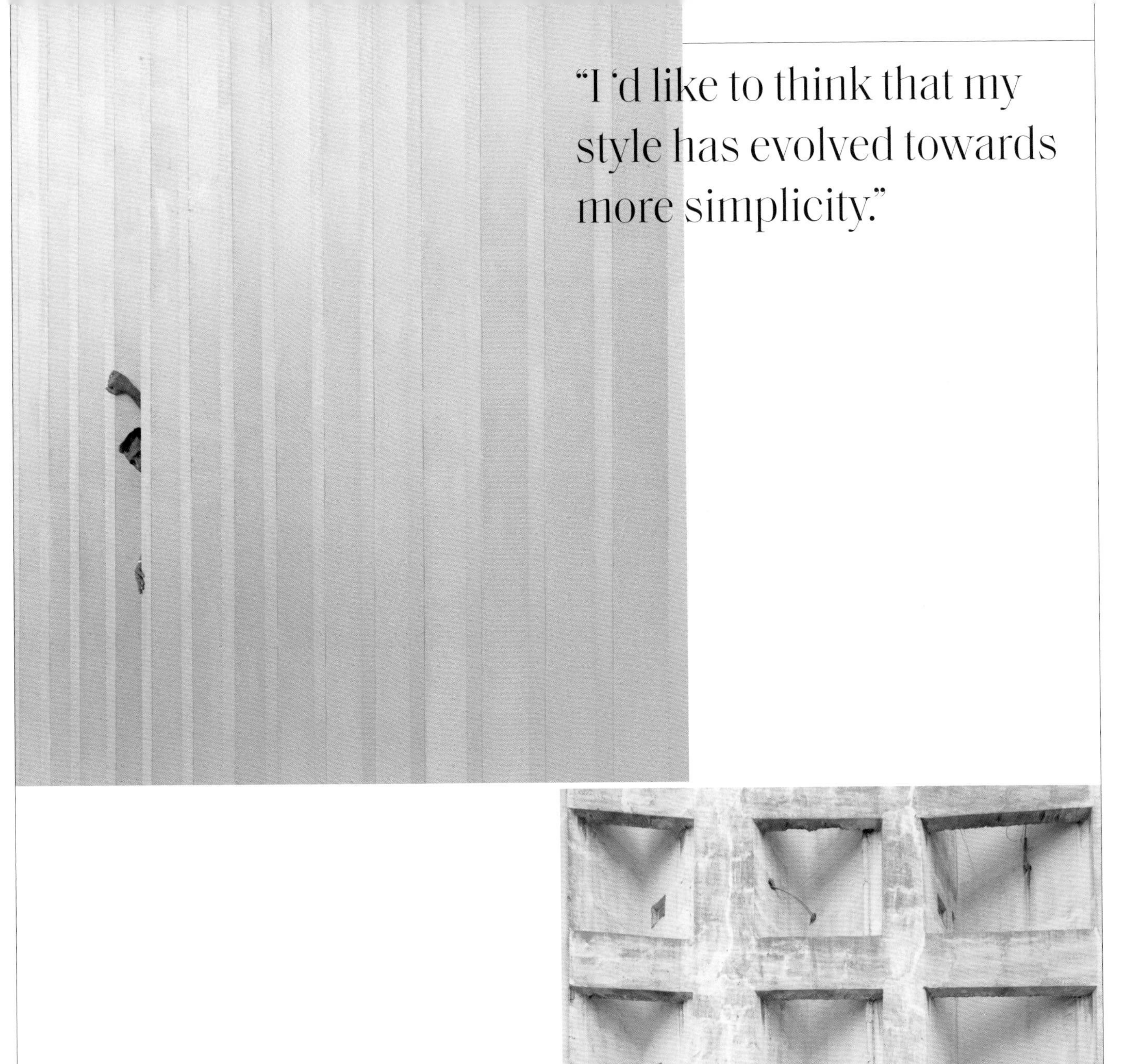

"I 'd like to think that my style has evolved towards more simplicity."

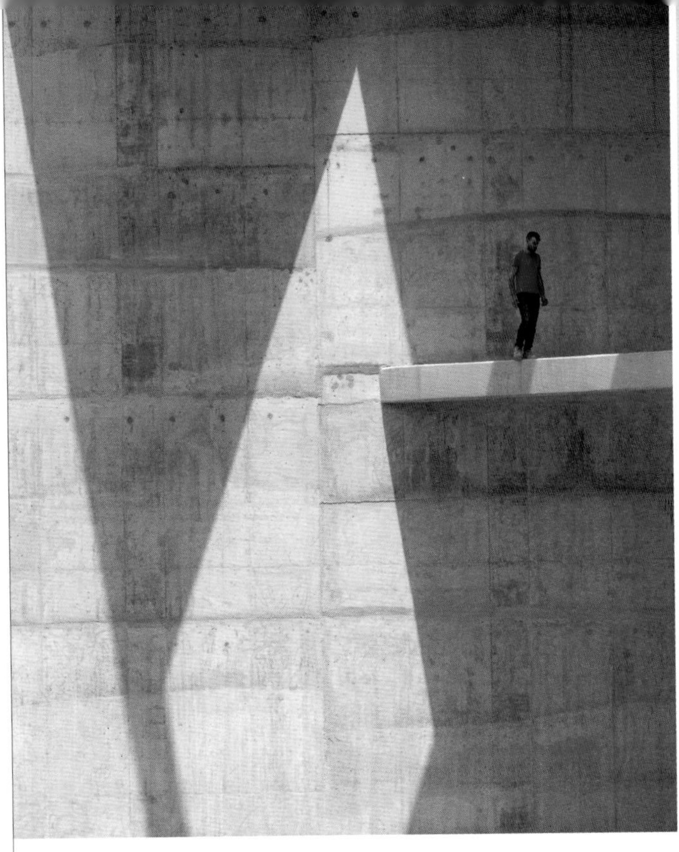

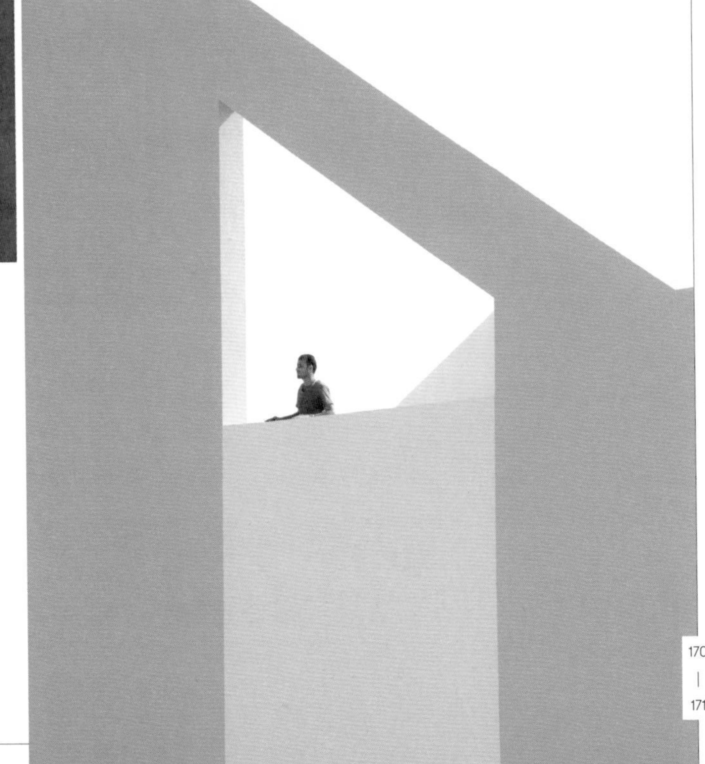

1. Tribute to Agnes Martin
2. Tic Tac Toe
3. Shadow Geometry
4. Turning my back on Light I

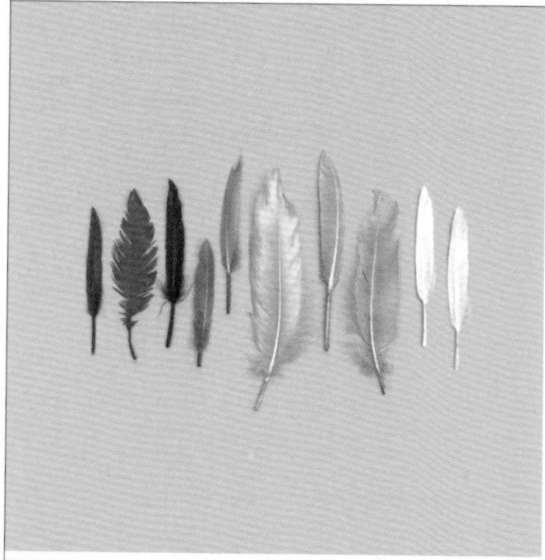

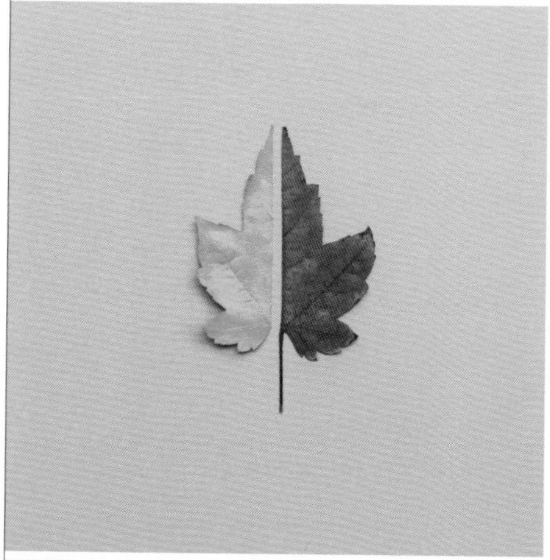

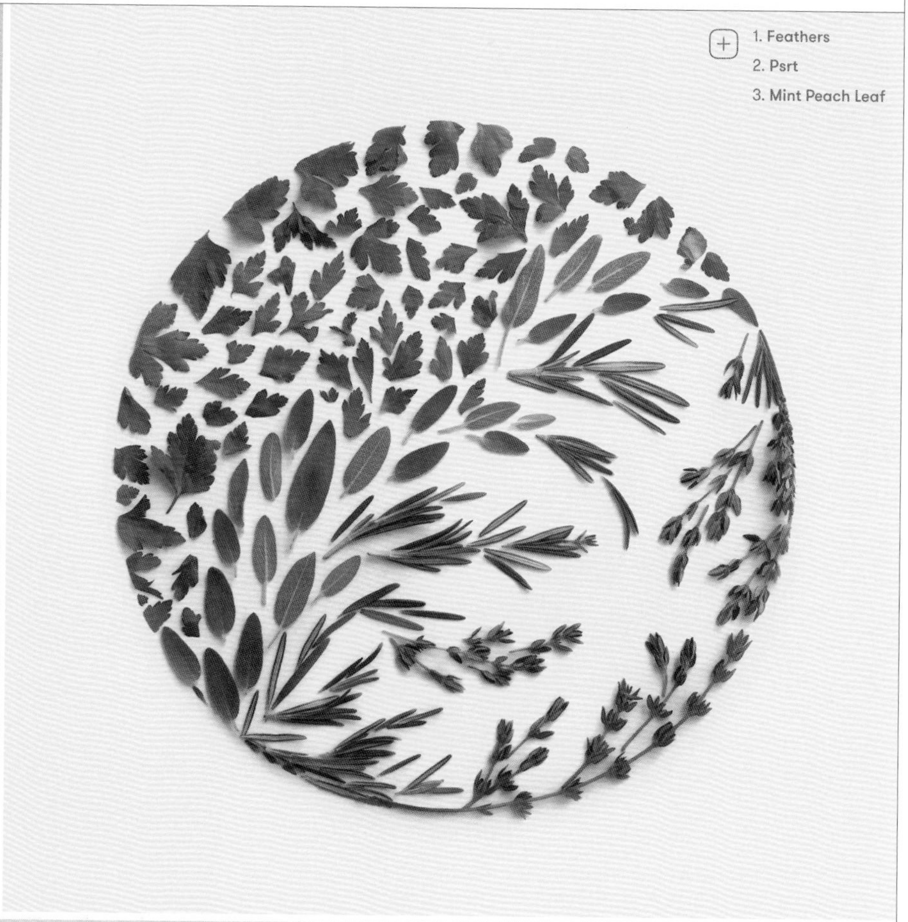

1. Feathers
2. Psrt
3. Mint Peach Leaf

4. Rock Formation
5. Ff
6. Cut It Out

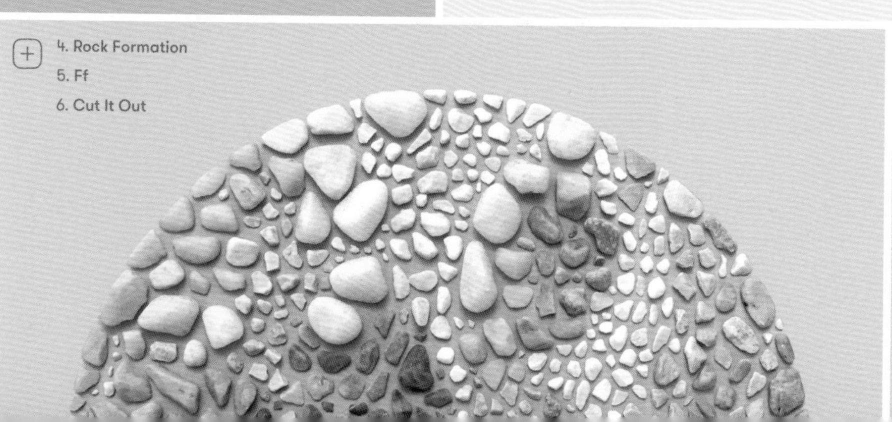

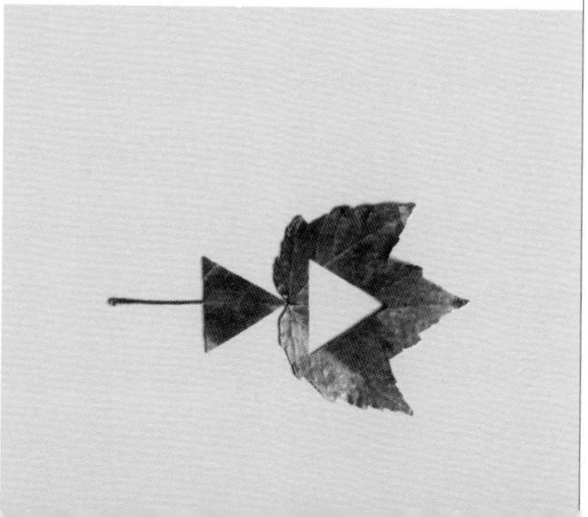

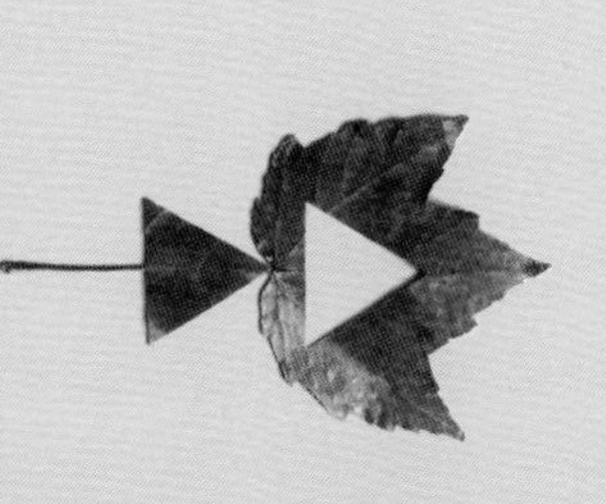

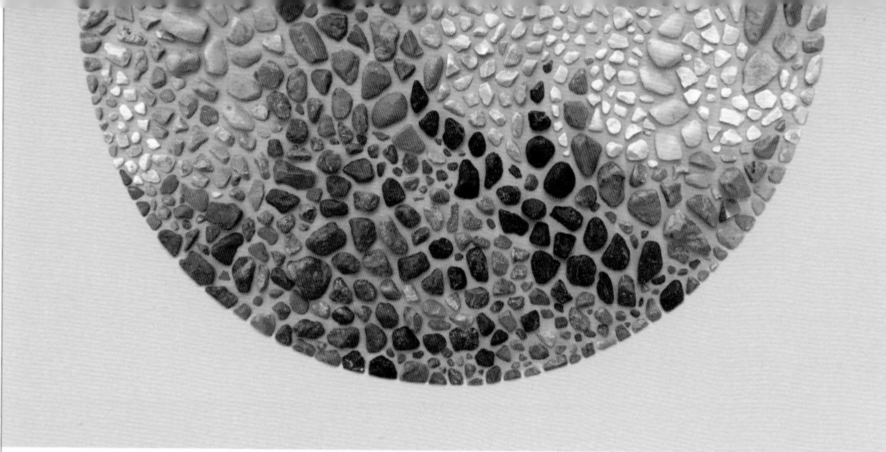

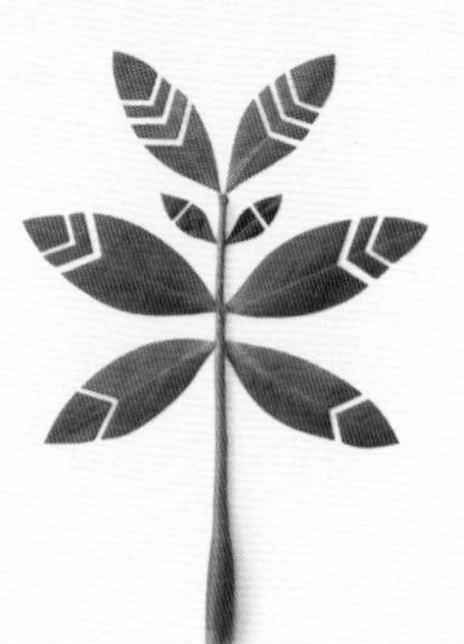

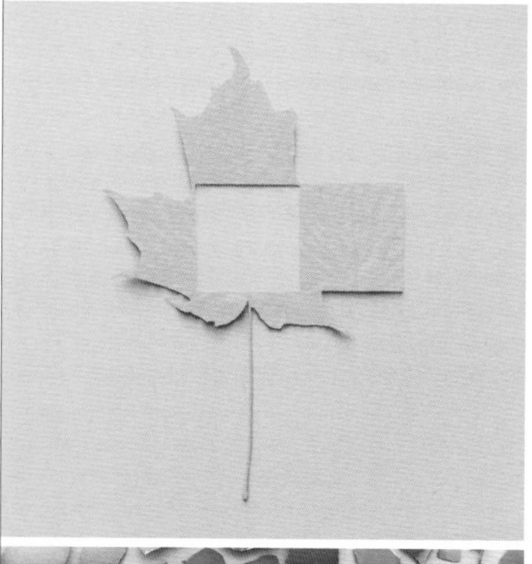

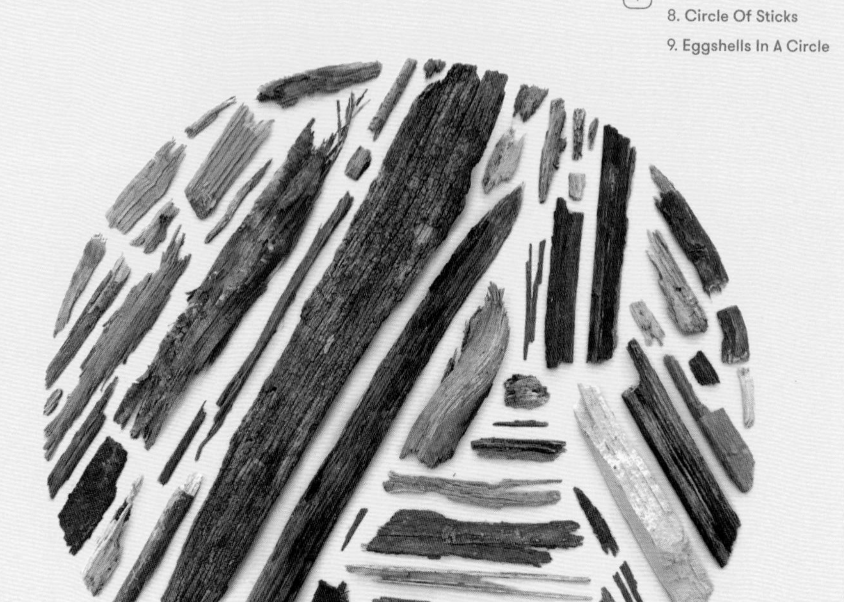

7. Blue Leaf 2
8. Circle Of Sticks
9. Eggshells In A Circle

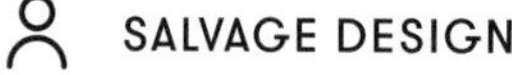

SALVAGE DESIGN

kmsalvagedesign

Salvage Design was set up by Kristen Meyer, a multimedia artist currently residing in New Haven with her husband and two daughters. The spectrum of her career has included work in floral design, interior decorating, window design, and prop styling.

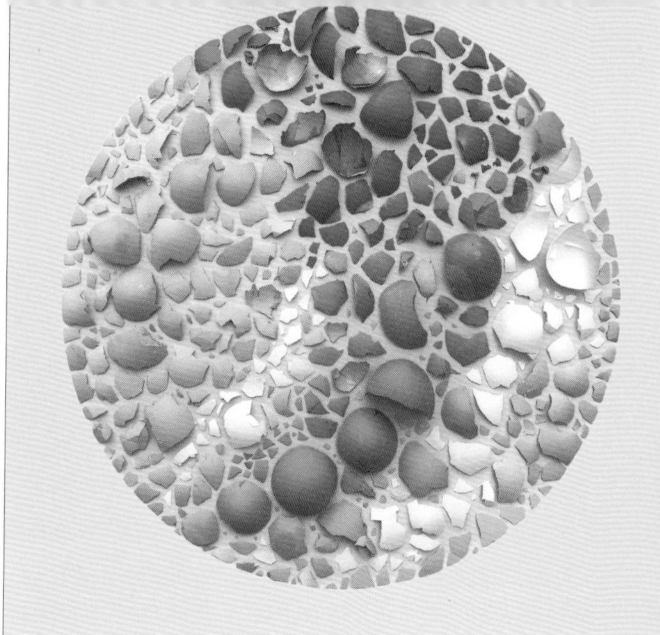

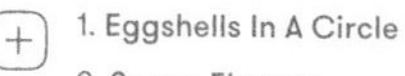

1. Eggshells In A Circle
2. Space Flowers

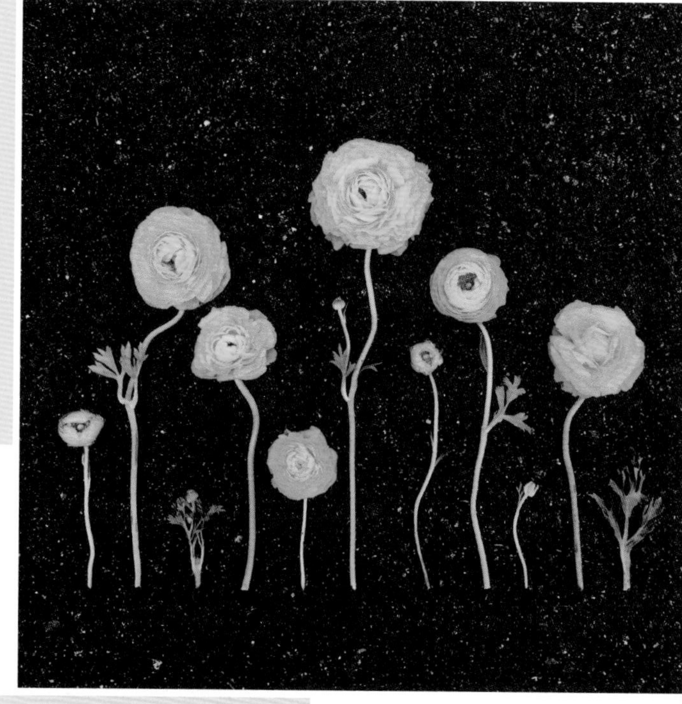

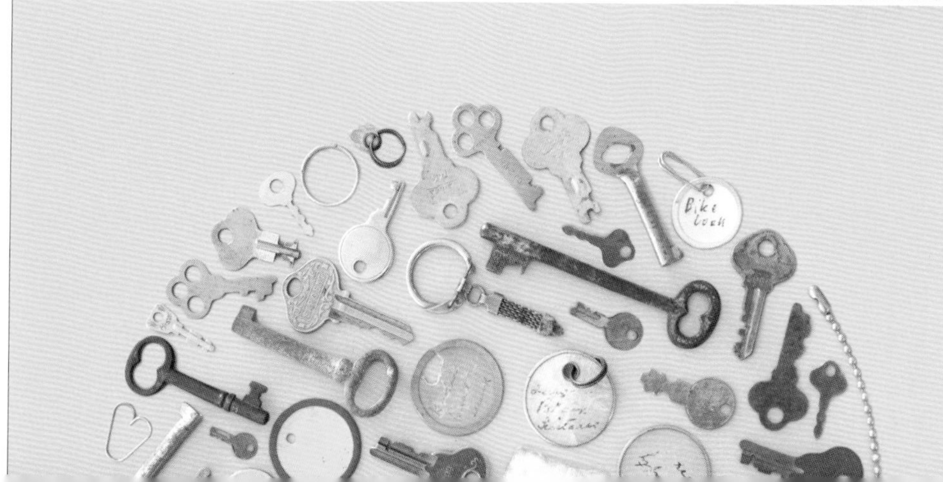

"There's something beautiful about finding ordinary objects and giving them new life."

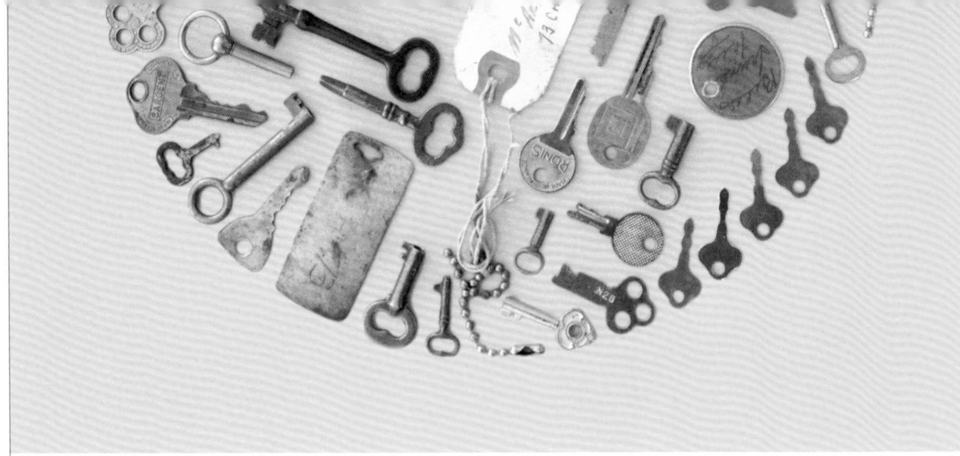

3. Open Up
4. Bananasplit
5. Ombre Cut Leaf

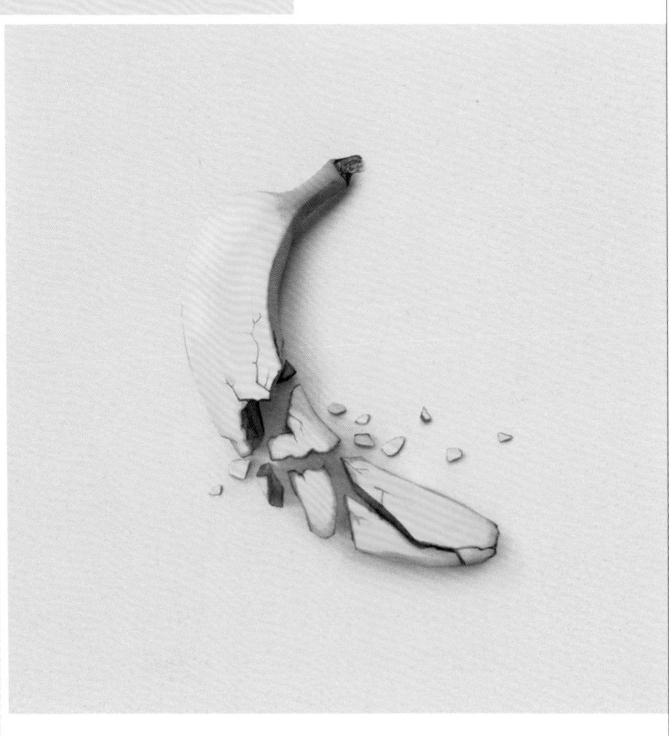

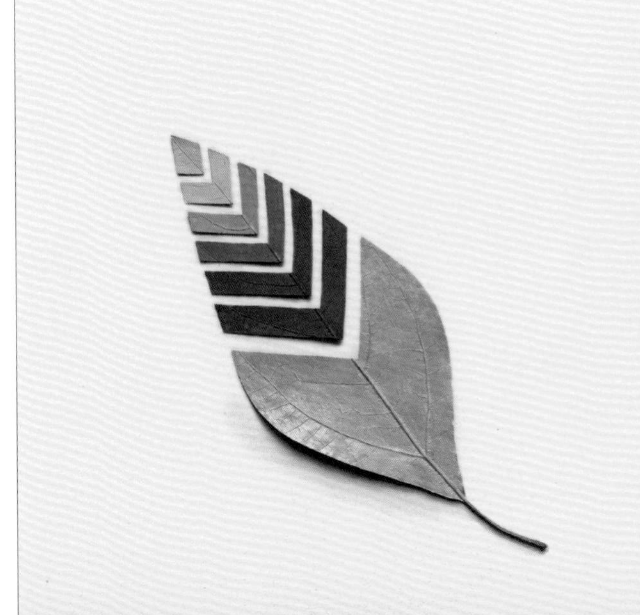

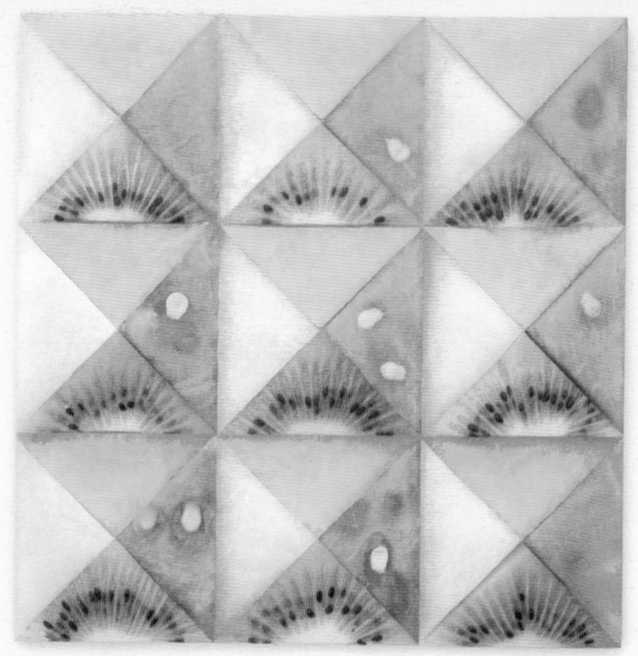

"I've always been obsessed with contrasts. I love the challenge of taking delicate, natural shapes and manipulating them into something graphic and structured."

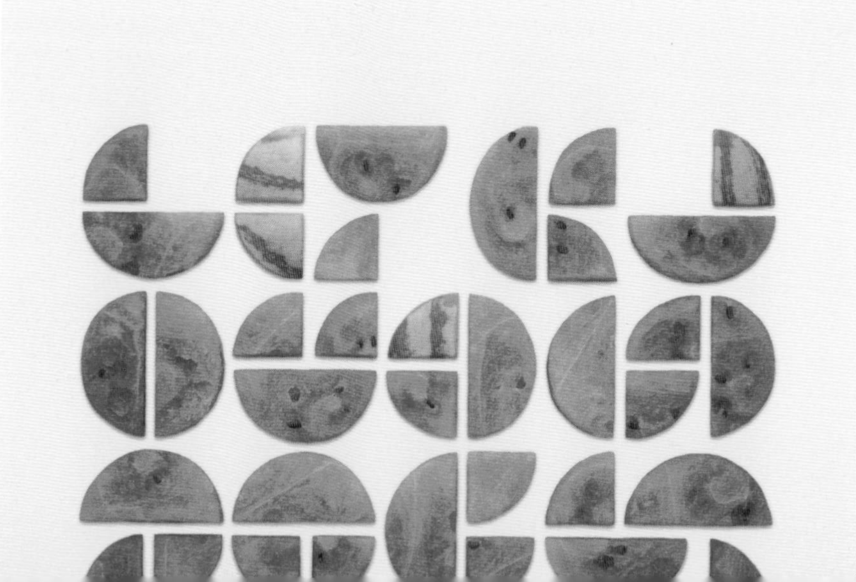

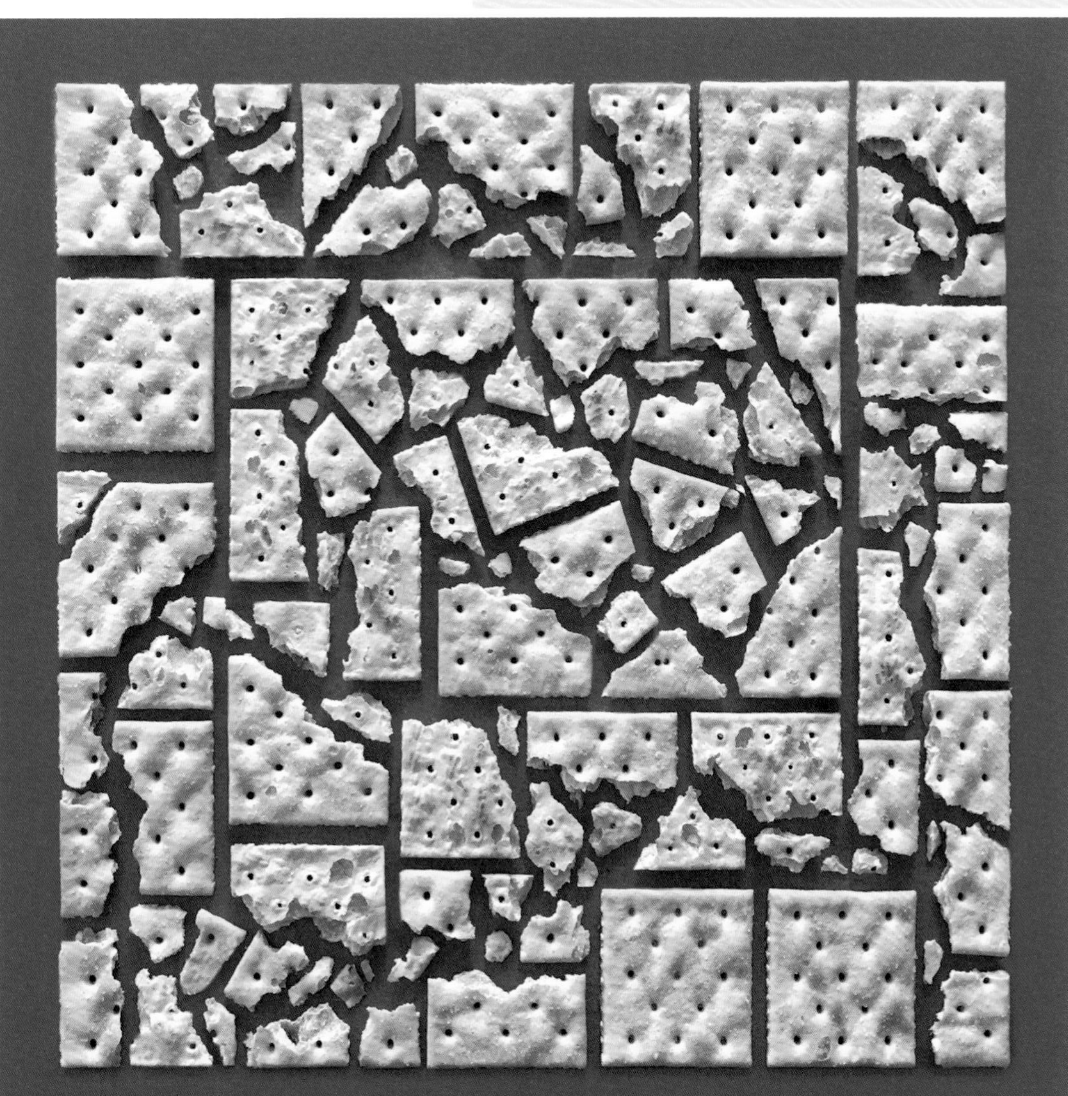

1. Melon Squares
2. Modmelon
3. Cracked

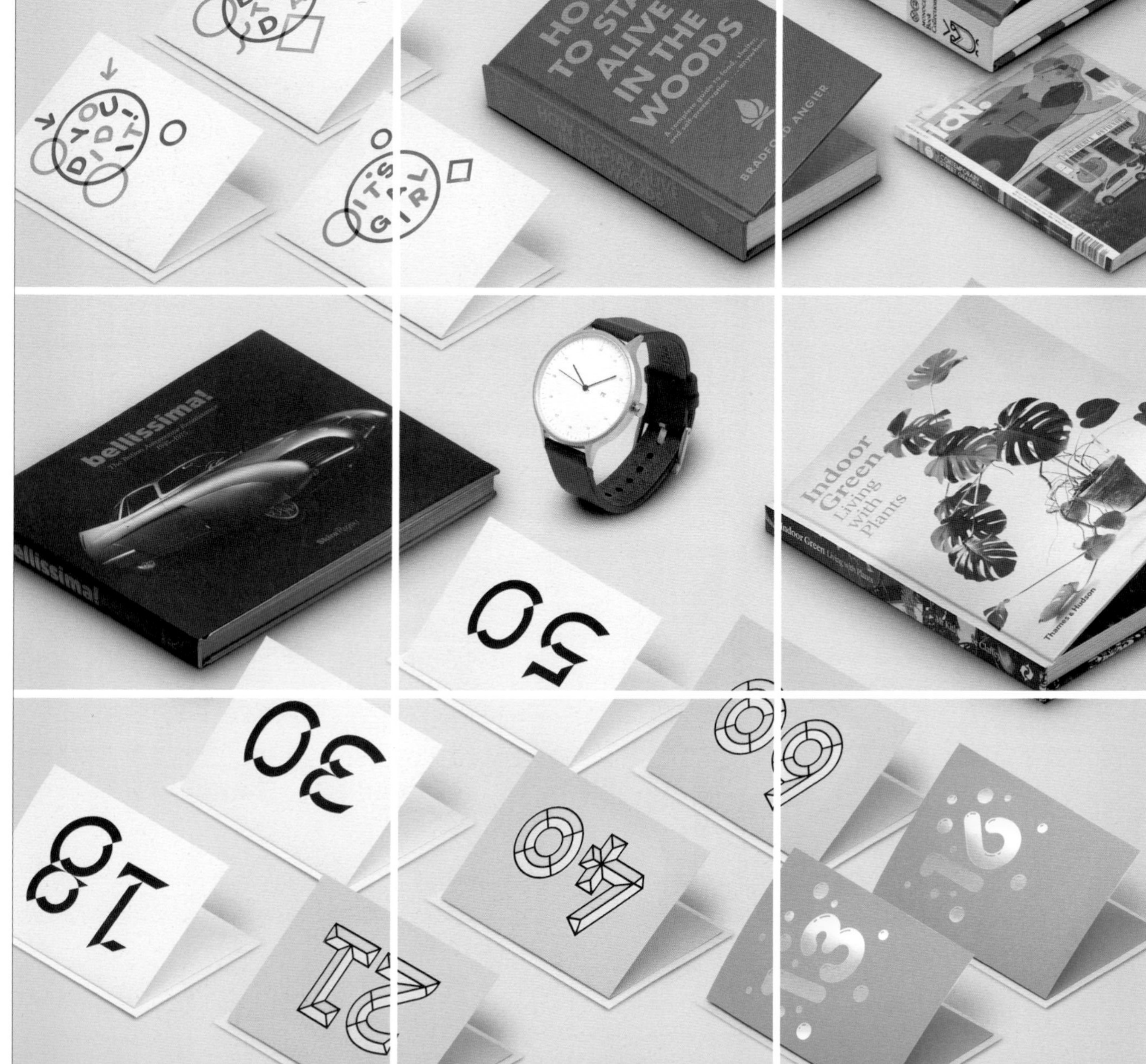

HOW TO STAY ALIVE IN THE WOODS
BRADFORD ANGIER
bellissima!
Indoor Green
Living with Plants
Thames & Hudson

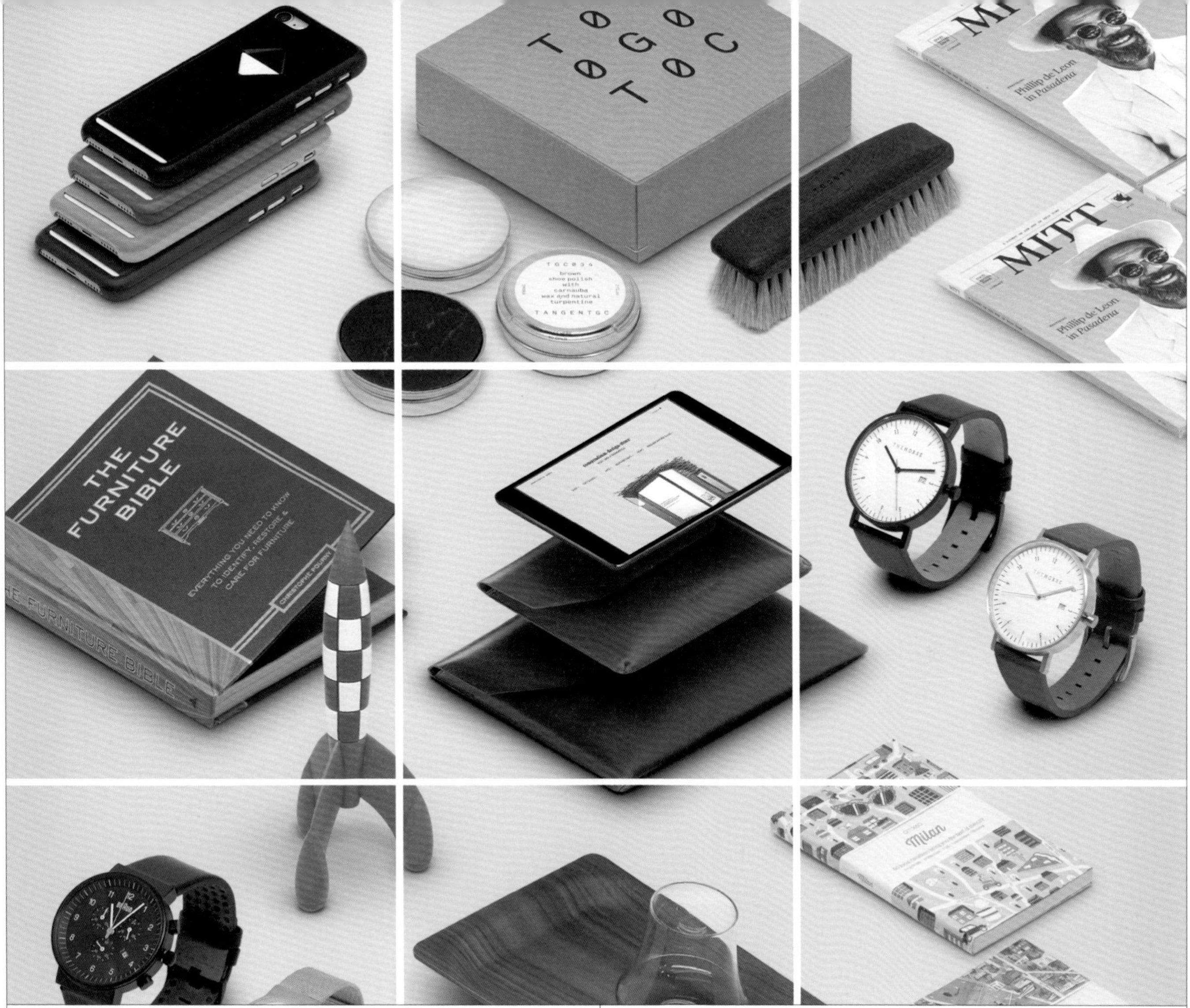

COMPENDIUM DESIGN STORE

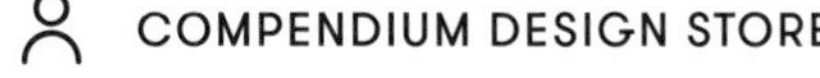

compendium.design.store

Compendium Design Store specialise in creative gifts for discerning people. Based in Perth, Australia, their collection features a concise collection of watches, ceramics, homeware, books, stationery, and other stylish objects from local and international designers.

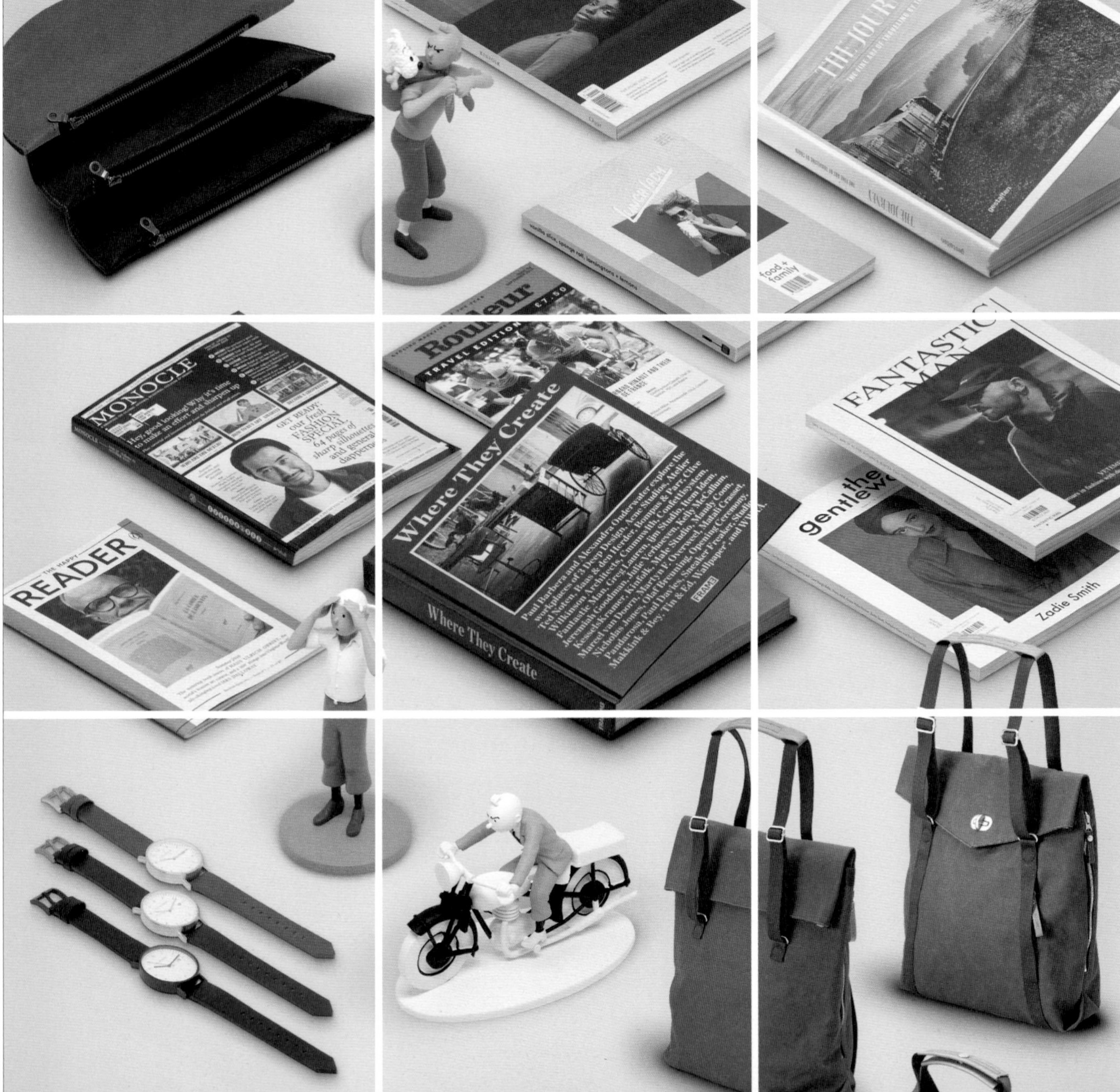

THE JOURNEY
food + family
MONOCLE
Hey, good looking! Why it's time to make an effort and sharpen up
GET READY: our fresh FASHION SPECIAL 64 pages of sharp silhouettes and general dapperness
Rouleur
TRAVEL EDITION
Where They Create
FRAME
FANTASTIC MAN
the gentlewoman
Zadie Smith
THE HAPPY READER

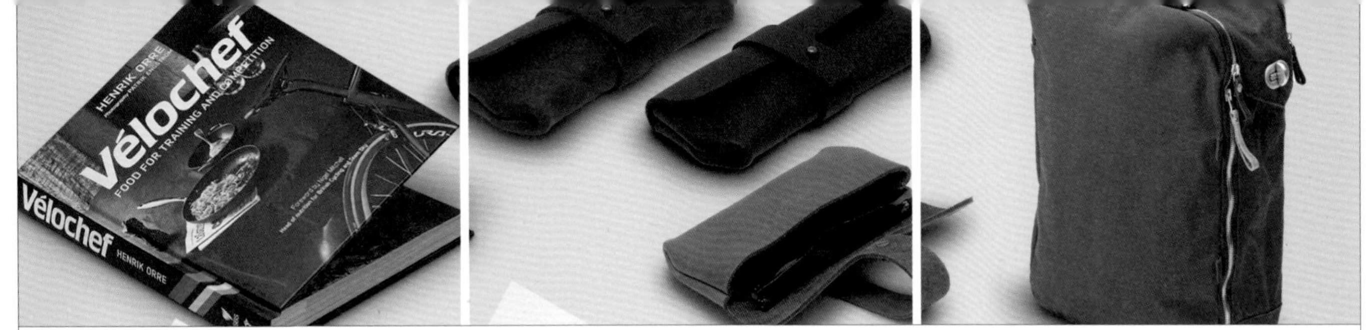

"We looked to create a 'continual grid'-style to encourage deeper exploration into our Instagram feed. We wanted to show what our store was about, in an overall sense, with just a few swipes by the visitor."

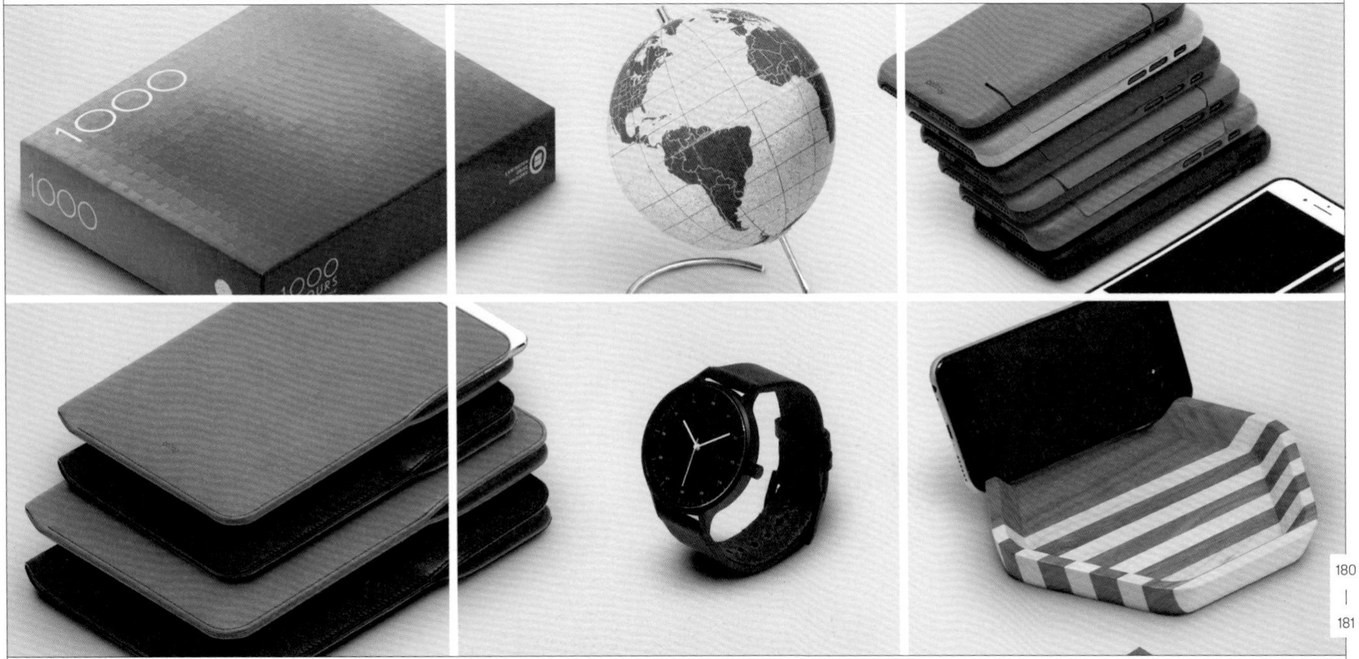

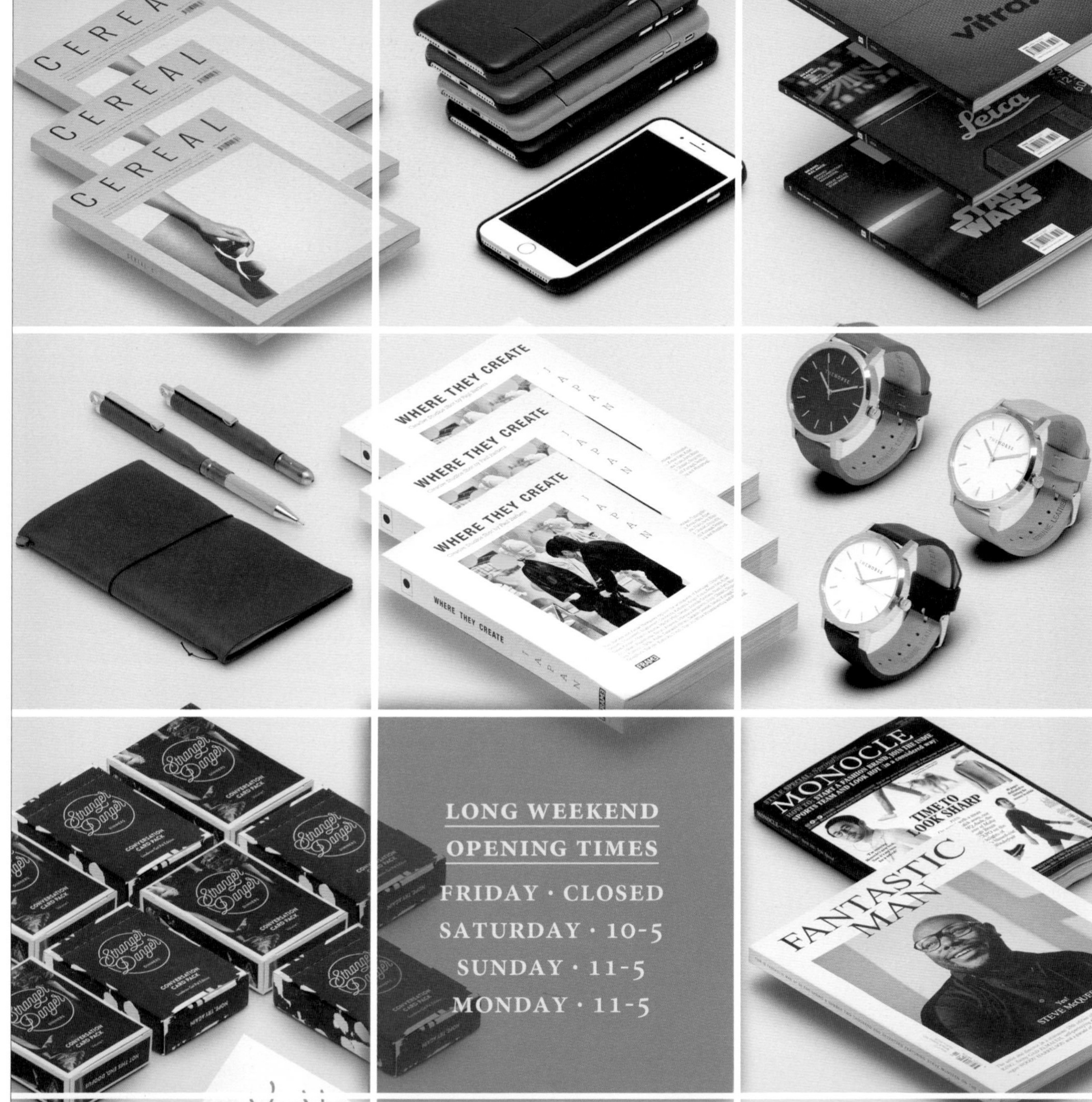
CEREAL
CEREAL
CEREAL
vitra.
Leica
STAR WARS
WHERE THEY CREATE
JAPAN
WHERE THEY CREATE
JAPAN
WHERE THEY CREATE
JAPAN
Stranger Danger
CONVERSATION CARD PACK
LONG WEEKEND
OPENING TIMES
FRIDAY · CLOSED
SATURDAY · 10-5
SUNDAY · 11-5
MONDAY · 11-5
MONOCLE
TIME TO LOOK SHARP
FANTASTIC MAN
STEVE McQUEEN

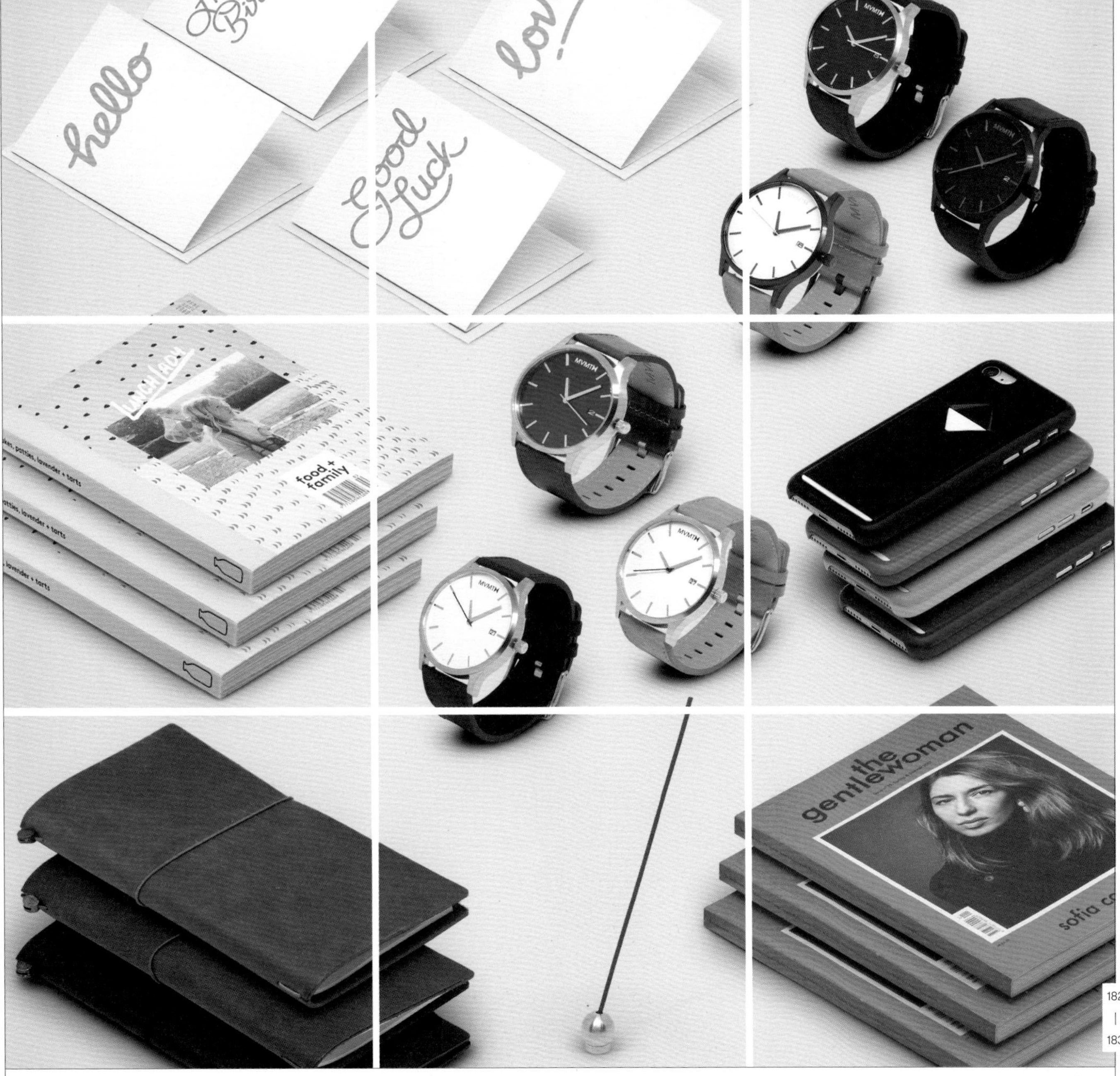
hello
love
Good Luck
MVMT
food + family
the gentlewoman

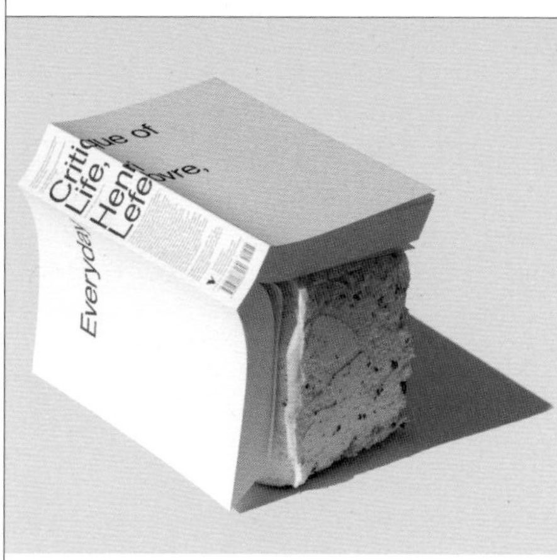

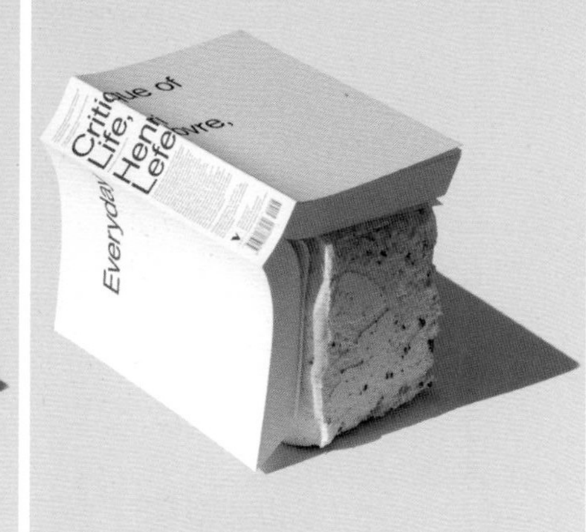

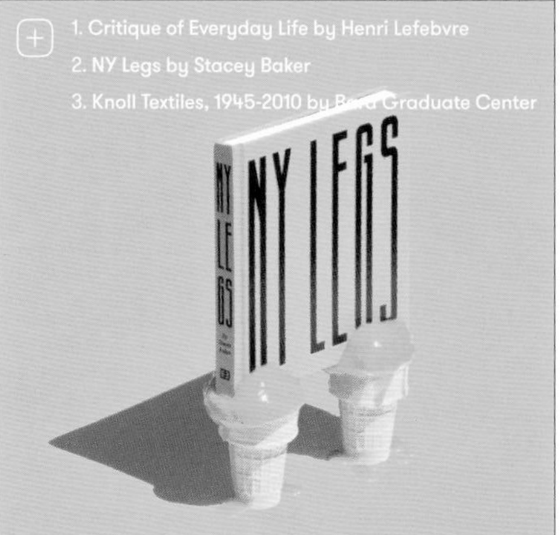

1. Critique of Everyday Life by Henri Lefebvre
2. NY Legs by Stacey Baker
3. Knoll Textiles, 1945-2010 by Bard Graduate Center

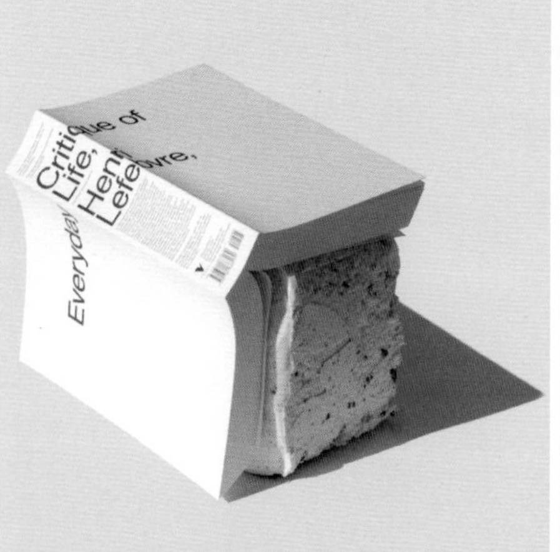

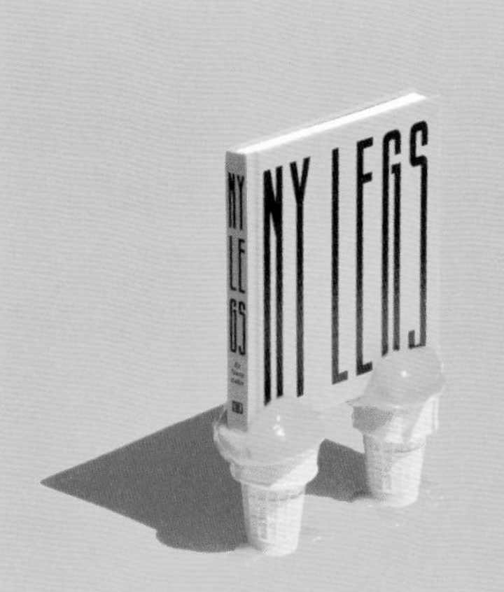

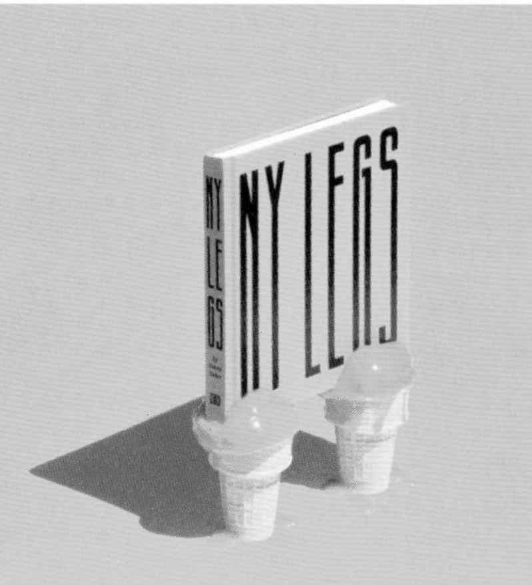

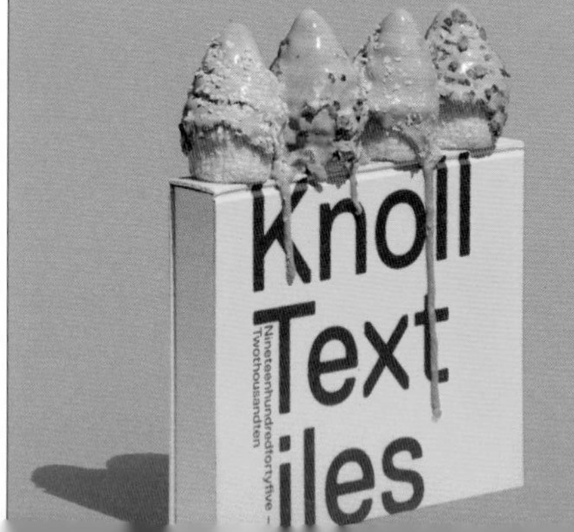

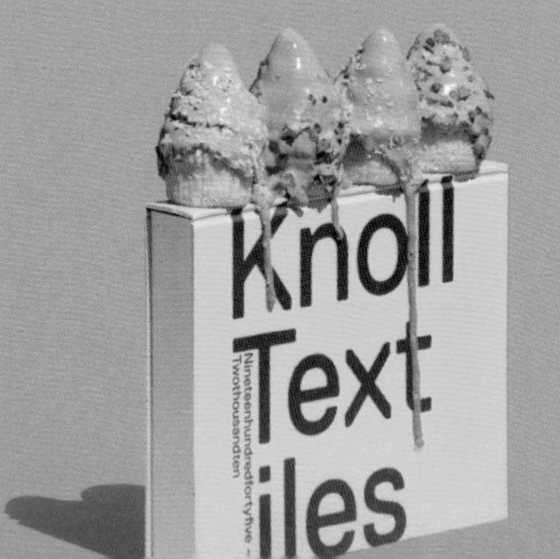

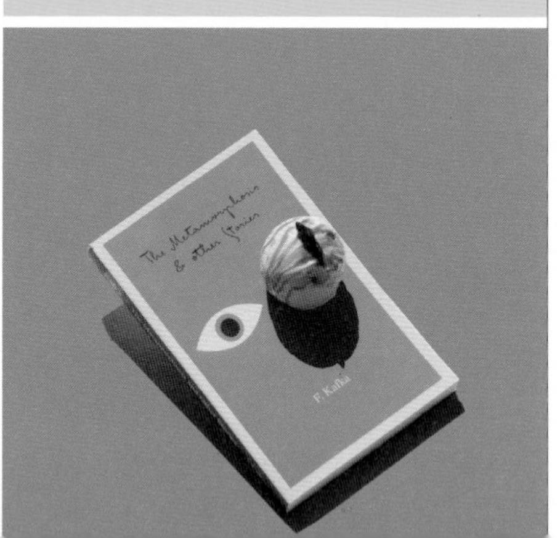

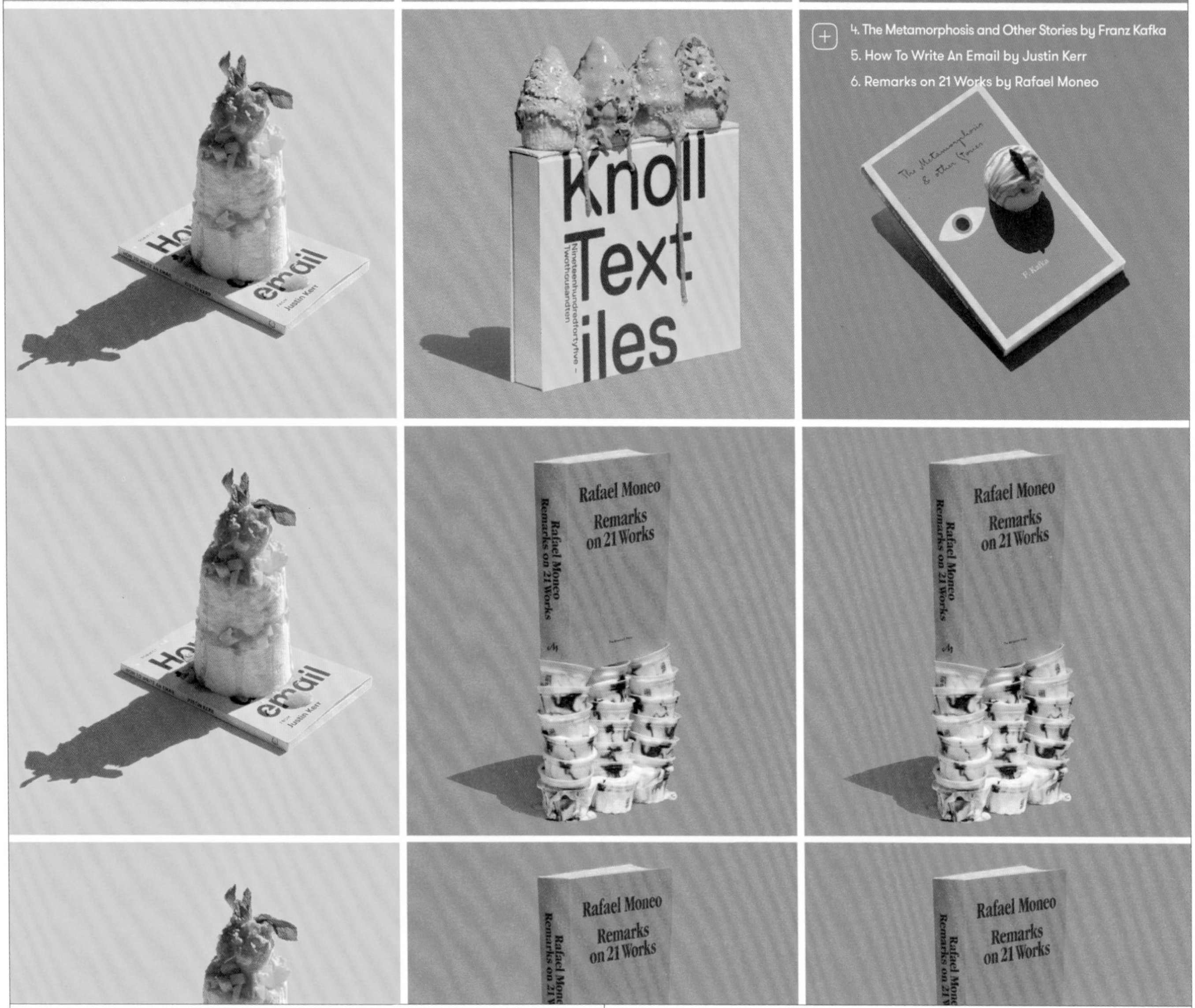

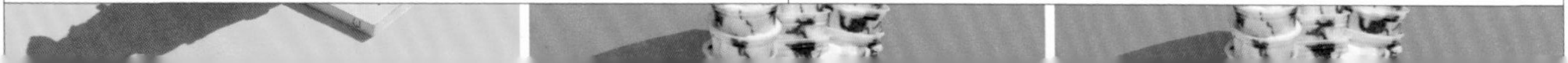

4. The Metamorphosis and Other Stories by Franz Kafka
5. How To Write An Email by Justin Kerr
6. Remarks on 21 Works by Rafael Moneo

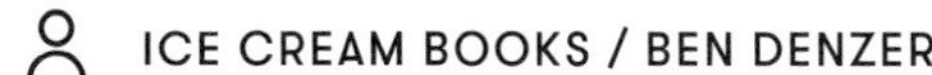

ICE CREAM BOOKS / BEN DENZER

ice_cream_books

Ice Cream Books pairs great reads with frozen desserts. The project was started by Ben Denzer, who is a designer and publisher focused on exploring the book as an object. His work has been awarded by the Type Directors Club, the Art Directors Club, AIGA, and AI-AP.

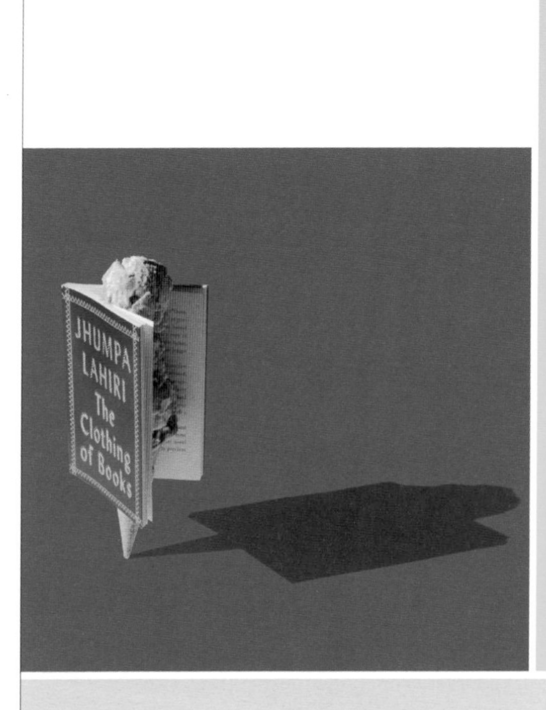
JHUMPA
LAHIRI
The
Clothing
of Books

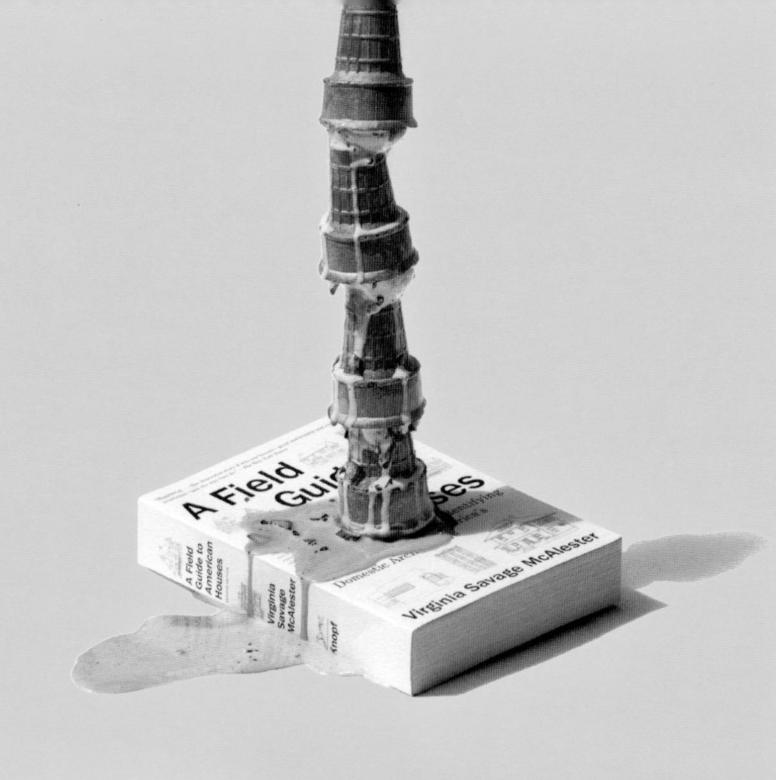
A Field
A Field
Guide to
American
Houses
Virginia
Savage
McAlester
Knopf
Virginia Savage McAlester

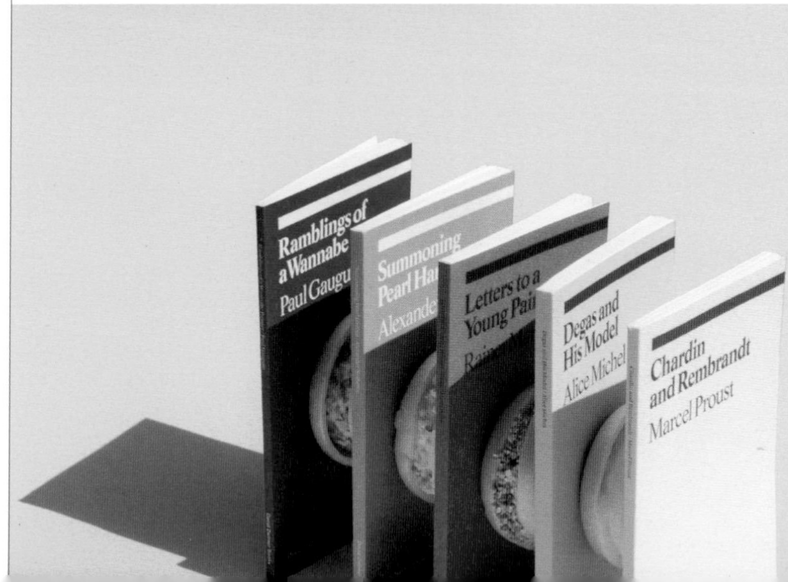
Ramblings of
Degas and
His Model
Alice Michel
Chardin
and Rembrandt
Marcel Proust

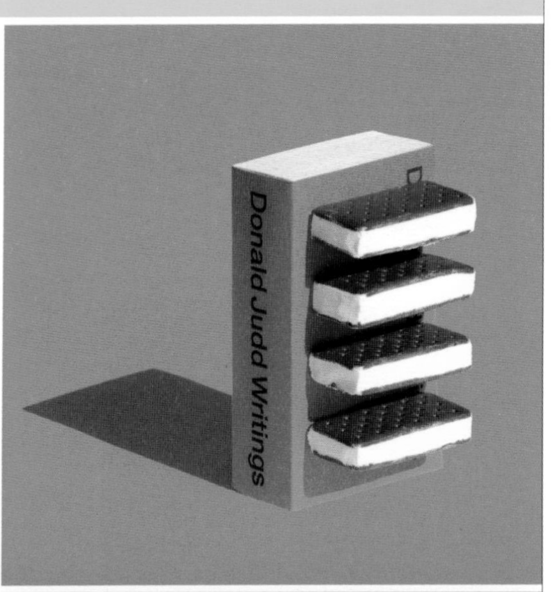
Donald Judd Writings

1. The Clothing of Books by Jhumpa Lahiri
2. A Field Guide to American Houses by Virginia Savage McAlester
3. Ramblings of a Wannabe Painter by Paul Gaugin, Summoning Pearl Harbor by Alexander Nemerov, Letters to a Young Painter by Rainer Maria Rilke, Degas and His Model by Alice Michel, Cardin and Rembrandt by Marcel Proust (Left to Right)
4. Donald Judd Writings by Donald Judd
5. Massin by Aprilsnow and Olivier Legrand
6. Things Are What You Make Of Them by Adam J. Kurtz

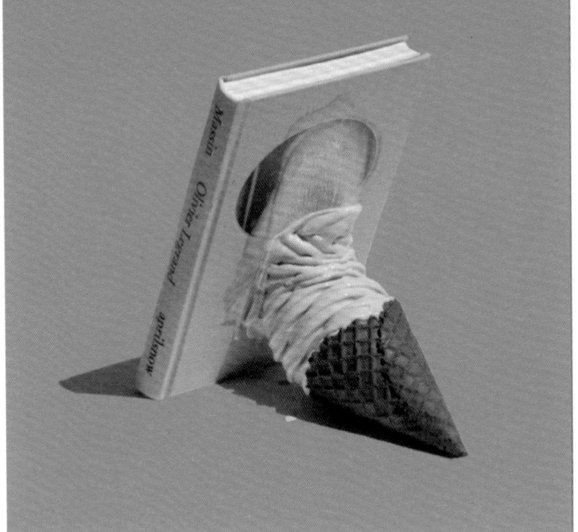

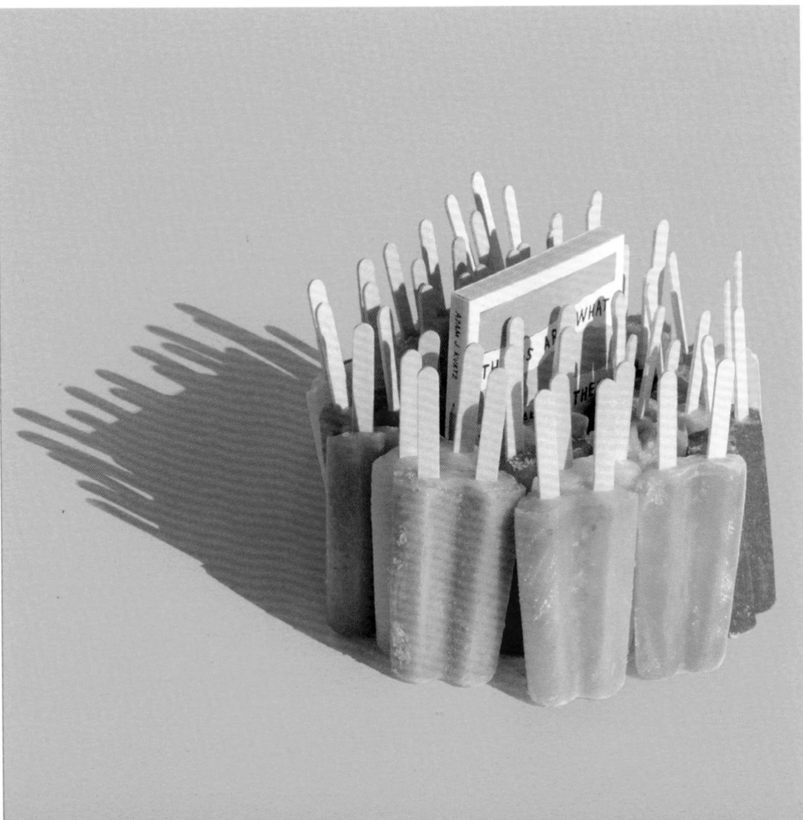

"Most people think of books as pure content, but they have always fascinated me because of their inherent duality. Books are both content and object, simultaneously the contained and the container."

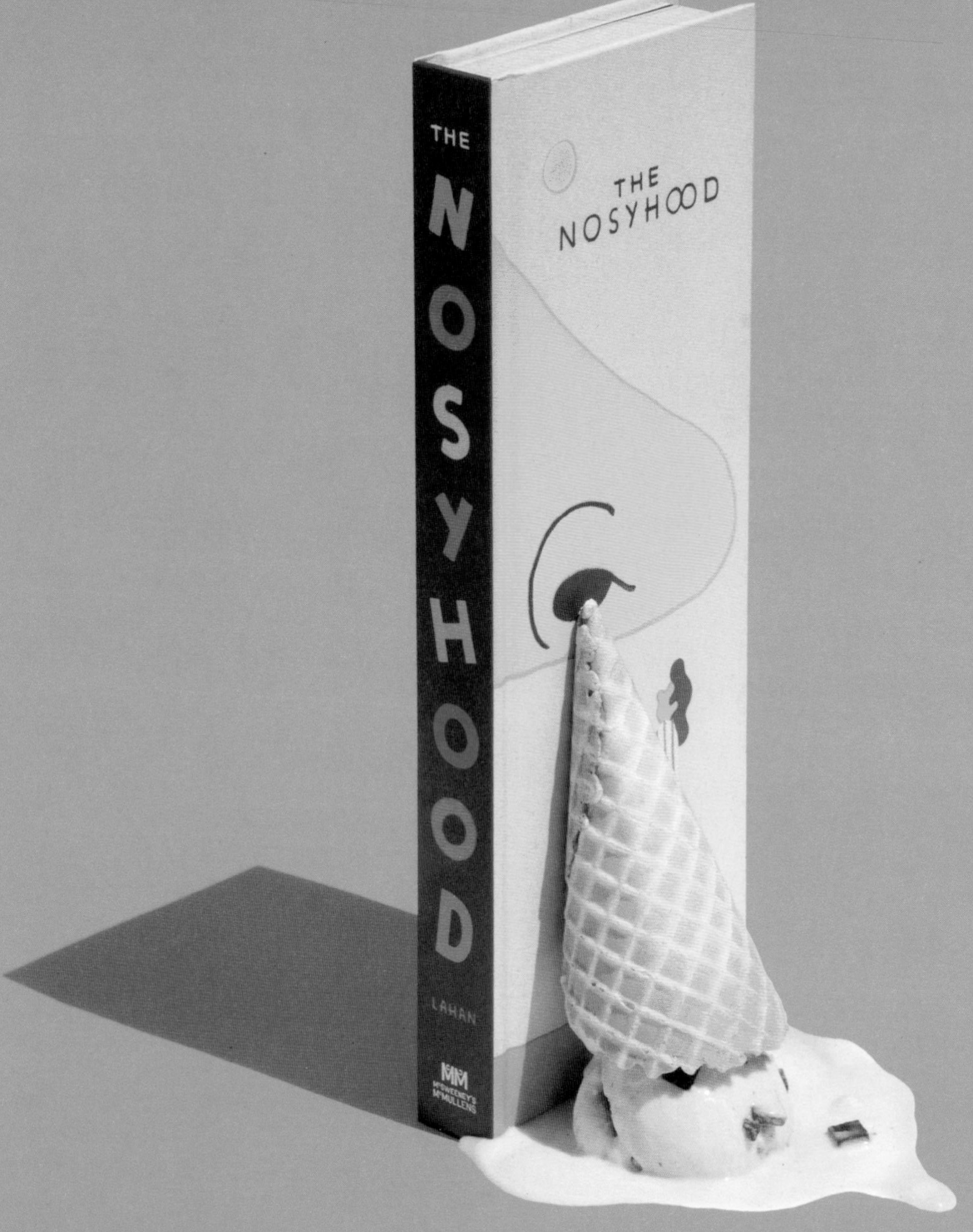
THE
NOSYHOOD
LAHAN
THE NOSYHOOD

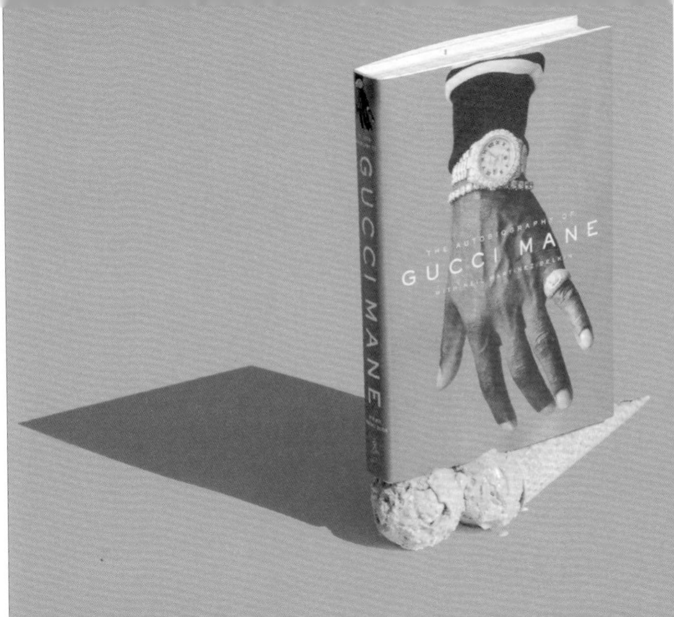

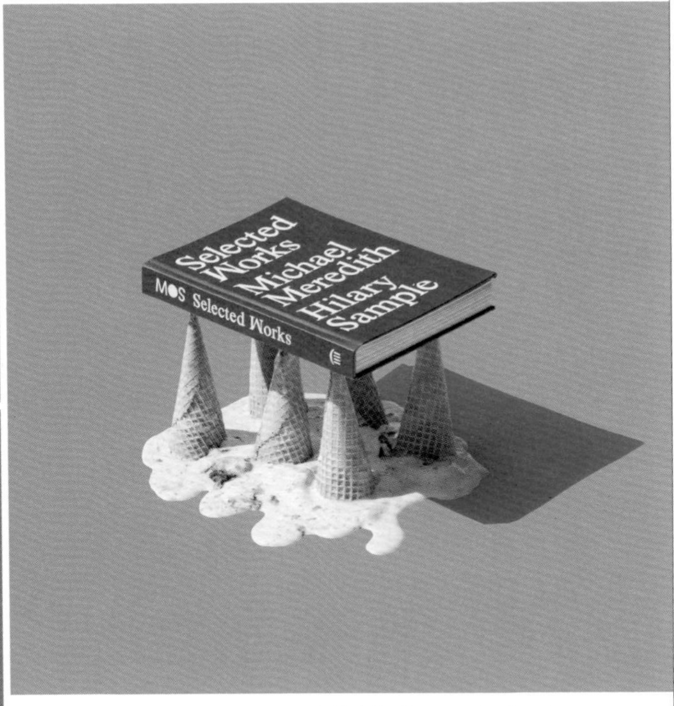

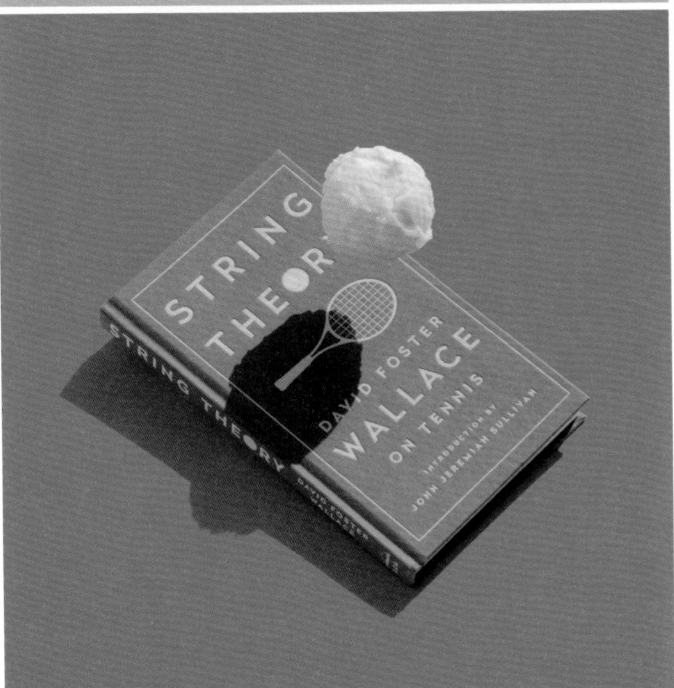

1. The Nosyhood by Tim Lahan
2. The Autobiography of Gucci Mane by Gucci Mane and Neil Martinez-Belkin
3. Selected Works by MOS, Michael Meredith, Hilary Sample
4. String Theory by David Foster Wallace

INDEX